SHOC
DOWN!

The Dramatic, Untold Story of the Police Response to the VIRGINIA TECH MASSACRE

By **John P. Giduck,** J.D., M.S.S., PH.D.
author of *Terror at Beslan*
and co-author of *The Green Beret in You*

With **Major Joseph M. Bail, Jr.,**
City of Chester, Pennsylvania SWAT Commander (ret.)

Foreword by
Brad Thor, *New York Times* No.1 Bestselling Author
of *Foreign Influence* and *The Athena Project*

With expert analyses by
Delta Force Command Sergeant Major Mel Wick (ret.)
and Mark Baganz, Esq.

ARCHANGEL GROUP LTD.

Published by Archangel Group, Ltd.

First Edition 2011

The Library of Congress has cataloged this edition as follows:
LCCN 2011902414

ISBN 0-9767753-4-4

For information about special discounts for bulk purchases or to purchase additional copies send an email to info@archangelgroup.org, call Archangel at 303 215 0779, or fax a request to 303 215 0780 including your name and contact information or visit www.archangelgroup.org

Designed by Michel Hogan
Manufactured in the United States of America

About Shooter Down!

Shooter Down! is an incredible book. A riveting, powerful, and *vitally important* book. The definitive, and complete account of one of the most horrific murderous acts ever committed on American soil. A masterpiece in the realm of "true crime" reporting and journalism.

The world must never forget Virginia Tech, and we must never forget the lessons to be learned from that tragic day. The men who truly know and understand what happened, *because they were there,* have made this information available to us, and we must listen and learn.

This is a lifesaving book, because we can save lives if we will learn and apply the lessons of Virginia Tech. This book is written with the noble and worthy purpose of preparing America's warriors to be better prepared to protect our citizens from future threats. And that purpose has been well and truly achieved. *Shooter Down!* gets away from the useless "blame game" and gives us a true, in depth and professional analysis, and captures *lessons learned*, that must never be forgotten.

The tragic "blood lessons" captured in this book make it *required reading* for *all* law enforcement, for all school administration (pre-school, elementary, middle school, high school *and* college), and for *every* parent of any student in any school across our nation. As we love our children, as we love our way of life, we must learn the lessons of Virginia Tech.

Dave Grossman Lt. Col. (ret)
Author of *On Killing, On Combat, Warrior Mindset,*
and *Stop Teaching Our Kids to Kill*

This book is dedicated to the brave men and women in America's police forces who every day drive the streets alone, ready to race into the worst hell that could befall their citizenry.

But most especially to those courageous officers who on April 16, 2007, fought frantically to enter Norris Hall as gunshots rang out about them.

Table of Contents

Does Anybody Care?

Is anybody out there?
Does anybody care?
There are other victims of April 16,
And we are hurting and in despair.

Can we talk to people who understand,
Can we meet with those in charge?
Those who have neither called nor asked,
We bear a burden too large.

While gunshots rang, no armored vests donned,
Into Norris Hall they raced.
Should they, too, die for others to see,
The courage that drove their haste?

Long hours of grief and lack of concern
Has brought this wife to her knees,
In prayer for her children who are confused by it all,
To a silent God, she pleas.

She prays for all those suffering,
And for her husband who endures long nights.
Haunted by the victims' faces,
He lives those families' plight.

Our officers did their very best,
To some they may have failed.
For even as they fought to save,
The bullets, they did hail.

The students to whom they pledged their lives,
They loved as though their own.
One life lost would have been too much,
But so many: who could have known?

All our lives forever changed,
And we are hurting and in despair.
But on my knees, I ask once more,
Does anybody care?

Written by Teresa Cook in the aftermath of her husband, Lt. Curtis Cook's rescue efforts at Norris Hall as the Virginia Tech Police ERT commander.

At 10:08 a.m. on Monday, April 16, 2007 a team of ERT operators from the Virginia Tech Police Department swept into room 211 of Norris Hall, followed closely behind by a team from the Blacksburg Police Department. There they found Seung-Hui Cho lying on the floor with a gunshot wound to his head, at which time Lt. Curtis Cook grabbed his radio and pronounced to all those who had responded to the attack: **"Shooter Down!"**

Foreword

By Brad Thor, *New York Times* bestselling author of *The Last Patriot, Foreign Influence* and *The Athena Project*

When horrific violence strikes, as it did that April morning of 2007 on the Virginia Tech campus, we are all affected. As rational beings, we have an innate need to make sense out of chaos, to tear down the dark veil of madness, and to try to impose order in its place.

In the wake of such a tragedy, we find ourselves possessed by the same questions – *Why did this happen? Where were the killer's parents, his friends? Where was law enforcement? Didn't anyone see it coming? Couldn't this have been prevented?*

As spectators viewing the aftermath of violence via our televisions, we often leave our questions there, trusting the talking heads to get to the bottom of what "really happened." While we await a reason, we grieve with our friends, neighbors, and co-workers, lamenting the injuries and unfathomable loss of life.

Soon, along with the news coverage, the remorse and the pain we feel dissipates. As the media moves on, and the tragedy is discussed less and less, we begin to feel better and are able to move on ourselves.

For the majority of the nation, the massacre at Virginia Tech will become but a distant memory. Some, though, will *never* be able to forget what happened that day. There are those who still have questions; those whose lives were directly affected, forever altered by a coward named Seung-Hui Cho.

There is another group of people who will never forget what happened that day. These are the brave men and women of our nation's law enforcement agencies. For them, Virginia Tech is both a tragedy and an opportunity to learn.

To all of you who have purchased this book in order to learn from that terrible day, I thank you. I thank you both as a father and as an American. The measure of our greatness is the degree to which we protect the weakest among us – our children. The children you help protect today - be it as a law enforcement officer, engaged PTA participant, government official, teacher, or concerned citizen - will grow to become the men and women who protect the children of tomorrow.

Yours is the noblest of causes and I wish you strength, speed, and safety.

Prologue

"For every one hundred men you send us, ten should not even be here. Eighty are nothing but targets, nine are real fighters. We are lucky to have them, they the battle make. Ah, but the one. One of them is a warrior, and he will bring the others back."

Heraclitus, 500 BC

You wake in the middle of the night to your own screams, your body twisted among sweat soaked sheets. As full consciousness returns the dreams fade to a blurry kaleidoscope of torn bodies, innocent faces, blood and brains leaking from skulls ruptured by bullets. It's been four years and still every night you relive the horror of what you experienced. You had thought you were ready. Everyone, including your own university officials, said repeatedly that it could never happen here. Not in America. They said they weren't worried. Still, as a SWAT operator on your department, you recognized that your job was to be ready for what no one else was; what no one else would allow themselves to even contemplate.

When it came you had done everything possible, everything in your power to save the lives of the students and teachers. It was brutal, horrific, unlike anything anyone in American law enforcement had ever faced before. Certainly, it was unlike anything they had ever prepared for. When it was over the killer was dead. Many of the students and teachers were dead. Some of you would forever wish that you had died as well.

Before the blood had hardened and the shredded bodies were identified, the legal wrangling had begun. First, the news media fueled both state and federal commissions to investigate "what had gone wrong." Then the lawsuits came. The families of the dead sued.

As though that weren't enough to deal with, all but two of those who lived filed suit as well. The dead were condemning you for an attack, and the living were crucifying you for making them endure the trauma of not having anticipated an unprecedented attack at a U.S. school. "You should have known," everyone seemed to say. You look at the alarm clock, knowing that in a few hours you will have to get up to face another day. Your wife tries to comfort you. But you wonder if you're beyond comfort, beyond saving at this point. Certainly you feel beyond redemption.

The battle you have continued to fight in your dreams since the last gunshot rang out was the work of a depressed loner, a graduating senior in the English Department. In the early morning of Monday, April 16, 2007, 23-year-old Seung-Hui Cho had entered room number 4040 in West Ambler-Johnston (WAJ) dormitory on the campus of Virginia Tech. This was the room in which 19-year-old Animal Sciences freshman Emily Hilscher lived. It is believed that due to some noise, possibly shouting by Cho or Emily in her room, Ryan Clark, the fourth floor male resident advisor who lived next door, had rushed over to render assistance. Upon entering the room he was shot in the head with a 9mm handgun. Cho then killed Miss Hilscher with a single 9mm gunshot to her head as well. This occurred by 7:15 a.m.

At approximately 9:40 a.m., Cho entered the Norris Hall Engineering building and began to systematically attack five rooms on the second floor of the north-south wing, ultimately killing another 30 students and professors, and wounding or causing the injury of an additional 27 people.

These premeditated attacks by Seung-Hui Cho represent the worst shooting mass-murder ever to take place at an American school.

Introduction

Hokie, Hokie, high, Tech, Tech, VPI!

More than a century ago when Virginia Tech was a military academy the cadets were known as the "Fighting Gobblers" as they were made to gobble their food quickly. The name and icon of the "Hokies" as a colorful rooster endures to this day.

After the Beslan school siege in southern Russia, just across the line that defines the Chechen War Theater that begins at the border of Ingushetia, I promised myself I would never do another investigation and assessment like that again. And certainly never another book. Quite simply, the horror is too great. The pain and terror of those victimized by such conscienceless predators is too much. The agony of the warriors who battle out such atrocities in a failing effort to save everyone wears on you. Worse is the agony they suffer at the hands of an uncaring public that merely looks to blame someone, anyone. Someone other than the perpetrators themselves. The families of the victims hate them for what they couldn't do. Then there's the blood. The remnants of bodies torn apart, left to lie in a shattered building as though it will forever serve as a solitary tomb, cradling in its cold embrace all that is left of the victims is a lot to walk into. The dead speak to you. What they say is haunting.

Making it all the worse is the news media: armchair quarterbacks that have never done a brave act in their lives, who destroy the very character, nobility and courage of those who race into harm's way for no other reason than their desire to protect the innocent. They publicly decimate the best that any nation has, merely for sport. They are defamed by people who care merely about generating readers and viewers with their all-too-skewed version of the facts, not on reporting the truth. Stories of courage and sacrifice don't sell papers and air time, disgraced heroes do.

After spending months in Russia over three trips, analyzing the Beslan battle, interviewing the brave men that raced into harm's way, who fought for more than ten hours on September 3, 2004 to save children and innocent adult captives, I had had enough. It was often difficult to speak publicly about that attack, to conduct the training that the Archangel Group existed to provide to America's government agents, police and military operators. Never again did I envision actually walking into another blood-soaked classroom, of having to see children's brains stuck to walls or drying on floors in sweltering rooms. The smell never leaves you.

Then the hostage-taking, brutal sexual assault of seven beautiful young women at Platte Canyon High School in bucolic Bailey, Colorado happened. And I was asked by the police into that crime scene immediately to assess their performance. My book on Beslan, *Terror at Beslan: A Russian Tragedy With Lessons For America's Schools*, had resulted in many police departments and military units asking me to help them prepare for the worst possible thing that might ever come to their communities. Cho got to see this attack. He got to see Duane Morrison's fortifications in that classroom and the one that came five days later in tiny and remote Nickel Mines, Pennsylvania. There the perpetrator, Charles Carl Roberts, IV, improved on what Morrison had achieved in Colorado. His superior fortifications resulted in five little girls wounded, with one left in a vegetative state, and five more dead. Through an odd quirk of fate I had been just a few miles away in York, Pennsylvania training area SWAT teams and deputy U.S. marshals when that attack occurred too. Two of the Pennsylvania State Police SRT[1] unit members that had responded had been in a week-long SWAT school that I had run with Delta Force Command Sergeant Major (ret.) Mel Wick two months before. Through York SWAT commander Lt. Ron Camacho

1 Special Response Team, one of the several names and acronyms for law enforcement SWAT teams.

(now captain Camacho) I was able to get as much information as possible to understand what they confronted, what decisions they made, and why.

Cho, who had been obsessed with the Columbine massacre eight years before and had studied it relentlessly, could not have possibly missed these attacks. They both drew national media attention and the attackers' plans were reported extensively. Cho's fortifications would be better than both of these predecessor attacks on students in schools, his tactics more difficult for innocents to survive, and for police to overcome. In a strange way, from Columbine where the FBI investigation was led by two Archangel founding directors to these predecessor attacks, my life would thus be intertwined with Cho's. It was as though all of these events would compel me to be at Virginia Tech, to witness the remnants of his work, his grand masterpiece of hatred and terror. I would quickly learn that Cho was little different from the terrorists that had taken the school in that remote small town in Russia. Blacksburg, Virginia was little different from that town, too. The country and the culture may have been thousands of miles apart, and the languages unrecognizable to each other, but small towns anywhere are similar. And the horror was the same. Even the victims were the same. They always seem to be.

For three years after the Virginia Tech shootings I had countless inquiries about why I didn't write a book on it. Most in law enforcement, after either reading the After Action Review Archangel produced, or hearing me speak on the Virginia Tech massacre at trainings, said that I should do for American police and the officers who responded to that horror what I had done for the Russian Special Forces at Beslan in that book: bring the truth of their courage to light.

Yet I always insisted that I would not write on it, that it was a story that belonged to others; most especially Donnie Goodman, Anthony Wilson, Curtis Cook, Wendell Flinchum, Kim Crannis and so many others. Then one day I received an email from Lt. Curtis Cook, the Virginia Tech Police Department (VTPD) Emergency

Response Team (ERT)[2] commander. In it, he said that he hoped someday I would do that very thing: write a book on the VT shootings and tell the world what really happened, and how they had all really performed, rather than the contrived, vicious and fallacious version put forth by the media and other ignorant experts. With that endorsement I spoke with former Blacksburg Captain and Operations Commander Donnie Goodman. At first he told me that horrible day should be left alone, that nothing more should be written on it. However, with the passing of time and the publication of numerous other books on it that either didn't address the law enforcement response, or cast it in inglorious terms, he said that "it might just be time." I had his blessing, and that of Anthony Wilson, the Blacksburg Police Department (BPD) ERT leader who was among the first into Norris Hall, having raced to that horror without even donning body armor. That was all the support I needed.

My first hope was to write this book in conjunction with Donnie Goodman, the newly minted chief of the city of Radford. Donnie and I had become friends over the years since Cho attacked VT, and we had met virtually the day after in the TOC (Tactical Operations Center) the police had established in the offices high up in the football stadium. I had come to respect him immensely and adore his family. Beyond even our friendship, Donnie was one of the few who had taken a critical role in both the investigation of the first two shootings at WAJ that morning and the response to Norris Hall. He had been a captain on the Blacksburg Police Department and was the oversight SWAT commander. Moreover, he was the only one who had assumed a substantial role in the law enforcement response yet who was no longer affiliated with either of the two departments, or the politics and liability concerns that swirled around them still at that time. However, such an undertaking was simply too much to ask of a man who continued to try to live beyond that day, or his wife and kids. He had a loving wife, Anne, a beautiful daughter in college and a son finishing up a star high school football career getting ready

2 Another name for SWAT teams which also include such titles as SERT for Special Emergency Response Team, and SORT for Special Operations Response Team.

to head to college. Still, I had his support and he said he'd provide whatever assistance I needed.

The only other people I needed to hear from had been on the Archangel Team that had traveled quickly to Virginia Tech immediately after the attack, and who had endured months there over seven trips, studying everything that Cho had accomplished and that the police from the Virginia Tech and Blacksburg police departments had done in response. From those efforts Archangel's 144-page AAR had been generated. But that was merely a report on an event. To do justice to the victims, and to answer the families, the media and critics as to what the police had done and why at every moment throughout that fateful day would require many more trips there. It would necessitate countless more hours of interviews of the officers and medics who fought mightily to meet the highest duty any society can impose on its warriors: the duty to protect and save the lives of the innocent. Simply, to do justice to those brave men and women I couldn't just *report on an event,* but had to *tell a story* of all that had happened and what had drawn all of those students, professors, police officers, medics, doctors, dispatchers and Cho himself all together in a single building in southwestern Virginia.

And so I turned to my years-long friend Major Joe Bail, a SWAT commander from one of the most violent and crime-ridden jurisdictions in the Philadelphia area. Most people found us to be as unlikely a pair to team up as could be imagined. I have always liked to harass Joe with my version of the first time we met one night in Chester when I was 17-years-old. Ten years my senior, and the son of the police chief, he had already been a cop for seven years. That first encounter saw him banging my head against the hood of his police cruiser while counseling me against scurrilous and immoral behavior. Decades later when we met again at a counter-terrorism training I hadn't forgotten him.

Since then Joe had traveled to Russia with me on my final trip interviewing the Russian Spetsnaz (Special Forces) who had fought out the battle to retake the Beslan school. We were in Mumbai, India together investigating and assessing that terror attack in November 2008 along with top Indian Special Forces commanders. We had also survived the Russian invasion of the Republic of Georgia together in the summer of 2008, assessing Russian military presence and behavior in a city that even the American president had assured the world they had already abandoned. We had even been to the border regions between Israel and Jordan, Lebanon and Syria together. Coming up on retirement after a storied 40-year career in law enforcement Joe was already looking for new challenges. He readily agreed to help, and he took a crucial role in many of the subsequent investigatory trips to VT and Blacksburg that yielded much of the information for this book, that had not been obtained previously when preparing our AAR. Of the more than half dozen additional trips to VT we did, Joe made all of those and some on his own. We had to attempt to make some sense of it all so that maybe all of those who suffered that day could have some understanding with which to go forward in life.

Joe and I had ended up at Virginia Tech in an unexpected way. Upon the occurrence of the shootings at the university (hereinafter referred to as "VT," "Virginia Tech" or simply "Tech") a team was immediately assembled with the expressed initial interest of several law enforcement agencies and associations, to conduct a tactical assessment of the law enforcement response.[3] This effort and our corresponding investigation had begun immediately, even prior to the announcement by Virginia Governor Timothy M. Kaine of his appointment of a special panel to review various aspects of the tragedy, and recommend steps to prevent and better respond to attacks on college campuses in the future. Reportedly, the governor's intervention had been initially requested by VT President Charles Steger. Certainly our investigation had begun well before the President of the United States commissioned his own federal report through the Secretary of the Department of Health and Human Services and Secretary of the Department of Education.

3 We were originally contacted by Washington, D.C.'s Frank Borelli to be part of this effort.

As so often happens when political considerations are at issue, support from the law enforcement groups quickly dissipated in the face of the Governor's Panel's formation. As our investigation had already commenced prior to the governor's announcement, the decision was made that it would continue under the auspices of the Archangel Group, Ltd. Archangel is an agency providing training and consulting to U.S. military, law enforcement and government agencies, in addition to schools of all levels, in the fields of terrorism, security and combat tactics. It was Archangel that had sent me to Beslan and so many other places. From the start, our team was comprised of a number of top law enforcement professionals, and some of the most experienced men the country could deliver. In addition to me, the following formed the core of our team:

Co-author Joseph M. Bail, Jr. a 40-year police veteran, and a major with the Chester, Pennsylvania Police Department in the Philadelphia area.[4] He was the oversight commander of the SWAT team, created the SWAT-integrated Tactical Dive Unit, and also commanded the Search and Recovery Dive Team, as well as the Narcotics and Internal Affairs divisions over the course of his career. He studied Criminology at Indiana University of Pennsylvania and graduated from Widener University's Paralegal Studies program. He was an adjunct instructor of Police Studies at Delaware County Community College. In addition to having traveled to Russia to assist me in Archangel's investigation into the mass-hostage taking and battle at the Beslan school that had taken place in September 2004, he traveled to Bailey, Colorado to review the hostage-taking and murder that occurred at the Platte Canyon High School on September 27, 2006. Then, in the aftermath of the Mumbai, India terror attacks, he traveled with me, along with his SWAT and Dive Team Leader Ernie Manerchia, to that distant place to conduct an assessment of those attacks and the military response with representatives of their Special Forces. He regularly provided training on school security to law enforcement and schools. Major Bail was present during every

4 Major Bail retired from the police department shortly before this book went to print.

research trip to Virginia Tech and Blacksburg conducted in order to produce the original Archangel After Action Review (AAR).

Mark Baganz, Esq. was a 35-plus year practicing attorney from Wisconsin, who had defended countless police officers in lawsuits. He was a national expert in law enforcement liability issues, such as training and use of force. In addition to having represented numerous officers over the years, he had been consulted by attorneys, law enforcement agencies and individual officers concerning law enforcement issues and provided legal training to agencies and officers throughout the U.S. He was a former member of the Advisory Board of *The Police Marksman Magazine*, and has authored many articles on the legal aspects of, and liability protection in, law enforcement. Attorney Baganz was present at Virginia Tech for certain critical aspects of the investigation and reviewed all available information on the training of the two primary responding agencies in order to conduct a legal assessment.

Walter Chi held the position of Director of Training with Archangel for five years. He is now a national manager with Securitas, the world's largest security company. He is a graduate of Boston University, with a bachelor's degree in Finance. As part of his work with Archangel he was an assistant civilian instructor to U.S. Army Special Forces, other military units, SWAT and patrol officers in defensive tactics (hand-to-hand combat) and close-quarters combat firearms through the REACT® course (Rapid Engagement and Close-quarters Tactics) taught by Archangel Group. He held a black belt and had been inducted into the USA International Martial Arts Hall of Fame. A former national Olympic weightlifting and state wrestling champion, in 2007 he was an honor graduate from a Colorado law enforcement POST academy[5] and worked for a short time as a police officer, while continuing to provide assistance to Archangel. Mr. Chi made several trips to Virginia Tech and Blacksburg as part of

5 Peace Officer Standardized Training, which are Colorado police academies which are "standardized" to insure all officers have the same minimum training.

this investigation and co-authored the initial report that Archangel published on the attacks.

Chris "Hollywood" Hays was an eight year Marine sniper who was assigned to Joint Special Operations Command (JSOC) in Mogadishu, Somalia from September 1993 to March 1994. He was a 17-year law enforcement veteran, SWAT team leader and sniper with the Orange County (CA) Sheriff's Department. Chris held a bachelor's degree in criminal justice from the University of Phoenix. He was – and remains - a lead instructor for the National Tactical Officers Association in Active Shooter response tactics and co-developer of the Multi Assault Counter-Terrorism Action Capabilities (MACTAC) training program for Active Shooter response. Mr. Hays was present during the first three of five research and investigation trips to Blacksburg and Virginia Tech. His expertise and tireless work, not to mention his peerless technological skill, were of inestimable value. Chris also responded immediately to the Ft. Hood shooting and conducted an investigation and assessment of that terror attack.

Thus the core team was comprised of people whose credentials included police officers, investigators, SWAT members and commanders, attorneys, and law enforcement instructors and trainers. In aggregate, all of those participating in this effort possessed close to 100 years of criminal justice, legal, criminal justice teaching, law enforcement and law enforcement-related experience, including academic and tactical training.

The original After Action Review ("AAR," the "Archangel Report" or simply the "Report") was intended to be used as a tool for law enforcement and school security for both tactical planning and response, and school emergency planning purposes. The goal of the Report was to offer relevant facts, findings and conclusions, concerning the tactical response of law enforcement and first responders to the shootings on the campus of Virginia Tech on April 16, 2007, and to offer recommendations for future preparedness and tactical response capability to all relevant agencies. The Report was prepared for distribution to U.S. law enforcement, security and first responder agencies, and was made available at no cost to all such agencies.

Just as with the AAR, many facts in this book rely on the in-depth investigation of the Governor's Panel and the report that it generated, as well as other sources. Countless news articles and the first four books published on the tragedy since 2007[6] were exhaustively reviewed and their respective assessments, reported facts, and conclusions independently researched in an effort to produce the most factually accurate recitation of events as possible. It was the belief of the Archangel Investigating Team ("Archangel Team") that no conclusion would be of value to U.S. law enforcement, first responders and schools if factual accuracy could not be assured, or at least attempted to the greatest degree possible.

Toward that effort, interviews, investigation and research were conducted over months spent in Blacksburg and at VT over an almost four year period. Debriefings and interviews were conducted with, or other information obtained from: responding patrol; Emergency Response Team (ERT) and Special Weapons and Tactics (SWAT) team members from involved local agencies and the Virginia State Police; command staff from agencies integrally involved in the investigation of the first murders and tactical response to the second; medical first responders; as well as information obtained from victims inside Norris Hall during the second attack and other students at Tech. Norris Hall was inspected, assessed and evaluated from the perspectives of Cho's attack, defensive efforts by victims to evade attack or barricade themselves in rooms, and the police response. Some of this was accomplished prior to the building being cleaned and its rooms sealed. Every route of travel, whether by foot or vehicle, of the murderer Seung-Hui Cho and the responding officers was

6 Roland Lazenby, et al., editors, *April 16th: Virginia Tech Remembers* (London: Penguin Group, 2007); Beth J. Lueders, *Lifting Our Eyes: Finding God's Grace Through the Virginia Tech Tragedy* (New York: Penguin Group, 2007); Ben Agger and Timothy W. Luke, editors, *There is a Gunman on Campus: Terror and Tragedy at Virginia Tech* (Lanham, Maryland: Rowman & Littlefield Publishers Inc., 2008); and Lucinda Roy, *No Right To Remain Silent: The Tragedy at Virginia Tech* (New York: Harmony Books, 2009). Others published later include Douglas Kellner's *Guys and Guns Amok: Domestic Terrorism and School Shootings from the Oklahoma City Bombing to the Virginia Tech Massacre* (Boulder: Paradigm Publishers, 2008).

traveled and measured with times of transit recorded for purposes of assessing both the movement of the attacker and police, particularly with regard to the law enforcement (LE) response to the Norris Hall assault.

However, early on in the process of, first, merely contemplating the possibility of this book, and then the actual writing of it, we decided that it had to be written from the perspective of a single author. Trying to tell a story from two perspectives is literarily difficult, tedious, and often confusing for the reader. Joe was a gifted writer and in fact had several law enforcement counter-terrorism articles published in magazines and journals. But he was in the process of wrapping up his career as a police commander in the Philadelphia area and simply didn't have the volume of time to devote daily to the project. With me in Colorado and Joe in Pennsylvania some 2,000 miles away, the manuscript was going to have to be written by one person, and the tasks that created the foundation of information on which it would be built parceled out.

Thus, while the burden of the writing was largely carried by me, Joe made numerous additional trips to Virginia Tech to continue the long series of interviews of those who had responded to the two attacks. He conducted much of the research into news media sources addressing different aspects of the shootings so that references to them could be accurately made. As well, he made every effort to speak with as many of the students who were at Norris Hall that day as possible. So, while the entire book is written from my perspective, it is in every way a joint effort of us both.

We realized early on that the strength of this book would be its unprecedented access to the many police officers, commanders, SWAT team members, dispatchers and tactical medics who had dealt with the WAJ and Norris Hall attacks in their respective capacities. Just as the strength of my book on the Beslan school siege in southern Russia in September 2004[7] had been my unprecedented access to the Russian Spetsnaz soldiers who had fought out that battle to retake the

7 *Terror at Beslan: A Russian Tragedy With Lessons for America's Schools* (Golden, Colorado: Archangel Publishing, Ltd., 2005).

school and rescue more than 1,200 hostages, most of them children. At Virginia Tech no one had made any substantial effort to hear what the police had to say, or to understand what decisions they had made and why. No one had reported on just how they had actually performed under fire. And to the extent those efforts were made, they were made by the very journalists who had already eviscerated them with no facts on which to base their onslaught. Even the blue ribbon panel commissioned by Governor Kaine in the days after the attacks spent very little time with the officers who actually handled those attacks. But again, as with Beslan the weakness of this book would be its limited access to the students and professors actually in Norris Hall: i.e., the victims themselves.

Though we spent some time speaking with students and parents in preparing our original AAR, our focus had been on the police side of the tragedy. Part of this was due to the fact that we were trying to be sensitive to all that the victims had endured. In writing this book we felt that they had been through enough, and after relentless hounding by the media would have been sickened at the thought of yet another interview asking them to relive the horror for yet another book. Nevertheless, effort was made to – in as respectful and sensitive a manner as possible – talk to those who were comfortable with discussing their experiences. In some cases the students were long since gone from VT and unreachable by us. Where possible, the parents of the students who survived were contacted first to explore whether asking to speak with their son or daughter would be appropriate. Part of this was to serve as a final check of the facts as recalled by all of the police officers and tac medics who had gone inside Norris Hall while still an "active" shooting scene.

And certainly there were discrepancies in the various accounts of events, particularly those inside Norris Hall. Famed law enforcement and military author, speaker and trainer, Lt. Col. (ret.) Dave Grossman, has made a science of the study of the manner in which human beings react to life-and-death experiences, including their capacity to kill. His books *On Killing* and *On Combat* are legendary. Through those years of research he amassed an enormous body of anecdotal evidence that demonstrated that with even trained, experienced police officers and combat soldiers, the human brain does funny things when confronted with deadly threats. Many – if not the vast majority – will remember things that never happened, and be completely incapable of remembering things that did happen. Police officers in the midst of a gun battle will see their partners shot and killed beside them, when in fact they had not been shot at all and were completely unharmed. The variations of fantasy the mind appears to conjure are endless. It seems that in life-and-death situations the brain creates enormous gaps and then fills those gaps, often in the most bizarre and unpredictable of ways. But for those who have experienced these things, the images they have in their minds of exactly what they saw and did are virtually unshakable.

It is from this psychological reality that we can only assume that some accounts of what took place inside Norris Hall derive. For if trained and experienced police officers and soldiers will still suffer from this, how much greater would it be for an average citizen who has never experienced a gunfight or a life-threatening attack – or any violence at all – in his or her life? Recognizing that differences existed in accounts, at times between students and police over the identical events, we made every effort possible to develop all of the information available to at least be able to report the most likely version of events. When confronted with these differences we would not be satisfied with a single police officer's account, but interviewed every available cop, virtually cross-examining them with regard to each small detail, in an effort to confirm what had actually happened. At times crime scene photos were examined in the hope of finding an answer from some small, possibly overlooked detail. Only where a substantial body of consistent information dictated a particular reality of events did we report it as such. To the extent that the information we present in this book may, at times, contradict what others' believe happened should not be seen as any criticism on our part of those other accounts, or that we are questioning their integrity. Our contention is simply that in high stress circumstances people recollect things differently.

This was something that I confronted in the six months during and after the Beslan school siege and battle, where over three different long trips there I interviewed everyone I could get access to. Even the several other authors who penned books on that event lamented the same thing: that in such situations every single victim's account of what happened, when it happened, and who did what, disagrees with the others. With the Virginia Tech tragedy we can only say that this book is the product of four years of research and interviews, crime scene and photo examination, all in an effort to present the most accurate version of events possible.

Another problem that we attempted to tackle arose during trainings that we would often do for police around the country on the events at Virginia Tech. After covering the technical and tactical aspects of the attacks, audiences were often left nonplussed over just who Cho was, where he came from, and how he reached the point where he could do such a thing? University police and school administrators in particular wanted to understand how one of their own students could arrive at such a point. They wanted to know how he could have had so many of the positive experiences he did in life, have the loving parents and sister he enjoyed, yet still end up as a monster stalking classrooms shooting defenseless students. They sought to understand what could possibly have been going through his mind as he worked his way through his education at one of America's premier schools, dealt with roommates, tried to meet girls, and interacted with his professors. They wanted to know how all of those experiences culminated in him staring expressionlessly down at wounded and cowering kids, as he pumped bullet after bullet into them with complete emotional detachment.

Much of the information presented about Cho's early life and the available information on his mental health issues was taken from the Governor's Panel Report that was published at the beginning of the following fall semester in 2007, as well as Dr. Lucinda Roy's book

No Right To Remain Silent. Toward this end, the university drafted a release form, and with the assistance of the Virginia State Police obtained permission from the Cho family so his records could be released. Other psychological assessments were developed by mental health experts forensically based on information given them about Cho and his life after the event. However, in an effort to make Cho – and others like him who may be out there plotting the next attack – real, to make them understandable, we have employed a literary tool that carries with it some inherent risks. At the beginning of various chapters and sections we present *in italics* up to several paragraphs on what we perceive to have been going on in the mind of this killer. This is, of course, our speculation and we have no evidence or information that these were his actual thoughts beyond our own examination of his experiences, writings and emails at different phases of his life, his planning for the attacks, the attacks themselves, and the conclusions we drew from them. With each phase we looked at what we knew was going on in his life and juxtaposed those experiences with the decisions he was making. We attempted to deduce what *could have been* going on inside his head in a way that would make some sense for the reader.

In so doing we express Cho's perceived thoughts in the way we believe he would have been thinking them. Therefore, at times these sections of mental dialogue are somewhat graphic and profane, though based on some of his writings and videos not nearly to the degree he would have actually thought them. They may even be seen as insulting to some of the people about whom he would have been having such thoughts, but we have tried to limit that to the absolute degree possible. In no way are these depictions reflective of how we see those people, or the type of people that they actually are. They are merely reflections of how those individuals may have been perceived by an evil-minded murderer as his life built toward that day in April 2007. Many of those we used as a test group of advance copy readers expressed their feelings that these were actually the best parts of the book, as without them it would have been hard to understand Cho at all. We can only hope that is true for everyone. If anyone is offended by this effort, or feel that he or she has been unfairly or insultingly portrayed, you have our sincere apology. That was not our intention. We are not saying that what we have created is exactly *what* Cho was thinking or *why* he made the decisions he did. There is no way to know those things with any degree of certainty short of someone, someday producing a journal that he kept. A journal which no one believes ever existed. We have included these dialogues of Cho with himself – as speculative as they are – in the hope that they will allow the reader to stop and exclaim, *Now I get it. Now I understand what he could have been thinking and how he could have ended up being the person he was, and doing the things he did.* We can only hope that we have succeeded in that endeavor.

For all of these reasons we are grateful to every single person – particularly the brave men and women from the police departments – who lent their voices to this effort. It is only through your willingness to relate what you experienced that this story can be told at all. We are also grateful to the students who spoke with us. Those students demonstrated that they were truly courageous young men and women, for no one wants to continue to relive the horror of such experiences. As well our gratitude goes to Sgt. Bob Hafley, Division 3 SWAT commander of the Virginia State Police; Radford Police Chief Donnie Goodman; Blacksburg Capt. Anthony Wilson; Virginia Tech Police Chief Wendell Flinchum; and Virginia Tech ERT commander Lt. Curtis Cook. Without them and their support for this effort, no one would have ever known all that their officers did. We believe that it was a tale worth telling. If we have come close at all to telling a useful story it was only due to the contributions of so many people whom this story is about.

In so doing, however, we have had to limit the number of accounts of the officers and others who did respond. Every single person who contributed to the response and investigation of the two shootings that day served a role that can never be appreciated, and each has his and her own story. Stories that are worthy of telling.

However, in order to be able to tell a comprehensible tale in a way that was not overwhelming and confusing to the reader, we have had to limit these significantly. Thus, the tale of Cho's attacks on innocent people at VT is largely told through the perspectives and experiences of a handful of people integral to those responses. Although we have tried to mention every single person at some point in the book we likely failed in that endeavor and apologize to anyone who went unreferenced. In having made the choices of who to highlight, we in no way trivialize the contributions of so many others and hope that someday their stories too will be told.

We owe special thanks to many times *New York Times* bestselling author Brad Thor for lending his own thoughts and perspective in the Foreword. Brad is a great friend and true American who works diligently to develop in our citizenry the very values, skills and warriorship that we are all doubtless going to need to deal with the exigencies and terror attacks of the future.

Most of all, to the victims who survived April 16 and the families of those who did not, we are sorry to have added ourselves to the long list of others who have used the subject of your grief for our own purposes. It has not been our desire to lay bare pain that we cannot begin to imagine. It is only due to our heartfelt belief that others can benefit from the information and knowledge that we have acquired, that we have undertaken this effort at all.

And to Mr. and Mrs. Cho and Sun-Kyung, please accept our sincere apologies. We can only imagine how the constant retelling of this event and the pain that each resurrection causes you only adds to a burden of suffering that a lifetime cannot wash away. In our efforts to make your son and brother's story understandable to so many who need to learn from its lessons we fear that we may have reopened wounds that perhaps had only just begun to heal. Our decision to attempt to present the torment of Seung-Hui's mind through our speculative monologues of his thoughts – though honest – cannot help but present your loved one in a light that may add to your grief. If it were not for the fact that our purpose is to prepare America's warriors to be better able to protect her citizens from all threats, foreign and domestic, and that the study of this event can better prepare them for attacks in the future, we would have limited our efforts to a much greater degree. We hope you can forgive us.

It is our hope that the information provided in this book, and the conclusions and recommendations drawn therefrom, will be of value to the brave professionals in America who are yet to be called upon to respond to future devastating and unpredictable attacks on our nation's children and citizens.

Chapter One
The Creation of a Monster

"Ninety-eight percent of the people are sheep. They are good, decent people who couldn't hurt another human being except by accident. One percent are wolves. They are evil predators who hunt and kill the sheep. One percent are sheepdogs. They live their lives to protect the sheep who cannot and will not protect themselves."

Lt. Col. (ret.) Dave Grossman

Cho's Early Years

Why did mommy and daddy send me away to these mean people? I hate the smell here and the people do not love me. I hate the pain. They stab me with sharp needles and hook me up to machines that make terrifying noises. They yell at me. I cry all day. I cannot sleep. I am terrified every moment. Why won't my Mommy and Daddy rescue me from these people? They come and stare at me, then leave. Will I ever get to go home? I miss my sister. Where is Sun-Kyung? Why don't they love me anymore? They must hate me!

I feel like I just got home and now they're taking me back! Why are they taking me back to that place?! I try to be good. I try to stay out of everyone's way and say nothing, hoping they won't think to send me back there to be tortured. I am terrified.

Cho was born on January 18, 1984 in South Korea, the second child of Sung-Tae and Hyang Im Cho. His mother had been a Korean War refugee. Sister Sun-Kyung was older by three years. Islamist conspiracy theorists' insistence that he was actually born in Saudi Arabia and raised Muslim, were incorrect. His was a lower class working family, and was reported to have been quite poor, though the Governor's Panel Report (GPR), entitled *Mass Shootings at Virginia Tech, Report of the Review Panel,* stated that "the families did not encounter the level of deprivation that many did in post-war Korea."[8] They lived in a rented three-room apartment in the basement of a house in Seoul.

When Cho was only nine-months-old he developed whooping cough, then pneumonia, and was hospitalized for an extended period of time. His parents were told he had a hole in his heart, which was possibly a heart murmur. When Cho returned from the hospital he was resistant to being touched. The family had already experienced his lack of communication and interaction, even with them. Cho underwent additional testing of his heart two years later, and this caused the almost three-year-old boy even greater emotional trauma.[9] From that point forward young Cho did not like to be touched by anyone. According to Cho's mother he cried a lot and was constantly sick.[10] An elderly great-aunt would later say that she thought he was autistic.

–

Why doesn't anyone like me? I have no friends, everyone hates me. I try to be nice and make people like me but I don't know how. Everything I do seems to disappoint my family and make others hate me. I hate it when people touch me. Only Momma and Sun-Kyung make me feel good. Daddy is mean and stares at me. He doesn't talk. I wish he would talk to me, to tell me why I displease him. I wish I could ask him what's wrong with me, why no one likes me. I hate school. I hate being out of my house. I am afraid each day that I will be sent back to the hospital. The teachers hate me. I cannot talk to anyone. My auntie hates me. They make me talk but I cannot. I cry. Why don't they love me?

8 *Mass Shootings at Virginia Tech, Report of the Review Panel,* August 2007, p. 31. Hereinafter cited as "Governor's Panel Report" or "GPR."
9 GPR, p. 32.
10 Ibid.

In South Korea, Cho had only a few friends who would ever come over to play. He was extremely quiet, and the family described him as "sweet" by nature.[11] In Korea, as with other Asian countries, quietness, calm and introspection were valued personality traits and reflective of intellect. However, in Cho's case his behavior was so extreme that the family became concerned.[12] Still, his medical records from Korea did not indicate any diagnosis of mental illness prior to moving to the U.S.

Cho attended Shin Cheng Elementary School in Seoul in first grade and part of second grade. News reports indicated that the only record of Cho's time there states that he left school on August 19, 1992. In South Korea the school year was divided into two terms. The first typically ran from early March to late August. Vacation then came in the summer. For elementary and secondary schools this was from mid-July to mid-August. For higher education it ran from mid-June to late August. The second term typically resumed in late August and went until early February. The winter break was from early February to early March.

That same year, Cho and his family arrived in the United States and moved to Washington, D.C. Cho was only eight-years-old. The GPR reported that the family's immigration was largely motivated by Mr. Cho's sister who had already emigrated from South Korea to America. The parents stated that they made this move to pursue educational opportunities for their children. The move was difficult due to the fact that none of the family members spoke English, the children felt isolated, and for the first time Cho's mother began working outside of the home. The young boy who wouldn't let his own family members touch him, and who had few friends and never spoke to anyone, had been ripped from his home, culture, language and all that he knew and transported 6,953 miles and dumped into a completely strange world.

11 Ibid.
12 Ibid.

–

During the year of Cho's birth an event like that which would occur 23 years later on April 16, 2007 was the furthest thing from Larry Wooddell's mind when he decided that he had to give up his job as a "turkey catcher" in Stanton, Virginia. Larry, who would be one of the first officers to enter Norris Hall, was a self-described farm boy. At the time he was tired of being filthy and dealing with the disgusting smells that were conditions of employment on the farm where he worked. Through friends he was able to land a job with a concrete company in Montgomery County, the very county in which both the town of Blacksburg and Virginia Tech were situated. The smell was better and the dirt washed off easier. Then, he never imagined he would become a cop. Nor did he imagine he would one day walk into the worst mass-shooting murder an American school had ever seen.

–

Wendell Flinchum, who would be the chief of the Virginia Tech Police Department when Cho launched his rampage in 2007, started his association with the department as a student employee in September 1983. He later became employed as a Safety Escort in January 1984, virtually on the day that Cho was born. Flinchum would end up holding many positions over his career at Tech: SWAT operator; narcotics task force officer; instructor, among others. Their lives would become two unerring paths leading straight to Norris Hall more than two decades later, as though from the very beginning they were both to be inextricably intertwined with Virginia Tech, and each other.

–

In January 1984 Curtis Cook was midway through his tour in the Navy. He had become a rescue swimmer and had two deployments to the Middle East, including one to Beirut right after the bombing of the Marine barracks. This was the year after he had married his high school sweetheart, Teresa Sasser. She was blonde and pretty, with a friendly and engaging personality, and Curtis was on top of the world when she said "yes" to him. That she would wait for him to return from long deployments made him the luckiest guy on the planet. Along with a number of the officers Curtis would later work with at the Virginia Tech Police Department (VTPD), he started his law enforcement career as a deputy with the Montgomery County Sheriff's Office in December 1986. Cho, then a toddler, was about to be readmitted to the hospital for a second long stay in his young life, this time for perceived heart problems.

—

In 1984, as a criminal justice student at Radford University, a short drive from Virginia Tech, Donnie Goodman never thought he would be in a position to command police officers as they responded to a massacre. In the ensuing 23 years Goodman rose from college student to FBI National Academy graduate, then Captain and Operations Commander in charge of the Emergency Response Team (ERT)[13] of the Blacksburg Police Department, and finally to the position of police chief in the city of Radord, having come full circle back to where his interest and career in law enforcement originated. Still, he was the type of man who believed that if something horrible, something unimaginable, could happen anywhere it could happen right where he was. He always prepared himself, and those who served under him, for the worst.

A southern gentleman of smaller stature than one would expect of a kick-ass SWAT commander, the anomaly was furthered by Donnie's boyish face and impish smile. But Donnie Goodman was a force to be reckoned with anytime someone crossed his family or his men. In the situation that he faced on "the 16th" Goodman did what all good leaders do: he led by example, and never from behind a desk. In 1992, as the Cho family was emigrating from South Korea, Goodman was a sergeant in the Blacksburg Police Department's Investigation Unit.

13 ERT is another name for a police SWAT team.

Cho's Childhood in America

Where am I? I don't know anything here, I don't understand what anyone is saying to me. It's a strange place with the meanest and most hateful people. Sun-Kyung and I are scared. We can't talk to anybody. We are left alone. Mommy works now with Daddy. They are hardly ever here. My aunt says how good it is here, but I'm afraid. All I knew is thousands of miles away. I even had a friend there. Another boy like me who everyone made fun of. I don't want to live here. I hate this language. They say I have to go to school here, but the children all make fun of us. I can't understand them, but I can tell they are being mean. We keep moving from place to place. Nothing is home to me. Just as I get used to a new home they make me move somewhere else. Just as I think I can start talking to other children I'm taken away again. Why did we have to leave South Korea? I want to go home.

Upon immigrating, Cho's parents took jobs at a dry cleaner near Centreville, Virginia. They worked long hours and were gone a great deal of the time. The Korean newspaper, *Dond-a Ilbo Daily,* reported that his parents emigrated from Korea to the U.S. in the hope of finding a better life for their children. Only Korean was spoken in the home. The media reported that Cho's classmates said that throughout the rest of his elementary and middle school education Cho was taunted by other students, though there does not appear to be any indication that he was physically assaulted.

For the first six months in the U.S. the Cho's lived with extended family members in Maryland. After that they moved to a townhouse for one year. They, then, moved again to Virginia where they lived in an apartment for the next three years. The move to Virginia took place when Cho was nine-years-old, and in the middle of third grade. At that point, this young boy who lived a solitary existence of social awkwardness and who struggled to even talk to another person much less make friends, had been ripped from every home and environment at just about the time he would have begun developing some comfort. Not only had he been removed thousands of miles from the only world he ever knew, but upon landing in this strange new universe where he couldn't even speak the language he had been made to move two more times. Thus, three times he was made to adapt to new surroundings and people. At this stage in his life he only ever had one friend, a boy who lived next door with whom he occasionally went swimming.

As soon as Cho arrived in Virginia from Maryland in the middle of third grade, his school enrolled him in its English as a Second Language program (ESL). Teachers reported that he would not "interact socially, communicate verbally" or participate in any activities. Sister Sun-Kyung said that once in America Cho became even more withdrawn. She related that at times they were made fun of at school, but nothing beyond that. It has been reported in the news media that Cho exhibited troubling behavior as a child. Other family members said that his silence as a preteen was a source of worry to his parents.[14] Despite concerns over the violent nature of his later writings, no known acts of criminal or violent behavior preceded his attacks in 2007. Within two years of immigrating the two children began to speak, read and write English. Though Korean continued to be spoken at home throughout his life, Cho could neither read nor write that language.

Dark Clouds on the Horizon

Why doesn't the school just leave me and my parents alone? Why do they bother them? Sun-Kyung hates it when she has to translate to our parents while they talk about how messed up I am. I just want to be left alone. Mom thinks she can force kids to be my friend, but they hate me. I can't talk to them. They laugh at me. I don't want to do things with them. I hate sitting on the school steps in the dark waiting for someone to pick me up. I'm scared. Why can't they just leave me alone at home, let me watch TV and play video games by myself?

14 N.R. Kleinfield, "Before Deadly Rage, A Life Consumed by Troubling Silence," *New York Times*, April 22, 2007, www.nytimes.com.

I hate our new house. Why do we have to keep moving? Now the kids all know exactly where I live. Why did we have to move right next to the school? I don't want them to know where I live. I don't want anyone to know. I don't want anyone to know I even exist. If I don't exist they can't make fun of me. Why did the school make my parents take me to a doctor for crazy people? I'm not crazy. I just want to be left alone. I hated that first one. This one tries to be nice, but I hate going. My Dad is so ashamed he can't even talk to me except to yell at me for embarrassing him. I hate them. I hate them all. I wish our house didn't have a door so that they could never make me leave. I wish it didn't have any windows so no one could see me.

A requested parent-teacher conference to address Cho's refusal to answer anything in class or talk at all resulted in Mrs. Cho assuring them that she would find friends for him. The school thought his problems were emotional, and therefore must have been skeptical that her efforts would see any improvement. She encouraged both her children to attend the church she belonged to in order to get involved in congregation activities. This did not last long. Cho - this slight, painfully shy young boy - could neither figure out how to make a friend, nor even how to talk to another boy. Due to the fact that both parents worked for a dry cleaner where much of the work was done overnight to have clothes ready for the morning, leaving work to pick him up from activities was difficult. Cho was completely incapable of going to another kid and saying, "Hey Billy, can you ask your mom if she could drop me off at home?" This would see him often sitting alone in the dark, for hours afterward, waiting for one of his parents to finally come get him. Other efforts to have people intervene with Cho met with similar failure. His isolation only grew worse.

During sixth grade Cho's parents bought a townhouse right next to the school so he could access the school and its resources more easily. This was his third move and fourth residence since arriving in America. For a time during his elementary school years the family felt Cho was doing better. He was reported to have gotten involved in Tae Kwon Do for a short time; however, his quitting so quickly should have warned his parents that things were not improving. They reported that he watched television and played video games like *Sonic the Hedgehog,* though his family denied that any of the games he enjoyed had violent themes. Still, the parents reported no disciplinary problems and said that he never threw tantrums or had angry outbursts. It was reported that violence was not tolerated in the household, and no family member had a gun or could use one. At one point while in college Cho's mother found a folding knife he had hidden in his bedroom and expressed her extreme disapproval.

Cho's parents finally threw their hands up in exasperation and decided to just "let him be the way he is." The GPR noted that his parents reported that at no time did he speak of imaginary friends, was not involved in any type of fantasy world, nor was he fascinated with any type of theme or behavior that caused them concern. These disconcerting behaviors would, however, manifest themselves while in college. At home he never talked of a "twin brother," as was reported by roommates at VT subsequent to the shootings. His parents described him as "very gentle, very tender," and a "good person."[15] At this point Cho was still just a little boy trying to figure his way through a school and life that he felt disconnected from and unable to fit into. The rage, however, was likely beginning to build.

Still, just before beginning seventh grade in 1996, and his first year in junior high school, Cho's parents acted on the elementary school's recommendation that he receive psychological counseling. Cho was about to be thrust into yet another new environment. He was taken to the Center for Multi-Cultural Human Services, a mental health group that provided treatment to low-income, non-English speaking or English-limited refugees and immigrants.[16] This flew in the face of strong Korean cultural biases against acknowledging problems of this type or receiving therapy, as they were cause for embarrassment.

15 GPR, p. 34.
16 GPR, p. 21.

Young and troubled, Cho did not react well to his first counselor, another Korean. His next therapist was unable to get Cho to communicate verbally at all, and resorted to having him engage in art therapy. This involved him supposedly expressing himself and his feelings through clay modeling, drawing, and making figures on a sand table. He was asked to draw and build houses in the hope that his outlook on life and the demons haunting him would be reflected from that symbol of unity, family, happiness, love and safety. It was noted by the therapist that none of the houses he drew or built had any doors or windows. Cho's therapist further noted that any time he was asked to explain his artwork his eyes would fill up with tears.[17] Cho also had limited access to a psychiatrist who diagnosed him as suffering from "severe social anxiety disorder."[18] The Diagnostic and Statistical Manual IV (DSM), the bible of the mental health profession, defined this as:

> A persistent fear of one or more social or performance situations in which the person is exposed to unfamiliar people or to possible scrutiny by others. The individual fears that he or she will act in a way (or show anxiety symptoms) that will be embarrassing and humiliating.[19]

Cho's parents were told, and the GPR confirmed, that his problems stemmed from his inability to fit into the new culture of America after immigrating, together with the fact that the tests he underwent for his heart as an infant had caused long-lasting emotional trauma. While the emigration from South Korea was a likely contributing factor to his behavior, he had already been demonstrating these symptoms prior to moving to the United States. The GPR also stated that Cho's school records - obtained with the cooperation of his parents - showed that he had been evaluated as being much younger than he actually was. This indicated social immaturity and a lack of

17 GPR, p. 34.
18 Ibid.
19 http://www.socialanxietyinstitute.org/dsm.html

verbal skills, but not retardation. His IQ tested above average. Cho was smart, and would graduate with an impressive GPA in addition to scoring well on the SAT while in high school. He simply couldn't relate to other human beings. Taunts increased and his anger grew.

A Monster Emerges

They all think I'm stupid. I'm not. I'm smarter than all of them. I don't talk because they are beneath me. I hate that they tease me, that they bully me. I want to just hide away from all of them, from life. Why can't I just be left completely alone? I don't want to go to school. I wish I could just bury myself under the ground where I never had to see people, and where they couldn't see me, couldn't find me. I never knew what to do before. But now I know. I know how to show them I am superior. I know how to make them pay. Dylan and Eric knew, they showed everybody. But I am smarter than even they were. I could do better. I could kill more. They all deserve it. That shrink thinks I want to kill myself. That's stupid. What I want to do is kill them. I don't want Sun-Kyung to leave. She's the only one I love, the only one who understands me. She's the only one who is nice to me. Mom is okay, but she doesn't understand. I hate my father. He is embarrassed by me. He yells at me. He thinks I'm a freak. I'm not a freak, but they put me on drugs anyway. They say they're for my health, like vitamins, but I know what they are. They all think I'm crazy, but what they don't see is how smart I am. I'll show them. I'll show them that I'm even smarter than Eric and Dylan. Maybe I'll really do it some day. Then they'll get it. Then they'll all be sorry for how they treated me.

Through junior high school Cho continued to isolate himself, though he was never in any trouble. Then in March of his eighth grade year Cho's therapist noted that his drawings of houses suddenly became illustrations of tunnels and caves. At the same time he became even more withdrawn. She was concerned that he was having suicidal ideation, though he denied it when she confronted him. She had him sign a contract stating that he would not take his own life.

The following month was April 1999, and the Columbine High School massacre in Littleton, Colorado. This single event not only changed the vision and response of police reacting to active shooting incidents across the nation, but also had a profound influence on Cho. The morning of April 20 two Columbine seniors, Dylan Klebold and Eric Harris, launched a devastating assault in their high school in the upper-middle class neighborhood southwest of Denver. The two disaffected youths aged 17 and 18 visited death and destruction of a magnitude never before seen in modern times. In less than 15 minutes they killed 12 students and one teacher. In addition to the dead, they also wounded another 21, and three more were hurt trying to escape. Untold others suffered non-physical, psychological injuries.

Jefferson County, in which Littleton sat, was composed of 512,000 residents and encompassed 777 square miles, within which were 11 cities and towns. Columbine High School was a 250,000 square foot modern facility with 2,000 students, 140 faculty and staff, and had 75 classrooms and 25 exterior doors in the single two-story building. According to Donn Kraemer, a Lakewood Police Department SWAT operator and long time head of the regional Rocky Mountain Tactical Team Association, at 11:14 a.m. on April 20 the two suspects placed two large duffel bags containing 20-pound propane bombs inside the school cafeteria. Each device was timed to explode at 11:17 when the largest number of students would be present for lunch. Approximately three miles away, and several minutes later, two diversionary backpack devices previously planted by the teens detonated and caused a small grass fire, drawing the attention of the sheriff's office and local fire departments.

When their cafeteria bombs failed to function, the two killers abandoned their similarly booby-trapped cars (which were timed to coincide with the arrival of first-responders) and - heavily armed - walked toward the school at 11:20 a.m. They shot at the school windows, exposed students, and at a responding deputy sheriff who was a school resource officer (SRO). Entering, the two suspects began randomly firing their weapons at any available human targets.

They also threw homemade pipe-bombs as they stalked the second floor hallways. Between 11:29 and 11:35 a.m. the two murdered ten students and wounded 12 others inside the library before exiting to throw more pipe-bombs. Going downstairs to the cafeteria, they then fired shots at the undetonated propane tanks but failed to explode them. A partial detonation soon thereafter caused a fire in one of the duffle bags which was subsequently extinguished by the ceiling sprinkler system.

Police had been outside and waiting on the orders of newly elected Jefferson County Sheriff John Stone for more than half an hour. Until then they had been ordered to hold where they were. At 12:06 p.m. the first officers entered the southeast doors of the school, and minutes later the two suspects killed themselves before being confronted. Donn Kraemer was the SWAT operator standing atop a van with "POLICE" emblazoned across his back, who was pulling a wounded student from a second story window in a famous photograph of the incident. He relates that not until after SWAT teams completed their searches of the vast building at 4:45 p.m., was the scene declared secure of any other gunmen.

The two teens had armed themselves with a 9mm Tec-9 semi-automatic pistol, two 12-gauge sawed-off shotguns, a Hi-Point 9mm carbine, and numerous knives. They also carried or placed 52 small "cricket" bombs, 27 pipe-bombs, 11 1.5-gallon and two 20-gallon propane explosive devices, and seven gasoline/napalm-type bombs, several of the larger ones of which failed due to faulty timers. A "cricket" is an empty CO2 cartridge (as for a BB pistol) that the user drills the top out of, fills with gunpowder or fireworks powder, then tapes strike-anywhere matches around the neck. The user ignites the matchhead via a striker/friction surface mounted on his vest or forearm and then throws the device. When it explodes the casing, and any BBs previously inserted, are projected as shrapnel. It's considered to be a "poor man's grenade." Together the two gunmen fired 188 rounds. Had their plans, as detailed in their journals and videotapes, succeeded and had all their homemade bombs worked, the death-tollwould have been much greater. Inside, Columbine High School already looked like a war zone. The carnage that would have been left if their plan had succeeded was beyond imagining. But Cho imagined it. He imagined so much more.

Columbine sat about a ten minute drive from our offices. I knew a number of the officers that responded to that horror, and attended two of the SWAT debriefings on it. Moreover, two of the founding directors of Archangel led the FBI investigation into the attack. The bodies of the kids had been left to lie there for a day-and-a-half – until 5:30 p.m. the following day – while these men and other forensic experts and investigators crawled around the school attempting to understand this emerging phenomenon.

After the massacre at Columbine, those closest to Cho became concerned that he was fixated on the mass murder. That and other increasing concerns resulted in his parents again meeting with the therapist. After consulting with Cho's parents and sister, the therapist contacted another psychiatrist who evaluated Cho in June 1999 at the Center for Multi-Cultural Human Services. The doctor who performed this evaluation was an experienced child psychiatrist and family counselor. He informed Cho's parents and sister that there would be a crisis in the fall when Cho's sister, Sun-Kyung, finally left home to attend college.[20] Though they were only three years apart in age, she had continued to progress, and even excel in her academic studies in the U.S. while her younger brother had fallen behind a year. Bright and disciplined in her studies, she was headed to Princeton on a full scholarship where she would continue to prove herself to be a success academically.[21]

She had been the most important factor in her family's life in dealing with her troubled brother. Though a very young lady, she was the major conduit between her Korean-speaking parents and

20 At some point subsequent to the family's emigration from South Korea, most likely around third grade, Cho fell a full year behind in school. As a result, although only three years older, Sun-Kyung would be graduating high school four years ahead of young Cho, who would only be completing eighth grade at that time. No information as to when and how his failure to progress in school actually occurred could be located.

21 Roy, p. 29.

American culture, and American schools and administrators. She was also the only means of communication between her parents and the myriad mental health professionals attempting to help their son. Moreover, she was the single person with whom Cho had any kind of relationship at all; the only one he ever talked to. The school, the doctors, her parents and her brother were all about to lose the only element holding this all together.

The psychiatrist this time diagnosed Cho with "selective mutism" and "major depression: single episode." Selective Mutism was reported by the GPR as being a type of anxiety disorder that was characterized by a consistent failure to speak in specific social situations, particularly where there is an expectation of speaking.[22] This is based on a painful shyness, although other mental health experts the Archangel Team contacted opined that it is a behavior selected by the individual, not something he is simply incapable of doing. The *Diagnostic and Statistical Manual IV* defined it exactly the same way. Major Depressive Disorder, in addition to addressing the basic symptoms of depression, dictates that an "episode" has ended – yielding "single episode" – when any of the criteria have not existed for two months. However, statistically 15 percent of those suffering from this ultimately die by suicide. Cho was about to enter high school, yet another new and stressful environment, was losing his sister and was imbued with notions of mass murder from Columbine. It was a perfect storm of adolescent revenge fantasy he would never recover from.

Cho was prescribed the anti-depressant drug Paroxetine which he took from June 1999 to July 2000. For perhaps the first time in his life Cho showed some improvement while on the medication. Reportedly, the doctor stopped its application a year later when he determined that Cho had improved. Cho would never again be on any regimen of medication to help with his personality and psychological issues or conditions.

22 GPR, p. 35.

Despite being on the anti-depressant medication, the following fall - Cho's freshman year of high school – he wrote an English class paper that contained Columbine-esque themes of homicide and suicide. It was inferred that "he wanted to repeat Columbine."[23] The school was forced to contact Cho's sister at Princeton, as the only English speaker in the family, and encouraged her and Cho's parents to have him evaluated by a psychiatrist. Yet again.

Sun-Kyung and the parents attended Cho's next regularly scheduled therapy appointment and were told of the disturbing themes from his paper. Not unexpectedly, the Governor's Panel reported that when this paper was discussed with Cho's parents and sister by their investigators, the parents expressed surprise that it had addressed any aspects of homicide. They said that they were aware he had used suicidal themes, but were unaware that he had ever contemplated taking the life of another. Cho did have a paternal uncle in South Korea who had taken his own life.

This was, quite possibly, one of the inherent problems with all of the schools throughout Cho's life, and the Governor's Panel itself: relying solely on a three-year elder sister to conduct all of the translations about critical issues to not only her brother, but exceedingly sensitive issues to her parents. It should not be dismissed that at the time he was suffering these problems in junior high school, she was nothing more than a 16 or 17-year-old girl, saddled with the responsibility of being the sole manager of Korean culture, her parents, American teachers, mental health professionals and her brother, and American society and its demands and stresses on her.

The biggest problem between Cho and his parents was his refusal to communicate on any level. As he grew, he would speak very little to them and almost never even make eye contact. His parents and sister reported that at times his mother would become so frustrated with him that she would shake him. While he did speak more to his sister, it was never about anything substantive, and certainly not about his feelings, hopes, likes or plans. If made to speak

23 Ibid.

with guests in the home he would become agitated, nervous and sometimes burst out crying.

As Cho grew, his mother became more aggravated with him being so withdrawn and uncommunicative. While his parents urged him to get involved in sports and other activities, his father put less pressure on him than his mother. Naturally quiet himself, Cho's father did not seem to see the problem that his wife did. Still, Cho's father was very strict on matters of respect, and he and his son would argue over Cho's lack of respectful behavior toward others, particularly adults who would visit the home. As Cho aged he often wrote stories that involved father-son relationships in which the father was portrayed negatively, and at times committed acts of abuse and anal rape. However there was no indication whatsoever that his parents were anything but devoted, responsible, loving people attempting to do all they could for their troubled son. Clearly, Cho was viewing life, the world, and every little thing that happened to him through a prism, a distorted lens that twisted and magnified the slightest negative experience or statement. This would continue to fester in his mind through the rest of his life.

Though Cho never had any type of job during summers or other breaks from school in his life, he was never a problem for anyone. In high school he was asked to write about his hobbies and interests:

> I like to listen to talk shows and alternative stations, and I like action movies… My favorite movie is X-Men, favorite actor is Nicolas Cage, favorite book is *Night Over Water*, favorite band is U2, favorite sport is basketball, favorite team is the Portland Trailblazers, favorite food is pizza, and favorite color is green.

—

In April 1997, just as Cho was finishing seventh grade and half a year of counseling for his problems, Curtis Cook transferred from his position on the SWAT team of the Montgomery County Sheriff's Office to the Virginia Tech Police Department. A year later, and exactly one year prior to Columbine, he earned a position on that agency's SWAT unit, the Emergency Response Team or ERT. He would soon become its leader. Wendell Flinchum was already there, as was Wooddell and others. Anthony Wilson, Donnie Goodman and Kim Crannis were all at the Blacksburg Police Department. Goodman was a sergeant in the Investigation Unit until his promotion to Lieutenant in Charge of Professional Standards, Internal Affairs, and Recruitment in 2003. Most of those who would be key players in the drama that would unfold a decade later were in place. Together with Cho, they were on a collision course toward each other and the pastoral campus that was to be their common destiny.

The High School Years

They did it again. Why do I have to go to another school? Why won't they ever just let me stay where I am and be left alone? My grades are good, so why don't they just leave me alone?! The kids think they're so smart. They tease me, they call me China Town and other racial things. They don't know who I am or what I'm capable of. I miss Sun-Kyung, I miss her so much. But with her gone the teachers and counselors at school can't screw with me as much, because they can't talk to Mom and Dad. Mom and Dad don't have a clue about what life is like for me. I've tried. I've tried to do what they want. I try to join things. Things like the Science Club full of other social rejects like me, the uncool kids, the ones who all get made fun of. But I'm even smarter than them. I get good grades, even in honors classes, without even having to talk. They have to talk and suck up to the teachers for good grades, but I don't. I've made them let me do what I want. I don't have to eat with others in school and I don't even have to talk in front of them like some performing monkey in a circus. They are all so stupid. As long as I don't talk, don't eat with them, don't talk in class, it's like I don't exist. I'm a void in space, like I'm invisible.

In September 1999 Cho began his high school years at Centreville High. The following fall, September 2000, a new school, Westfield High School opened in Chantilly, Virginia to handle the population overflow in the area. Cho attended his next three years there, from fall 2000 until spring 2003 whereupon he graduated. This increasingly angry and disaffected young man had just been, yet again, torn from a place he had come to know and maybe have some comfort in and shipped elsewhere. Again without the support and protection of his older sister.

During high school his behavior was marked with the same concerns and reports from teachers over him being withdrawn, refusing to engage in any substantive way in classes, and refusing to even talk or make eye contact. The usual requests and suggestions to his parents to have him psychologically evaluated occurred again. Guidance counselors asked Cho if he had ever received any mental health counseling or therapy, and he duplicitously told them that he had not. By then he had learned when confronting these well-meaning interlopers, to tell them what they needed to hear to get them to leave him alone. And without the involvement of his sister any longer, it was virtually impossible for them to even talk to his parents who had never developed any capacity to speak English. It was now Cho who had become the interface between his parents and American society, and he could keep them isolated.

Westfield's Screening Committee considered Cho's situation and behavior on October 25, 2000, in order to determine whether he fell within federal statutory requirements for providing special services and accommodations, and a special educational plan for students with disabilities.[24] This is called an Individual Educational Program or IEP. They managed to interview Cho's parents, who in turn gave permission for them to work in tandem with Cho's therapist in devising a plan that would help him. This was interesting in light of the fact that all reports indicated that he always did his school work, that his work was essentially good and always timely, and that

24 GPR, p. 22.

he received decent grades. The committee determined that Cho was entitled to be enrolled in the Special Education for Emotional Disabilities and Speech and Language program. Cho's IEP would begin in January 2001, halfway into his sophomore year.

There were problems for the school in meeting all of the requirements of Cho's IEP, however, although he continued to do good school work and was even enrolled in some honors classes. He excelled at science and math in particular. Relatively, his English skills and writing were never very good, but it was in his work for that subject that most of his perceptions of those in his life and aberrant thoughts became obvious. As part of his IEP Cho was permitted to eat lunch alone and was allowed to provide verbal responses to his teachers in private rather than in front of a class.[25] With this arrangement Cho's grades were excellent. No record in the school, nor any information Cho's parents or sister ever obtained, indicated that he was the victim of bullying, and certainly not excessive or physically assaultive bullying.

In December 2001 - the following school year and his junior year of high school - Cho stopped attending his weekly therapy sessions. There had been a small improvement in his behavior but the one thing he could, and did, verbalize was that he felt there was nothing wrong with him and didn't want to go anymore. With Cho turning 18 the following month, January 2002, his parents felt there was little they could do but accede to his demand as he would shortly be in a position to make his own decisions legally. Simply, there was nothing more they could make him do as his parents.

Under the artificial environment created by his IEP, Cho's grades continued to be impressive through high school. He graduated with a 3.52 GPA, and he scored a 540 verbal and 620 math on the SAT. The yearbook for 2002, the end of his junior year, listed Cho as a member of the Science Club. However, upon graduating in 2003 his yearbook did not list either his name or include his picture. Cho's behavior of always walking with his head down and never speaking

25 GPR, p. 37.

was well developed at this point. For all intents and purposes he had ceased to exist.

Conditioned By America

I know the answer. So many people who have come before me did as well. They reach the point where they cannot take it anymore. They make those bullies, those tormentors, run like the cowards they are, scurrying about like terrified rats waiting to be shot. How I would love to do that, to be famous like Eric and Dylan, to show them all. But they lived in Colorado and there were lots of guns there. I don't have guns. I've never shot a gun. Maybe someday I'll show them. I have studied all those who have come before me, just as I am certain Eric and Dylan did. They were not the first to use bombs as diversions and plant bombs in the school, only to drive them to the parking lot where the big ones would tear them apart. They got that from William Keogh in Bath, Michigan all the way back in 1927. The information is there, the tactics have all been proven. It's all available on the Internet. It's just a matter of studying them and improving on them. I'm smart, I can figure it out.

Through his childhood and teen years, during which America saw many school attacks, how could Cho not have been impacted by the brutality of these incidents? Certainly the decision he would ultimately make with only one month left before graduation from college would bear silent testimony to the influence such acts – and the media notoriety they generated – had on him. None more so than Columbine.

Since 1966 when Charles Whitman, a student with previously diagnosed psychiatric problems, climbed to the top of a 30-story observation tower at the University of Texas-Austin, killing 14 and wounding dozens more in a 96 minute sniper assault, at least 49 schools would be attacked in the United States by both students and – in the case of two schools during Cho's senior year at Tech – adults. Some of the major school attacks included

Pearl, Mississippi; West Paducah, Kentucky; Jonesboro, Arkansas; Springfield, Oregon; Tucson, Arizona; Littleton, Colorado; Red Lake, Minnesota; Bailey, Colorado; and Nickel Mines, Pennsylvania.[26]

But this has not just remained an American problem, as this level of atrocity has been successfully exported to other countries. There was the 1996 Dunblane, Scotland massacre. Others nations that have joined the sad fraternity of those suffering attacks on their young in schools have included Canada, Finland, Germany, India, Argentina, Russia, Denmark, Yemen, the Philippines, Australia, the Netherlands, Sweden and Bosnia.

Coming To Virginia Tech

I know what I'm going to do. I'm going to get out of this place. This stinking place. They all want me to stay, to go to some pathetic, stupid little community college so I can stay in my parents' house, keep running into the same jerks who have tortured me for years. They're the ones who kept wanting me to move, to never stay in one place and be happy. They're the ones who never let me stay in one home, stay in South Korea where I would have been like everyone else, stay in the same school. Well I'll show them. I'm going as far away as I can. I'm going where no one will know me, where I won't have to keep seeing these same people all the time. I'll go somewhere that is so big that no one will notice me. Someplace I can be invisible. I'm going somewhere they're all too stupid to get into. I'm getting out of here. Yes, that's the answer: get far away. Maybe I'll let them all live after all. As long as I can get away.

Cho's GPA and SAT scores were the basis for his acceptance at Virginia Tech. There was also an optional essay about oneself that could be submitted with a student's application. Cho submitted a short piece on rock climbing, which was written in the first person and spoke about human potential that often cannot be achieved because of self doubt.[27] It is questionable whether Cho had ever gone rock climbing

26 For an excellent, in depth study of the majority of the major school shootings, read Joseph A. Lieberman's *School Shootings: What Every Parent and Educator Needs to Know to Protect Our Children* (New York: Citadel Press, 2006, 2008).

27 GPR, p. 38.

in his life. Due, however, to federal and state laws no information was made available to the university with regard to Cho's IEP which had propped up his academic success, nor of his complete refusal to participate in class. In light of Cho's problems, his guidance counselor strongly recommended that he attend a small school close to home, to aid in the transition from home and high school to college. Cho refused. The guidance counselor gave him the name and number of a school district resource in the Virginia Tech area whom he could call if he encountered any problems at college. He never made any such call.

In fall 2003 Cho began his studies at Virginia Tech, majoring in Business Information Systems.[28] After the VT shootings there was much speculation that he had applied for admission to the Engineering College at VT, but was rejected, and that was the reason for his assault on the Norris Hall Engineering building. This was untrue. Despite his predilection for science and math, he never pursued higher education in those fields. As he entered VT he was not on any medication, had no support group, no counselors, no friends, and had no special academic accommodations for his problems. No one at the university would ever know of these mainstays of his earlier life until after he was dead. In interviews with the news media after the shootings, Cho's roommates would be reported as saying that he rarely made eye contact with them, and never spoke to them at all. In the report to the President of the United States on the VT shootings, titled *Report to the President on Issues Raised by the Virginia Tech Tragedy*, it was pointed out that many people with serious mental illnesses exhibit them at the age they enroll in college.[29]

Though no one in his life had wanted him to go so far from home, or to a school as large as VT, Cho had insisted. This included teachers, counselors and family members.[30] In order to support him and help with his transition, during his freshman year his parents made the eight hour roundtrip drive every weekend to visit

28 GPR, p. 22.
29 *Report to the President on Issues Raised by the Virginia Tech Tragedy*, June 13, 2007, p. 5.
30 Roy, p. 279

their son. Though they would not be able to continue this schedule beyond that first year, they continued to call him every Sunday he was away at school.[31]

—

Two hundred fifty miles away in June 2003, just as Cho graduated from high school and headed to VT, Donnie Goodman became a lieutenant in the Professional Standards Unit of the Blacksburg Police Department. Wendell Flinchum – then a lieutenant with VTPD - married his second wife Sharon, a strikingly attractive southern lady, one month later. That fall, as Cho was settling into his first year at Virginia Tech, Curtis Cook was an instructor in ERT, and also working as an Emergency Response Diver. Good and evil had all come together in the place that would ultimately become their battleground.

History of Blacksburg and Virginia Tech

The school that Cho had selected for his college studies had a long and proud history. Long before he decided to enter Virginia Tech the area known as Blacksburg was not a stranger to massacres. In July 1755, during the French and Indian Wars the Draper's Meadow Massacre occurred, a tragic event which is currently memorialized by a dedicated bridge near the Virginia Tech Duck Pond. Over 250 years later that same Duck Pond may have played a part in the events of April 16.

The area that everyone sees today was first settled by European pioneers back in 1671. The land that is now Blacksburg and Virginia Tech was purchased by Samuel Black for his two sons. John Black's property covered most of the current main campus and his brother William's encompassed the current downtown area. William Black petitioned the state legislature to establish a town on almost 39 acres of his property, and the request was approved and the town was established on January 13, 1798. On August 4, Black signed over the

31 Ibid.

deed to the town trustees, and the town was named Blacksburg in his honor. In the years before, a young Daniel Boone was even known to have lived, hunted and trapped in the area that is now the nearby city of Roanoke.[32]

In 1801 the log cabin now known as "Solitude," was built and remains the oldest building on the Virginia Tech campus.[33] In 1827 a post office was established, and in 1832 a cemetery was deeded on a few of the acres by the town trustees. One of the first educational opportunities for women was established in 1840 as the Blacksburg Female Academy. It was then chartered as the Olin and Preston Institute in 1851. Within 20 years the institute would fall on financial hardship and requested monetary assistance was made from the Morrill Land Grant passed by Congress in 1862. The assistance carried with it the condition of mandatory military education for all students. The school then became a full-fledged military academy.

The funds were also assured on the condition that Olin and Preston relinquished its charter and property to the State of Virginia, and that the institute be reorganized as an agricultural and mechanical academy. Blacksburg, as a town, was not incorporated until 1871, and one year later the Virginia Agriculture and Mechanical College (VAMC) opened its doors on October 2. The college grew and became the Virginia Polytechnic Institute and State University, which informally became known as Virginia Tech. The governing body of the new institution was known as the Board of Visitors and according to *A Short History of Virginia Tech* by Dr. Duncan Lyle Kinnear, the Board established the purpose of the new college as being to "further the education of the industrial class."

During the tenure of Tech President John McBryde from1891 to 1907, the school fielded its first football team as part of an official athletic program. During the 1903-1904 school year he also organized the Corps of Cadets. One of the more noticeable and lasting contributions of McBryde was construction of the first building

32 Robert Morgan, *Boone: A Biography* (Chapel Hill, North Caroline: Algonquin Books, 2008), p. 30.
33 It sits on the shore of the Duck Pond.

with native limestone, now known as "Hokie Stone." In 1896, Burnt Orange and Chicago Maroon were picked as the official colors of the growing educational institution and were first displayed at a football game in October of that year.

Then during November 1916, with the United States becoming enmeshed in World War I, a Reserve Officer Training Corps (ROTC) unit was requested at the college, and then two months later in January 1917 an infantry unit was established. The Virginia Tech Corp of Cadets required Corps participation for every able-bodied male for four years until 1923, and then for two years until 1962, after which participation became voluntary. This would forever imprint the university with the look and feel of the military academy it maintains to this day. Today Virginia Tech is one of only three public institutions of higher education that have both an active corps of cadets and a civilian lifestyle coexisting on campus. Texas A&M and North Georgia College and State University are the other two.

Virginia Tech continued a long and successful relationship with the United States military. During the years of World War II, Virginia Tech graduates numbered over 7,000 with more than half of the alumni being officers ultimately achieving rank from major general down to lieutenant junior grade and ensign. Several hundred graduates have been decorated in combat, and 300 killed in battle. Three VT graduates have received the Medal of Honor, with Femoyer, Monteith and Thomas halls named in their honor.

Traditions run deep in Virginia Tech from the Corps of Cadets to the Athletics Department, and no book about Virginia Tech would be complete without the mention of the "Hokie Bird" mascot. From 1909, when Tech sports teams were referred to as "Fighting Gobblers," to its present day status as a football giant the Virginia Tech "Hokies" mascot has evolved to resemble a bantam rooster. Today's Hokie Bird made its first appearance in 1987. Tradition has it that no one at the university is to know the identity of the student who dons the Hokie Bird costume every game day until graduation, when that student is allowed to wear the giant orange bird feet to the ceremony.

The original word "Hokie" had nothing to do with either a turkey or a rooster, however. It was coined by O.M. Stull in 1896 who used it in a spirit cheer he wrote for a competition to represent the then-new college, Virginia Polytechnic Institute. Stull stated that it was a word that he simply made up to grab attention. The word has been grabbing attention, and has been a part of Virginia Tech, for the more than 110 years since.

Blacksburg and Virginia Tech Today

Virginia Tech University – today officially The Virginia Polytechnic Institute and State University – is 38 miles southwest of the city of Roanoke, in the New River Valley of Montgomery County. The university has over 28,000 students and approximately 9,000 live on campus. The university actually sits within the town of Blacksburg, which is approximately 19 square miles. The population of Blacksburg is approximately 40,000, which includes off-campus college students. On weekdays the daytime population increases to 75,000 with visitors, area residents commuting into Blacksburg for employment, and other students driving into the town. On April 16, 2007 the campus population was 34,503 and consisted of 26,370 students; 7,133 university employees (including student employees there were approximately 13,000 employees); and approximately 1,000 visitors, contractors, transit workers, etc.[34]

The Blacksburg Police Department (BPD) Emergency Response Team (ERT) leader, Sgt. Anthony Wilson (now Captain Wilson) well described Virginia Tech as "a city placed within a smaller city." The Virginia Tech campus is approximately 2,600 acres or 4.0625 square miles. The school has 131 major buildings on campus with a total of 150.[35] VT's website boasts "over 100 campus buildings." Of the 16 road entrances onto the campus, there are no guarded roads or gates.[36] There are approximately 19.6 miles of road on campus,

34 GPR, p. 11.
35 Ibid. Other sources claim 153 total buildings both on and off campus.
36 Ibid.

leading to 14,369 parking spaces. Virginia Tech also has a private airport and a corporate research center.

Blacksburg Captain Donnie Goodman, who was the Operations Division Commander, which included serving as the ERT oversight commander, stated that crime both on and off campus – and other matters demanding police attention - were typically limited to assault, theft, some date rape, order control, intoxication, rare suicides, and death investigations. This last category largely involved deaths from accidents. Typically, neither police department required day-to-day assistance investigating crimes or with enforcement activities.

The 2006 Virginia Tech Police Department's annual report included crime statistics for the years 2004, 2005, and 2006. The total number of incidents of larceny in 2006 was 232, with merely 23 assault cases. Alcohol violations were common, as was the case with virtually any college.

Chapter 2
Cho's Early Years at Virginia Tech

"Courage is doing what you're afraid to do. There can be no courage unless you're scared."

Eddie Rickenbacker

I hate the dormitory, hate my roommates. They try to be nice, unlike the idiots from high school, but I just want them to leave me alone. Why can't anyone ever just leave me alone? I don't want to meet girls. They would just laugh at me. Like they've always done. I hate my classes. The work is easy, but even here the teachers want me to talk in class. Why do I have to talk in class? If I do good work, isn't that enough? I've got to get out of the dorms. I don't think I can have a career in business. I thought if I picked Business Information Systems I could just work with computers, wouldn't have to work with people. But I realize now that I'll have to work in an office with people, and they'll make me talk to them. They'll make fun of me.

I need a job where I can just do my work in my house and never have to talk to anyone. I know, I'll be a writer! That's the best job in the world. All they do is sit in their studies in their houses and write. They send their books into publishers and get money for them. And they make a lot of money. They're famous. I bet a lot of women want to meet them, but they never have to talk to anyone. They never have to meet anyone. They never have to leave their houses! I can write, I know I can. Those teachers of mine in high school didn't think I could write, but that was only because they were afraid of "what" I wrote, not how well. They were afraid of the truth of what I wrote, how those bullies and tormentors and abusers in my stories all needed to die. But I can write. I'm going to be a writer. And I will be famous. Maybe meeting girls isn't such a bad idea. The girls here are so "hot!" Everyone has sex here, I hear it all the time, hear them talking about it all the time. Even the girls. Maybe I can get lucky too. But I've never talked to a girl, not other than Sun-Kyung. Maybe I'll let my roommates try to fix me up after all, then see how it goes.

Cho ended his freshman year with an overall GPA of 3.00. For his sophomore year he made arrangements to share a rented condo with a senior at Virginia Tech, who worked long hours and was rarely home.[37] Again he was alone. Again he had intentionally arranged it that way. He was a void in space, he was a question mark to everyone. Perhaps this self-imposed exile wasn't as good for him as he believed, however. His grades began to slip during the fall semester of that year, 2004.[38] While living in the condo Cho became convinced that he had bed mites, due to research he did on the Internet.[39] He went to a doctor who diagnosed him with severe acne and put him on medication.[40] The demons in his mind were beginning to take over.

Also, during his sophomore year Cho became interested in writing, and in the spring of 2005 he decided to change his major from Business Information Systems to English.[41] The GPR stated that after his sophomore year and during the summer of 2005 his sister noted Cho's growing passion for writing, but he was always secretive about what he actually penned.[42] His family was thrilled that he had found something he could truly be excited about.[43] On November 6, 2004 during fall semester of his sophomore year, and before changing his major to English, he exchanged emails with

37 GPR, p. 40.
38 Ibid.
39 GPR, p. 41
40 Ibid.
41 GPR, p. 22.
42 Ibid.
43 GPR, p.41.

Dr. Lucinda Roy, chairwoman of the VT English Department with whom he had a poetry class. He explained an idea he had for a book to her, and asked if she had any advice for getting his book published.[44] She recommended two resource books and tips for finding a literary agent.[45] Unbeknownst to her, however, she would confront the seething Cho time and again the following year.

Cho submitted his book idea to a New York publishing house, but it was rejected.[46] Rejection from publishers is something that all authors expect and live with, and certainly something that all new, unproven writers expect in volume. It's simply part of the process and of the profession. I've known of writers who claimed to have wallpapered their offices with rejection letters. Yet for the thin-skinned Cho, whose life had become marked by both feelings of overwhelming rejection by everyone magnified through the distorted prism of his mind, and ceaseless efforts to arrange his life to avoid interaction with others and thereby avoid rejection, this was simply too much. According to his family the rejection from a single publishing house depressed him.[47] Professor Roy formed the impression that Cho "yearned for fame." It was a yearning that was crushed when his book idea was rejected.[48] But could the fame that he yearned for have been that of Klebold and Harris? The fame of Columbine and murder? Perhaps his desire to write, to have his fantasies in that regard published, would have been the only thing to spare the nation the product of his yearning.

During the 2005 fall semester of his junior year, Cho's sister noticed that he was writing less. She believed that the rejection letter he received had curbed his enthusiasm and reversed his improving attitude. He had also moved back into a dormitory. During that semester Cho's suitemates took him to some parties, but this proved disastrous. On one occasion he was seen stabbing the floor in a girl's

44 GPR, p. 40.
45 Ibid.
46 GPR, p. 22.
47 Ibid.
48 Roy, p. 116.

room with a knife in the middle of a party.[49] They stopped taking him with them after that.[50] Cho's roommates that year never saw him play video games, but did see him watch movies on his laptop.[51] Cho also listened to, and downloaded, heavy metal music.[52] That fall someone had also been writing heavy metal lyrics on the walls of their suite, and in the hallways during the spring.[53] Several of his suitemates believed Cho was responsible because the lyrics were similar to those he had posted on Facebook.[54]

Several times, when the suitemates came home, it smelled like Cho had been burning something, but they didn't know what. Cho would also go to different lounge phones and call the suite phone. He would identify himself as "Question Mark, Cho's twin brother," and ask to speak with Cho. He would also access one of his roommate's Facebook page and identify himself as Cho's twin.[55] The rejection from the publishing company may have been too much. Cho was facing graduation in a year. He was going to have to leave the safe, cloistered environment of Virginia Tech, where somehow he had made himself a home. Somehow he had become comfortable there. His parents, who were paying for his college studies, could not afford to send him on for a master's degree. Cho had to face leaving in a year, and going back out into the world that had been so cruel to him in his early years of life. Things were beginning to unravel for him.

Also during that fall semester Professor Nikki Giovanni complained to Department Chair Dr. Lucinda Roy, about Cho.[56] Prof. Giovanni, who taught *Creative Writing: Poetry*, told Professor Roy that she would resign if Cho was not removed from her class due to concerns over the violent nature of his writings. It was also reported from female students and Prof. Giovanni that he was taking cell

49 GPR, pp. 22, 42.
50 GPR, p. 42.
51 Ibid.
52 Ibid.
53 Ibid.
54 Ibid.
55 Ibid.
56 GPR, p.22

phone photographs of the girls from under his desk. Prof. Giovanni had even asked a student what was going on when she noticed nobody was attending class anymore, and he responded by telling her everyone was afraid of Cho.[57] Certainly Professor Giovanni was concerned about him: he was beginning to freak people out. Professor Roy was equally disturbed by the content of one poem in particular, seeing in its tone both anger and accusations that seemed to be directed against the professor and the students in the class. But she was soon to learn that "it could be hell trying to get help for a troubled student at Virginia Tech."[58]

Dr. Roy had had Cho in her *Intro to Poetry* class in the spring of 2004. Though there had been more than 250 students in that class, she remembered him as the one who had expressed concern that he would be penalized due to his poor language skills and his "small and tight" handwriting. She had given him advice on how to get private tutoring at the English Department's Writing Center.[59] He had been extremely concerned about his grade, and though an attentive student, had emailed her wondering if the "F" he had received on a test meant a zero or a 59 in the averaging for his ultimate grade for the course. He wrote, "That's a huge difference between 0 and 59 and I wanted to know where I stand now."[60] Professor Roy routinely handed out a questionnaire at the beginning of all of her classes, which included asking the students if they had any disability that would affect performance. Cho had not indicated he did.[61]

More than a year later, when confronted with her former student's most recent behavior, Dr. Roy consulted with close associates in her department, including Professor Fred D'Aguiar, who was her co-director of *Creative Writing*, as well as Cheryl Ruggiero, then-assistant chair of the English Department. The group unanimously agreed with Prof. Giovanni. When Cho had read the one disturbing poem aloud in class, it had a viscerally threatening

57 GPR, p. 43.
58 Roy, p. 30.
59 Roy, p. 33.
60 Roy, pp. 33-34; Cho's email to Roy
61 Roy, p. 37.

undercurrent.[62] Cho's behavior and the tone and content of his writing was such that she believed security would be necessary if Cho were left in the class. Moreover, his surreptitious photographing of students in the class, predominantly girls, she believed to be an issue for the police.[63] The monster was emerging, and everyone was beginning to feel its menace.

On October 18, Dr. Roy had begun notifying relevant "units" within Virginia Tech of a potential problem with this student. "Units" was the term used at Virginia Tech to refer to all of the various departments, colleges and divisions within the university.[64] In one email, she characterized the problem she saw as follows:

> In the poem he castigates all of the class, accusing them of genocide and cannibalism because they joked about eating snake and other animals. He says he is disgusted with them, and tells them they will all 'burn in hell'. He read the poem with dark glasses on.... His name is Seung-Hui Cho and I had him in my large lecture class last year. The students in Nikki's class have asked for assistance because they are intimidated by him.... Nikki no longer feels comfortable teaching the student, and the students have also requested relief. As I understand it ... I can remove Seung from Nikki's class as long as I offer him a viable alternative. I will be suggesting that he take an Independent Study in lieu of the class, and that he work with either me or Fred D'Aguiar. Nikki, who is never rattled about anything, is genuinely concerned about this student's behavior.[65]

As part of this effort, Professor Roy contacted Tom Brown, the Dean of Student Affairs, the Cook Counseling Center (CCC), and the College of Liberal Arts concerning Cho's writing in Prof. Giovanni's class.

62 Roy, p. 31.
63 Roy, p. 32
64 Ibid, footnote.
65 Roy, p. 31

She asked each whether the picture taking was a violation of the student code of conduct.[66] Dean Brown sent an email to Dr. Roy and advised her there was no specific policy concerning cell phones in class; however, Section 2 of the University Policy for Student Life, Item Number 6, spoke to disruption: "Behavior that disrupts or interferes with the orderly function of the university, disturbs the peace, or interferes with the performance of the duties of university personnel."[67] Dean Brown also contacted a counselor concerning the content of one poem in particular, but she did not discern a specific threat. Dean Brown spoke with Frances Keene, Judicial Affairs Director, whereupon he agreed with Dr. Roy that they would make it clear to Cho that if this behavior continued in the future he would be referred for disorderly conduct.[68]

Cho's conduct was discussed at the university Care Team meeting and it was ruled that with Professor Roy tutoring Cho individually, that this problem had been resolved and therefore the team made no referrals to the Cook Counseling Center.[69] In response to her email to Cho he had written back that he was agreeable to coming in to meet with her, as it was clear he was in a lot of trouble, and that he would "come and get yelled at or whatever you want to do to me."[70] Dr. Roy then emailed Cho and asked him to contact her for a meeting. Cho responded with an angry two page letter without paragraphs or page breaks in which he harshly criticized Prof. Giovanni and stated that she would cancel class and not instruct, but rather have students read their assignments and discuss them. Contradictorily, he also stated in this letter to Dr. Roy that he knew that it was his fault because of his personality.[71]

The next day, October 19, 2005, Lucinda Roy had her first tutorial meeting with Cho. Cheryl Ruggiero had agreed to be present for the meeting for security sake. Dr. Roy later recalled:

66 GPR, p. 43.
67 Ibid.
68 Ibid.
69 Ibid.
70 Roy, p. 33.
71 Ibid; authors' review of Cho's email exchanges with professors.

> Seung-Hui Cho enters my office in sunglasses and a cap. He sits down and speaks in the softest voice I have ever heard coming from a full-grown man; it is so soft in fact that I have to lean forward to hear him. He has already tried to persuade some of us in the English department that we have misunderstood him – that he isn't angry at all, that we overreacted to a disturbing poem he wrote, a poem he claims was meant to make us laugh.[72]

Dr. Roy specifically asked him about the nature of the poem, which was about an "animal massacre butcher shop."[73] Cho had written it in response to a class discussion about eating animals, rather than discussing poetry, which had upset him. Dr. Roy asked Cho if he was a vegetarian, or did not eat meat for religious reasons, and he answered "no" to both.[74] He insisted the poem was merely "satire."[75] Dr. Roy informed him of the seriousness of what he wrote and he informed her that he was "just joking."[76]

When specifically asked about the complaint of his instructor and fellow students regarding the picture taking, he insisted that photography was a hobby of his and that he took pictures of many different things. As Professor Roy attempted to explain why taking secret photos of students from under his desk was inappropriate and that his poem was disturbing he said "that all he was doing was making fun of things."[77] When she read some of the lines from his poem out loud to him, he did admit that he could see how some of the students would think he was angry, and tried to convince her that he was not.[78]

Professor Roy told him that he didn't seem like the same student she had come to know a year before, and asked if "something

72 Roy, p. 29
73 GPR, p. 42.
74 GPR, p. 44
75 Roy, p. 37.
76 GPR, p. 44.
77 Roy, pp. 37-38.
78 Roy, p. 39.

had happened to him."[79] He said nothing had happened, but that he was concerned about losing the credits he needed from Nikki Giovanni's class. Using that opening, Dr. Roy asked him if he would be willing to work with her and Dr. D'Aguiar privately. He said he would think about it.[80] But when he told her he was still working on his novel and she offered to work with him on it, he responded more positively.[81]

Dr. Roy offered to tutor Cho independently so that he did not lose credit for the class. After this first meeting, Prof. Lucinda Roy began tutoring Cho with the assistance of Professor Frederick D'Aguiar, so that he could complete the course.[82] Throughout that first meeting, other than his responses to direct questions, he "was so silent it was alarming." He remained completely motionless and would take up to 20 seconds to begin to respond to any questions.[83] Throughout this meeting Ms. Ruggiero took notes in the form of a transcript that provided information concerning Cho and his behavior. Cho seemed depressed and troubled. In, perhaps, a harbinger of things to come, Roy was equally disturbed by the fact that while Cho spoke in a whisper, and acknowledged that he was shy, he had, in fact, read his poem aloud to the class. It told her that "there was a lot more to Seung-Hui Cho than simple shyness."[84]

She urged Cho to go to counseling. She wrote that when she asked him to see a counselor he actually said, "Sure," but it carried with it the resonance of someone who was just telling her what he believed she wanted to hear.[85] This was something Cho's entire life - incessantly interrupted by interloping administrators and counselors - had taught him to do and do well. Roy has stated that she believed Cho's isolation may have been largely self-imposed. Still, she reported that "he seemed to acknowledge that he needed to seek assistance to

79 Roy, p. 38.
80 Roy, p. 38.
81 Roy, pp. 38-39.
82 Roy, pp. 38-39.
83 Roy, p. 36.
84 Roy, p. 40.
85 Roy, p. 39.

deal with his depression."[86] When he walked out of her office she was concerned that he might have been suicidal.[87]

After the session on the 19th, Roy emailed her report on the meeting with Cho to all of the same units at the university. Among her impressions, she wrote:

> …he appeared to be very depressed – though of course only a professional could verify that. At one point, when I went into the corridor to give him a book, he was near tears. He characterized his piece as a satire. He also said he understood why people assumed from the piece that he was angry with them. I strongly recommended that he see a counselor, and he didn't commit…. I requested that he get permission from others before taking their photos in class and he agreed to do so.[88]

Two days after his meeting with Roy, Cho wrote a long email to her. Clearly he was not through with the discussion they had and wanted to reassert himself. While he did agree to meet with Prof. Roy as an accepted substitute for the course, he also "launched into a long defense of the poem he had submitted to Nikki's class."[89] "The poem was supposed to be ha-ha," he wrote, "I had no anger when I wrote it." At the end he told her: "Sorry, sorry, sorry." This email, too, was two full pages, single-spaced with no breaks.[90] His 1,800 word diatribe that he would mail to NBC in between his two attacks at Virginia Tech a year-and-a-half later would look much the same. The tone of even this quasi-capitulation on Cho's part disturbed Lucinda Roy, and she forwarded his email to all the same units, yet again hoping for guidance if not outright assistance in dealing with the student who was worrying her.[91] Was she the only one seeing the danger in

86 Roy, pp. 2-3.
87 Roy, pp. 39.
88 Roy, pp. 40-41.
89 Roy, p. 42.
90 Ibid.
91 Ibid.

Cho, the seething anger and the threat to others? Clearly not. Cheryl Ruggiero had seen it. Nikki Giovanni and her students all felt it. They were all worried. Why couldn't she get others to listen? In her book written two years after the attacks she described the dilemma she faced:

> When he looked at me sometimes it seemed as though there was a startling cruelty in his expression; at other times, however, he looked at me with a kind of gentleness. I realize that this suggestion of gentleness seems unlikely, even offensive given the horror of April, but it was there. I saw it. Sometimes I wish I hadn't.
>
> I have experienced a lot in my life, including several robberies when I lived in Sierra Leone, one of which was carried out by intruders armed with machetes, but I didn't relish the idea of meeting one-on-one with students who could be unstable. It was a catch-22 situation: put Seung-Hui Cho in another class and lie awake at night worrying, or meet with him myself and lie awake at night worrying. I chose the latter.[92]

Lucinda Roy would learn from Cho that high school had been traumatic and he felt persecuted.[93] Westfield High School classmate Chris Davids would later say that Cho never spoke, and when forced to read by teachers he spoke "like he had something in his mouth." On one occasion the class began laughing and telling him to "go back to China."[94] Others called him names such as "China Town." After one month of meeting with Drs. Roy and D'Aguiar, Roy wrote an email to Mary Ann Lewis, Dean of the College of Liberal Arts & Human Sciences, who shared her email with the Dean of Student Affairs, and Ellen Plummer, Assistant Provost and Director of the

92 Roy, p. 43
93 Roy, p. 116.
94 MSNBC.com, "High school classmates say gunman was bullied," April 19, 2007, http://ww.msnbc.com/id/18169776/.

Women's Center.[95] In the email, Dr. Roy wrote that the meetings with Cho had "gone reasonably well, though all of his submissions so far have been about shooting or harming people because he's angered by their authority or by their behavior."[96] Dr. Roy was impressed by his writing skills but was always encouraging him to seek counseling, which he refused. She would eventually be told by a counselor that intervention by the Cook Counseling Center was impossible. Given Tech policies, the CCC couldn't get involved unless a student came voluntarily. Her pleas for a counselor to come to her office and sit in on one of her meetings with Cho went ignored.[97]

Through the weeks of fall semester 2005 Cho continued to meet with Drs. D'Aguilar and Roy together or individually, though mostly with Dr. Roy alone. He always showed up with his trademark dark glasses and ball cap. Dr. Roy continued to try to pry responses out of him:

> Each time he walks into my office, I am seized with the desire to fill the void he creates. There is something melodramatic about his entrance. He knows what impression he is creating and it seems to give him satisfaction. As a result, I talk a lot. It is partly nerves, but it's also because I want him to grow accustomed to my voice. Sometimes it's like talking to an inanimate object with limbs and an attitude. The core of his identity is impenetrable, his gaze is strangely neutered, as if he has spent his entire life ridding it of expression.[98]

Other observations she made about Cho and herself as her meetings with him continued were:

"He still seems wary of me at times …. Once in a while I see a flicker of what seems to be anger or resentment…." [99]

95 GPR, p. 45.
96 Ibid
97 Roy, pp. 43-44.
98 Roy, p. 46.
99 Roy, p. 47.

"…he rarely laughs or even smiles." [100]

"…I feel almost sick as the time for our session approaches." [101]

"It's not simply that [he] seems … depressed; it is his anger that troubles me, particularly when I am never sure how he will react to my suggestions that he seek counseling." [102]

"…sometimes he gives me a look so full of pain that I am not sure what to do with it." [103]

Cho Encounters the Enemy

I am a question mark in everyone's mind. A void in space they can't make sense of. That's how I hide who I am, what I am, the power that I have. They're all so pathetic, so weak. They are afraid of what I write. Even Dr. Roy is, I can see it in her eyes. She tries to be calm, to show me she is not afraid, but she is. She cannot figure me out either. So I write the things she is afraid of, each one worse than the other. So long as she is afraid I control these ridiculous meetings. She doesn't even realize it, but I've made her recreate that stupid special program they let me have in high school. They've let me finish any class I don't like the way I want to. I like her though. I wish she had been my teacher for all my classes. I wish she had been my high school teacher. Maybe things would have been different then. She wants me to know I can talk to her about anything. I want to ask her about girls, but don't know how. I know I'm going to be famous. If I can't be a famous writer, then maybe I'll make others write about me! Eric and Dylan are famous. They knew how. They had all those girls who probably made fun of them cowering, afraid of their power. All those who teased them, or wouldn't talk to them, suddenly begging. They probably deserved it. I've been around a

100 Roy, p. 49.
101 Ibid.
102 Ibid.
103 Ibid.

couple of them in class though, and they didn't seem to hate me. Maybe they will talk to me. But I've never talked to a girl before.

My roommates kept trying to fix me up with girls. Oh, how I want one. I tried to talk to some, but I got so nervous when I got close I couldn't say a thing. My stomach was in knots. I didn't know what to do. Everyone emails and texts and sends instant messages to girls. That's what I'll do. Then they can't laugh in my face. But girls only want guys they can respect. I'll make them respect me, show them that I'm powerful. They don't know me. I'll tell them I have a twin brother and get them to talk to "him" about me, see what they say, see if they like me. Girls like poetry. I know Shakespeare. I'll leave a message on the one girl's board. I'll be strong and romantic and sensitive, all at the same time. That's what girls like.

But the girls didn't understand. They feared me. They saw how powerful I was and it scared them. The police came and said they would arrest me if I did it again. They came twice. What did I do wrong? What did I do that every other guy at this university doesn't do to girls every day?! Why do they treat me like a freak? I hate them. Dr. Roy's the only one who's nice to me, who understands me and sees my abilities, my genius. She keeps telling me to get counseling. I tell her I will. Maybe I will just so that she can see I'm trying and like me more.

It is easy to understand why Cho liked Lucinda Roy, why she was, perhaps, the first person he had ever let down his walls with and opened up to. She was probably the first person, and certainly the first woman, he had ever really talked to other than his sister and mother. Even his therapist could never get him to talk. Lucinda is an attractive woman, possessed of an exotic look which is the product of a Jamaican father and British mother. Her features give her more of a hint of Asiatic heritage than either of her white British or black Jamaican inheritances.

She is petite, stylish and elegant in an old world sort of way. When you sit in her well-appointed and immaculate home speaking to her, she is poised like a princess on a chair beside her husband.

Though casually attired, he appears more like a professional athlete in the relaxed confines of his own castle than a VT employee. Pastoral scenes of meadows, woods and grazing horses through the windows across the room frame her. She speaks in well-modulated tones, gentle and kind. The soft lilt of her British accent puts one instantly at ease. It is easy to become entranced. She is inquisitive, with a quick mind, and you can see how she would have had the effect of making Cho comfortable, relaxed. Only at that moment can I understand how he, even with his anger and tortured thoughts, could have shoved down the monster that was growing inside him after minutes with her at each meeting. Easy to see how she, perhaps, managed to spare Virginia Tech his wrath for an entire year.

On November 27, 2005, a female student who lived on the fourth floor of West Ambler-Johnston Hall (WAJ),[104] filed a report with VTPD complaining that Cho was "annoying her on the Internet, by phone, and in person."[105] Cho had also shown up at her room wearing sunglasses and a hat pulled down and said, "I'm Question Mark." Needless to say, she was disturbed by this.[106] VTPD contacted Cho, and he was referred to the school's disciplinary office: the Office of Judicial Affairs. Perhaps unnerved by the appearance of police officers who threatened him with arrest, and with Lucinda Roy's pleadings for him to get help echoing in his head, on Wednesday, November 30 at 9:45 a.m. Cho called the Cook Counseling Center (CCC) and was given a preliminary screening over the phone.[107] He was interviewed by Maisha Smith, a licensed professional counselor. A "preliminary screening" meant that no diagnosis could be made[108] and Ms. Smith has no recollection of Cho's call. Her notes were missing up to the conclusion of the Governor's Panel's investigation and report.[109] In fact all of the CCC's records on Cho were missing. It was

104 This would be the dorm and floor on which Emily Hilscher lived, who would be Cho's first victim on April 16, 2007.
105 GPR, p.22.
106 GPR, p.45.
107 GPR, p.23.
108 Roy, p. 62.
109 GPR, pp. 45-46.

a great mystery until they were discovered on July 15, 2009 at the home of Dr. Robert Miller. He had been the director of the CCC. Dr. Roy wouldn't learn of this contact by Cho, or the other three times he contacted the CCC, until she was interviewed by two of the representatives of Governor Kaine's special panel during their investigation in the aftermath of the attack.[110]

In December 2005, emails among resident advisors (RAs) reflected complaints by female students in Cochrane Hall, stating that Cho had been instant messaging them under strange aliases.[111] Emails also reported that Cho went in disguise to a female student's room.[112] On December 9 Cho sent an instant message to another female. Sometime during the night from December 11 to 12 Cho wrote an excerpt from Shakespeare's *Romeo and Juliet* on this female's dormitory dry eraser board that hung on the outside of her door. It read:

By a name
I know not how to tell thee who I am
My name, dear saint is hateful to myself
Because it is an enemy of thee
Had I written it, I would tear the word

Poet Lucinda Roy inferred that Cho wanted to write like Shakespeare and make women love him, writing in her book that "this was passion in extremis, the kind of passion he had written about in his novel. It was centered on idealized, unattainable beauty, agonizing insecurity, and an immature possessiveness."[113] She concluded that, like all stalkers, Cho was writing about himself as "the object of his own affection."[114] On December 12, 2005 this student – who was a friend of Cho's roommate Andy Koch and a resident of East Campbell Hall[115] – filed a report with VTPD that Cho was harassing

110 Roy, p. 62.
111 GPR, p. 23
112. Ibid.
113 Roy, p. 230.
114 Roy, pp. 230-231.
115 GPR, p. 23.

her.[116] It had been in this young lady's room where Cho was stabbing the floor with a knife.[117]

On December 13, 2005 VTPD contacted Cho concerning a report they received the day before from the young woman who was the recipient's of Cho's affections, and instructed him to cease further contact with her. If he didn't, he would be arrested. Cho did not again contact either of the females who reported him to VTPD. Subsequent to the shootings, the Collegiate Times reported Chief Wendell Flinchum as saying, "The outcome of that report [was] outside the scope of the police department." This was an accurate statement, but did nothing to quell the highly critical and accusatory nature of news media reporting of the police response to the shootings that day. VT police were reported by local newspapers as stating that the two young women declined to press charges against Cho. Neither were victims of either of Cho's shootings on April 16, 2007.

After police contacted Cho on December 13, 2005 he sent an instant message to roommate Andy Koch stating, "I might as well kill myself now."[118] This message was alternatively reported by other sources to have read: "Maybe the world would be better off if I wasn't here." Upon receipt, Andy Koch called his own father and asked him what he should do. Mr. Koch senior phoned the Christiansburg police to ask their advice. They said to have Andy call VTPD whereupon they were informed of the message. Tech officers arrived at Cho's dorm room and took him away in handcuffs. He was transported to a voluntary counseling evaluation at New River Community Services where he was examined by Kathy Goodbey, who recommended Cho for hospitalization. The New River Valley Community Services board concluded Cho to be "an imminent danger to self or others."[119]

The New River Pre-Admission Screening Form, under the section for "Present Situation" contained the following notes:

116 Wikipedia.
117 GPR, p. 46.
118 Wikipedia
119 GPR, p. 23.

> Cl[120] seen for face to face eval @ VTPD at the request of Officer Lucas.[121] Per Officer Lucas VTPD had initial contact earlier this AM after a dorm resident complained that Cl was harassing her by sending unwanted instant messages and leaving message [sic] on a dry erase board outside her room. Police report also note [sic] that officers were contacted by Cl's room mates father after Cl left an instant message indicating he might as well kill himself. Officer Lucas said Cl readily admitted to IMing the statement but said it was all just a joke.

Under the form's section for the intake person to "Explain clinically significant findings," she wrote:

> Cl presents with flat affect and states he is here because his friend Andy was concerned about the statement he had made in the instant message. Cl says he was just kidding. Cl denies being upset by having to talk to the officers re: harassing the female. Cl says he does not feel he was harassing her but understands she is not interested in his attention. Cl denies any feelings of depression or anxiety. Cl denies any his [history] of suicidal thoughts, intentions or desires and denies any such thoughts today or currently. Cls roommate Mr. Eide states Cl's behavior has been bizarre lately. Mr. Eide says he is Question Mark and Seung is his twin brother. Mr. Eide says VTPD had been by earlier in the semester because Cl had been bother [sic] another female dorm resident. Cl is unable to come up with a safety plan to adequately ensure safety. Cl unwilling to contact parents to pick him up although he indicated this was the only other option beyond TDO.

120 Client.
121 This would be the same Dean Lucas who would ultimately shotgun his way into Norris Hall during Cho's attack.

Based on Mrs. Goodbey's findings regarding the threat Cho posed, she requested that a temporary detention order (TDO) be issued,"[122] and at 10:12 that night a judge issued the TDO against Cho due to his depression and possible suicidal tendencies, declaring Cho a danger to himself, and ordered a psychiatric evaluation. Cho was transferred to Carilion-St. Albans Psychiatric hospital, and admitted at 11:00 p.m. He was evaluated by Dr. Roy Crouse[123] at 7:00 o'clock the following morning, December 14. Roy Crouse, however, concluded that Cho did not present an imminent danger to himself or others.[124] This was supported by a Carilion-St. Albans staff psychiatrist a few hours later during a noon evaluation. On the Carilion screening form the box was checked that allowed Cho to purchase a firearm.[125]

In his report on Cho, under the patient history section, psychiatrist Jasdeep (Bobby) Miglani, M.D. wrote:

> According to the available information, a complaint was lodged with Virginia Tech Police regarding patient instant-messaging a dorm resident. Apparently, he had been told by this girl not to instant message her anymore. The message was left outside on the erase board outside this girl's room. Patient claims that he did not leave this message. However, he became upset at being accusing of leaving these instant messages and the message on the erase board outside the girl's room. Later he told his sweetmate [sic] that he may as well kill himself because 'everybody just hates me.' He did not have any plan or intent to hurt himself. The sweetmate [sic] contacted Virginia Tech Police, who further proceeded with a mental health evaluation and he was TDO'd here.

122 Roy, p. 64.
123 *Wikipedia*; GPR, p. 23.
124 GPR, p. 23.
125 GPR, p. 47.

> On presentation he denies any suicidal or homicidal intent, he denies any prior history of depression, anxiety, psychosis or delusions. There is no indication of substance abuse.

Under the "Mental Status Exam" section Dr. Miglani wrote:

> The patient was casually groomed, he was oriented times three.[126] Speech showed increased latency due to anxiety that he was experiencing and he came across as somewhat scared of the whole process. He mentally denies any psychosis, delusions, suicidal or homicidal ideation. Cognitive exam is within normal limits. Fund of knowledge is average. Attention and concentration appear to be adequate. There is no indication of psychosis, delusions, suicidal or homicidal ideation.

Under "Hospital Course," the report stated:

> The patient spent overnight in the hospital, essentially it does not appear that he had any serious intent when he made the suicidal statement. It appears to be more an act of frustration. He was counseled about the need to need to [sic] act responsibly and the fact that in his adult life his actions will be followed by consequences. He seems to receive that message fairly well. Seems to be remorseful and apologetic about this situation leading up to this point.
>
> It is recommended that he be offered some outpatient counseling culturate to proper norms.

The "Disposition" read simply: "Condition at discharge: It is recommended that patient follow up in counseling. Access will also do some safety checks. Follow up and aftercare to be arranged with

126 He was oriented to person, place and time.

counseling center at Virginia Tech. Medications, none." This entire report was faxed to the Cook Counseling Center at 2:25 p.m. on December 14, 2005.

After having been held overnight at the mental hospital, Special Justice Paul M. Barnett, in a 30 minute hearing[127] chose not to commit him, even though he disagreed with the Carilion examiners and found that Cho posed an "imminent danger" to himself due to mental illness.[128] Special Justice Barnett reviewed Cho's paperwork, certified the findings, and ordered follow-up outpatient treatment.[129] Cho then made and kept an appointment with the campus Cook Counseling Center. This would be the first of two mental health evaluations.

The person at the CCC who met with Cho on December 14 was Sherry Lynch Conrad, Ph.D. A handwritten note appended at the top of the first page said: "I met with student for about 30 min – he denied any suicidal or homicidal ideation." The form noted two prior triages on November 30 and December 12, 2005. Dr. Conrad crossed out all the sections dealing with potential problems, noting "Did not assess – student has had 2 previous triages in past 2 wks – last 2 days ago." Cho was allowed to go home after his last final exam that semester upon the following disposition:

> Encouraged him to return for intake in January but did not schedule appt. because he doesn't know schedule. Provided emergency numbers for CCC, Connect, Respond and Access and encouraged him to call one of these #s if he begins to have suicidal or homicidal thoughts."

In her book, Dr. Roy cited the Panel Report as indicating that Cho had contacted Cook and that, "A note attached to the electronic appointment indicates that Cho specifically requested an appointment with Cathy [sic] Betzel, a licensed clinical psychologist, and indicated

127 Roy, p. 65.
128 Lawrence Hammack,"Focus Shifts to Gun Laws," *The Roanoke Times*, April 24, 2007, p. 1.
129 *Wikipedia*; GPR, p. 23.

that his professor had spoken with Dr. Betzel,"[130] What the records actually show are that on November 30, 2005 Cho made an appointment for December 12 at 2:00 p.m. to see Dr. Cathye G. Betzel. The note on the intake form read: "Ref to CC by prof. He has been depressed & has difficulty in social situations. Would like to see Cathye since the prof. has talked to her about the student." From the notations he obviously told Maisha M. Smith, the intake person, that he did not have, and had never had, either homicidal or suicidal ideation, or that he had ever attempted either. His case was not marked as "urgent."

On December 12 Cho did not appear at the CCC, however. Dr. Betzel did a phone triage, which meant that she had to call him. Her intake form indicated that he was suffering from panic episodes, anxiety, and self-destructive behavior. However, her handwritten notes read: "Responding to follow up call after cancellation of intake appointment. Stated difficulties were about the same – no worse – but did not want to come in at this time."

At the time, the Cook Counseling Center did not maintain a staff psychiatrist.[131] The staff psychiatrist at Carilion-St. Albans found that Cho's "insight and judgments are normal," and he was released. Neither the Cook Counseling Center nor the Care Team took any action to follow up on Cho.[132] Still, despite all this, Dr. Roy believes that Cho repeatedly contacted the CCC, but that the response he "received was tragically inadequate." She wrote, "Even after he actively sought help, treatment was not administered by the Cook Counseling Center, nor did Cho receive follow-up treatment from on-campus or local counseling services following the order by a judge that he be treated on an outpatient basis."[133] Cho's parents were never informed that he was committed to St. Albans Hospital at any time.[134] The GPR was harsh in its criticism that, "…the university

130 Roy, p. 62, footnote 2, citing Panel Report, p. 46.
131 Roy, p. 130.
132 GPR, p. 23
133 Roy, p. 3.
134 GPR, p. 49.

did not intervene effectively. No one knew all the information and no one connected all the dots." Of course, how university officials and staff were to have "intervened" with family members when dealing with a student who was over 21 years of age, and who was entitled to privacy and confidentiality of his medical condition and records from even his own parents, was never explained.

Throughout this time, Professor Roy's private meetings – her personal hell – with Cho continued. She tried to not only help him with his writing – believing that he was a gifted writer – but with his life and personal happiness as well. At every session she tried to persuade him to get serious counseling, even telling him about the times in her own life when she was struggling with life's challenges.[135] She was disturbed by his description of himself as "secret," "covered, silent waiting." When she asked what he was waiting for, he refused to say.[136] Alternately, he described himself as "unkempt, sad, solemn," though she noted there was never anything unkempt about him at all, describing him as "religiously neat."[137] His poetry continued to be mocking and accusatory, even unforgiving with regard to some people in his life.[138]

She tried to talk to him about empathy, though he seemed incapable of such a selfless emotion. His own pain was too great for him to care about others.[139] Then, again, this was one of the fundamental indications of a true psychopath. He didn't have any friends, and knew nothing about his roommates. He didn't know what his sister did for a living, or much about her, though she was the person he had always been closest to in his life. He vaguely told Prof. Roy that he had taken her advice and was receiving counseling. She offered to go with him if it would help.[140] She worried constantly that the backpack he was never without might contain a gun.[141] Her concern over this, when there had never been the slightest evidence of its possibility,

135 Roy, p. 50.
136 Ibid.
137 Roy, pp. 50-51.
138 Roy, pp. 51.
139 Roy, p. 51-52.
140 Roy, pp. 54-55
141 Roy, p. 52.

demonstrated an almost prescient awareness on her part. When the semester was finally over Cho received an "A" for the class. He had finally succeeded in convincing someone to acknowledge his ability as a writer.

Still, Cho provided Professor Roy with draft chapters of his novel framed by two poems, the first of which was titled, *A Boy Named LOSER*. The novel was a sad tale of flawed characters and violated adolescent trust. She wrote a page of comments and left it for him to pick up in January 2006, after the Christmas break, emailing him to let him know it was ready. One day the novel was just gone.[142] Professor Lucinda Roy stepped down as department chair in May 2006, at the end of Cho's junior year. She moved to Sierra Leone temporarily to pursue a research project, not returning to Virginia Tech until January 2007 for that spring semester. When she returned she believed Cho had already graduated. He was out of her life forever. Or so she thought.

Spring Semester 2006

I'm back in class. I hate it, I hate him, ... hate them. It's the same thing all over again. Why didn't Dr. Roy tell them? Why didn't she tell them I was a genius and that they should respect my writing. She said I was good and even gave me an A, and she's the head of the department. She can order them to respect it, to give me the grades I deserve. She saw. She knew. I'll make her take over my studies again. It's easy, I'll just continue to scare them. They are beneath me. They don't understand. They don't know who I am. I am powerful. I will make them respect me. If they won't respect me I'll make them fear me. It's easy to do. They are all such sheep. My roommates make fun of me now. I tell them I don't need to meet their girls, that I already have a girlfriend. But they say I'm lying and ask why they never see her, why she never calls. So, I tell them the truth: that she lives in outer space. She's a beautiful model, but can't see me much. She's real. She comes to me in my dreams. Sometimes

142 Roy, p. 56.

I daydream about her in class. They don't believe me about her. I tell them I know powerful people, too. That will make them realize how powerful I am. They ask who. I had just read an article about Vladimir Putin, so I told them I knew him and that I was with him last summer. They didn't believe me. I could see they were making fun of me behind my back, so I sent him an email at the Russian Embassy and when he writes me back I'll show them.

According to Prof. Roy, in January of spring semester 2006, "Cho returned to his classes ... without medication, without counseling, without any support system whatsoever."[143] Though things would continue to unravel for him, at no time did he contact the school district resource his high school guidance counselor had given him in the area. Back in a traditional classroom environment his problems continued due to the nature of his writings and his own peculiar brand of participation. Professor Robert Hicok experienced this with Cho in his *Creative Writing* class and reported him to Dr. Roy asking her for advice on how to at least deal with his shyness.[144]

Cho then wrote a paper about a young man who hated the students at his school and planned to kill them and himself.[145] This was little different from the paper he had written in the fall of his freshman year of high school, just months after Columbine, detailing how he could outdo that attack and kill more people there. The GPR noted that the writing contained a number of parallels to the attack that Cho would undertake on April 16, 2007 and the manifesto he would ultimately create and mail to NBC in New York.[146]

Rather than ask him to be removed from his class for largely the same behavior Cho had exhibited with Nikki Giovanni, however, Prof. Hicok, decided to just deal with Cho on his own and he received a D+ for the course.[147] On April 17, 2006, exactly a year before he

143 Roy, p. 65.
144 Roy, p. 66.
145 GPR, p. 23
146 GPR, pp. 23-24.
147 Ibid.

would massacre everyone he could in Norris Hall, Cho's *Technical Writing* professor, Carl Bean, suggested that Cho drop his class after repeated efforts to address shortcomings and inappropriate choices of writing assignments. At one point after class Cho followed the professor to his office, raised his voice and was asked to leave. Prof. Bean did not report this incident to the university, nor did Prof. Roy learn of it until after the attacks of April 2007.[148]

Also, through his junior year Cho was known to insist that he had a twin brother, that he had vacationed with Russian President Vladimir Putin, and that he had a supermodel girlfriend, named "Jelly," who lived in outer space. Though the media and countless experts would conclude that Cho was stalking the females that complained to the police, our team, in its investigation into Cho's life and experiences leading up to the attacks, believed that he had no such intention. After a lifetime of having no social experiences, and neither friends nor contact with young ladies, at age 21 he seemed simply interested in spending time with members of the opposite sex. However, a young man who was emotionally, psychologically and socially incapable of making even a male friend, could not possibly begin to figure out how to navigate the often turbulent and uncertain waters of courting women. We had come to believe that Cho was only interested in dating these females, and simply had no idea – or experiential basis – of how to go about it. As with everything in his life, the manifestations of these normal human urges in him were disturbing to others.

Dr. Roy described Cho's behavior in this regard as the unsuccessful pursuit of women,[149] which turned into stalking due to his desire to make certain they saw that he was "frightening" when he didn't receive the opposition to his generally strange and threatening behavior that he had expected from everyone. He wanted these women "to be afraid of him." She formed the belief that on one hand Cho valued his isolation, while at the same time he craved putting an

148 Roy, p. 67
149 Roy, p. 119.

end to it. She wondered if he hadn't lived in such isolation for so long that he couldn't conceive of anything else.[150] While this might reflect a certain pop-psychology perspective, no one can discount the substantive time the professor spent with him, or her prescient concerns about his mental state and possible future conduct.

Notwithstanding his problems in class, Cho was still making an effort at being a writer. Perhaps Lucinda Roy had a far greater impact on him than she realized. Unbeknownst to her, at this time Cho entered one of his poems in a poetry competition. Its theme of melancholy desperation and loneliness would very likely have been one more thing the kindly professor would have worried about.

> "Spear me down, Heaven"
> By Seung-Hui Cho
>
> This thing, my life, all an agony, of Hell of torture... And years of bludgeoning torment tiny nuisances.
>
> The disgust eyes, dirty frowns, and red fingers pointing at me. Feeling all the patheticness and humiliation.
>
> What time is right to abort the null existence and retire from sick lifeblood. And yet feelings — thwarted by sun's beams ready to attack, averted by smiling faces ready to rape — come, a wish to annihilate my self...
>
> If this wasn't true in my plaguing conscious. But Jesus Christ! Another day comes tomorrow, a shade better than present,
>
> If I can imagine, a day anew like a new born or an old dying, when nothing is everything and everything is nothing and all is mere shutting of eyelids.

150 Roy, p. 120.

> Good Christ! Rip me apart, tear me to shrivels, eat me to help me see a better day's worth and salvage this decaying thing from myself.

—

At the same time, in 2005 Donnie Goodman was the Lieutenant of the Criminal Investigation Unit of the Blacksburg Police Department. He was promoted to captain in January 2007, and would be that department's ERT Operations Commander with barely a few months experience under his belt when Cho's attacks came. In the spring of 2005, during the second semester of Cho's sophomore year, Wendell Flinchum was the Operations Lieutenant, and attended the FBI National Academy in July, graduating with class 222. As Cho was beginning to flounder in the waters of academic and social demands during his junior year, Curtis Cook continued on as a SWAT instructor, which he had done since the fall of 2003. They would need all of their experience, capability and training merely one year later.

Cho Begins His Senior Year

What am I going to do? I can't leave here. I sit in my room, I go to my classes. But I can't be a writer. Those publishing idiots were like all the others. They couldn't see my brilliance. Couldn't see the genius of my writing or even my ideas. How can they not see that I am like the next Stephen King? Only I deal with reality, not hocus pocus witches and ghosts. I deal with real people who are actually lurking in our society. People who hate. People who have been tortured and tormented and have reason to hate. Reason to take revenge. They are the real werewolves and vampires: predators all. That is my genius. It's all too real for them. They can handle the kind of violence I write about in pointless slasher films, but my work reveals an entire strata of society who are all plotting their revenge. We're out there. The others just need to know that they're not alone. They just need to know that I am here. This new teacher acts like he cares, but I know better. We'll see when I first reveal myself to him, to the rest of the spoiled rich brats in class. Then they'll all see. They'll see me for who I am and what I'm capable of. They will go from thinking I'm an idiot because I don't talk to being terrified of what I'm capable of when it is revealed to them through my writings. They keep telling me to go to counseling. But how can they be so stupid as not to see what I am showing them through my writing; how I am going to take my retribution on all of them? In literature they call that foreshadowing. Now that's funny. Could they really be that stupid?

I'm being thrown out of class again. So what? Professor Roy acted like she cared about me. Then she left. Left, and left me alone. Just like they've all done my entire life. I might have gone to counseling for her. Maybe could have done it with her. She offered to go. To help. Now I'm beyond counseling. Counseling can't fix the fact that soon I have to leave school. But I can't. I can't possibly go out there. My parents can't afford to let me stay and do a master's degree, and certainly not a Ph.D. And I can't go home and show them that all of their effort and money were wasted. I can't let them see that for the rest of my life I couldn't leave their house. I can never leave here. My new roommates will be so shocked. They're stupid like the others. Kissing teachers' asses, doing all their school work like good little boys. Making fools of themselves, too, in the hope that some girl will notice. Soon they'll all know the power that they have lived with, that they were too stupid to even notice. I have hid it all well, kept my mask in place. I am a mystery to them. I am still Question Mark. I am a hidden secret to all of them. But soon they'll know.

I know how I'll do it! Where I'll do it. I will go out like my brothers Dylan and Eric, united in our grand efforts to strike back at this messed up society, at all its screwed up people: martyrs. That building I have my Sociology class in is perfect. Not too many people, but enough to exceed their bodycount. The doors are perfect. There's only three public entrances, and you can't see them from the hallways. Those old swing bars on the doors will let me chain them just like Roberts did in Pennsylvania. Wire ties kept the cops out for almost three minutes. Wait'll they see what chains and locks will do. What will I need for it?

I don't know how to make bombs, and couldn't do it in my dorm room even if I wanted to. Guns will have to do. Can't very well conceal rifles, but at close range handguns should do the trick. Just need lots of bullets and magazines is all. And some way to carry them all and get to them quickly once I start killing. This will be perfect. I'll be more famous than them. No one will ever forget Virginia Tech or the name Seung the way they've never forgotten Columbine or Eric and Dylan.

During his senior year, from fall 2006 to spring 2007, Cho lived in a three-bedroom suite in Harper Hall, number 2120. Cho's bedroom was designated room 2121. Harper Hall was two buildings west of West Ambler-Johnston residence hall (WAJ), with only the crescent shaped Cochrane Hall in between. The other two bedrooms in Cho's suite were 2122 and 2123. The suite was on the east side of Harper Hall, facing WAJ, with the top two floors of the taller West Ambler-Johnston Hall possibly visible from Cho's room. With Cochrane Hall standing between the two, and at the top of a rise in the ground above WAJ, speculation that Cho would have sat in his room, staring at WAJ and obsessing about launching an attack there seems fanciful. Cho's bedroom was at the farthest north end of the suite, with the other two bedrooms being on opposite sides of the entrance to the suite. Cho turned 23 years old January 18 of his senior year, preparing to graduate with his degree in English at the end of the spring semester.

The Roanoke Times reported that Karan Grewal and five others shared a three bedroom suite with Cho. This would mean there were seven men in that three-bedroom dormitory suite, though no one has been reported to have shared a bedroom with Cho.[151] It may very well be the case that no one wanted to room with him. The suitemates had moved into the dormitory apartment together in August 2006 to begin the 2006-2007 academic year. Due to Cho's recalcitrance to engage in any interaction, they assumed he was a foreign student, new to

151 Mike Gangloff, "Finding Comfort in Front of Camera," *The Roanoke Times*, April 24, 2007, p. 4. This may be a mistake as the rooms each typically accommodated two, but even with only six in the suite no one was said to share a room with Cho.

America and either unable or reluctant to converse in English. They were later shocked to learn that he was, in fact, an English major.

Grewal confirmed what others suspected: that Cho seemed to have no friends, either male or female. His only pastimes, until shortly before the shootings, were working on his computer and watching television. Suitemate Grewal, 22, an Accounting senior from Falls Church, Virginia who moved to the U.S. from India in 2001[152] reportedly told *The Roanoke Times* and other media sources that Cho was "so uncommunicative that the first time he really heard Cho's voice was on television, in the ranting videos the killer left behind."

According to *The Roanoke Times,* Grewal said that "he and the others in the suite tried to reach out to Cho, but were rebuffed every time. Cho never made eye contact and rarely spoke, not answering if someone spoke to him." "I learned to pronounce his name correctly when I heard it on the news," Grewal said.[153] *The Roanoke Times* also reported Grewal as saying, "In the beginning, I just thought he was quiet and reserved. Later I thought he just got tired of life." No more prophetic words could have been spoken as an epitaph of Cho's tragic and largely self-tortured life. "But I don't understand why he killed so many people," Cho's roommate lamented. Cho had truly become the Question Mark he had so desired to be.

Dr. Roy is convinced that, one way or another, Cho was "determined to make a name for himself," and when he was denied the ability to do that through publishing his books, he decided that he would do it another way. [154] She believes that Cho could not allow himself to go out and have fun with other students, for by being their peers "how could they recognize his power?" Having spent much time with Cho, she concluded that by such actions as stabbing a knife into the floor of a dorm room during a party, he was signaling to all that he was not one of them, and never would be. After a lifetime of

152 Ibid.
153 Ibid.
154 Roy, p. 116.

rejection Cho was turning the tables and communicating to all that it was now he who was rejecting *them*.[155]

By fall semester 2006 Professor Roy had resigned as department chair and was on research leave in Africa. She received a call from Professor Ed Falco who, also, was concerned about Cho's excessive shyness, though she was pleased to hear that overall he was being "cooperative and polite."[156] However, up to that point Cho had not yet been asked to produce much in the way of writing assignments, which had become the window into his mind. Dr. Roy advised Professor Falco to speak with the new department chair, Carolyn Rude. He also sought the assistance of English instructor Lisa Norris.[157] From September 6 through 12, 2006, during the fall semester of Cho's senior year, Prof. Lisa Norris alerted Associate Dean of Liberal Arts and Human Sciences Mary Ann Lewis about Cho, but the dean did not find any mention of mental health issues in the police reports. She, too, encouraged Cho to go to counseling with her. Cho declined.[158]

During that fall Cho submitted two screenplays for a class. Disturbed by the intensely violent nature of these writings, classmates complained to Prof. Falco, who then removed Cho from the class. His days of politeness and cooperation in class had obviously come to an end. In its Monday, April 23, 2007 Special Edition, *The Collegiate Times* reported classmate Stephanie Derry, a senior English major in Cho's 3000-level playwriting class, as saying: "His writing, the plays, were really morbid and grotesque. I remember one of them very well. It was about a son who hated his stepfather. In the play the boy threw a chain saw around, and hammers at him. But the play ended with the boy violently suffocating the father with a Rice Krispy treat."[159] In reality, in the play entitled *Richard McBeef*, the main character was a 13-year old boy who falsely convinced his mother that his new former-NFL football player stepfather was trying to molest him.

155 Roy, p. 119.
156 Roy, p. 67.
157 Ibid.
158 GPR, p. 24.
159 Kevin Anderson and CT Staff, "Week of Follows Day of Horror on Campus", *Collegiate Times*, p. 2.

She turned the chain saw on and attacked her husband who fled outside to sit in his car. The boy then went out and attempted to choke the man to death with a cereal bar. The monster was revealing itself. If this was, in some fashion, a cry for help, there was nothing the university could do.

Chapter 3
Evil Begets Evil

"I'd rather go down the river with a few good men.
I know I can count on, than a boat full of people that
have not been tested proven and reliable."

Col. Charlie Beckwith[160]
Creator of the Delta Force

This is too good to be true! First Morva and now this! It's about time someone figured out how to fix those girls always tormenting us. They start that crap in high school. Even earlier. Snotty, stuck up bitches. And it's perfect that he did it in Colorado, so close to Columbine. I'd like to go there someday. Just walk around inside the buildings. "Feel" what they all did. Wonder what's up with Colorado anyway, that they treat so many people like crap that they have to do things like that. This guy was probably treated the same way I was in high school. Who could blame him? He held the cops off for four hours while he did whatever he wanted to the girls inside. That must be some kind of a record. Everybody's talking about it. It's all over the news. He's famous, just like Eric and Dylan. Just like I'll be someday. The cops had to stand outside that classroom and listen to what he was doing to those girls. And when they finally went in they couldn't get to him. Couldn't even shoot him! Desks and chairs. That's all it took: desks and chairs piled up to slow the cops down. They couldn't shoot him without risking shooting her. Good choice fellas

160 Per Delta CSM Mel Wick (ret.), Col. Beckwith was using the RB-15 rubber boat with a 15 man crew as an example and talking about the importance of the Assessment and Selection process for selecting the "right" man and ensuring that the other team members had confidence in each other. At the time he was under pressure to lower the standards for entry into Delta to increase the numbers faster.

You should've taken your shot. But when it comes right down to it, cops are cowards. I would have shot.

Wait! I can't believe it! Another one! It's only been five days, and someone else has done it. This time in Pennsylvania. This guy though, he took little Amish girls. What a bastard. They hadn't done anything to anybody. How could he hurt little girls? I don't hate them. That's just sick. Those Amish are outcasts like me. In fact they're nice to everybody. Still, he was smarter than the Colorado guy. He didn't just pile stuff up to keep the cops from shooting once they were inside, this guy kept the cops from getting inside. That's why they've already stopped reporting on the Colorado thing and everyone's only talking about this Amish school thing now. He took more girls, he shot more girls, and he killed more girls. That's the only way to do it. Just like I've always known. Beat the record and you're famous. Dylan and Eric beat the record, and look at them. No one will ever forget their names. Maybe no one will forget this guy and the Amish school either. But look at how he did it. Boards nailed up over windows. Brilliant.

But the doors, how he did the doors was the best of all. Just simple flex ties keeping them from being pulled open. The cops didn't know what to do. How funny is that? He tied the little girls up. I probably couldn't do that with the girls here. There's too many of them and they're too big. And there would be guys in the building too. No, I'd have to trap them inside with me. And me the only one with a gun. Whatever I used would have to keep the cops out, too. Probably wouldn't be too tough to figure out. Even if the little Amish girls had been loose, they couldn't have opened up those doors with the wire ties holding them shut. I just need to think about it. And start looking around at the buildings here. Who knows, maybe I will do it. I know I can't be an author. And I can't leave here either. Maybe I really will do it.

In late summer and into the fall of 2006 a series of tragic incidents involving schools rocked the nation, and were the subject of round-the-clock news media coverage.

The Morva Manhunt

On the morning of Sunday, August 20, 2006, Sgt. Tom Gallemore was the VTPD supervisor on duty. William Morva, who was coming to the end of a sentence in the county jail but facing felony charges for armed robbery in another case, had faked a wrist and leg injury on the same side of his body in order to be taken to Montgomery Regional General Hospital by a sheriff's deputy for treatment. He was due to be charged in the felony matter, and most likely held pending prosecution. While at the hospital Morva insisted on using the restroom. The deputy waited outside. After an extended period of time the deputy went in to retrieve him. Morva attacked the officer with a metal toilet paper dispenser he had prized off the wall of the stall, beating him into unconsciousness. Morva took his handgun and then tried unsuccessfully to choke him to death with the chain from his handcuffs. He clearly did not want to alert others by the sound of gunfire if he killed the deputy with the gun. Upon exiting the men's room Morva was confronted by hospital security guard Derrick McFarland who attempted to stop him. McFarland was shot to death by Morva who then fled the hospital into the nearby town of Blacksburg with the deputy's handgun. Morva was hampered by one arm that was cuffed to his waist chain. The other arm had not been secured due to the supposed injury. He also had one leg chained but not the other, also due to a feigned injury.

Blacksburg PD and the Montgomery County Sheriff's Office were both immediately dispatched to respond to the attack and the escape of Morva. They requested the assistance of Virginia Tech's ERT to help in the search. VT's Emergency Response Team responded to the command post at the hospital and assisted with a ground search for Morva. Geoff Allen, studious looking and articulate, recounts all of the facts of the Morva manhunt and killings with an eidetic memory. He looks like he could be a young professor at Tech, rather than one of its top law enforcement operators. Within three hours of Morva's assault, murder and escape, more than 400 cops descended on Blacksburg and Tech. From this overwhelming law enforcement response, the commanders of both the Blacksburg and VT police departments learned some valuable lessons that would be immediately implemented in the morning of April 16 the following spring.

With hundreds of police officers combing the town and campus, Morva for a time was hiding in bushes just outside the Blacksburg police headquarters. Then he slipped onto the campus just a block away. He was hiding in the foliage along the Huckleberry Trail jogging path when he saw Montgomery County Deputy Sheriff, Corporal Eric Sutphin walking down the trail alone searching for him. As the officer passed, Morva stepped out from the bushes and shot him in the back of the head. This was his second killing that morning, and he was now an official "cop killer."

During the search VT's special operations team secured the area around the hospital and checked all vehicles in the parking lot. It then checked the Medical Arts buildings before moving to the area of Davis Street beside the hospital. Several houses with suspicious conditions were searched, but nothing found. The VT team's next assignment was to assist other departments' K-9 units, providing security during tracking operations. VTPD's Daniel Hardy was assigned to the Pulaski County Sheriff's Office K-9 handler, and together they began a track starting with a bloody bandage that was located on Hospital Drive. At a decrepit house that a friend of Morva's lived in on Hightop Road they found his t-shirt, handcuffs and leg chains by a parked pickup truck. He had used the handcuff key he took from the unconscious deputy to escape his restraints.

The second request for the Tech ERT was at 8:30 that night when they were ordered to stand by at the Blacksburg Police headquarters, to be ready to respond to any sightings of the fugitive. They were called out to a possible sighting on Laurel Drive, which merely resulted in a juvenile being taken into custody on a different matter. Other homes in the area were checked, with nothing found.

The third call-out for VT's ERT was the next day, Monday, August 21, 2006. This was the first day of fall semester at VT, and the university's elite unit was no longer just involved to assist other departments. A cop had been killed on their ground. The university imposed a lockdown of the entire campus and cancelled classes. The VT team responded to the area and secured the university airport by searching all buildings and aircraft. They then returned to the command post and waited for new assignments. While at the CP the team was tasked with searching numerous locations both in town and on the Virginia Tech campus.

The last area to be searched was the area on Tech Center Drive on campus. There the Tech ERT conducted a joint search with the Blacksburg ERT. Blacksburg`s team searched and cleared all buildings on the left side of the road, while the VT team searched and cleared all of the buildings on the right side up to the Huckleberry Trail crossing. Hours later, while searching the area beside the Health and Safety Building near the trail the Blacksburg ERT located Morva. He was found and captured while hidden deep inside dense weeds and bushes on a hilltop just beyond the football stadium, still with the first deputy's gun. He did not resist and was placed in custody, then transported to the magistrate's office and then on to the county jail. VT's ERT then did an area search to look for evidence for the Blacksburg and Virginia State Police evidence technicians. No new evidence was located during the search, however. The team then reported back to the VTPD headquarters and conducted a debriefing. All equipment and weapons were then secured from the operation. The team had done a lot in two days in a critical and potentially dangerous situation in conjunction with a host of other departments. Among others, both police chiefs, Captain Goodman, both ERTs and team leaders, in addition to Larry Wooddell, Daniel Hardy, Tom Gallemore and Geoffrey Allen had all worked together to capture Morva. They would once again be thrown together, only the next time in a desperate race to enter a barricaded building in an even more horrific event just eight months later.

Thus the Morva manhunt locked the entire Virginia Tech campus down on its very first day of class in August 2006. Hundreds of uniformed police officers, search and attack dogs, and SWAT teams fully geared up and attired for battle raced everywhere for two days looking for a killer. A security guard and a police officer lay dead, and another cop was wounded. Cho would have sat in his dorm, perhaps wandered the campus like many other students, looking at the enormity of it all. He would have seen the unprecedented law enforcement response. The news media would have explained to him how long it took those 400-plus cops to arrive. He would have seen that the security guard and police officers had been defenseless against a single armed prisoner who had easily wrested an officer's gun from his hand, almost killing him too. "How easy they were to shoot," he probably thought. Perhaps he would have seen how terrified the students were at the thought of a killer being loose on the VT campus. He would have wondered if he could do it too. Whether he could kill in cold blood. At close range. He would have seen all the media trucks and reporters. He would have watched the coverage over hours on national cable news channels. How he would have craved that fame, and the greatness it would have bestowed on him.

Bailey, Colorado

Exactly one month after the tragedy caused by Morva, the media and the nation would again be scope-locked on another event. This time high in the Rocky Mountains; in the tiny, bucolic villa of Bailey, Colorado. Columbine had sat in Littleton, just in front of the foothills that serve as the doorstep to the towering Rockies, what singer-songwriter John Denver called "rocky cathedrals that reach to the sky" in his hit song *The Eagle and the Hawk*. Cho had remained obsessed with Columbine, with exceeding the bodycount of his heroes Harris and Klebold. Bailey was a mere 40 miles from there, yet more than half a mile higher in elevation. It was a different world from Denver and its environs. The remote town boasted one bar then-called the Bailey Deport (later closed and then reopened as the Rustic Station), a tiny breakfast and lunch cafe that served great food at low prices called the Cutthroat, and a gas station. It also had a post office no bigger than many suburban homes, an actual country store (also closed as of the printing of this book), one Chinese restaurant, and a small but well stocked hardware and lumber business. It was completed by a decades-old shop called the Knotty Pine that sold local souvenirs, clothes, animal pelts tanned by Native Americans, with an old fashioned counter and stools where a visitor could get a homemade milkshake right out of the 1950s, a good sandwich and even hunting gear and ammunition. The entire town was one block long. It made the hamlet of Cicely, Alaska of the hit 1990s TV series *Northern Exposure* look metropolitan.

Situated toward the eastern end of Park County, Bailey was another 40 miles from the county seat of Fairplay, which sat in the middle. This was where the sheriff's headquarters was. In between the two was the chain of beautiful and vast mountain valleys called South Park, the inspiration of the cartoon of the same name. Bailey sat along what the locals called a river, but that anyone else would think of merely as a rushing creek. Each summer the tiny burg's one street closed down to host something called Bailey Day, where people could stroll the single street drinking beer, and kids got to take turns trying to drop the sheriff into the dunk tank. Fairplay proudly hosted its own summer event, the annual World Burro and Lama Races, which saw people come from around the country to drag, push and pull the stubborn pack animals over a 30 mile course through the high mountains. It was Park County's Iditarod. This hidden spot in Colorado was America at its most idyllic.

The county was more than 2,200 square miles, with merely a 30 man sheriff's department and a tiny handful of state patrol officers to cover the vast area. The entire state of Delaware was only 1,800 square miles. Within the county's expanse were merely 18,000 residents. With a total of 20 patrol deputies on that small department, there would typically be only four on duty to cover the whole county on any weekday morning. One school resource officer - cops assigned to work inside a school called SROs - was assigned to the 80,000 square foot building with a middle school attached at one end, and about 450 students. It was one of only two high schools in the county, yet Platte Canyon High typically graduated fewer than 80 students a year. Fielding a complete wrestling team was difficult; a full football team without everyone having to play both ways was nearly impossible.

Into this pastoral setting came horror, torture and death in the form of one Duane Morrison, an angry 53-year-old man from Denver with a history of violent and threatening behavior. Denver was some 60 miles, and an entire world, away from Bailey. Divorced, vengeful, and living in his Jeep Rubicon he had traveled the distance to the remote town. It was a place with which he had no prior affiliation. Simply, he didn't belong there.

On the morning of Wednesday, September 27, 2006, with Virginia Tech still reeling from the trauma that Morva had wreaked, Morrison pulled his Jeep into the parking lot of the Platte Canyon High School at approximately 8:00 a.m. The school was as well prepared as it could have been for the horror he had planned. Corporal Jeff Wood had been an SRO since February. He had just trained at the School Safety Summit in Las Vegas in June. That was the second time I had met him; the first not nearly so propitious. For Bailey is my home; it's where I live. The sheriff was a friend of mine, and I knew many of the deputies, including Sergeant Glenn Hardey, a sniper on the SWAT team who would be filling in for Wood when Morrison struck.

Earlier in the year I had undergone some rather delicate surgery, including repair of a hernia. The following day I was recovering at home with some friends who had made the long drive up the mountains to visit. In the middle of the day, wearing my loosest sweat pants to avoid further discomfort, the phone rang. The security company with which I had my home alarm system called to say they had gotten a panic alert from the house and already sent the police. I told them that the system hadn't been turned on all day, that there was no alarm sounding and that they must be getting a crossed signal from somewhere else. They told me it was too late to recall the police.

Like every place in Bailey my house is surrounded by mountain ridges, pine and aspen trees. You cannot see another house. But as I looked out the window what I could see was a skirmish line of Park County Sheriff's deputies emerging from the woods some fifty yards to the front of my home. Assault rifles pressed to their shoulders, they were yelling at me to show them my hands.

With his rifle held in one hand, a young Asian deputy spun me around into the front wall and roughly frisked me with the other. The pain nearly drove me to my knees. I explained who I was, what had happened with the false alarm, and that there were others in the house who were friends, along with my 110 pound male Akita who had spent his entire life around cops and wouldn't be aggressive upon seeing their uniforms. I told him about my surgery and fussed that I would be grateful if he'd be a bit more gentle. They quickly searched the house, and the deputy who had reached me first, Corporal Wood, apologized. I told him it was no problem and that I appreciated how quickly they came, and *the way* they came when they thought someone might be in trouble. What I couldn't figure out, however, was how with a small department in which I knew the sheriff and many of the deputies and commanders, that somehow none of the ones who arrived were officers I'd met before.

The next time I met Jeff Wood was at that very School Safety Summit in Las Vegas where I was a speaker. He came up and we chatted, laughing about the incident at my house. Shortly after that, and just two months before Morrison would take a classroom of hostages in the school, the Park County SWAT team updated and improved the school's emergency response procedures against an event like an active shooting. Everyone had been trained to go into immediate lockdown the moment the "Code White" alert was issued over the P.A. system. The teachers were also to turn out the lights in their classrooms, move the students to the back corner of the room, beyond the sight of anyone peering in and assess any injuries or wounds. The deputies had implemented a paper triage system, where teachers slide different colored pieces of construction paper under their doors so that arriving law enforcement can see what rooms have wounded inside and move directly to them for evacuation first. At Platte Canyon, upon approaching a room the deputies would slide their badges and ID's under the door, alerting the teacher to the presence of police, whereupon the teacher would open the door and the students would be moved under the protection of the officers.

Platte Canyon High School was also, perhaps, one of the few schools left in America that didn't have an open campus. When students arrived for school in the morning they were to remain there until the day's end. They could not leave campus, or drive on and off at their leisure during free periods or for lunch. The Sheriff's Office had mandated that the only doors that would be unlocked during class periods were the front doors that led directly into the main lobby. Across that lobby was the administration office, with a large, open front facing the entrance. It would be difficult – if not impossible - for anyone to enter the building and not be seen immediately by school staff. Though students could exit and enter the building from the other external doors during passing periods, once the bell rang for each class period to begin the teachers with rooms adjacent to those doors were to pull them shut, automatically locking them against outside entry.

The vice principal, Mr. Mike Schmidt,[161] was not one of those administrators who believed in sticking his head in the sand and pretending that violence could never come to his school. Despite the remote and tranquil setting, he believed that if it could happen anywhere it could happen there, in his school. And he was going to make sure everyone was as ready as they could be. The SWAT team not only trained the school employees and teachers in emergency response, but the students as well. For two full days in August, the SWAT team ran a full FTX – field training exercise – using actual flashbang grenades[162] inside the school, with the kids participating. Everyone was also taught how to handle such situations as an active

161 Now the principal.
162 In certain jurisdictions flashbangs are now referred to as "Noise Flash Diversionary Devices," particularly in California, as a result of a U.S. 9th Circuit Court of Appeals decision.

shooter, someone with a grenade, a jealous boyfriend with a gun, and even a hostage situation.

Still, a few of the teachers objected to the new security measures. A couple resisted pulling the external doors shut. One complained to Sergeant Hardey that he was making them feel like prisoners. "There is no good reason for me to have to pull that door shut," he was told. That teacher could easily have looked eastward, down the long slope of mountains called the Front Range that drop all the way to Columbine High School for her answer.

Glenn Hardey – on duty that day - had grown up in Bailey, and spent most of his entire life there. He is muscular, with a cleft chin and chiseled jaw that makes one think of the actor Ed Harris, or perhaps even a rugged, thicker mountain version of Viggo Mortensen. Though numerous students, and even some parents, saw who they later described as a dirty, angry looking old man sitting in his vehicle in the parking lot drinking from a bottle in a paper bag, no one thought to tell Glenn.

Morrison had arrived early that morning and sat in the parking lot. He drove off a few minutes later, returning again at 9:45 a.m. The security camera high up on a pole in the parking lot recorded him leaving his car at 10:53 that morning and begin walking toward the school. It is not known for certain how he entered the building, but police quickly concluded that most likely he entered through one of the side or rear doors that had not been pulled shut and locked. By the end of the day, after seven beautiful girls had been terrorized and raped, and one lay dead, that teacher would have her answer to the question of why they should have been shutting those doors in the middle of the day.

Morrison remained inside the building, hiding in the boys' room part of that time, for at least half an hour. He waited six full minutes after Sergeant Hardey drove off campus in his marked patrol car at 11:30 a.m. before striking. The young sergeant had to conduct a witness interview in another case over the lunch hour. During that half hour period Morrison was seen by many students and even some teachers. Not a single person thought to alert the one man who was in the school to stand between them and any threat to their safety. Hardey drove off campus knowing nothing about the danger that lurked within.

At 11:36 a.m. Morrison entered room 206 in the English pod. He brought with him a backpack, a .357 magnum revolver, a .40 caliber Glock, a .22 caliber semi-automatic handgun, ropes, handcuffs, dildoes and spare ammunition. The room was part of a series of internal classrooms that wrapped around the library which formed the central portion of the building. The only windows in these internal rooms looked down over the library, like the upper level in a mall that allows shoppers to stand at the rails and look at all the activity below them. At the far southern end of the library was a large, 40 ft. high atrium window overlooking a spectacular view of the mountains. This window, and the sun streaming through it, would create an impenetrable glare on the interior window of 206, preventing Glenn Hardey and another sniper from the Jefferson County Sheriff's SWAT team from ever being able to take a shot at Morrison from their positions in other interior classrooms across the library.

Morrison walked into the classroom that hosted 25 students and a teacher. Brandishing his .357 magnum revolver, he ordered everyone to face the walls. He selected eight beautiful girls – most of them blonde - and screaming, ordered everyone else out of the room. The female teacher and some of the boys resisted. Threatening them, he fired one round into a poster on the wall with students on both sides of the bullet as it blew past, forcing all of the others out. He screamed that he had enough C4 to level the entire building. One of the eight girls managed to slip out with the others in the chaos. He was left alone with seven girls who were to feel the brunt of his rage at all that had gone wrong in his life.

At the sound of the shot the office was immediately alerted. An office administrator quickly dialed 911. It was then 11:41 a.m. He had been inside the room for five minutes. Her conversation with the police dispatcher was chilling, the school was desperate to get Glenn

Hardey back:

First Dispatcher: *Nine One One, what's your emergency?*

Office: *This is Carol at Platte Canyon. We've got somebody with a gun. Please get Glenn.*

Second Dispatcher: *Where is the person with the gun? We're getting Glenn.*

Office: *It's upstairs, it's the English pod. [Pause] … Okay?*

Second Dispatcher: *Please don't hang up.*

Office: *I'm not.*

Second Dispatcher: *I'm talking to my officers.*

Office: *Tell Glenn to get down here as soon as he can.*

Second Dispatcher: *I am. I've let everybody know. They will be responding. Who is…? Does anybody know who this guy is?*

Office: *No, I don't know, the kids… the principal just went up to check and the kids came down and said he's already shot one.*

Second Dispatcher: *He shot somebody?*

Office: *No, he shot the gun.*

With an enormous territory to cover, it would not have been unusual for law enforcement to have taken more than 20 minutes to reach any particular point in the county. In fact, Hardey and others have told me stories of having to "run code" for as much as an hour. However, due to a fortuitous set of circumstances, cops swarmed the building in less than five minutes. Sheriff Fred Wegener and former Marine and then-Lieutenant Mark Hancock (now Captain Hancock) were en route to the sheriff's substation just two miles up the road. They were preparing to leave for Denver for an awards luncheon. Glenn Hardey had just reached the same substation. When he heard the radio call he flung the door through the dry wall in his race to get back to his car, and spinning the wheels of the patrol Durango raced back to the school, lights and sirens slicing the mountain stillness. His kids were in danger. At the same time Detective Amy Frank was there to do interviews. She was in plainclothes. Darren Lougheed was there doing paperwork and Jerry Brigham had just gotten off shift. Sitting in his patrol car in plainclothes doing end-of-shift paperwork Brigham, too, tore out of the parking lot toward the school. Some of them might have been in civilian attire, but they were still cops. And they were needed.

By 11:45 a.m. six officers descended on the school. Forming up, and employing active shooter response tactics, they converged on room 206. Morrison had turned the lights out inside, but peering through the narrow window in the classroom door and the 18 inch wide mesh safety glass window next to it they could see him standing across the room. He held a young girl in front of him, with the others behind him. They couldn't risk a shot, and certainly not through the glass.

Talking to him through the door, Lt. Hancock made contact with Morrison. He screamed that he had enough C4 to blow the building up. He ordered police to back up and get out. Hancock got him to agree to let a hostage go in half an hour. The sheriff and his deputies had switched from active shooter to hostage rescue mode. At 11:57 a.m. Sheriff Wegener contacted the Jefferson County Sheriff's Office and requested its bomb squad be immediately dispatched to him. Jefferson County sits contiguously along the eastern border of Park County, with Denver on Jeffco's far eastern edge. Sheriff Wegener also asked that Jeffco's Regional SWAT team be placed on standby.

The call went out to its members at 12:02 p.m. This was the lead SWAT team in the response to the Columbine shooting seven-and-a-half years before. Though only two of its members from that attack were still on the team, they had been training up for another such event ever since.

Morrison released the first girl at about the same time the Jeffco SWAT team was being paged. Negotiations had been turned over to Sgt. Sven Bonnelycke (now Lieutenant Bonnelycke). Though not a certified negotiator, he had some training and was the best immediate choice. Attempts to converse only escalated Morrison's behavior. He told the police that he couldn't hear them, and to turn the cell service back on so he could talk on his phone. But they hadn't shut cell service off. It was just that that section of the school was a dead zone for reception. He refused to identify himself. He would ultimately release another three girls in approximate 30 minute intervals, but not in response to any efforts by the police negotiator. I was told that he would just periodically say to a girl: "Get the fuck out of here!" However, none of the girls was released without first being abused. He had ordered them to all face the wall containing the white board. There they were stripped down. Their breasts were pulled from their blouses and their pants opened. His ex-wife would tell police that he couldn't perform sexually, but he had brought a variety of implements to accomplish this for him. He would stand behind each girl, with a gun to her head, while he molested her. Before being freed, each girl was taken across the room and bent over a desk, where she was further brutalized. The police were powerless to enter without risking the girls' lives.

One of the girls said, "The thing that kept me going through it all was I kept thinking that what was happening wasn't real." She knew the other girls were being molested even though she was facing the board and was afraid to turn around. "You could hear the rustling of clothes and elastic being snapped and zippers being opened and closed," she said. Another girl, who had been molested above the waist, reported that 16-year-old Emily Keyes "got it worse." "We kept facing the blackboard because we didn't want him to fire any more shots. But you could hear Emily saying, 'No, please don't.'"

By 1:00 p.m. the Jefferson County Regional SWAT team had arrived. It was constituted of operators from the Jefferson County Sheriff's Office, as well as the police departments from the suburban cities of Golden and Arvada to the west and northwest of Denver. They immediately moved to room 206 and joined up with Park County SWAT. Sheriff Wegener immediately set up snipers across the large atrium expanse, in other second floor interior rooms facing directly at the single small window of room 206. Glenn Hardey, the SRO, had the further shot, approximately 90 feet. The Jeffco SWAT sniper was closer, with about a 60 foot shot to make. They each had a second officer crouched just below the window in front of them. The moment one of the snipers would have his shot the other officer would bash out the window, just as the bullet was sent flying. Even a slight deviation in the bullet's path from penetrating the glass couldn't be risked with the girls inside. Another cop was put at the top of a ladder just under the window to 206, set up in the library. Wegener immediately gave both of them the kill order. If either could get a shot on Morrison, he was to take it immediately. However, with the sun blasting through the enormous window to the south, and Morrison having turned out the lights in the room, the glare on the window kept the snipers from seeing the interior. A telephone sat on a table just inside the window. The police kept ringing the phone and telling Morrison to answer it so they could talk to him without having to yell. They were literally trying to talk the hostage-taker and rapist to the window to kill him. He never went near the phone.

An incident command post – or IC – was established on the football field across Colorado Highway 285 which the school fronted, and which wended its way southwest from Denver all the way to Fairplay and on toward Aspen. With the larger, more experienced and better funded SWAT team from Jeffco on site, plans began to be developed for a "dynamic entry," using explosives, into the room. Park County Sheriff Wegener remained in command; however, he had to make the call that the Jeffco team should take the lead role in an entry using violence of action to engage Morrison. No more difficult decision could be asked of any commander to make. Fred, himself, had grown up in Park County. Tall, with thick, muscular arms and chest that stretched his uniform shirts, he continued to sport the flattop haircut from his six years as an Air Force military policeman. Despite his hulking size and military bearing, he is a quiet, almost gentle man, with a modest demeanor. His smile is shy and almost self-deprecating, as though he is forever embarrassed at some small social faux paux he has committed. He is the type of sheriff who not only listens to every single police call on a radio 24-hours a day, but can often be seen helping lost tourists and stranded motorists. Now in his fourth term as sheriff, he is highly popular in the county.

Wegener had gotten part of his early law enforcement experience down in the city of Aurora that sits just to the east of Denver. Aurora was originally an area comprised of new middle class and upper middle class neighborhoods built for the huge influx of young college graduates and businesspeople and couples that invaded the Denver area in the late 1970s due to the economic boom from domestic oil production as OPEC placed a stranglehold on the nation. During that period countless oil and gas companies had moved their headquarters to Denver, many from Dallas and Houston. However, the economic bust that followed immediately after in the 1980s saw Aurora quickly descend into a city with gangs, violence and drugs. It was often one of the most dangerous areas for police to work. After one-and-a-half years on those mean streets, Fred had returned to the mountains. First he worked for another year-and-a-half as an investigator for the Idaho Springs Police Department. Then he went back to his home in Park County where he was quickly elected sheriff. Though the size of the county was immense, it retained its small and quaint atmosphere and was the kind of place where he could know almost everyone in his jurisdiction. And they could know him. His own two kids were inside the school that day, as was the son of SRO Jeff Wood. Wood was also the driving instructor and Hardey the swim team coach. The head of the Colorado Highway Patrol for that area, Sgt. Gary Rhoads, was the wrestling coach. For the officers there, this was very personal.

By 1:30 p.m., not only were the snipers in place, eyes scanning, desperately trying to penetrate the glare and gloom behind it to take their shot, but plans had been developed for the dynamic entry. At this same time the last of the five girls Morrison would release came through the door with no warning. He was alone inside with the last two girls: a German exchange student and 16-year-old Emily Keyes who had been suffering the brunt of his sexual rage. Emily was slender and modest, with long blonde hair and a sweet and engaging personality. She worked part time as a waitress at the Cutthroat café.

As the afternoon wore on, Morrison was 30 feet across the room from the door, with his back to the wall and the two girls in front of him. Yelling into the room, new negotiator Stacy Jarvis asked the girls if they are okay, and they were able to respond. One officer, who spoke German, began conversing with the coed exchange student in her native language. Morrison freaked out and threatened to shoot her if it continued. He demanded that the air conditioner be turned off.

The bomb squad had arrived at 1:40 p.m. The police attempted to snake fiber optic cable into the room, but Morrison saw this and screamed that he would blow up the entire building. At 2:32 p.m., efforts by another team of officers to inspect the roof of the building for possible entry yielded much the same result. The roof was covered with river rock and "it sounded like a herd of elephants up there," according to Sheriff Wegener. Morrison was escalating and the likelihood of having to end the siege in violence was increasing.

At 3:05 p.m., Morrison was still refusing a throw phone, and wouldn't answer the ringing phone on the table against the window. Though there was no ability to use cell phones, enough signal existed for text messages to be sent. Emily Keyes had been texting her parents, John-Michael and Ellen, waiting pensively with their son outside on the football field. The police were increasing the tempo of their negotiation efforts. They were insisting he come out, that he release the hostages. He just kept telling them to wait. At no time did he ever make any demands.

At 3:23 p.m., all preparations in anticipation of a dynamic entry had been put in place. An explosive charge would bisect the door into the room, while a water impulse gun port would be blown through the south wall, just to the left of the door. As these explosions were occurring, the officer on the ladder under the window would break it and throw a flashbang grenade in toward Morrison. He had had Emily yell out that he was going to blow up the whole building and kill everyone. "It would all be over at four o'clock," he had her tell the police arrayed just beyond the door. The threat had to be taken seriously. Emily sent a last text message to her parents outside. It read simply, "I love u guys." At 3:32 p.m. the girls inside began screaming. The police believed they were about to be killed. Fred Wegener gave the order to "go." At 3:36 p.m. they went in.

The door blew, as did the water port. The flashbang was thrown in and detonated near Morrison. Morrison barely flinched at all of this going off around him. He stood crouched against the far wall, 30 feet from the door that was the SWAT entry point. He had a girl in each arm in front of him, his arms around their necks, a pistol in his hand. He had stacked all of the furniture – desks, chairs, tables – in a pile between himself and the door. At the detonations the German student dropped from his arm and ran scrambling away, straight across the line of fire of the first two officers to enter. They were short, stocky Grant Whitus and tall, lanky A.J. DeAndrea. They were also the only two SWAT operators from the Jeffco team that had been at Columbine.[163] At the front was Grant with a protective shield held before them in one hand, and a handgun in the other. Taller, A.J. was behind him, with an assault rifle held over the top. Grant took a round in the shield immediately upon entering. Still they pressed the battle. Everything was moving at lightning speed. Morrison held petite Emily Keyes in front of him, with a gun to her head. The officers

163 In 2010 Grant Whitus left the SWAT team.

were fighting and kicking their way through the furniture, yelling at Morrison to "put the gun down!" The police were unable to take such a thin margin shot from that distance. Morrison fired one round into Emily's head, then another into his own. The officers hit him twice more as his body was falling to the ground. The entire event, from detonation to end took a mere 3.7 seconds. Emily Keyes was dead.

The media was consumed by the tragedy at Platte Canyon High School. It had returned the specter of Klebold and Harris to Colorado. And to the nation. Yet America had never before seen an attack of this type, where her young girls were held hostage and sexually assaulted and the press was scope-locked on it. News programs carried the story around-the-clock. But only for five days. Cho would have seen this. Having studied and obsessed over Columbine for years, he would not have missed this event or its significance to what he, perhaps, was already contemplating. After all, hadn't he already written a second paper at Tech on how he could "do a Columbine" at VT? Cho would have seen the unprecedented tactical hurdle that the police had been confronted with. Out of all the attacks on U.S. schools, never before had anyone used any type of fortifications. Morrison had merely used the furniture for interior obstacles for law enforcement upon entry. But that had been enough to slow them down, to stymie them for seconds, and allow him the time he needed to shoot his hostage.

Cho could not have missed the press conference shortly after. There, a crushed Fred Wegener, with tears unashamedly streaking his face, told an enormous crowd of students, family members, townspeople and reporters, that Emily had died. Cho would have seen Emily's father embrace the sheriff before all the cameras, and tell the world that he knew that if Fred could, he would give up his own life in an instant to bring Emily back. There would be no threats of lawsuits. John-Michael and Ellen Keyes knew the police had done all they could. They knew that Fred Wegener and every officer there was destroyed by the outcome, that their souls were damaged beyond repair at what they were unable to do. They only wished things had turned out differently. With that solemn thought, they made their way home to their house high atop a nearby mountain. A house that suddenly seemed so empty.

I was called into the school by the Park County Sheriff's Office as soon as they regained control of the crime scene that day. I didn't want to go. I didn't want to see Emily's blood on her classroom floor. I thought that horror followed the physics principle of gas, that it expanded to occupy all available space. Certainly all available mental space. In Beslan an entire city had been brought to its knees by the taking of 1,217 hostages and the deaths of 314 of them, 186 of them children. In Bailey, the same thing had been accomplished with the taking of seven girls, and the death of a single beautiful young lady. It was all the same. For me it was Beslan all over again.

But the sheriff and Park County SWAT team wanted an assessment of everything they had confronted, and how they had responded at each turn of events. I entered room 206 with Jeff Wood, Glenn Hardey, investigator Amy Frank, Mark Hancock and others. You could feel the horror and sense the evil that inspired it. Blood streaked the far wall. I found myself wondering if it was Emily's blood I was looking at. I hoped not. She used to serve me breakfast at the café in the mornings when I would return from another week of travel for work. She was always sweet and friendly. I didn't want to remember her like this. As we walked through the school that night, looking at each point, reliving each minute of the entire four hour operation, they only wanted to know how they could be better prepared. They wanted to know how they could do it better "the next time." And Fred Wegener said, "You know the next one is coming." The next one did come, only five days later. Though it would take place 1,800 miles from remote Bailey, I would be just a few miles away when that one occurred as well. I would have the opportunity to study that attack and the next evolution in fortifications that police would face in an attack on a school. Cho would have been doing the same.

Nickel Mines, Pennsylvania

Most people in the country don't remember the Bailey school attack. But they knew all about it for five days. For five long days the media reported on a never-before-seen type of attack on our children. While America had seen more than its share of school shootings, never before had someone taken hostages in a room for the purpose of sexually assaulting young girls. Stories ran day and night. And then they stopped. They were superseded by another man who decided that he, too, could wrest revenge for all the wrongs done him in his life. He knew intuitively, through the sheer evil of his own mind, something that al Qaeda taught as formal doctrine and factored into all of its strategic level attacks. Al Qaeda strategized that in order to spread fear throughout the world, that they needed each strategic level attack to be made famous. And they needed the media to give them that fame. To do that they sought to surpass the number of captives in any hostage-taking attack. But in all attacks they had to set a record in the number of deaths. But for that, the press would cover the story only superficially, then quickly move on to other, more recent events. Klebold and Harris had known this. They had wanted to be more famous than the student shooters from West Paducah, Kentucky; Jonesboro, Arkansas; Pearl, Mississippi; and Springfield, Oregon, among others. And they knew exactly what they had needed to achieve that fame: they had to kill more students than anyone ever had before. The Columbine killers achieved that infamy with the deaths of 12 of their fellow students and one teacher. Cho recognized it too. That is why he had been dwelling on surpassing Klebold and Harris' record.

Now Charles Carl Roberts, IV had figured it out too. Though Pennsylvania State Police investigators would find that he had begun accumulating some of the things that he would need for his own attack even before Morrison took room 206 in Colorado, he could not have helped but be fascinated by that assault. Already contemplating some type of an attack on innocents, Roberts must have watched in awe as events unfolded at that obscure school in the mountains of Colorado.

He could not help but be aroused at the thought of doing what he wished, whatever he wanted, to helpless girls. But in the black and twisted labyrinth of his thoughts, his tastes ran even more to the dark side, to inexplicable evil. He wasn't going to sexually brutalize older teenage girls. He wanted little girls. Girls too young to understand, and from a culture so simplistic and innocent that they couldn't begin to comprehend all that he was going to do to them.

He may have been thinking about such an attack for a long time; perhaps months, maybe years. But Morrison showed him that he could do it. He likely made Roberts believe that he, too, could be made famous by catharsizing all of the myriad sick fantasies that he had held at bay in the catacombs of his mind for so long. But he needed to be more famous than Morrison, and he knew how he was going to do it.

Roberts had bought the first of the items he would need to restrain little girls, and hold the police off sufficiently to shoot them all, on September 26, the day before Morrison drove into the Platte Canyon High School parking lot. He would have realized that after Bailey, police all over the country were already deciding how they would handle Morrison's interior obstructions should they ever be encountered again. His fortifications would have to be better. If the police were ready to deal with such obstructions faster than the cops in Colorado had, then he needed to throw one more tactical hurdle at them that they had not seen before. He needed time to kill. He needed to slow the cops down to give himself that time.

He purchased flexible cable ties, large screw-in eyebolts and an electrical stun gun; the last being purchased the day after the Bailey siege. His list of equipment for his attack also included duct tape; carpentry tools; nails; wrenches; KY Jelly for assaulting the littlest girls; guns; ear plugs; batteries; a flashlight; candles; lumber; hose; and rope. He would bring 600 rounds of 30.06, 9mm and 12 gauge ammunition into the tiny, one room school house. He was not planning on coming out alive.

Roberts was as unlikely a person to go on such a rampage as could be found anywhere. Thirty-two years old, he had lived in the rural Lancaster area all of his life. He looked like the neighborhood dad who coached his kids' little league baseball team. He had been a regular churchgoer and had even met his wife at a church function years before, though he had begun moving away from the church in the months leading up to his attack. He was employed as a milk delivery truck driver, and even made deliveries to several of the families of the girls who would be his victims. When he walked into the school several of the kids would recognize him. They would trust him. He had no criminal record, nor had he ever been treated for mental health problems. His neighbors described him as being upbeat and jovial.[164] He had lost his first daughter, Elise, nine years before when she was born prematurely. She had only lived for 20 minutes. He and his wife had three other children. Though he lived a mere mile-and-a-half from the school, he was not Amish and had no connection to that community beyond milk deliveries and the casual contact of all those who lived in close proximity to the gentle and God-fearing farmers and craftsmen.

The school he had targeted sat out in the open in Bart Township, in the Older Amish Community of Nickel Mines at the intersection of Nickel Mine and White Oak roads, both remote rural lanes. It was situated in the midst of more than 600 yards of flat, open space, and was a one room building without electricity, phones or any modern technology. The school roof held a bell to signal the start of class to the children walking in from their farms. Merely nine miles from the Pennsylvania State Police Lancaster Barracks, the stucco and wood frame structure had two doors, one in the front center and another on the right side, to the rear as you approached the building. Both were metal and opened outward. Harkening back to the days depicted in Little House on the Prairie, it was one of 180 similar one-room Amish school houses in Lancaster County.

164 *Wikipedia*, "Amish School Shooting."

The remote location and lack of telephones among the school's occupants guaranteed Roberts the time he would need. He came fully prepared to improve on Morrison's example. With Bailey as a model, he determined that exterior fortifications would significantly delay law enforcement's penetration of the building. He must have thought that at Platte Canyon High Morrison had stupidly let the cops stand just outside the door the entire time. Breaching the room was easy for them. All Morrison had done with his pile of desks and chairs was to buy himself a couple of seconds to shoot a single girl. Roberts intended to increase his record by 1,000 percent. The school was perfect, and standing outside with the doors and window shutters closed the cops wouldn't even know what they were up against until it was too late.

At 8:45 a.m. on Monday, October 2, 2006, Charles Roberts walked with his wife Marie to drop off two of their children at the school bus stop. He watched as they clambered aboard the bus amidst a host of giggling school children. By 9:14 a.m. he was in a local store purchasing more large screw eyebolts and cable ties. At 10:10 passersby noticed Roberts sitting in his milk delivery truck at the nearby intersection watching the schoolhouse. The milk truck would later be located at the auction building by that very intersection. At 10:00 a.m. the children had raced, clambering and laughing out of the cottage-sized building for recess. Roberts sat and watched it all. He saw the innocent glee of little children at play. And he imagined raping and killing them. Much like Cho six months later, he thought only of how they would cower and fall before him. How they would fear his power. It was a bright sunny morning in central Pennsylvania. The beautiful fall weather, the laughter of children, the pastoral scene, all should have served as a reaffirmation of the existence of a beneficent God. However, none of this, not even the innocence of the tiny Amish children, did anything to assuage his rage or make him reconsider the horror he was about to unleash.

At 10:15 a.m. the children were called in from recess. Roberts then left his milk delivery truck at the auction parking lot which served as a staging area for the drivers to leave their personal vehicles and begin their rounds in the milk vans. He got back into his own pickup truck, laden with all of the tools of his plan, and drove the quarter mile to the school. It was only ten minutes later that Roberts backed his truck up to the front door of the school. Once again, death had arrived at a school full of innocent children.

At 10:26 a.m. he walked through the unlocked front door of the school. He was carrying a piece of metal and proceeded to tell the 20-year-old female teacher, Emma Mae Zook, 15 boys, 11 girls, and the teacher's mother, sister, and two sisters-in-law who were there to assist with class a concocted story of needing help finding a clevis pin that he had lost outside. One of the women was pregnant. He asked them if anyone had found one out on the road. Being a kind and helpful people they offered to assist him and several students followed him back outside. Roberts was mumbling his words and not making direct eye contact.[165] At 10:27 a.m. he walked straight to his truck and retrieved a 9mm semi-automatic handgun. One of the boys saw him chamber a round. The metallic echo of the weapon's slide slamming forward must have seemed eerily out of place in so picturesque a setting.

Roberts forced those who had come out to assist him back into the school at approximately 10:30 a.m. Upon seeing him re-enter the building armed with a gun the teacher and her mother fled out the side door. They raced the half mile to the closest farmhouse north of the school to summon help. Roberts told an older boy to "get her or there will be shooting." The boy raced out of the building and saw the women fleeing across the fields. He was terrified Roberts would kill them all if he didn't bring them back. He had promised to do just that, and a classroom full of terrified people were left to his mercy. But mercy was beyond him.

From 10:30 to 10:35 a.m. Roberts made several trips from his pickup truck into the building, carrying all that he had prepared for his siege and massacre. He made some of the older boys help him.

165 *Wikipedia*, "Amish School Shooting."

They carried in the 600 rounds of ammunition for his rifle, shotgun and handgun, as well as gunpowder. He also had prepared a headlamp for the gloom in the electricity-less building once the doors and shutters were closed. As well he brought a bucket of tools, chains, nails, change of clothes, toilet paper, candles, plastic flex ties, and ear plugs against the shock of gunfire in such close confines that he knew would take place. He ordered all of the male children, the pregnant woman, and the teacher's sister and sisters-in-law with infants, out of the building. He was only there for the little girls. There were eleven, well beyond the seven Morrison held, and they would do. Nine-year-old Emma Fisher, who spoke only Pennsylvania German and did not understand his instruction to "Stay here, do not move, you will be shot," slipped out with her brother Peterli. Then there were ten.

He ordered the girls to line up against the blackboard, exactly as Morrison had done. Roberts then began fortifying his position. He secured the side door with the flexible wire ties so that it could not be opened. He closed the shutters over the windows and began nailing up the lumber he brought over them. The police couldn't know that they had been fortified. He had prepared another board with ten large eyebolts set ten inches apart. He seemed to know exactly how many hostages he would keep from the beginning. Either that or his original plan was for one to always be unsecured to be raped. Roberts had the ten girls lie down on their stomachs with their heads under the blackboard and he tied their hands and feet. He told them that he was sorry for what he was about to do, but "I'm angry at God and I need to punish some Christian girls to get even with Him." He bound each girl's ankles to the girl's next to her. He then nailed the wooden plank into the blackboard. Later he was going to stand them up and chain their wrists to the eyebolts to be raped. These girls were between the ages of six and thirteen-years-old. He took out the KY Jelly and told them what he was going to do to them. They were sobbing and screaming, exactly what he wanted. Some of the older girls volunteered to be raped first to spare the younger ones for as long as they could.

As this was occurring the young teacher and her mother had been racing to the farm of Amos Smoker. Though the Amish eschew modern conveniences and technology, they are not completely ostracized from the world, and many keep cell phones in barns or woodsheds outside their houses for emergencies. At 10:32 a.m. she arrived, panting from her long race, and told Smoker what was happening. The farmer's 911 call was received by the county dispatch center at 10:35 a.m. It was transferred to the Central Dispatch Center of the Pennsylvania State Police. By 10:38 a.m. the first state trooper had been sent from the Lancaster Barracks nine miles away and was racing to the remote schoolhouse. As he rocketed toward the school, the Ford Crown Vic highway patrol vehicle hugged the pavement as the siren and lights tore through the distant farms. The teacher continued to feed information to the dispatcher, that was then relayed to the trooper. She described Roberts and the gun she had seen. The boy who had chased after her reported seeing him binding the girls. And them screaming.

With the police on their way, and Emma Mae Zook continuing to relay information to the dispatcher, Amos Smoker and his two large dogs stealthily moved from his farm up to the windowless back wall of the schoolhouse. According to reporter Rick Armellino, "Hoping for an opportunity to help the little girls, he slowly crept around one side of the wooden structure and positioned himself as an observer next to a side window." Armellino reported that as he was attempting to look through the shuttered windows Smoker saw that the first police patrol vehicle was not slowing down to stop. He sprinted toward the road to wave down the trooper, who made a quick U-turn and slid to a stop outside the school.[166] It was 10:45 in the morning.[167]

When the state police arrived Roberts ordered them to leave the property or he would shoot. He told the girls, "I'm going to make

166 Rick Armellino, "Revisiting the Amish Schoolhouse Massacre," *Outside the Box*, August 22, 2007; *Wikipedia*, "Amish School Shooting."

167 *Wikipedia* places this arrival at 10:42 a.m., though Pennsylvania State Police Deputy Commander Lt. Col. Jon Kurtz places it at the slightly later time of 10:45 a.m., Presentation on the Nickel Mines attack by Lt. Col. Jon Kurtz, Delaware County Community College, April 7, 2008.

you pay for my daughter." One of the girls, 13-year old Marian, said, "Shoot me first." The next troopers on scene were right behind. They checked the doors and windows and reported the license number on Roberts' truck, still parked before the front door. They immediately ordered the State Police SRT – Special Response Team[168] – be alerted and deployed. A team of officers was positioned just behind a shed attached to the rear corner of the schoolhouse. They could hear children screaming and asked for authorization to breach the school, to rescue the girls. They wanted to move up to the windows to assault. The permission was denied. They were ordered to stand down and wait. They were afraid of what was being done to the girls. "Do not approach the building," they were told. Roberts had been inside for 15 minutes.

Roberts was hailed on troopers' cruiser PA systems. They ordered him to throw his weapons out and surrender. He screamed back at them, demanding that they leave immediately. By 11:00 a.m. a large crowd including police officers, emergency medical technicians, and Amish residents, was gathered outside the schoolhouse and at a nearby ambulance staging area. County and state police dispatchers had briefly established telephone contact with Roberts as he continued to threaten to kill the children.[169]

At 10:58 a.m., Mrs. Roberts called 911 after arriving home from a prayer study group meeting. She had discovered a suicide note left on the kitchen table addressed to her and had received a brief and disturbing emotional phone call from her husband. She called 911 and identified herself. She explained who her husband was and gave a physical description. She told the dispatcher that it sounded like a suicide note, and that he had written of "never coming home." The 911 dispatcher put her in touch with state police. She had suddenly and inexplicably been thrust into a nightmare and must have only wanted to wake from it.

168 Another name for a law enforcement SWAT team.

169 "Family friend:Amish girl asked to be shot to save others". *CNN.com.* 2006-10-06. Archived from the original on October 9, 2006; *Wikidpedia,*"Amish School Shooting." http://web.archive.org/web/20061009002325/http://www.cnn.com/2006/US/10/06/amish.girls.reut/index.html. Retrieved 2006-10-06.

Having quickly "run" Roberts' truck plates, the police called his wife at home and explained the situation. She was shocked. Between 10:45 and 10:50 she tried to reach him on his cell phone. As she was frantically trying to reach her husband, at 10:47 a.m. other units had arrived and established a perimeter around the school. Roberts brought them under fire. They fell further back. At 10:49 a.m., the troopers on site radioed that the windows were all shut. Deputy Commander Lt. Col. Jon Kurtz, en route to the school and concerned that something might happen before he got there, ordered them to "stay back unless there is an immediate danger or you see a threat." He told his troopers that it was considered "a lockdown barricade situation." He said that no one was being injured.[170] The shrieking of the girls must not have constituted children being threatened. Moreover, how could they even "see" a threat if one existed with the doors and shutters closed?

With police holding impotently outside, and girls continuing to scream, the supervisor continued on to the school. At 10:50 Roberts called his wife from his cell phone. He told her "the police are here." She couldn't believe that this was her husband that she was talking to. Nor could she believe what he was doing. Ultimately she would find four letters, one each written to her and their three children, ages one through seven. He rambled seemingly pointlessly about "getting revenge." But revenge for what? He told her that he had molested two girls who were family relatives 20 years before. His note to his wife confessed the same thing. His cousins were four and five years old at the time. But he would have only been 12-years-old then. What on earth was he talking about?[171] At 10:51 a.m. the girls inside were still screaming. Flashbacks of Columbine, where officers stood outside while children were being tormented and shot, often at pointblank range, must have burst into the troopers' minds. They couldn't possibly have wanted to live with that guilt. But just as at Columbine, they'd been ordered to do nothing. At 10:53 more frantic

170 Briefing by PSP Lt. Col. Jon Kurtz.

171 Extensive investigation into Roberts' life and background in the aftermath of this event would fail to yield a single female he knew from that period of his life that he had molested.

radio requests from the officers outside to assault the school were made. The supervisor was still on his way.

At 10:55 a.m. Roberts called 911. He told the dispatcher who he was. He gave her exactly two seconds to tell the cops outside to leave the area. She put him on hold. His rage grew. Two minutes later at 10:57, a police negotiator arrived. From a position in his vehicle 45 yards away from the building he attempted to contact the hostage-taker with his hailer. There was no response. Dispatch notified the officers on scene of Roberts' 911 call and demand. The cops were told that an aviation unit was 20 minutes out. But what could it do? And did they have that much time? The troopers outside, hardened veterans used to working alone in remote areas of central Pennsylvania with no backup, felt that the situation was unraveling. These were tough men, with a time honored and tough tradition. For years after World War II the Pennsylvania State Police preferred to select only Marines who had seen combat. And for years after that it still had a penchant for Marine drill sergeants. Stories were legion of a single, lonely state trooper arriving in the midst of a riot in one of Philadelphia's many violent neighborhoods. In story after story that sole trooper would take a shotgun from his trunk and chamber a single round, resulting in an entire angry mob dispersing, so feared and respected were they. Knowing nothing of the Texas Rangers, the reputation of "one riot, one trooper" had long been cemented in the minds of Pennsylvanians.

Though perhaps not all former combat Marines anymore, the ten troopers arrayed outside the school were hardened men virtually chiseled from Pennsylvania granite, well trained and armed, yet standing idly by while little girls were screaming for someone to save them. It had to have been destroying them. Just as standing outside room 206 in Bailey had eaten away at those officers. The troopers had more than enough men to do the job, and they knew it.

By 11:00 a.m. a four-man element of the Lancaster Barracks' Special Response Team had been formed and was staged behind the outhouses, some 30 yards beyond the rear left corner of the school.

At 11:02 the negotiator who had obtained Roberts' cell number from the 911 dispatcher, was desperately trying to call into the school. The calls went right to voicemail. Roberts had both his own and his wife's cell phones inside with him. The negotiator tried to reach him three times with no success.

At 11:05 a.m. Roberts had been inside for 35 minutes. The police commanders on site continued to think they had a fairly stable barricade situation. In their minds it was a standoff. At 11:06 the troopers took fire from Roberts through the front door. Rounds pinged against his pickup truck. He then pulled the front door shut and secured it, too. Then with no warning, shots rang out from inside the building. But these were different. The police were not being shot at. The troopers all immediately raced across open ground, hitting the walls of the building. Gunfire inside continued. Upon reaching the building they pulled frantically at the doors that were wired shut. They tried to bash the shutters in but were learning too late, with too little time, that lumber had been nailed over them preventing their entry. One trooper tore out every fingernail trying to rip wood from a window.

At 11:08:30 the troopers finally breached the front door. They darted into the interior, eyes straining to adjust to the dark and the smoke inside. As they entered Roberts shot himself in the head. But they were finally inside. It had taken almost two-and-a-half minutes from the first gunshot for the police to gain entry. Though that was fast to cross open ground, move quickly to a door while expecting to be brought under fire, encounter such fortifications and overcome them, what they were only then learning was that Roberts had discharged 13 rounds into the bound and helpless girls in eight seconds, according to Pennsylvania State Police Deputy Commander Lt. Col. Jon Kurtz.[172]

Other reports of the children's wounds differed dramatically. Pennsylvania State Police Commissioner Jeffrey Miller said Roberts shot his victims in the head at close range, with 17 or 18 total shots

172 Other law enforcement officials placed the shots having been fired in ten seconds.

fired, including the one he used to take his own life as police stormed into the school. Janice Ballenger, Deputy Coroner of Lancaster County, Pennsylvania, told *The Washington Post* that she counted at least two dozen bullet wounds in one child alone before asking a colleague to continue for her.[173] Some reports even insisted that the police first entered through a window, rather than the front door as recounted by Lt. Col. Kurtz.[174] Shortly before Roberts opened fire two sisters, Marian and Barbie Fisher, 13 and 11, requested that they be shot first that the others might be spared. Barbie was wounded, while her older sister was killed.

He had used both his 9mm handgun and shotgun. They had been too late. From beginning to end the entire thing had taken 41 minutes. All ten of the girls had been shot. The troopers inside, still trying to discern the situation through the smoky haze and darkness in the unlit room, first called for emergency transportation for nine or ten victims. Eight of the ten girls had head wounds. At about 11:10 a.m. a message was broadcast on the police radio of "a mass casualty on White Oak Road, Bart Township, with multiple children shot."[175] And "at 11:11 a.m. police radioed dispatchers again, estimating ten to 12 patients with head injuries. The first medical helicopter was dispatched."[176]

The situation was desperate. Due to the darkness, and the fact that the girls were wedged shoulder to shoulder under the blackboard with their ankles bound to each other, they had to be moved. The troopers could only pray it didn't aggravate their injuries. One girl was already dead. Nine troopers immediately attempted to provide casualty care to an equal number of little girls with whatever they had at hand. The kids' clothing, jackets, anything they could find, were used to try to stop bleeding. Children were dying in their arms and first aid kits were in cars too far away. Ambulances began arriving

173 Tamara Jones, Joshua Partlow, (2006-10-04). "Pa. Killer Had Prepared for 'Long Siege'" The *Washington Post* (Washington Post). http://www.washingtonpost.com/wp-dyn/content/article/2006/10/04/AR2006100400331.html. Retrieved 2010-04-23.

174 Kurtz briefing.

175 Lancaster newspaper reporter and author Janet Kelley, *Horror and Heroism.*

176 Ibid.

just as the wounded girls were being carried out of the schoolhouse. Troopers and local police officers assisted the surviving children and EMTs, administering first aid on the school playground. Helicopters landed shortly thereafter and those still living were whisked away for medical treatment at hospitals in Lancaster, Hershey, Reading, and Delaware.

In the end five little girls died. For four of them nothing could be done, and they died at the school house. The fifth died on October 7. Of those wounded, one would remain brain damaged the rest of her life. She can neither walk nor talk. Reports stated that most of the girls were shot "execution-style" in the back of the head,[177] which would dictate that the girls were lying on their stomachs and explain how Roberts was going to stand them up while lashed to each other, and chain them to the eyelets that had been nailed into the blackboard just above them. Inside the school, Deputy Coroner Ballenger said, "there was not one desk, not one chair, in the whole schoolroom that was not splattered with either blood or glass. There were bullet holes everywhere, everywhere."[178] Roberts had won. On October 12 the schoolhouse was demolished. The site where it stood remains an empty field.

I had spent much of the night of September 27 inside the Platte Canyon school. I finally made it home in the early morning. I sat in my mountain home, alone in the dark. And got drunk. Four days later was Monday, October 2. I, along with a team from Archangel including founding director and retired Green Beret Sergeant Major John Anderson, were in York, Pennsylvania training area SWAT teams and deputy U.S. marshals. Early that morning all of the officers' radios crackled to life with panicked calls regarding

177 Chris A. Courogen, (2006-10-03). "AMISH SCHOOL SHOOTINGS: 'ANGRY AT GOD'". *The Patriot-News.* http://www.pennlive.com/news/patriotnews/index.ssf?/base/news/1159845919211960.xml&coll=1. Retrieved 2006-10-03: Raymond McCaffrey, Paul Duggan, and Debbi Wilgoren,(2006-10-03). "Five Killed at Pa. Amish School". *The Washington Post.* http://www.washingtonpost.com/wp-dyn/content/article/2006/10/03/AR2006100300229.html. Retrieved 2006-10-03.

178 Jones and Partlow (2006-10-04). "Pa. Killer Had Prepared for 'Long Siege'". *Washington Post* (Washington Post). http://www.washingtonpost.com/wp-dyn/content/article/2006/10/04/AR2006100400331.html. Retrieved 2010-04-23.

the school takeover. We monitored its progress from start to finish. Two of the Pennsylvania State Police SRT operators who had raced into that building had attended a SWAT school I had run with Delta Force Command Sergeant Major Mel Wick outside of Philadelphia just two months before. York SWAT commander Lt. Ron Camacho (now Captain Camacho) got in touch with them right away, so I was able to talk to them. I had been told by Fred Wegener late that night at Platte Canyon High School that because of what I did for a living he wanted me to know what had happened so that I could pass the lessons onto every other police officer I trained. He was right, it was important information and I wanted to know what the state troopers just a few miles down the road had gone through for the same reasons. I had to study these events so that I could try to make sure other officers were ready for the next one. And, as I had already been told, the next one was coming.

Cho would have sat in front of his television set in his dorm room in Harper Hall and watched all this with fascination. Maybe even glee. He had just been shown how to do it. Morrison had taught Roberts how to slow the police down enough to kill a single girl. But those were interior obstructions, not actual fortifications. From that Roberts had discerned how to keep the police from even entering. At least long enough to kill more children, more girls. His external fortifications had impeded the police penetrating the building. He had had all the time he needed. But Cho wasn't going to be able to bind and secure his victims. The numbers he had in mind were far too great. And they were grown up, not tiny little girls. No, he'd need better fortifications. He'd need something that would allow him to both contain his target victim population, and slow down a police response. A plan was beginning to formulate in his mind.

Chapter 4
A Monster Prepares to Reveal Itself

"There is a great streak of violence in every human being. If it is not channeled and understood, it will break out in war or in madness."

Sam Peckinpah

I am preparing for the inevitable. This has been inevitable since the day I was born. Inevitable that they would drive me to this. Inevitable since the day they abandoned me in the hospital to be tortured. They think I don't remember, that I was too young. But I do. And they've all been doing the same thing ever since. I will show them just what they created. What they drove me to. But I am doing it for others, not for me. I am strong, I can handle it. They will see just how powerful I am. I am preparing. I love lifting weights. I wish I had tried this long ago. The strength I see developing in my body matches the power that is also growing within me. I love to see my muscles grow. I will be ready for them. If they try to rush me, try to attack me, maybe when I'm reloading, I will mess them up with my hands and feet. I will have the power. I have been practicing my Tae Kwon Do from years before alone in my room. I will kick them in the face. I will toss them off. No one can stop me.

The .22 won't be enough though. I should have known that. One gun won't be enough anyway. I need to make sure I can hit each room and shoot everyone at least once before I risk having to reload. But the .22 is just too small, the rounds too small even with hollowpoints. I'll have to look for head shots with that. I should have figured that out from all that I had read on the Internet. Glocks are the "in" gun, especially with all the police departments. That's what everyone says. All the cops have gone to Glocks. Fine. I'll give them a taste of their own medicine. I bet the irony of it will be lost on those idiot cops: that I killed everyone with their favorite gun. The guns they were wearing last year when they came to threaten me. And then when they took me away. They'll see. Maybe I'll get to kill some of them with that same gun. Then maybe they'll get it.

I need lots of bullets and magazines, though. It's hard to get around to buy them and I'm running out of time for buying them on the Internet. And I need to practice. I've never shot a gun before. I'll rent a car. I can put it on the old man's credit card. Wait til he sees what I spent all his money on. I need to practice, too. The Internet is full of information on how to do this. Lots of blogs telling me tactics. I need to remember to take my time reloading. "Slow is fast," they all say. And I have to remember to count my rounds. Don't fire til the magazines are empty. Reload at every opportunity and before moving to the next target, to the next potential threat site. That means reload before I leave each room. I have to remember that. I won't be doing tactical reloads, where you take a magazine out and keep it in case you need the remaining bullets or have the time to reload it from loose ammunition. I won't have someone to cover me, and I won't have the time. I'll be dead. I'll do speed reloads, just dump the magazines when I put fresh ones in. I'll need other stuff too. At least one combat knife, maybe more. Maybe I'll get to stab one of them to death. Maybe I'll get to bash their skulls in with my hammer.

The doors in Norris Hall are perfect. Those old swing bars will make it easy to chain them. Perfect fortifications. Will they see the genius of my tactics? No one before me has ever done anything to keep those who need to die from escaping, and at the same time keep the cops from getting in. It's so funny really. They'll be stuck outside listening to me kill and they won't be able to do a thing about it. That will show them my power, and my brilliance. They should have paid attention to the papers I wrote about this. How I could outdo Eric and Dylan. Even they didn't think of doing this.

I know I am going to die. But I've been dead for so long already. They all made sure of it. I didn't exist for them at all. An unperson as Orwell called it. Funny, that I learned that as an English major. Now that's ironic. But that's me. A Question Mark. A non-human. Dead. A void in space. Well, they'll soon see what's it's like to be killed by others, when there's nothing you can do about it. To simply not exist. Professor Roy tried. I thought she liked me. She said we could write together. I know she's back. She's been back since January. But she hasn't called me once or even sent me an email. Hasn't even wanted to know how I was doing. She's just like all the others. I should have known it was all just crap to make her feel good about herself. The one thing I'm going to do, though, before I do all this is get laid. I'm going to have some bitch. Maybe she'll see. If she sees my power, gets a glimpse of who I really am, I may have to kill her. I can't let her warn the others. I want to do this on April 20, the anniversary of Columbine. But a lot of classes don't meet that day. I can do it on the 19th, the anniversary of Waco, but that would be Thursday when my class in Norris Hall meets. But there aren't as many people in the building then. Should I do it on Wednesday the 18th then? I'll have to wait and see.

By spring semester 2007 "Cho seemed to be listening only to the crazed voices in his head."[179] Wendell Flinchum had just been appointed chief of the Virginia Tech Police Department in December 2006, just four months before Cho would strike. By then he was a 20-plus year veteran of law enforcement, all of it spent at VT. *The Roanoke Times* would report that he had beaten out 93 other candidates,[180] something Chief Flinchum acknowledged, but only in the humblest of terms. Lucinda Roy would report in her book, *No Right To Remain Silent*, that Flinchum's colleague Lt. Vince Houston described him as "having 'unbelievable decision-making skills, even in a rushed situation, you know he's always thinking the next step.'"[181]

179 Roy, p. 65.
180 Shawna Morrison, "Tech police chief studying up on his job," *The Roanoke Times*, December 21, 2006; cited by Roy, p. 20.
181 Roy, p. 20.

Before we ever met him we had been warned that Flinchum could be taciturn, even dour at times. But while a deliberate and careful professional, hardly given to excesses or bursts of emotion, he was courteous and decent in all of his dealings with us. That said a lot for him given the circumstances in which we came to know each other, and the obvious harm our work could do to him and his department. As he explained all that he had done that day, and the decisions he had made, we realized that his reticence as a hero had only fueled the flames of media predation.

Preparing

I need to know more about the cops that will be coming. The jerks that threatened me last year. I hadn't done anything wrong. Who did they think they were? I hope I get to see them. I hope I get to kill them. And the ones who took me away. I got to see how they all were running around scared back in August just because a couple of them got waxed. Big deal. They're just cops. Who cares? It took hundreds of them to handle one man on campus. But unlike him, I won't be unarmed. Or untrained. They won't know what to do when they realize all the ammo I have. But I still need to know more about them. How fast they are, how fast they'll get their SWAT teams ready. I'll need time to kill everyone. To surpass Dylan and Eric's numbers, I will need to slow them down.

In February, at the commencement of spring semester 2007, Professor Roy was teaching a graduate poetry class that met on Mondays from 6:00 p.m. until 8:45 p.m. She had stepped down from the position as chairwoman of the English Department where she supervised close to 50 professors almost a year before, though she was still co-directing the *Creative Writing* program.[182] She hadn't heard from Cho in a year.

But Cho was no longer interested in English assignments, passing classes or graduating. At 1:41 p.m. on February 2, 2007, he

182 Roy, p. 15

submitted an order for a semi-automatic .22 caliber Walther P-22 handgun over the Internet from TGSCOM, Inc., in Illinois. This would be the same business that Stephen Kazmierczak would use to buy two 9mm magazines and a holster in preparation for his shooting rampage on February 14, 2008 at Northern Illinois University, ten months after Cho's attack. On February 9 Cho picked it up at a local pawnshop, J-N-D Pawnbrokers, across the street from campus.[183] On March 13, 2007 he purchased a semi-automatic 9mm Glock and a box of ammunition for it at Roanoke Firearms in Roanoke. It had taken him six weeks of preparation and training to realize he needed more firepower and a lot of ammunition. He asked for eight additional magazines for it, but they only had four so he had to satisfy himself with that, at first.[184] Cho had to wait another 30 days by Virginia state law for the dealer to perform a background check, but no record of mental health issues was found.[185] Nor did Cho disclose the fact that he'd been ordered to undergo outpatient treatment.[186] He knew better than that. Cho's purchase of the firearms was reported to have been an arguable violation of federal law by the Governor's Panel due to fact that he had been judged to be a danger to himself and ordered to outpatient treatment.[187] However, in his medical and adjudication records from when he had been taken in for evaluation in December 2005 the box on the form had been checked that indicated he was capable of purchasing a firearm. On March 22, Cho purchased two 10-round magazines for the Walther P-22 through his eBay ID – "blazers5505" – from "bullelk14" of Elk Ridge Shooting Supplies in Idaho.[188] Hanni Durzy, an eBay spokesperson, said that the purchase from a vendor in Idaho was legal. On March 23, Cho purchased three more 10-round magazines from another eBay seller.[189] Durzy also said that Cho had used eBay to sell VT football tickets and horror-

183 *Wikipedia*, GPR, 24.
184 GPR, 24; training presentation by VSP Lt. Timothy Lyon January 22, 2010, Safe School Summit, Delaware County, Pennsylvania.
185 Ibid.
186 Roy, p. 224.
187 GPR, p. 2.
188 *Wikipedia* – "Virginia Tech Massacre Timeline."
189 GPR, p. 24.

themed books "that were assigned in his classes."[190] Other magazines were purchased at a Wal-Mart and Dick's Sporting Goods stores near campus.[191] Cho was stockpiling arms and ammunition for his grand assault on the society that had rejected him for so long. Ultimately he would purchase all hollow point bullets to be used in his attacks.

During his senior year, as with all of his other years at Tech and throughout his life, Cho appears to have spent most of his time outside of class working alone on his computer, or watching TV. At 8:58 a.m. on March 12, 2007, Cho rented a red minivan at Enterprise Rent-A-Car at the Roanoke Regional Airport and used it to travel to local gun ranges and carry out training and reconnaissance on his target, Norris Hall.[192] Beginning in January or February 2007, just months before the shootings, he began what seems to have been a disciplined exercise program, and spent time lifting weights according to his suitemate Karan Grewal.[193] On March 14, 2007 Cho was seen at a national forest shooting range outside of town. What the range managers and other shooters recalled that was so unusual was a young Asian man putting paper targets on the ground in two long columns with a narrow aisle between them. He was walking down the aisle, a gun in each hand, shooting down into the targets on both sides of him. Cho had figured out how to deal with the jammed desks full of students and narrow aisles between them in Norris Hall classrooms.

On March 22, 2007 he practiced for one hour at PSS Range and Training, an indoor pistol facility.[194] Cho was getting ready for his one-man assault. This was little different from the intensely physical terrorist training camps in Afghanistan, Chechnya, the Philippines, Indonesia, Pakistan, Somalia and Libya, or the flying, martial arts and scuba diving lessons al Qaeda operatives have been known to seek in the U.S. At no time did Cho's suitemates have any idea that he had purchased two guns, or that he had begun practicing at local gun

190 "Law Would Focus On Gun Buyers' History of Mental Illness," *USA Today*, April 23, 2007, p. 5A.
191 Roy, p. 225.
192 GPR, p. 24.
193 Gangloff, p. 4.
194 GPR, p. 24.

ranges. "The isolation he was in was self-induced, mostly," Grewal told Mike Gangloff of *The Roanoke Times*.

On March 28, he checked into the Mainstay Suites hotel in Roanoke and, according to police, attempted to arrange to have sex with a woman from a Roanoke escort service.[195] In an interview with Denis Eck of *WSLS10 News* out of Roanoke, Virginia on April 23, 2007, Miss Chastity Frye had been retained by Cho for a social evening through the escort service she was employed with. She says Cho hired her, and the two met at a Valley View motel. "I'm just so shaken by this, I don't know what to say," she told Eck. She said that she spent an hour, all alone, with the Virginia Tech killer. "He was so quiet, I really couldn't get much from him, he was so distant, he really didn't talk a lot. It seemed like he wasn't all there." She said:

> I danced for a little while and I thought we were done because he got up and went to the restroom and began washing. And I said, 'well, do you want me to go? I'm going to go ahead and go'. And he's like, 'I paid for the full hour, you've only been here for 15 minutes', and then he came back in the room. And I started dancing and that's when he you know, touched me and tried to get on me and that's when I pushed him away.

"Well, they asked me what happened, and then they asked me if anything stuck out. They wanted to know three words that described him," Frye said. What three words represented Cho to her? "I used dorky, was one of them, maybe timid and pushy, there at the end he was a little pushy. Now she thinks about the victims, and how lucky she was.

> I don't know what to think. I'm just very grateful that nothing happened then. Sometimes I wonder if I could have said something or done something differently or maybe talk to him a little bit more you know, get him

195 Presentation by VSP Lt. Timothy Lyon.

> to open up? Right. But I wasn't thinking about that at the time. I was thinking, he was creeping me out, I was thinking about getting out of there.

Cho checked out the following morning. It should be noted that until that encounter there was no indication Cho ever had any personal or social relationship with a female in his life, outside of his mother and sister.

On March 31, 2007 he was issued a speeding ticket by the Montgomery County Sheriff's Office. That same day Cho went back to Wal-Mart and Dick's Sporting Goods and purchased additional ammunition, magazines and a hunting knife,[196] then went to Home Depot where he bought several chains.[197] Then on April 3, 2007 Cho purchased a four-pack of Brinks solid brass keyed padlocks, a "Signatures" black mesh baseball cap, shooting targets and a Dremel multi-pro 7.2 volt cordless tool.[198] The Dremel tool was used to attempt to file the serial numbers off the firearms. He was issued another speeding ticket on April 7, 2007, this time by VTPD. Perhaps he was armed when the officer walked up to the side of his van. Perhaps he contemplated shooting that cop. The monster was growing beyond control, and was daring the police who he knew he would soon go head to head with. On April 8, 2007 Cho spent the night at the Hampton Inn in Christiansburg, Virginia videotaping a large portion of his manifesto.[199] Per Virginia State Police Lt. Timothy Lyon, who was responsible for all of the coordination of the VT investigation, Cho also brought a second escort to this room, obviously continuing in his efforts to have at least one sexual encounter with a woman before he died.

On April 9, 2007 Cho was again seen at a Blacksburg shooting range, and later observed sitting in the back of the minivan he had

196 GPR, p. 23.

197 GPR, p. 24.

198 In a training presentation by VSP Lt. Lyon it was stated that Cho purchased the chains and locks on April 3, 2007.

199 Ibid.

rented. Additional portions of his videotaped manifesto were filmed while sitting in the back of the van in that parking lot. A father and son at the range collected the expended brass he left for reloading. This was still in their possession after the shootings and they turned it over to police who were able to match it to the crime scenes.[200] The following day Cho returned the Kia Sedona minivan. True to form for him, he drove it onto the lot at 12:15 a.m., well after normal business hours, dropping the keys in the overnight delivery slot. He may have wanted the world to see his power, to fear his name, to tremble at his deeds and capacity for violence, yet he remained incapable of talking to another human being merely to return a rented car. He took a cab back to his dorm.

Two days later on April 12, 2007, Cho purchased a 26-pocket fishing vest from a sporting goods store in Christiansburg. He needed a tactical vest along the lines of what military special operations and SWAT teams used. He needed as many loaded magazines as possible within easy reach. Having returned his van two days before, it's unknown how he got there from Tech. Records indicate that Cho purchased the ammunition and firearms with his parents' credit card. Cho's parents stated they did not receive the bill for the credit card until after the shootings, and so had not known what he was doing. After his death they said that they received a bill for more than $3,000.00.[201]

On April 15, 2007 at 5:27 p.m. Cho made his weekly Sunday telephone call to his family in Fairfax County, but they reported that there was nothing unusual about it.[202] This would be the last personal call he would ever make, with no indication of what was to follow. This would also be the last time his mother and father would ever hear from him, until his image appeared on television following the worst shooting mass-murder at a school in U.S. history.

200 Lt. Lyon presentation.
201 GPR, p. 71.
202 GPR, p. 24.

Virginia Tech Police Department and ERT

The 41-person Virginia Tech Police Department Cho was to go up against oversaw a college campus as large as many United States' cities. Prior to the formation of the police department at VT in the late 1970s, the university only had a security department. For almost twenty years after its creation, however, the police department languished. Then beginning in 1995, it evolved into a nationally accredited law enforcement agency. As the university continued to grow, the department was often tasked with keeping up under tremendous budget constraints and a staff of aging officers. Starting just several years before the attack numerous command staff and officers retired and younger ones were hired in their places.

This was the time when Curtis Cook and so many others joined or transferred in from other agencies. They brought with them high-risk criminal experience, and a desire to see their new department function as a top agency. In conjunction with the presence of a new police chief, this constituted dramatic change for the department. Then Chief Wendell Flinchum took the helm in December 2006. He had an immediate stabilizing effect, and adopted a more cooperative and proactive stance with regard to campus law enforcement than had been seen before. In that position he reported directly to a university vice president.[203] However, on April 16, 2007 the department was below full strength, with merely 35 officers due to six vacancies.[204]

The reason for the existence of the Virginia Tech campus police was stated in the university's Emergency Response Plan: "The primary purpose of the VTPD is to support the academics through the maintenance of a peaceful and orderly community and through provision of needed general and emergency services." Typically, at VTPD the day shift came on duty at 7:00 a.m. with five officers. In addition, nine officers worked in the office, including the chief.[205] All VTPD patrol vehicles were equipped with 12-gauge shotguns. On

203 GPR, p. 11., and interviews with VTPD officers and commanders.
204 Ibid.
205 Ibid.

April 16, 2007, 34 of the 35 officers went to work at some point that day.[206] One was away on vacation.

Both primary agencies that would respond to the Norris Hall attack – Blacksburg and Virginia Tech – were certified by the Commission on the Accreditation of Law Enforcement Agencies (CALEA). Virginia Tech PD was initially accredited in November 1995 and reaccredited in November 2006. This certification provided a proven modern management model to its member departments, which included preparedness programs to address natural and manmade incidents. One of the purposes of CALEA was to maintain a body of standards covering a wide range of up-to-date public safety initiatives. The commission's credentialing authority came through the efforts of the International Association of Chiefs of Police, the National Organization of Black Law Enforcement Executives, the National Sheriffs' Association and the Police Executives Research Forum.

Both departments also had tactical or SWAT teams, called ERTs. Tech's had between eight and ten operators, including a volunteer student serving as a tactical medic. A tactical medic is different from a medic or paramedic. A tactical medic – or "tac" medic – functions hand-in-hand with his assigned law enforcement or SWAT team. He is trained in their tactics, wears body armor, and takes a position within the SWAT team when entering a dangerous or "hot" zone, as opposed to other first responder medical professionals who typically will never enter a building until it has been declared secured and safe by the police.

The tac medic is right in the thick of things, ready to use his skills to save a wounded teammate, or those who are the victims of violence. They are even ready to save the criminals themselves, right then, in the moment, and long before others might arrive to help. In addition to providing critical life-saving treatment while bullets fly around them, in many cases tac medics are also fully qualified and certified police officers.

206 Ibid.

According to information supplied by VTPD, its ERT was established in 1991 and had a competitive selection process. Each applicant had to have appropriate letters of recommendation, a flawless background, and must have successfully negotiated grueling firearms and PT[207] tests. The team was led by Lt. Curtis Cook and was comprised of officers who volunteered their services at no additional pay. They didn't do the most dangerous job in law enforcement for the money. Unlike the military, they got no combat or hazardous duty pay. And they certainly did not do it for the fame, as there was none to be had. They only wanted to be part of the best unit their department could field, and handle the most dangerous police operations with the best trained operators from that department. The ERT specialized in high-speed weapons and tactics, and bragged expertise in such disciplines as sniper operations, team entry and rappelling. The team's equipment had been completely replaced in 2005 with a grant from the Department of Homeland Security, including the addition of night vision for every operator.

Up to the date of the VT attacks by Cho, the team had completed numerous high risk search and arrest warrants, partnering mostly with the Blacksburg ERT, its sister unit. The VTPD ERT had also operated with the U.S. Secret Service in warrant service and presidential protection. Upon initial entry onto the team each member had to undergo a Basic SWAT course, though training and assessment continued throughout time in service. Each ERT member had a specialty within the unit, which required him to function as an instructor for both the team and the department, exactly the model used by the U.S. Army Special Forces. This included chemical and specialty impact munitions instruction; PepperBall instructors; rappelling mastery; firearms instructors; general instructors; police divers; H&K armorers; and snipers. Though led by Lt. Cook, and including two sergeants, one detective and four officers, there was no recognized rank hierarchy among the members. This, too, was the very model and behavior found on the vaunted A Teams of the

207 Physical Training

Green Berets, who were famous for eschewing rank and the stiflingly obsequious behavior that idolatry of rank causes in the conventional military. With top special operations units, whether military or law enforcement, the bond between a team of elite operators was the most important thing of all. Each one was devoted to his teammates and cared more for them than he did for himself

Blacksburg Police Department and ERT

The 57-person Blacksburg Police Department (BPD) had a 13-man tactical team, which also included a tac medic who was not a sworn officer, supplied by the Blacksburg Volunteer Rescue Squad. Prior to the shootings at VT on April 16, 2007, the BPD tac medic had experience with two gunshot incidents, a massive manhunt and an attempted suicide. The BPD ERT had been in existence since shortly after 9-11. Though not a written policy within BPD, Captain Goodman activated the ERT on all violent calls.

The Blacksburg Police Department was initially accredited by CALEA in July 1993, and was reaccredited in July 2007, shortly after Cho's rampage. The department had never been fully staffed, however. At full complement, on April 16, 2007, BPD would have put nine officers on the day shift, 11 on swing shift and nine more on night shift. All shifts overlapped by two hours. The town of Blacksburg had not increased the number of police officers in ten years, but their duties had increased significantly over that period. In short, they were stretched very thin.

All Blacksburg patrol officers had assault rifles, though not all of the vehicles had racks to carry them up front, those others being relegated to the trunk. In a meeting with Captain Goodman in July 2007, months after the VT attacks and almost a year after the Morva double-homicide and massive manhunt, he stated that BPD had received funding for more rifles. All BPD officers were trained on both shotgun and rifle, and they were schooled in the use of shotgun rounds for breaching. Captain Goodman felt that every police officer in America should have a tactical mindset, and he had made strides to ensure that the department he served employed those with the greatest capability of functioning successfully in a life-or-death environment.

BPD and VTPD Preparedness and Inter-operability

In the months and even years leading up to Cho's onslaught, the Blacksburg and Virginia Tech ERTs trained jointly once every month. These multi-agency trainings, as rare as they were for contiguous departments to engage in on a regular basis throughout the country, included training with the Virginia State Police and Montgomery County Sheriff's Office. In Blacksburg, the tactical team members were spread throughout the patrol shifts and the police department attempted to use them as leavening for the patrol officers, by seeing the specialized tactical training raise the overall level of the patrol capability on each shift. This, too, was a model found in the military. Blacksburg's most highly trained operators were spread among all others in much the same way the Army traditionally used those who had graduated from Ranger School at Ft. Benning, Georgia, by placing them in regular units with the expectation that they would increase the overall performance level of the other soldiers they served with.

Historically the BPD and VT ERTs responded to every call of each other, and the two units trained and operated together constantly, always maintaining a mutual aid agreement. Per Capt. Goodman: "The two departments' teams were virtually interchangeable." Each of the tac medics for both departments had trained recently at the NTOA[208] National Conference in Los Angeles in September 2006.

Former BPD Capt. Goodman stated that the two tac teams had conducted a Columbine-type active shooter FTX together at a local middle school, merely two months before the VT shootings. The design of the middle school closely resembled the layout of Norris Hall, which ultimately aided in both agencies' ability to organize and execute entry from multiple points in rapid fashion.

208 National Tactical Officers Association.

Capt. Goodman stated that this training included every single officer with BPD. As well, both the Blacksburg and VT police departments had conducted mass casualty and terrorist response full field exercises jointly within the prior two years. They were as ready as they could possibly have been. As ready as any departments could ever be.

Despite this, Blacksburg and VT had no common radio channel between the two departments, a frequent problem between many police departments. Even the two ERTs lacked this ability during joint operations. Historically, during major incidents BPD's tac team communicated with VT's and others via Nextel. The VT campus had its own dispatch center, though due to the area communications system all 911 cell phone calls made from campus got routed directly to either BPD or the Montgomery County Sheriff's Office (MCSO) dispatch. On the day of the event calls were received by VT, BPD and MCSO.

In addition to the Morva manhunt, Virginia Tech and its police department were no strangers to terrorist threats and other potential critical incidents. VT had been targeted by both ELF, the Earth Liberation Front, and ALF, the Animal Liberation Front, in the past. For two small town police departments they had clearly entered the world-at-large, and were dealing with big city threats.

Chapter Five

The First to Fall

"When you look long into an abyss, the abyss looks into you."

Friedrich Nietzsche

So the cops come quickly when someone screams "Bomb!" But they hold outside. A long way away, too. They wait for other cops and dogs to show up. They take their time securing the area and evacuating the building. That should give me some time. I'll put bomb threat notes up outside first. That'll make them wait some distance away before the dogs show up. It'll give me enough time to kill everyone inside. I can't believe this place was actually going to give me a degree. After throwing me out of every class they could and trying to tell me and everyone else that I was nuts. The cops, my roommates, my teachers, the damn girls. They just wanted to be rid of me finally. Well, they're gonna be rid of me all right. But not the way they think. They'll never forget my name or what they did to me. Would it have really been that tough for them to just help me get my book published? It would have sold, I know it would. After that I could have just kept writing. But without that, and without a master's degree or Ph.D., what am I going to do with an English degree? I can't get a job with it. Wouldn't matter, I couldn't go work anywhere anyway. I hate people, and they all hate me. I can't leave this place. Save my parents the embarrassment of having me back home. But no one's ever gonna forget me. I'll use all that great writing training they gave me to leave them with something that will make me famous. It'll be like the book of my life, my piece de resistance. *I'll tell them all what they did. I'll tell the world. All the others like me, like Dylan and Eric and everyone else, will use it as their bible. But that's not enough. I'll videotape myself. Take photographs. They need to "see" that I hate them, not just "know" it. They need the visual imagery to see me, to see what they did to me, what they made me become, how they destroyed me.*

I want to do this on April 20, on the anniversary of Columbine. Dylan and Eric did it then, on Hitler's birthday. They could have done it on the 19th, which was the anniversary of Waco and Oklahoma City. God, how famous we all become just by killing. It's not so hard really: to kill. They're not even human. I shouldn't think of them as human. They certainly never showed me the slightest bit of humanity. But the 20th will be on a Friday and none of the classes meet on Fridays. They're all Monday-Wednesday or Tuesday-Thursday classes. I'll do it on Thursday then. I'll kill all of them in my own class. Maybe I'll start right there. Walk in and take my seat, then just stand up and start shooting. Decadent, disgusting jerks. The Muslims are right. Americans deserve to die. I'm not even an American. They live unforgivable lives, drinking their cognac and vodka, driving around in cars they've done nothing to earn, showing off their jewelry.

I've spent all weekend getting ready. Trying to get ready. I don't even go to class anymore. No reason to. I'm not sure that I can do it, though. I need to know. I don't think I can wait until Thursday.

It's Sunday night, and if I'm going to do it, I have to do it now. I have to get this over with. I don't know how I'll handle shooting everyone in Norris. I know, I'll make sure I can do it first. Where to go? Maybe West AJ. It's right over there. I could go to Cochrane, but I don't know it and the fucking football team lives there. That's all I need, not that I wouldn't like to teach those hotshots a lesson too. I can get into West AJ easy. Even early in the morning I can just walk in through the open door. I do it every time I go to get my mail there. There's lots of girls there. Like that one on the fourth floor from last year. All I wanted to do was talk to her. I thought she was an English major, thought she liked Shakespeare. Maybe she's still there. Maybe I'll run into her. That'd be ironic. Talk about poetic justice. If I can't find her, I'll just kill the first one I see. They all have their doors open in the mornings. If anyone catches me I'll just shoot up the whole floor. Maybe kill everyone in the whole dorm. Whatever. It won't matter at that point.

Okay, I have to do it now, this morning, or I'll never do it. It's Monday. Eric and Dylan did it on a Tuesday. I wonder how they could take the waiting. I can't. It has to be today. I'm going to go about my usual routine, though. Don't want my roommates thinking anything's strange. I could just kill them. That would be a great way to start. Gonna brush my teeth for the last time. Put zit cream on my face like always. I have to, Grewal just came in. Always says, "Good morning." Cheerful shit. Wait'll he learns just what he's been living with all this time. Damn zit cream. Live fast, die young and leave a good looking corpse, right? I just need to know that I can do it. Then if I can get out of AJ I'll go to Norris. Then I won't have a choice. I'll be screwed for the first killing, so I'll have to go through with it then. May as well take out as many as I can after that. How many times can they give me the death penalty? Doesn't matter. I don't plan on coming out anyway. I'll have to mail my package in between. By then I'll be fucked so I might as well send it. But first I have to know I can do it.

The Morning of April 16

Charles W. "Charlie" Smith, the Director of Engineering and Security at Montgomery Regional General Hospital in Blacksburg, the same hospital Morva had escaped from, described the morning of April 16 as "unseasonably cold" with sustained winds of 30 to 40 mph, which would gust up to 60 mph. Before that day was over Smith would have a greater understanding of mass casualties and site security than he had ever imagined. Though he and his staff had trained for these kinds of crises, like many others he never thought that they would have to bring it all to bear in a single overwhelming event.

—

The 16th would become the worst day in the 24 years that Wendell Flinchum had spent on the Virginia Tech campus. Even the worst in his life. It was not as though Wendell was unaccustomed to tragic events occurring in his police career, however. There had been the airplane crash at the Virginia Tech Airport on July 17, 2006 and the tragic Morva manhunt the previous August. But "the 16th" would never be the type of event that you filed away in your sub-conscious and only resurrected as a talking point when the need arose. To Wendell Flinchum and his family April 16 would become a lasting and life altering event. To the world, and before scores of television cameras, he would initially become the face of the massacre, a position that he was not comfortable with. But he understood that was what leaders were required to do. He still bristles at the way the national media hurt the members of his department.

5:00 a.m. to 7:01 a.m.

At five o'clock on the morning of Monday, April 16, 2007 Cho was seen by one of his suitemates at his computer.[209] He had stopped going to class two weeks before, and it is certain that he was not completing any of his assignments before graduation. The only documents that he would need completed for the day were his rambling 1,800 word diatribe against society and his fellow students whom he was about to gun down, and a letter to the English Department complaining about one of the professors he had not liked, but which didn't mention his planned massacre at all. Suitemate Karan Grewal had been up all night studying, preparing for final exams.

At 5:30 a.m. Grewal walked into the bathroom and saw Cho brushing his teeth and applying acne cream to his face. He may have been about to commit the worst mass-shooting murder on a campus in America's history, but he wanted to do it blemish free. Like most days Grewal said, "Good morning." And like all days he got no response from Cho. In eight months of living together none of Cho's suitemates had ever heard him utter a word. They had never even

209 *Wikipedia,* GPR, 24.

heard his voice. They thought that he was a foreign student who couldn't speak English. The first time they would learn that he was, in fact, an English major or hear him talk would be two days later when NBC aired his videotaped rants attempting to justify what he had done. Cho left the bathroom, got dressed – including tucking at least his 9mm Glock handgun under his coat - and left the suite shortly before 7:00 a.m.[210]

According to the Governor's Panel Report, Cho was next observed by students outside the external doors of West Ambler-Johnston Hall at 6:47 that morning. Amanda Weakly saw him in between the two sets of doors on the western side, which would have been the side facing toward Cho's dormitory. West Ambler-Johnston Hall is a dormitory located in the southern quadrant of buildings on the campus of Virginia Tech. It is seven floors, houses 895 students and is one of the largest dormitories on the Virginia Tech campus. WAJ had post office boxes and a post office distribution area on the ground floor, so many students who didn't live there had access to this area with their key cards, but could not gain entry to the interior living area or elevators of the dorm. This was the dormitory where Cho received his mail, but the access cards for non-resident students did not let them into the building at all until 7:30 a.m. each day. All non-residents needed authorization to access the living areas from 10:00 p.m. to 10:00 a.m. every day. It was also the dorm in which 19-year old Emily Hilscher lived, and where one of the girls Cho had been harassing the previous year had lived; both on the fourth floor. It had been on the whiteboard outside her door that he had left the Shakespearean message that had compelled her to call the police.

Cho must have entered through a door that was opened by a resident either coming in or going out - called "tailgating" - as his key card would not have let him in that early. This explains his initial presence loitering outside the building.[211] There was no video surveillance at any building on the campus.

210 GPR p. 25.
211 GPR, p. 77.

Bomb Scares Foreshadow Cho's Attack

In the two weeks prior, VT had suffered two bomb scares. The first was by note and involved a single building, Torgersen Hall. On April 13, 2007 a second bomb threat was made, also by note which included the statement: "This will continue." It involved three buildings, Torgersen, Durham, and Whittemore Halls.[212] In both bomb scares all of the targeted structures were Engineering buildings. On April 23 the news media reported that there might have been a third bomb scare the morning of the shootings. Police later confirmed the threat had been against Norris Hall. In the book, *April 16th: Virginia Tech Remembers*, the authors criticized VT for its response to the scares: "The university took a low-key approach in the reporting of these bomb threats, which in turn left some students with an almost casual attitude toward them."[213]

While the university administration may not have reacted as strongly as it could have according to the quoted students, in Archangel's interviews with VTPD and BPD, both confirmed that they had taken them very seriously. Police expert analysis later confirmed that Cho had not been the author of the bomb threat notes leading up to April 16. Nevertheless, the notes and the police reaction would have given him much needed information on the response times and tactics of both police departments. With both bomb scares the ERTs from the departments checked and cleared all of the threatened buildings. Certainly the commitment of, both, large amounts of time and resources by the two police agencies in responding to these bomb threats demonstrated the seriousness with which they were taken.

Cho's Selection of Targets

The Virginia Tech campus was laid out along the lines of the military academy it had been for a century and a half. For many years all students had served in the Corps of Cadets, creating a military legacy

212 GPR, p. 24.
213 Lazenby, p. 5.

and atmosphere that continues to this day. The center of the campus was a large military drillfield. The older buildings were made of stone blocks, distinguishing them from more modern construction. Today, students can volunteer to serve in both the ROTC program as well as Marine and Air Force Cadet programs, and students in military uniforms can been seen everywhere on campus.

Ambler-Johnston Residence Halls were located south of the Drillfield and sat approximately 50 yards north of Washington Street. The entry doors were 80 yards from the opposite street. The Ambler-Johnston Halls were divided into two distinctly different dormitory buildings: East and West.

Cho's second target, 270,000 square foot Norris Hall, was built in 1960, and was located on the northern side of the Virginia Tech campus, and north of the Drillfield that sat between the two buildings and was the center of campus. Norris Hall was connected to Holden Hall to the east by a covered breezeway with public entrances to each building beneath the portico. Norris Hall was made of solid stone blocks and the interior walls were cinderblock. In 2007 the rooms had wooden doors that opened inward. Some classroom doors had windows, but not any of the rooms Cho would attack. To the northeast of Holden Hall, cattycorner to the building, a new multi-story building was under construction leading up to the time of the attacks.

Additional construction was taking place in the interior of Burruss Hall, approximately 20 yards to the west of Norris Hall, and immediately across from the point where the police assault teams would breach a wooden door to gain entry. A chute for construction materials and debris was evident outside the upper floor windows for dumping materials out the window and into a large trash dumpster in the direction of Norris Hall. Constant construction noise, including hammering, jackhammering, sounds of walls being torn out, and trash noisily being dropped two stories into the dumpster was heard coming from the buildings on a regular basis throughout the semester. At times the teachers had to stop talking, so overwhelming was the noise. As the sounds of this construction had become well known to all of the students and professors, when Cho began shooting it had the predictable effect of being mistaken for the omnipresent construction noise. Whether Cho intended this, and whether it was a factor in the selection of his target, is unknown.

Figure 1 – Diagram of Burruss, Norris and Holden Halls, with new building under construction to northeast.

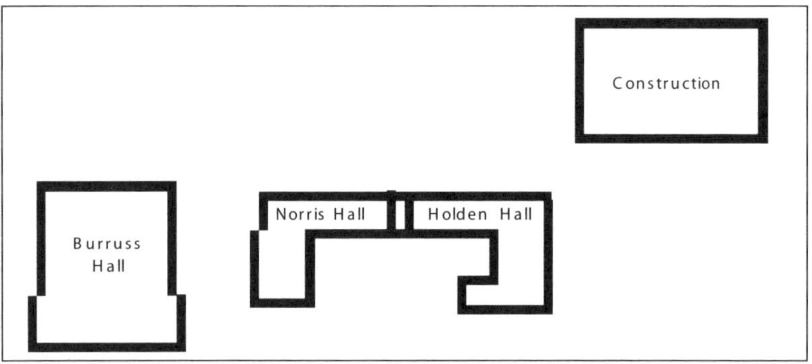

Note the covered breezeway separating Norris from Holden Hall.

7:02 a.m. to 7:20 a.m.

I'm in AJ. That was easy. Cold as hell out today though. I'm shaking from the cold. The wind was a killer. Maybe it's nerves. Actually I'm not afraid. I feel alive. The best I've ever felt. I should have done this years ago when I first started thinking of it. I just walked right in. Idiots even held the door for me. Can't they feel it? Can't they feel that death is stalking them? I remember the security camera video of Eric and Dylan walking into Columbine. They were gods, powerful. Anyone who saw them would have known, would have felt it. Can't these fools feel it? I would think they could. The elevator ride up was easy. No one heading that way. Everyone going out to class.

I'm on the fourth floor. What room was that girl in? I'll walk down the hall and see if she's there. Wait. This door's open. I can see some girl inside. Nice looking. I'm inside. She's freaked. I can see the fear in her eyes. She knows. She knows who I am, what I am here for. I tell her to stay quiet but she screams. I yell at her to shut up but she keeps screaming. I hear a door opening. Some idiot coming. Door opening. I pushed the door shut but it's not locked. I have to hide. He comes right at me. Big black dude. In his underwear! I do it. I didn't even think about it. It was just a reflex. She's sobbing. Now it's her turn. Nothing bothers me. I am revenge itself. If I had asked this one out she would have laughed at me like the others. If anyone sees me walk out I'll kill them too. Now I know I can do it. I feel great. If any of my suitemates are still there and see all this blood on me, I'll kill them too. Nothing can stop me.

From the computer log that tracks the use of the students' key cards, at 7:02 that morning 19-year-old freshman Emily Hilscher entered her dormitory after being dropped off by her boyfriend Karl Thornhill, with whom she had spent the weekend. He was a student at nearby Radford University.[214] Thornhill had driven his pickup truck to the back entrance of the building by the loading dock, where he could get his girlfriend just short of the door, rather than make her walk the 80 yards in from the main road to the front doors in the cold, bitter wind and snow. Whether the skulking Cho was already inside or not will never be known. Karl Thornhill had sat in his truck and watched Emily walk through the door and saw no one follow her in.

In all probability Cho had entered one of the main doors on either side of the lobby, not the remote back service entrance that would have seen little traffic. No one would have noticed him going through those doors, and in fact no one reported to police ever remembering seeing him in the dorm that morning. At that time of the day, with final exams looming and the first class about to begin in less than an hour, the volume of students moving in and out of those doors would have been heavy. Like at most universities and even security apartments in America they all held the doors open for

214 GPR, p. 25.

each other, or he would have simply slipped through a door before it closed. Gaining entry would not have been difficult for the murderer.

Karl Thornhill turned his truck around and began the 20 mile drive back to Radford to begin his own class day. He had no idea that he would never see his girlfriend alive again. Emily took the elevator to her fourth floor room that she shared with Heather Haugh. Haugh, too, had spent the weekend away and the two young women had chatted briefly on their cell phones that morning. They had agreed to meet up at their room, get ready for class and go off to have breakfast together first. Heather had just spoken to Emily before she entered the building.

Emily was inside her room. Whether she was all the way across it from the door, under her "loft bed" when Cho entered, or she retreated to that remote spot will also forever remain a mystery. Many of the beds in the dorm rooms were up on high poles, like top bunks, as a space saving measure, allowing the university to take advantage of the areas beneath for desks, tables and dressers. Emily entered her room, and like most kids in their rooms on a busy morning on the floor, probably did not lock her door behind her. After all, Heather would be there in just a few minutes and her friends were everywhere. More importantly, large and athletic Ryan "Stack" Clark, the male RA for the floor, lived just next door and was in his room. He was a great friend and confidante to the girls on his floor. What could she possibly have had to worry about?

Suddenly Cho was inside her room. He must have either seen her enter or seen the door ajar. He stepped inside and closed the door behind him. She likely yelled at him to get out. Seething and menacing he produced his 9mm Glock handgun. Now she was scared. More yelling ensued. She needed someone to help. Ryan Clark, asleep in his underwear next door was awakened by the heated sounds. Clark was a fifth year senior with triple majors in Biology, English and Psychology. He leapt from bed and raced next door. Pounding on the door, perhaps hearing Emily whimpering or calling to him, he threw the door open and entered the room. At the warning of Clark's presence, that his first kill was about to be interrupted, Cho appeared to have retreated behind the far end of a standup closet inside the door along the left wall as Clark entered. In an instant Clark was inside. He started to move across the small room. He must have either seen Cho trying to hide there, or Emily would have told Clark the intruder was right there, just a couple feet away. Perhaps Cho even let himself be seen with his gun held behind the closet. Suddenly he stepped out from behind the closet, his gunhand swung up and shot Ryan Clark in the head. Clark went down, just inside the partially opened door.

Emily would have been terrified; probably in shock. Cho then crossed the few feet to the space under the far bed where she was cowering. With the same cold and rage-filled voice that would shock the world in his pre-recorded videos, he forced her down onto her knees. She was shot execution style in the back of the head, the bullet entering the right rear quadrant of her skull just behind her ear and lodging inside the front portion of her face. Blood from the entry wound splattered the desk and microwave under the bed. The floor beneath her was covered with her blood. Inside the door, blood from Ryan's head wound began to spread across the floor. It was just shy of 7:15 a.m. Cho quietly walked out of the room, pulling the door shut behind him. He appears to have taken the stairs down, exited the building and calmly walked back past Cochrane Hall, the crescent-shaped dormitory that stood between West AJ and Harper Hall, and entered his own dormitory. No one saw him.

Cho's access swipe card was used by him to enter Harper Hall where he lived at exactly 7:17 a.m. Depending on which way he would have walked around Cochrane Hall, it would have taken him two-and-a-half minutes to traverse the 334 yards in one direction, or only two minutes to cover the 270 yards going the other direction. Therefore, he would have walked out of WAJ no earlier than 7:14. Accounting for the approximate two minutes it would have taken him to walk down the fourth floor hallway, descend the three sets of stairs to the first floor, and exit the building, both Emily Hilscher and Ryan Clark would have been shot by 7:12 a.m. When Emily Hilscher had hopped out of her boyfriend's truck and entered the building she could not have known that she was in the final ten minutes of her life.

Cho went up to his second floor room to change out of his bloody clothing. His room was adorned with dozens of ducks. There were duck toys, stuffed ducks and duck pictures. Students later reported seeing him enter Harper Hall at approximately this time, though no one remembered seeing blood on Cho's clothes or shoes. He stripped out of his blood-spattered pants and blood-covered sneakers and shoved them down into his dirty clothes hamper. At this point he dressed in the assault clothes he had intended to wear for his rampage in Norris Hall from the very beginning, climbing into tan cargo-pocket BDU-type pants, a dark shirt, the tan 26-pocket vest he bought to hold his knife and spare magazines, and hooded sweatshirt. These were the same clothes he had videotaped himself in in the month leading up to the attack. The exception was that he did not put on the menacing black baseball cap he had specially purchased and worn in his videos and photos that he had taken of himself, but a maroon VT cap. His handguns were carried in two right hand draw holsters, one on his right hip and the other a cross-draw shoulder rig worn under his left arm. He would have wondered whether he could actually do it, whether he could actually take a human life. Just minutes before he had put bullets into the heads of two innocent people at pointblank range. And he felt nothing. At this point he was calm. If anything he felt high, euphoric. It was perfect. And he couldn't wait to do it again, to go on with the original plan that had been festering in his mind for almost ten years.

At 7:20 a.m. the Virginia Tech Police Department received a call on its administrative telephone line from a third floor female RA of WAJ, advising that a female student in room 4040 had possibly fallen from her loft bed. Per the GPR, the caller had been given this information from another WAJ resident, Molly Donohue, who lived next door to Emily Hilscher and Heather Haugh in room 4036, on the opposite side of Ryan Clark. From accounts of that morning told in the book *Lifting Our Eyes* by Beth Lueders, freshman Molly Donohue had returned to her dorm room at approximately 4:20 that morning, after a late night studying with her boyfriend. She had set her alarm for 6:50 a.m. and dozed off at 4:30. Miss Donohue stated in the book that she woke up before her alarm, shut it off and then lay in bed half awake. She must have dozed off again, as next she heard a scream which shocked her awake. She looked at her clock, which read 7:15, and realized she was late meeting her boyfriend for breakfast. Miss Donohue began to get dressed when she heard a pounding followed by a strange scream, which came from next door. Despite the fact that all four interior walls were cinderblock, she heard more pounding which woke her roommate, who opened her eyes to see Molly standing in the middle of their room.

Miss Donohue reported that she ran to the door and paused there. She then heard a door slam loudly, followed by someone running down the hallway past her room. She opened the door and saw bloody footprints right outside her door. She said that she initially thought the pounding was someone falling out of a loft bed. After she saw the bloody footprints she thought it was Emily Hilscher running to get help. Miss Donohue recalled that she then proceeded to Emily and Heather's room and tried to open the door, but there was a body pressed against it, and she saw an arm in the doorway. She yelled, "Is everything all right? Is everything all right?"

Miss Donohue further reported to author Lueders that she then ran to RA Ryan Clark's room, but he wasn't there. His door was open and she feared something was wrong. Miss Donohue ran back to her room, and her roommate went to find female RA Carrie Johnson on the third floor. Molly went back and finished getting dressed, then met her roommate in addition to two other girls from a neighboring room and the RA in the hallway. Donohue said that RA Johnson approached Emily Hilscher's room and forced her way through the door. VSP Lt. Lyon says that she used her passkey to gain entry, which means the door would have been shut. The RA returned seconds later with horror on her face and kept repeating, "I need a phone. I need a phone." Reportedly, the RA then made a 911 call, as she had just observed Emily Hilscher and Ryan Clark with gunshot wounds to the head.

Law enforcement accounts cast some doubt on this version of events, however. Reports that the first call was a 911 call alerting VTPD to a shooting at WAJ were inaccurate. According to police, after making the report Miss Donohue went to breakfast and class, and could not be located for some time. Per BPD ERT leader Sgt. Anthony Wilson, the dispatcher stated it "was a very generic call," and came in on the Tech administrative line at 7:20 a.m., not an emergency 911 call. VTPD Dispatch confirmed that the initial call came in on the administrative line from room 4038 and was made by the third floor female RA, but that she only alerted them to a student who had possibly fallen from her bed. If it had been a 911 call from a cell phone it would have gone to BPD or MCSO. Further, it does not appear that Miss Donohue mentioned seeing bloody footprints. If so, it didn't get communicated to the police. When the first officer and paramedics arrived they believed they were there merely to help a student who had fallen from a bed.

There was no evidence that Cho followed Miss Hilscher into WAJ, that she had been targeted in any way, or that Cho knew her. One reporter at the Wednesday, April 25, press conference after the shootings asked if police could confirm that Miss Hilscher had been working at a local escort service and that Cho had met her through her services there. Police refused to even respond to that question, so outrageous and vile was it. The police were certain that the selection of Miss Hilscher was completely random and that Ryan Clark died attempting to save her. Anonymous sources in law enforcement were quoted by the media as saying that Cho committed the first murders for no other reason than to divert police from his planned attack on Norris Hall across campus. However, based on our assessment of the events we did not believe this was true. It was the Archangel Team's conclusion that Cho committed the first murder of Emily Hilscher simply to see if he could go through with all that he had planned. There was no evidence evinced from investigations that he had planned the killings in WAJ in advance.

If Cho needed a diversionary murder he could have simply killed someone in his own dormitory and walked out the door. He would have waited outside, watching the police arrive in droves and then simply turned and walked on to Norris Hall. He should have also realized that such a "diversionary" killing would have only served to mobilize law enforcement on campus, whereas police resources would otherwise have been few that morning. No, he needed to see if he could kill, and to do that he was going to go to the source of so much of his humiliation and rage the prior year. Between his knowledge of WAJ from his mail collection, and the potential presence of the young lady he had harassed who lived on the fourth floor the previous year, he was drawn to it. As well, it was in proximity to his dorm. If he needed to kill someone first, just one person, to prove to himself that he could do it, he would have needed to pick someplace close to his dormitory. While Cochrane Hall was closer and sat between Harper and WAJ, VT alumni told us that Cochrane was where most of the football team lived, which would not have made nearly so viable a target for an initial killing. Simply, Cho wasn't that brave. He needed an easy victim. A petite 19-year-old girl was perfect.

Whether he followed Miss Hilscher into the WAJ elevator or was simply walking down the hall on the fourth floor when he saw her enter her room, or came upon her already opened door, he took his opportunity to "get his hands bloody" by trying to kill her. In Cho's mind, he was then forced to kill Ryan Clark who came to her rescue. This is why he had not mailed his manifesto, videos and photos to NBC prior to these killings: he had to know he could go through with it first. He had to get the scent. Once he committed those murders he would have felt that he would be caught, and so had to go forward with his real plan of attacking Norris Hall.

7:21 a.m. to 7:49 a.m.

One minute after the RA's call was logged at 7:21 a.m. the VTPD dispatcher notified the Virginia Tech Rescue Squad (VTRS) of the report that a female student had possibly fallen from her loft bed. Curtis Cook also confirmed that this was a generic call that came in on the police department's administrative line, not a 911 emergency call. The Rescue Squad was comprised of first aid-giving medical personnel only, and did not include any police officers, nor was any member of the VTRS armed. The Rescue Service was located on the campus and was the oldest of its kind nationwide. The GPR noted that the VTRS was a student-run organization and had 38 members.[215] Highly trained paramedics, they traveled around the campus in completely equipped and stocked paramedic vehicles. A VTPD officer was dispatched to room 4040 to support the medical response. This was standard procedure.

—

ERT Tac Medic Jason Dominiczak's early morning response to West Ambler-Johnston dormitory on the south side of the Virginia Tech Campus as "Rescue One" had begun as the result of hearing the "student fell out of the loft" call that Virginia Tech Rescue Squad Number Three was responding to and he knew that VTRS was short on personnel. He had been asleep at home that morning as he had been pulling backup duty. He got up and headed in to provide assistance in the event of a back injury to the student. Like every other person in the Blacksburg and the Virginia Tech communities that day his life would change forever that morning.

The northern New Jersey Chemical Engineering major at Virginia Tech never thought that he would be a pivotal cog in the emergency medical wheel that would be in motion throughout the day on April 16, 2007. Dominiczak had been involved in medical first response since he was merely 16-years-old and worked for a volunteer

215 GPR, p. 101.

fire department in his home state. It was during his sophomore year at VT that Curtis Cook had come to him and said that they were looking for a tactical medic for the SWAT team. So Dominiczak joined and became a certified Emergency Medical Technician-Intermediate Provider for the state accredited Virginia Tech Rescue Squad as well as the ERT. During his half-year probation he underwent the identical training as the ERT operators, including CS/OC,[216] explosives, and room entries and clearings.

In an interview on October 22, 2009 at Sharkey's restaurant in Blacksburg, Jason Dominiczak, or simply "Jersey" to his co-workers who struggled to pronounce, much less spell his name insisted that the biggest part of his job as a tac medic was not the "blood and guts stuff," but team care. He insisted that despite what might be a rather romantic notion of how tac medics functioned, that his primary purpose was "keeping my guys healthy and operational." He said that "team health, team wellness and operational medical support is critical and the most rewarding and most fun part of my job." This bespoke a modesty and commitment to his team that would help him when put to the ultimate test of his skills in Norris Hall.

—

At 7:24 a.m. the dispatched VT police officer and the VT Rescue Squad Number Three medics arrived, expecting to find a possibly injured and sobbing coed in need of a quick patch-up, and maybe some ice and aspirin. Typically such falls resulted merely in a sprained or fractured wrist or ankle. At worst a student might have bumped his head, suffered a concussion or injured his back. Pushing the door open against Ryan Clark's still form, they saw the pool of blood and two victims.[217] Both of their skulls were ruptured by bullets. The responding Rescue Squad members and police officer immediately requested "additional VTPD resources."[218] Dominiczak was already

216 Chlorobenzalmalononitrile, which is tear gas, and oleoresin capsicum which is pepper spray.
217 The book *April 16th: Virginia Tech Remembers* states that VTRS was dispatched at 7:24 and arrived 2 minutes later, Lazenby, p. 6.
218 GPR, p. 25

on his way. The squad members immediately began treating the students, attempting to stabilize them, to keep them alive.

—

Per the GPR and the panel's review of university computer records,[219] at 7:25 a.m. Cho had already changed his clothes, taken the elevator down to the lobby of his dormitory and accessed his university email account. It was merely eight minutes since he had returned to the building, and none of his suitemates had been home to observe him. If they had, they might have paid with their lives at seeing his bloody appearance. He erased all of his files in the email account. They were irretrievable. It is believed that at this time Cho made final edits to the video clips of himself to be mailed as part of his visual and written manifesto to NBC. This was supported at a July 7, 2007 debriefing with the Archangel Team, by commanders of both Blacksburg and Tech police. Beth J. Lueders, in her book, *Lifting Our Eyes*, stated that he accessed his computer one minute earlier, at 7:24.[220]

—

Hearing the new call, Dominiczak hit the gas pedal on his Chevrolet Tahoe designated Rescue Vehicle Number One, and raced to the dormitory. The VTRS always responded with fully equipped vehicles. According to Jersey, the medical "golf cart-looking things" cited by the media "were only used at football games." The VTRS service was a highly trained, excellent first response program for those on the VT campus. It handled between 900 and 1,200 calls each year, including 60 to 70 patients at each home football game. In 1997 the service had won the JEMS[221] award for the best program in the nation. Jersey arrived just two minutes after the first rescue truck at 7:26. As he approached WAJ another call came over the radio, this one saying that there was a lot of blood in room 4040. He had just arrived and leapt into the elevator, trying to get to the fourth floor as fast as he could.

219 Ibid.
220 Lueders, p. 9.
221 *Journal of Emergency Medical Services*

As the elevator labored slowly up to the fourth floor he heard that there were, in fact, two patients, not one. But he only had one IV bag. "I had been thinking that maybe one kid had fallen from bed and cracked his head," he told us. As soon as he heard there were two victims and "a lot of blood" he called for a second ambulance. Medics Suzie Thomas and Ben Foster of VTRS Three were already on scene. A third female medic was also on scene. VTPD police officer Darrell Sheppard was also there.

Three minutes after arriving, at 7:29 a.m., Dominiczak entered the room.[222] What he saw put him into autopilot. He could see blood on the floor and a single bullet casing. He gave only fleeting thoughts to this bloody scene as possibly being a murder-suicide or a "love triangle gone wrong." He had patients to save. Ryan Clark and Emily Hilscher lay bleeding on opposite sides of the room. Paramedics Suzie Thomas[223] and Ben Foster were working to stabilize the victims. Jason knew that the "Golden Hour" clock – the approximate 60 minutes time span within which severely injured patients could be saved by getting to a hospital - was ticking and transportation to the hospital was critical.

"Suzie was working on Ryan Clark; he's really bad at that point," Jersey says seeing the event as though it was playing out all over again in his mind. "Ben was on the female. She was moaning; he was unresponsive, very shallow breathing, weak and thready pulse. I started helping with her, and they got the male out. He was more critical so he came out first."[224] Jersey had requested helicopter evacuation for both. Roanoke's medical chopper was Lifeguard 10 and typically only eight minutes out, and came out of a Level I trauma center. The other, Lifeguard 11, was 12 to 15 minutes out. He knew that with the winds that day "the chances were slim they could get a chopper in the air" but felt that he had to try. It took one-and-a-half minutes before he was informed that it was impossible for the

222 The book *April 16th: Virginia Tech Remembers* says VTRS 3 arrived at 7:35, Lazenby, p. 6.
223 Suzie would leave the service to finish her degree elsewhere shortly afterward.
224 The book *April 16th: Virginia Tech Remembers* states that VTRS was dispatched at 7:24 and arrived two minutes later, Lazeny, p. 6.

helicopters to get into the air. "With the winds they weren't coming," he said.[225]

Jersey continued to work on Emily Hilscher. "She was moaning, unresponsive, also very shallow breathing, with a weak and thready pulse," he recalled. Neither of the students had been conscious, but Emily was at least responsive to pain. Despite his training and high level certifications, these were the first gunshot wounds he had ever seen. "Emily had been shot in the back of the head behind the right ear, execution style, and had a lot of facial swelling," he told us. He couldn't tell if the round had exited her face, although it hadn't. "It was just a mess. All I could see was clotting blood mixed with her hair."

With no choppers going up, ground transportation was the only option. With two ambulances already on-scene he called the hospital and alerted them that he had "two victims with GSWs" and that they were on their way from Tech. The hospital worker on the other end of the phone was shocked. "You have what!?" he yelled into the phone. The two ambulances took off within three minutes of each other.[226] As they pulled away, the lights and sirens could barely be discerned above the howling wind.

Montgomery Regional General was a small, 146 bed hospital with a 16 bed Emergency Department. But it was only a Level III trauma center. Situated a three to four minute drive from the Virginia Tech campus it also served as the teaching hospital for residents and students from the university. Charlie Smith was the Director of Engineering Services and Security for the hospital.

Nestled in this southwest Virginia community, Montgomery Regional Hospital and Charlie Smith still were no strangers to violence in the emergency room. It was here that in August of 2006 Smith had had one of his security guards killed by a prisoner named William

225 Lazeny, in the book April 16th: Virginia Tech Remembers, reports that VTRS didn't request air rescue until 7:48 a.m., p. 7. This is inaccurate as the request had already been made and denied, and an ambulance dispatched which had arrived prior to Miss Hilscher being transported to the hospital at 7:43 a.m.

226 Lazenby says that Ryan Clark's ambulance left fully six minutes after Emily Hilscher's, at 7:49 a.m., p. 7. However, it was the first to leave with hers three minutes behind.

Morva. The Morva event helped prepare him and the staff for what was to take place that morning, but no one would have ever expected the magnitude of the carnage that was to come bursting through their doors.

At 7:45 a.m. the Emergency Room staff at Montgomery Hospital was advised by radio that they would be receiving gunshot victims from the Virginia Tech campus. People were shocked. Gunshot victims?! That never happened at the university. Six minutes later the first VT Rescue Squad pulled up with Ryan Clark dead on arrival with exposed brain matter. Four short minutes later the second student, Emily Hilscher, was brought in with a gunshot wound to her head. Jersey was in the back of the ambulance with her, working feverishly to keep her alive. "I got IVs into her, I was monitoring this slender, little girl," was all he could manage to say during our interview. The loss of this beautiful teenager was something he clearly still struggled with. Upon arrival Emily was whisked into the Emergency Room by a waiting team.

Jersey gave his oral report to the Emergency Room staff, restocked his IV and plasma units, and then after getting himself together sat down to write a detailed report. He knew that this was a report that was going to require that he "dotted all the i's and crossed all the t's." He was only thinking that because of what he witnessed he expected to end up in court testifying to the events of the morning. Little did the young tac medic know that the whole world would be reviewing his actions at West-Ambler Johnston Hall that morning and his later performance at a bloodbath in Norris Hall.

From what little he had seen in the WAJ dorm room he still continued to suspect that it was a love triangle gone bad. He had done a quick visual sweep but saw no weapon. "At 7:00 a.m. you don't see a guy in a girl's room unless they're in love, sort of a relationship," he explained. At the hospital they took x-rays and were trying to stabilize Emily. The harsh weather meant that she would still have to be transported by ambulance to Roanoke's main hospital, a Level I trauma center 45 minutes away. Still clinging to a thread of life Emily was prepared for transport at 8:30 a.m. A paramedic-intermediate and an enhanced provider accompanied her to make every effort to keep her alive. Cho's second shooting victim would also not survive the attack and she died en route to Roanoke. "What a horrible morning," Smith thought.

By 7:30 a.m., additional VTPD officers began arriving at West AJ and room 4040. The crime scene was secured and a preliminary investigation begun.[227] Initial contact with other dormitory residents resulted in no suspect descriptions, and no one on the fourth floor had observed anyone leaving the girl's room after the initial noise was heard by Molly Donohue. At 7:40 a.m. VTPD Chief Wendell Flinchum was notified by telephone of the shootings.[228]

—

For VT ERT commander and former Navy rescue swimmer Curtis Cook, the 16th had started off badly. Cook had actually once aspired to be a firefighter. Before the day was over he would wish he had pursued that career option. He was almost late for work, something he never allowed to happen, and was already frustrated when he hustled into police headquarters. Upon arrival Cook was advised by Detective Stephanie Henley that the "big news" for the morning was that a student had fallen out of her loft bed. However, as he settled in for the day he was quickly briefed by two members of the department command staff, Captains Vince Houston and Joseph Albert, that the simple accident had turned into a homicide scene at West AJ.

Cook lived for SWAT. He was a special operator at heart, and didn't much care whether it was military or law enforcement, although he was happy to be at Virginia Tech charged with the command responsibility of handling the worst cases to keep the kids and university safe. And Cook looked every bit the part. Stocky with short, dark hair, he was exactly what you would expect from a SWAT commander. His face bore the faint remnants of an acne problem

227 GPR, p. 25.
228 Ibid.

from childhood, which only served to add to his generally serious, if not menacing, visage. But when he smiled his entire face would crinkle up, revealing the vulnerable, kind and caring person that he really was. "Curtis Cook is a great commander," Jason Dominiczak would later tell us. Cook liked the work, liked the operators on his team, liked his bosses, and liked working with their sister team, the Blacksburg ERT. He had a wonderful wife and two great kids. For a man who lived to serve, life couldn't be better.

Per the GPR Hilscher's roommate, Heather Haugh, arrived at their room to walk with her to Chemistry class.[229] She was immediately questioned by detectives. Until her arrival police had not been able to tell which of the two girls had been shot, so distorted was Emily's face from the bullet that had entered her head from behind. They kept looking at photos around the room of the two girls, but just couldn't figure out which one she was. Heather explained that, typically, Hilscher's boyfriend, Karl Thornhill, would drop her off early Monday morning after spending the weekend together. She believed that Emily had been dropped off at the dorm at approximately 6:50 that morning. She informed police that Thornhill was a student at nearby Radford University and that he was an avid shooter and gunowner. Heather Haugh also informed investigators that he frequented a shooting range, and he had taken both of the girls to the range with him. This was at 8:16 a.m.

This information, together with the fact both victims died from gunshot wounds and the presence of numerous photos of Thornhill in the room, always with guns, made him a *person of interest* and potential suspect. Even Miss Hilscher's computer screensaver was displaying photos of Thornhill with firearms. The desire to speak with Thornhill was further supported by the information from Miss Haugh that Emily had, in fact, just been deposited at her dorm by Thornhill minutes before, and was found shot with another man in her room, clad only in his underwear.

229 GPR, p. 25.

7:50 a.m. to 8:20 a.m.

At 7:51 that morning, merely 11 minutes after receiving notification of the double shooting, VTPD Chief Flinchum was already on the phone with Blacksburg Police Chief Kim Crannis, making a mutual aid request for the assistance of a BPD evidence technician and detective for the WAJ crime scene and investigation. During that call both chiefs decided to send in back-up and support in terms of investigators, crime scene technicians and other officers to lock WAJ down, establish a perimeter around it, begin searching it, and interview other residents. A number of Blacksburg's ERT were immediately dispatched to West AJ to perform these other functions. All of these groups began screeching up to the dormitory by 8:15 a.m.

Flinchum also alerted elements of VT's ERT. Curtis Cook went immediately to West Ambler-Johnston dormitory. "When I arrived on scene I was told by Officer Darrell Sheppard that two students had been shot and were being transported to the hospital," he said. He recalled seeing a 9mm shell on the floor at the scene. This was important to Cook so that he could advise his ERT members what type of weapon they might be facing. His people were being supported by members of the Blacksburg Police Department with patrol officers, detectives and its Crime Scene Investigation Unit which had also arrived. VTPD's George Jackson was already processing the crime scene with the Blacksburg evidence technician. There were also some university officials at the scene when Cook arrived.

No sooner was Chief Flinchum off the phone with Chief Krannis at 7:57 a.m., when he notified the Virginia Tech Office of the Executive Vice President of the WAJ shootings. The two chiefs, who had been friends and colleagues for years, had taken barely five minutes to discuss the critical aspects of the shootings, arrive at joint decisions on needed officer deployment, and get off the phones to issue the necessary orders. Flinchum's subsequent call to VT President Steger at 8:10 a.m. resulted in the university's Policy Group immediately convening a meeting at 8:35 a.m. This was the crisis management team that came together to make decisions during campus emergencies. It was to meet at Burruss Hall, the main administration building for the university, which was just 20 yards to the west of Norris Hall. With the flair of the poet, Professor Roy described Burruss Hall as a building that:

> ...dominates, with its castlelike appearance and its multicolored façade, sitting majestically at the top of an imposing flight of stone steps. This was the seat of Virginia Tech's central administration – where the offices of the president, the provost, the treasurer, the vice presidents, the vice provosts, and other administrators are located.[230]

At eight o'clock as the calls were being made to the Policy Group members, and both police departments' command staffs were mobilizing resources, classes were beginning on campus. At the same time Chief Flinchum arrived at WAJ and contacted the detectives on scene from both departments. He was also looking at alerting the Virginia State Police. He was going to leave no stone unturned in tracking and finding the monster that had shot two of his kids.

–

Friday the 13th was an omen of bad luck, harkening all the way back to Friday, October 13, 1307 when French King Philip IV and Pope Clement V ordered the overnight arrest of thousands of brothers of the Poor Fellow-Soldiers of Christ and the Temple of Solomon – more commonly known as the Knights Templar – which ultimately saw several hundred of them burned at the stake. Ominously, for Lieutenant George Jackson of the Virginia Tech Police Department, Friday the 13th of April 2007 was his graduation day from the Virginia Forensic Science Academy. In less than fifty hours he would become involved in crime scenes that would become the focal point of both national and international news, and certainly the worst crime scenes

230 Roy, p. 18.

that he had seen in his ten years in law enforcement. On that morning Jackson responded to the initial homicide at the West Ambler-Johnston dormitory and in his own words, "I didn't even have my pencils sharpened yet." Fresh from his Crime Scene Investigation training, he started to process the bloody scene in room 4040 and the surrounding area.

–

April 16 was also opening day of spring turkey hunting season. That made Tech police Sergeant W. Morgan Millirons a happy man. That was, until he spoke with his wife who reminded him about the federal income taxes that were due that day. Taxes were never filed on Sunday so Monday was the untraditional taxman day. By the end of that day Millirons - who today is the Sheriff of Giles County - would remark, "You hear of it happening but never dream of it happening on your own ground." Millirons had just finished the midnight tour of duty with the Virginia Tech PD and was quickly called back into work because of the West Ambler-Johnston shootings. The sergeant had been with the Virginia Tech Police Department for 12 years and fondly remembered his time there as "phenomenal." All kinds of training had been provided to him and he served many collateral duties, including K9 and SWAT.

–

Virginia Tech police officer Rebecca Hawkins, a young, attractive Radford University psychology and criminal justice major, had also gotten off duty at 7:00 that morning, after completing an uneventful night of duty. Rebecca had been with the department for less than eighteen months. As Hawkins was driving home Cho was about to proceed up to the fourth floor of the West Ambler-Johnston dormitory. Within two short hours of completing her night shift Hawkins was called back to work and would be on standby with other officers at the Blacksburg Police Department lunch room when the horrifying radio call was broadcast.

The unfortunate part in the whole picture of this young officer's professional life was that twice in less than eight months she would become part of a violent death-ridden criminal episode. She had been a friend of Deputy Sheriff Eric Sutphin who was killed the previous August during the Morva manhunt, and now she would be part of the largest school shooting in American history.

—

When Shannon Combs left the Radford Police Department in 2005 after four years on the job, he was looking forward to being a member of the Blacksburg Police Department's ERT. He had no idea that on April 16, 2007, not only would he be a member of that special operations team but would also be involved in one of the most horrific SWAT deployments in history.

—

Tom Gallemore was born in Germany because his father was in the military and stationed there. He had served his own tour in the Army as a military policeman. In 2003, at age 30, he started with the Virginia Tech Police Department, eventually passing selection for a position on the ERT and moving up to the position of team leader. When he was called to stage at the Blacksburg Police Department that cold morning he was one of the last officers to arrive. A short time later he would be one of the first officers into Norris Hall to assist in putting an end to the rampage. He would be the first into room 211 and the first to see the carnage inside.

—

Based on at least one witness account, Cho was seen near the Duck Pond between 8:10 and 8:20 that morning. The Duck Pond was approximately one-quarter mile to the southwest of Norris Hall, and 645 yards to the northwest of Harper Hall, Cho's dorm. At a normal walking pace, it took six minutes to cover the distance from Harper Hall to that point at the Duck Pond. With Cho having logged onto his university email account at 7:25 a.m., police investigators assessed that it would have taken him approximately 30 minutes to delete his email account and make the final edits to his diatribe and videotapes, before printing the pages and downloading the images for his NBC package. That would have seen him leaving his dormitory somewhere around eight o'clock. The six minute walk would have put him at the Duck Pond at exactly the time he was reportedly seen.

The pond itself covered more than three surface acres and was about sixteen feet deep in the middle, at its deepest point. In addition to the flocks of colorful ducks squawking happily about the water were countless geese guarding their domain on both the water and shore. Cho was observed on the far shore, across the water from Duck Pond Road, near the parking lot. He was just standing there, looking out over the water. For the loner, self-exiled to a life of no human interaction yet who found solace in the many representations of the gaily feathered and web-footed creatures in his bedroom, maybe he was seeking some peace after what he had just done. Long after that day speculation would continue that his missing cell phone and computer hard drive may have been thrown into the pond at that time.

—

Her cell phone rang at 8:11 a.m. on the morning of April 16, 2007. April Blankenship wondered what the department could want at that time of the morning since she had just left work at 7 a.m. after completing her midnight shift as a dispatcher for the usually quiet university police department. The term "quiet university police department" would never again be used by anyone in relation to Virginia Tech. April was being called back to help deal with the turmoil that was erupting from the double murder at West Ambler-Johnston dormitory. Just one hour before Cho began his rampage in Norris Hall, April walked back into the Virginia Tech Police Communications Division with "no idea what I was walking into." Despite the seeming panic over the two homicides, the situation appeared to her to be calm when she first arrived on that cold, snowy morning. She thought to herself, "But nothing ever happens on a Monday morning." April would be proven very wrong.

Between 8:10 and 9:25 that morning the police had been working feverishly to identify, track and find the killer of two kids, searching everywhere on the sprawling campus and the network of rural roads and towns that satellited Blacksburg. During this period Chief Flinchum provided updated information via telephone to the Virginia Tech Policy Group (VTPG) regarding the status of the investigation into the WAJ shootings.[231] Chief Flinchum informed the VTPG that a possible suspect had been identified, and that he was most likely off campus. This "possible suspect" was Hilscher's boyfriend, Karl Thornhill.

—

At first police considered the possibility of the double murder having actually been a murder-suicide, until the point at which Clark had been moved and no weapon found. But there was a set of bloody footprints that appeared to be exiting the room. First arriving officer, VTPD Patrolman Darrell Sheppard, reported that the footprints were present on his arrival and that the crime scene had been documented from the outset. He had ensured the scene had not been disturbed beyond rescue personnel rendering life-saving first aid to the victims prior to transport. Initial indications were that the shooter had exited the crime scene and was "at large." From the wounds and location of the victims in the room police concluded that one had been shot "execution style" (Hilscher), and the other "ambush style" (Clark).

After VTPD called out BPD, it responded with an evidence technician; the chief of police, Kimberly Crannis; Capt. Donnie Goodman as the Incident Commander; ten extra officers for perimeter security; two SROs; two administration lieutenants; and five detectives. BPD investigators were quickly teamed up with Virginia Tech personnel to locate witnesses and begin interviews. BPD helped

231 GPR, p. 25.

establish a perimeter around WAJ and to secure Washington Street to the south, which was the closest thoroughfare to the building, some 50 yards away from the southeast corner of WAJ. The initial command post was established in the fourth floor WAJ lounge.

There was seamless cooperation between the agencies as investigators, forensic staff members, supervisors and command staffs were quickly paired to form investigative teams. Pairing investigators from each department had also been utilized during the Morva manhunt in August 2006 and had proven to be extremely beneficial. Both Blacksburg and VT police units were heavily concentrated on the campus, and Montgomery County Sheriff's deputies were directed into Blacksburg to assist with patrol and other calls for police service. This early coordinated effort would prove critical to aid in locating witnesses and persons of interest.

Heather Haugh had confirmed that the relationship with Ryan Clark, the male RA, was strictly platonic. He appeared to have responded in an attempt to save Emily from whatever had made her scream. Further follow-up was done on the relationship between Miss Hilscher and Thornhill, and although it was described as "loving," nobody could attest to the activity of that weekend or the final moments of the morning. The Virginia Tech Police Department had started a preliminary criminal investigation and it was reported that one victim was a confirmed fatality and the second was in extremely critical condition and en route to Roanoke Memorial Hospital Trauma Center.

Additional information was provided to all suggesting that Thornhill had weapons and lived inside the town limits. At this point, locating the boyfriend became an immediate priority. The evidence gleaned up to then was consistent with domestic murder. With address, vehicle and physical information confirmed, by 7:30 a.m. police were following up information on Karl Thornhill, and a BOLO[232] was issued for him as a "person of interest."

232 Be On the Look Out, a broad radio and computer message communication for all law enforcement agencies that immediate assistance is being sought locating a particular individual. Formerly known as an APB or All Points Bulletin.

—

At 8:11 that morning, merely 20 minutes after her department had received a call from Wendell Flinchum, Blacksburg Police Chief Kim Crannis arrived at WAJ to assist in the investigation. This really wasn't her problem; however, she was going to make sure that the VTPD had every resource at her disposal that they could possibly need. After all, two kids were dead and no one was treating this as a routine matter. Though the original request by Flinchum for the Blacksburg police was only for forensic support on the crime scene, it had been quickly upgraded to investigative assistance and man-power to secure a large perimeter around WAJ. VTPD did not have a substantial amount of experience with processing fatal crime scenes, and certainly not homicides, and did not hesitate to call in support from its sister agency. At 8:18 a.m. Virginia State Police Special Agent Eaton was requested to assist with blood splatter analysis.

—

It was about 7:00 that morning when Captain Donnie Goodman had reported for duty at the Blacksburg Police Department. A short time later he was advised of the shootings at West-Ambler Johnston Dormitory and the Virginia Tech PD request for assistance in the investigation. Goodman responded to the scene and met with Chief Flinchum and his own chief who had beaten him there. It was a "brutally freezing cold morning," he recalled later.

At 8:13 Chief Flinchum requested additional officers from both VTPD and BPD to secure WAJ entrances and assist with the investigation. Due to the growing enormity of the event, and the need for multiple police to secure the perimeter, those officers that had gone off duty from the nightshift were recalled and assigned to Ambler-Johnston. Upon arrival officers were put in as many two-man teams pairing one each from Tech with one from Blacksburg as possible. They were assigned either to door security positions or were part of roving patrols. They were looking for Thornhill, or anyone or anything else that might give them a lead in the murder investigation.

The perimeter around West AJ was to be secured and checked for dropped or discarded articles of evidentiary value.

Blacksburg lieutenants Joe Davis and Kit Cummings were coordinating these assignments, with flexibility built in to respond to investigative leads passed through Captain Goodman or Blacksburg Lieutenant John Glass who was the direct ERT commander serving immediately under Goodman, the ERT oversight commander Anthony Wilson, then a sergeant, was the actual leader of the team when it came to kicking in doors and taking out bad guys. Wilson was an excellent choice for team leader. With his boyish good looks, blue eyes and bright smile reminiscent of the childhood actors from 1950s and 60s television shows like *My Three Sons*, *Father Knows Best* or even *Dennis the Menace*, he had the look of an All American Hero, which he nearly was. A former Marine, he had returned to his hometown to continue to serve. Only now he wore the uniform of the Blacksburg ERT leader as well as that of the assistant fire chief. Wilson knew nothing but service to his town, his community, and his country - and Virginia Tech. Always in uniform.

At 8:15 a.m. Capt. Goodman ordered Lt. Glass to activate the full Blacksburg ERT. That meant the full complement of both ERTs had been called out, though elements of both had already been on scene. According to the GPR, however, it was not until 8:19 that BPD Chief Crannis alerted and assembled the full BPD ERT. No matter the specific minute, four of its members were already at WAJ, as they were among the first BPD officers deployed to assist with the investigation. During a meeting we had with BPD and VTPD commanders on July 7, 2007, it was confirmed that both ERT teams had actually been activated at 8:15. Due to the level of violence that had already occurred, and the probable encounter with an armed suspect, both Blacksburg and VT emergency response teams were staged for deployment, with half of each held at the Blacksburg Police Department for deployment and the other half at West AJ. This practice of also combining the two special operations teams had been utilized on many previous occasions and allowed for the deployment of joint units of specially trained police to the higher risk callouts.

Up to that point the four Blacksburg ERT officers already on duty had been serving such functions as investigation (as some, including BPD ERT leader Anthony Wilson, were detectives); security; perimeter; and search and patrol. Lt. Glass was functioning as the Investigations Liaison and Tactical Team Commander. Lt. Cummings was also on site and serving as the IC[233] of Ambler-Johnston Perimeter Control. Lt. Davis was IC of Ambler-Johnson Building Access Control; and, Sgt. Wilson was the CID[234] Supervisor and Tactical Team Leader. A lot had taken place in less than the hour that had passed since the first call for a Tech paramedic had come in to tend to a girl who had fallen from her bed. The police were moving at lightning speed.

8:21 to 9:16 a.m.

Deborah Morgan was the lieutenant in charge of the VTPD communications center, where all 911 calls and dispatch radio calls came and went from. That morning her daughter had an eight o'clock orthodontist appointment. While in the waiting room she received a call that she had to report for duty, "NOW!" There had been a homicide on the campus and all personnel were being summoned to work. Her job was a critical one in such an event, and she was at police headquarters within 20 minutes. Upon arrival her first task was to take some crime scene supplies to West Ambler-Johnston. When she returned to headquarters she began to handle the duties of the communication center. She fielded whatever questions that her dispatchers had and assisted in answering the phones. Some people that had a "need to know" called in and were given what information was available. Many of the callers had "just wanted to know" what had happened at West Ambler-Johnston. It was hectic, but it paled in comparison to what would transpire in the next several hours.

233 "In Charge" or "In Command" officer.
234 Criminal Investigation Division

The BOLO was issued at 8:30 that morning, and officers from Tech, Blacksburg, the Montgomery County Sheriff's Office (MCSO) and the Virginia State Police (VSP) all joined the search for Karl Thornhill. He had not been at his scheduled class at Radford University, nor was he at his residence. His vehicle had not been found in any of the VT campus parking lots. Per the GPR, officers were increasingly confident that he had left the campus. Their first desire was to ensure that no other students were in jeopardy from whomever had murdered the two West AJ residents. Investigators continued looking for witnesses in the dormitory where those shootings had taken place. VTPD and BPD continued processing the crime scene in room 4040.

At 8:35 a.m., VT officials, in the form of the university Leadership Team or Policy Group, which included the university President, Charles Steger; and Executive Vice President, James A. Hyatt, met to assess what was known about the situation, and to determine what information they should provide to the students and faculty about the homicides. At 8:50 a.m. Virginia State Police blood splatter expert Special Agent Eaton arrived at WAJ.

The Governor's Panel reported that at 8:52, upon hearing of the incident at WAJ from their security chief, who had overheard the transmissions between the two departments on his police radio, Blacksburg public schools locked their outer doors.[235] However, both departments' commanders insisted that this information was actually conveyed by one of the Blacksburg PD school resource officers who had been called to provide perimeter security at WAJ.

At nine o'clock, Chief Flinchum was still at WAJ overseeing the investigation. Therefore, VTPD Capt. Joseph Albert was sent by him to begin briefing the VT Policy Group on the shootings. At this time Provost Dr. Mark G. McNamee joined the Policy Group. At 9:01 a.m., approximately one hour and 50 minutes after the WAJ shootings, Cho mailed a package to *NBC News* in New York, from the downtown Blacksburg Post Office. The package contained a 1,800 word written

235 GPR, p. 26.

"manifesto," or "rambling diatribe"[236] of his anger, 43 photos of himself, and a DVD with 27 Quick Time video files of his beliefs, complaints and positions on issues important to him.[237] Essentially the videos were rants of his hatred and malice. Lucinda Roy would call it "his crazed, misanthropic video missive."[238] He "alludes to a coming massacre" and otherwise expressed his desire to "get even" with "oppressors," she wrote.[239] The GPR described the videos as nothing more than performances of his enclosed writing.[240] The package which contained all of this was opened at NBC's headquarters in New York two days later. *NBC News* President Steve Capus would later defend his network's airing of these by saying that, "This is as close as we'll ever come to being in the mind of a killer."

Cho also mailed a letter to the VT English Department verbally attacking Professor Carl Bean, with whom he had had an earlier disagreement. Strangely, this letter - and the killings - would take place almost exactly one year after Cho's fight with Professor Bean in his office, leaving Lucinda Roy to wonder if it was in some way intended to punish the English professor.[241] Second period classes would begin four minutes after the post office time stamped the package at 9:01 that morning; thus, no warnings would be issued to students before they commenced.[242]

One of the biggest mysteries about the massacre was just where the gunman was and what did he do during that two-hour window between the first burst of gunfire at a high-rise dormitory, and the second fusillade at a classroom building? Some of that time was spent walking into town, waiting in line at the post office among the myriad citizens ensuring the date stamp on their tax returns, mailing his package at the counter and then returning to Norris Hall. What is not definitely known, however, is what Cho did for the rest

236 Ibid.

237 Kevin Anderson and CT Staff, "Week of Strength Follows Day of Horror on Campus," *Collegiate Times*, p. 1.

238 Roy, p. 107.

239 Ibid.

240 GPR, p. 26.

241 Roy, p. 81.

242 Roy, p. 107.

of that time. It is certain that he would have had to walk directly to his own dorm room from West AJ, as the computer log for his card swipe showed he re-entered Harper Hall at 7:17, with the first two shootings having occurred by 7:15.

He accessed his university computer account at 7:24 a.m. The interim would have been just enough time for him to change clothes and go down to the lobby to access his email. Investigators had reason to believe that while on the computer, he not only completely erased his email account with VT, but did final edits to his manifesto and video clips that he would mail to NBC.

Assessing that Cho would have spent the estimated 30 to 40 minutes on his computer and preparing his package for NBC, it was estimated that he would have departed Harper Hall between 7:55 and 8:05 a.m. The shortest walking distance from Harper Hall to the post office in Blacksburg is 1,220 yards and took Archangel's Chris Hays and Walter Chi 13 minutes and 37 seconds to traverse at an average pace. The shortest walking distance from the post office directly to Norris Hall is approximately 850 yards and took Archangel's team members 10 minutes 37 seconds to travel by foot. If Cho had gone straight from Harper Hall to the post office, and then directly to Norris Hall he would have been traveling merely 24 minutes 23 seconds. Assuming, both, that Cho finished with his computer and departed Harper Hall at 8:05 (the latest estimated time) and spent ten minutes at the post office, he would have arrived at Norris Hall at approximately 8:29 or 8:30. This well preceded the times he was seen at Norris Hall at both the breezeway and outside the west entrance by a minimum 45 minutes.

From Archangel's investigation, the most likely answer lies in the reports from students that Cho had been at the Duck Pond between 8:15 and 8:20. It is important to note that much information on the preparations and other activities of Cho leading up to the attacks is missing, due to the fact that the hard drive to his computer has never been found. With Cho never having had a friend throughout his life – much less his time at VT – it was seen as doubtful that he had an accomplice who would have assisted him or disposed of his computer information for him. Thus, we must consider that he took steps to ensure it would not be recovered through the police investigation into the atrocity he was about to commit. Since his computer was still operational at 7:24 a.m. – and he never left Norris Hall alive once he entered - he would have had to discard it after leaving Harper Hall and either arriving at the post office or after leaving the post office.

However, with his package being time-stamped at 9:01 a.m., and Cho being seen by witnesses outside Norris Hall as early as 9:15 a.m., he would have barely had enough time just to make the almost 11 minutes walk. One professor saw him outside the western doors at 9:18. Simply, there would have been no time for him to secret the hard drive away in a manner that would keep it from ever being found despite massive efforts by police to locate it.

Thus, we are left to assume that Cho eliminated the hard drive between leaving Harper Hall at approximately 8:00 and arriving at the post office. The distance from his dorm at Harper Hall to the closest point of the Duck Pond is 645 yards and takes six minutes to walk. The Duck Pond sits approximately one-quarter mile southwest of Norris Hall, and is a large expanse of water covering between three and four surface acres. It is approximately 16 feet at its deepest point in the center with a bottom that is several feet deep in duck and goose excrement. This is the pond that police divers have searched underwater on two occasions since the shootings, with no success. Later that year the police attempted to drain the pond, still searching for Cho's computer hard drive. However, even when emptied about four feet of water was left at its deepest point. Without completely draining the pond and conducting a veritable archaeological dig in the muck, sifting through each layer inch by inch, there would be little to no possibility of the hard drive ever being found. If, in fact, that was where Cho had disposed of it. Due to the nature of that computer part, metal detectors and magnets could not be used to locate it without erasing the memory. Whether it would still be in tact at all after having been submerged for so long is another concern.

Had Cho walked directly from his dorm to the Duck Pond, leaving at 8:05, he would have arrived at the far point he was seen at, at approximately 8:11 to 8:15, placing him there during the 8:15 to 8:20 time frame exactly when reported. From the Duck Pond to the post office in Blacksburg is another 1,593 yards and takes 16 minutes 40 seconds to walk. Assuming he spent just a few minutes at the Duck Pond, and walked around the more remote far end – where he was seen - it would, again, place him in that facility with sufficient time to wait in line, obtain the Express Mail envelope, address it and pay for it at the counter, accounting for the 9:01 a.m. time stamp. One of the postal workers recalled having to help Cho address his package to NBC.[243]

At 9:05, just as the police were cancelling all trash collection on campus in order to contain and preserve any possible evidence that the killer had discarded, classes were beginning for the second period of the day at Norris Hall. At 9:15 both full ERTs had arrived at their assigned locations and were in position in full force. Elements of both the VTPD and BPD ERTs were divided between WAJ and the BPD headquarters, ready to respond and affect a possible arrest of Thornhill when found, and to execute corresponding search warrants that were being hastily issued by a local judge. Per Anthony Wilson, some were dispatched to Thornhill's home. As well, the ERTs were ready to answer any calls of more violence. In short, they didn't know what to expect and, therefore, were poised and ready, or "locked and loaded" in military parlance.

The overall BPD manpower resources requested by VTPD Chief Flinchum to augment his agency's investigation and search for a suspect, and the locations to which they were assigned and responded to the Norris Hall call out, were: Chief Crannis and Captain Goodman as part of the WAJ Command Group; Lts. John Glass and Bruce Bradbery, along with Detective Quinton Self and

243 Roy, p. 115.

Officers Scott Craig and Brian Roe at the Prices Fork Road stop of Thornhill; Sgt. Wilson as part of investigations at WAJ; Sgts. Steven Taylor and Gary Thomas, and Officer Mark Mitchell at Blacksburg PD for patrol staging; Officers Jeff Robinson, Brian Cross, Sedrick Hayes, Todd Rutledge, Nathan O'Dell, Shannon Combs and Ben Machingo all part of the ERT staged at Blacksburg; Officers Johnny Self, Greg Evans, Fred Carlson, Gary Green, Mike Czernicki, Erin Purdy, Chad Horne, Jeff CiChocki, Eric Harris, and Steve Workman on Ambler-Johnston Hall perimeter.

This represented more than half of the entire Blacksburg Police Department which, combined with all but one of the officers from VTPD, constituted a substantial force. It also represented exponentially greater numbers of law enforcement responding to a double homicide than would typically be seen in major metropolitan area police departments possessed of far greater resources.

Chapter Six
The Massacre of Norris Hall

"Greater love hath no man than this: That a man lay down his life for a friend."

Jesus Christ

Have to make sure no one sees me, sees what I'm doing. Just stop at each door, pull the chains out and lock them around the bars, then walk away like nobody's business. Inside the breezeway was easy, no one hardly ever uses that door. Straight down the hall then down the steps to the door by Burruss. Still no one around. Coupla' kids and construction guys saw me, but they can't tell what I'm doing. Class already started so no one is really coming and going. Maybe it's a good thing it took a while at the post office. Now down the first floor hall to chain the Drillfield doors. Up the Drillfield steps and I'm here on the second floor, looking at my killing field. Gonna change here in the first room by the steps. I know there's no class here this morning. Need to make sure they're all in their places, waiting for me, waiting to die. I look in all the rooms. Perfect. Leave my backpack at the end so that I can get to it and my knives and hammer and other ammo once I have hit all the rooms in the hall. I'll walk all the way back down and start from this end and work my way back to my backpack. I figure by the time I get done with 211 I'll be out of ammo and will need to grab the rest. Can't help but look back in the rooms as I walk down the hall. My prey. Shit! The teacher in 206 is looking at me funny. I think he suspects something. Need to start here then, kill them all here first.

Journalists and pundits alike speculated that Cho had applied to the VT Engineering Department and failed to get in, and that was the reason for his attack against Norris Hall, an Engineering building. This was false. He did, however, have class in Norris Hall that semester. It was a second-semester Sociology class called *Deviant Behavior.*[244] On March 29, 2007 Cho had missed his class in Norris Hall. He never made another one. From February 2007 to April 2007 he was seen in the vicinity of Norris Hall several times. This would not be unexpected, except he was reportedly pacing off distances of the building. Police believe he was conducting reconnaissance and intelligence-gathering on his target. In the military this would have been the precursor to a mortar barrage. For the students, teachers and police in the building it would be little different. Cho was assessing shooting distances from different points, sectors and vectors for attack. He may have also been estimating the ranges and angles of shots police would have to take in the hallways. He did not have class in Norris Hall on April 16, 2007, nor did his class meet on Mondays at all. It met on Tuesdays and Thursdays in room 200, a room which would be empty on the day of the shootings.

Cho's target was one of the best choices of the 131 major buildings on the Virginia Tech campus. Norris Hall is a three story "L" shaped structure with a long base that runs west to east. The building contains offices and laboratories on the ground floor, with classrooms on the north-south arm of the "L" on the second, and offices on the west-east wing of that floor. There were both faculty offices and classrooms on the third. The book *April 16th: Virginia Tech Remembers*, reported:

> He has selected an old building on campus because it has just a few escape routes. He can chain the doors on the exits to the building and quickly trap the people inside. He knows the second floor of the building is filled with students in their classes. He also knows that

244 Lueders, 15.

> the classroom doors have no locks. The occupants will be defenseless. The classroom windows are too small in many cases to exit through.[245]

In addition, the building was one of the few remaining ones on campus where the doors had the old style emergency swing-bars that made it easy to chain, rather than the newer solid push-bars found in most buildings today. The GPR noted that on Saturday, April 14, 2007 a faculty member in Norris Hall remembered seeing an Asian male wearing a hooded garment. The Report said that this may have been Cho practicing.[246] It was certain that he wasn't there for class.

Also, according to the Governor's Report Cho was observed outside and then inside Norris Hall between 9:15 and 9:30 a.m. Construction workers saw him outside the breezeway door at the east entrance. He chained the external doors shut from the inside in the alcoves of the stair wells at the three external public entrances to the building, one at the northwest elbow of the building ("western" or "central" entrance and stairwell), one in the breezeway at the east end, and one at the far southern end of the north-south wing facing the Drillfield. Though he was later reported as having been seen reaching into his backpack inside the western entrance,[247] no one observed him chaining any of the doors. This was because the doors were not set into the walls at the end of the hallways as might be expected. When you looked down the halls you only saw a bare wall at the end. To the side were doors that led into alcoves at the far side of which were the external doors. By chaining the doors after classes began Cho ensured that there would be little traffic coming and going from the building, and anyone in the halls could not have seen the chains. Before Cho began chaining the doors a student left Norris Hall to get a snack at Burruss Hall. By the time she returned the breezeway doors were chained. So were the other doors. She found an open

245 Lanzenby, pp. 3-4.
246 GPR, p. 24.
247 This is the same entrance the entry teams would ultimately attempt to breach with shotgun rounds before moving to a set of doors to the immediate left or north.

window and crawled through, then quickly went into hiding on the first floor when she heard gunshots.

As there were no witnesses to Cho chaining any of the three public entrances, the sequence of him implementing his fortifications is somewhat speculative. However, it was generally concluded by the responding officers and commanders that Cho chained the eastern breezeway entrance first. This was on the second floor. He then would have walked westward down the second floor hallway, descended the stairs at the western elbow of the building, then chained the west entrance on the first floor. From there he would have walked southward down the first floor, finally chaining the southern or Drillfield entrance. The chains were effective in both delaying law enforcement and keeping his prey from escaping.

The GPR reported that Cho had also put a note on the eastern breezeway entrance doors, stating that if the chains were removed that a bomb would go off.[248] A building maintenance worker found the note and took it to the Engineering School's dean's office on the third floor.[249] Supposedly, they were about to call the police when the shooting started.[250] Other sources reported that the building's maintenance manager insisted that no such call be made, deciding that the note was not genuine and so there was no need to bother the police. The GPR reported that had this note been reported immediately, as university instructions to faculty stated, it might have saved the police a crucial few minutes.[251] Students and faculty who did see the chains assumed that it was done by construction workers. When the police arrived, frantic to gain entry to save the lives of those inside, they would make the same assumption - at first.

Once on the second floor from the west or central staircase, one has to make a right turn to enter the hallway containing the classrooms in the north-south corridor that Cho ultimately assaulted. The first room on the left (east side of the wing facing into the courtyard

248 GPR, p. 89.
249 Roy, p. 109
250 GPR, p. 89, reports that the person who found the note was a faculty member.
251 GPR, pp. 89-90.

surrounded by the long northern leg of the "L" that formed Norris Hall, along with Holden Hall and its north-south wing on the eastern edge of the yard) was room 210, followed by rooms 206, 204 and 200. There was no room 208. Room 200 was the last room on the left at the end of the hall before reaching the stairs leading down to the south end of the building. It is believed that Cho chained the Drillfield entrance last, ascended the stairs and entered the empty room 200 to prepare for his assault. Students later reported seeing him inside there. Dr. Lucinda Roy reported that he pinned bomb threat notes to each of the doors, though police would confirm merely one such posted threat. It was then approximately 9:30 a.m. and well into the second period of the day.[252]

If Cho had been conducting surveillance on the building on Monday and Wednesday mornings prior to the attack, it can be inferred that he knew room 200 would be empty. As with most universities, classes typically met either Mondays and Wednesdays, or Tuesdays and Thursdays. He was seen rummaging through his backpack inside room 200. It is certain that he was withdrawing and preparing his weapons, and getting dressed for battle. Cho then walked down the second floor hallway (northward) and looked into each room, even to the point of opening closed doors to look inside the occupied classrooms.[253] He left his backpack on the floor next to the water fountain just outside the men's room and across from the second floor landing of the western staircase. Many students recalled Cho poking his head into classrooms. In the book *April 16th: Virginia Tech Remembers*, a student reported the teacher saying it was weird that someone was lost that late in the semester.[254] Having confirmed the presence of his target-victim population, he was then prepared to attack the students and teachers sitting studiously in classes in *Intermediate French* taught by Jessica Couture-Nowak, *Elementary German* under the guidance of Christopher Bishop, *Advanced Hydrology* with G. Vasudevan Loganathan, *Scientific Computing* being covered that

252 Roy, p. 1.
253 However, student Heidi Miller in room 211 did not remember seeing him look into that room at all.
254 Lazenby, p. 13.

day by grad assistant Haiyan Cheng, and *Solid Mechanics* being taught by 76 year-old Holocaust survivor, Professor Liviu Librescu.[255]

At 9:24 a.m., just as Cho was entering Norris Hall, a Montgomery County Sheriff's Office (MCSO) deputy sergeant saw Karl Thornhill driving his pickup truck off campus and inside Blacksburg city limits on Prices Fork Road. Alerted by the BOLO, the sergeant threw his patrol car's light bar on and forced the pickup truck to the side of the road, right by the Blacksburg Middle School where the two SWAT teams had recently run an active shooter FTX. He was on the radio instantly, alerting all that he believed he had found the boyfriend of the then-dead girl. The sergeant didn't wait. He approached the vehicle and asked for license, registration and proof of insurance, identifying the driver as Thornhill. Detectives and ERT members were immediately dispatched to assist with the roadside stop and begin questioning Thornhill. When Daniel Hardy - "Boomer" to his friends - arrived, Detective Self from BPD and VTPD Detective Stephanie Henley were just beginning to question him. Hardy and Henley then continued with the questioning.

When you first see Daniel Hardy his stature immediately gives the lie to his nickname of "Boomer." He could, perhaps, most accurately be described as almost petite. Though small in size he has lived his entire life with a burning desire to serve, and to serve in dangerous conditions protecting the innocent. He started as a law enforcement Explorer as a boy, ultimately beginning matriculation at Tech where he would graduate in December 2003 with a degree in Political Science. As a freshman he first worked as a night monitor in the dorms, then in 2002 began as a campus security guard within the VT Police Department.[256] During his work with the PD he came to be known to the cops as "the little guy who always shows up to everything." His zest and energy for the job had not waned; not even in the aftermath of April 16. When he graduated college he wanted to enlist

255 Roy, p. 2.

256 Since April 16 all security guards are DCJS trained and certified in addition to receiving an additional 40 hours of training from the police.

in the Marines and become a fighter pilot. However, poor eyesight forced him into the arms of the Virginia Tech Police Department. He wanted to join the ERT immediately and sheepishly confessed that he may have gotten on quickly in large part due to the fact that no one else could fit into the extra small equipment that they had. Today he is also a sniper and has responded to every single operation VTPD ERT has done with only the exception of a couple of drug raids.

—

"A great place to raise a family" was how Ben Machingo described the town of Blacksburg where he had been a police officer for five years on April 16, 2007. That day hasn't changed his opinion of the town, but he now admits it certainly seems to have put a negative connotation on anything associated with the term "Virginia Tech." Ben's wife had already left for work that morning. He had been off the night before and was still at home when the call came in early in the morning for all officers to report because of the first two homicides. Machingo arrived at the Blacksburg Police headquarters just about the same time that Karl Thornhill was stopped on Prices Fork Road, not far from the Virginia Tech campus.

—

With the consensus of the university Policy Group, just two minutes after Thornhill was stopped, at 9:26 a.m. a recorded message was placed on the VT Emergency Weather Line, a telephone message was sent to campus phones, and an email sent to the entire VT community attempting to notify everyone of the first two shootings. A news release was drafted and posted on the VT website.[257] The email stated:

> A shooting incident occurred at West Ambler-Johnston earlier this morning. Police are on the scene and are investigating.

257 The *Collegiate Times* says this email was at 9:28 and *Lifting Our Eyes* states 9:26.

> The university community is urged to be cautious and are asked to contact Virginia Tech Police if you observe anything suspicious or with information on the case. Contact Virginia Tech Police at 231-6411.
>
> Stay attuned to the www.vt.edu. We will post as soon as we have more information.

9:25 a.m. to 9:50 a.m.

A Virginia State Police special agent, who would ultimately inherit the investigation into the Norris Hall rampages, also quickly arrived at the traffic stop of Thornhill on Prices Fork road by the elementary school and assisted with the questioning. Thornhill was put in the backseat of a police car, and Daniel Hardy got in the front passenger seat. At first they thought they probably had their man. But Thornhill wasn't acting quite like someone who had just murdered two people, including a young woman he loved. It was just a feeling they had, but he was answering questions directly. Someone who had just put bullets in the heads of two human beings at point blank range should have been behaving differently. At least a little. He said that he knew that Emily was dead. But that was only because someone had called and told him that the police were looking to talk to him. It had never occurred to him that they thought he might have done it. Innocent people never do. The police asked if he would allow them to administer a field gunshot residue test (GSR) right there. He said, "Sure." They were baffled. If it wasn't Thornhill, then who was it?

The GSR was administered, though results would not be known for some time as it had to be sent to a lab for processing. Though relatively calm, Thornhill was also agitated as he didn't understand why the police were focusing on him. He was being asked when he dropped Emily off, where he had been since then, and similar accusatory questions. He insisted that he had gone directly to class at Radford University and was on his way back because someone had called or texted him that something had happened to her. If the cops were wasting time talking to him, then the real murderer of his beloved Emily was still loose. The initial interview and his willingness to submit to the GSR at the traffic stop left investigators beginning to doubt Thornhill's involvement in the shootings at West AJ.

Daniel Hardy recalled that the boyfriend was aware that Emily had been shot but insisted that he was not involved. He and Det. Henley were conducting the interview of Thornhill at the traffic stop. The units were "clearing" from the stop to return to the BPD with Thornhill and continue to assist in the investigation when the police radio blurted: "Active shooter on second floor of Norris Hall." The boyfriend, seated in the back of the patrol car erupted: "That's the guy that killed my girlfriend!" Neither Hardy nor Detective Henley realized just how right Thornhill would prove to be, or that Emily and Ryan were not going to be the only victims that day. Having been with the ERT since 2005, Hardy headed straight for Norris Hall. He felt in his bones, in the deepest recesses of his cop instinct, that they were going to need every skilled shooter they had.

At the same time VTPD Sgt. Tom Gallemore was at the BPD headquarters staging area. He had been the last Tech ERT member to arrive that morning. When all officers were called back on duty he had been more than an hour away and had not been to WAJ that morning at all. When the radio call of an active shooter at Norris Hall blasted across everyone's radio he was standing at the back of the tactical van outside the building. It took him but seconds to jump in and be ready to roll.

In her book, Prof. Roy was highly critical of the way the police handled locating and questioning Karl Thornhill; however, she could not have been more rash in her judgment. It was this very attitude on the part of the public and media that did such an injustice to these two departments. A masterful poet, Dr. Roy ventured beyond her expertise in concluding that, "A seasoned officer would have suspected as soon as he questioned the young man that something wasn't right – that perhaps they had been tracking the wrong person all along."[258] However, it often takes hours, and sometimes days, to induce a perpetrator to tell the truth about a crime. And if that person demands an attorney it may never happen at all. The most experienced investigators, including the iconic professionals in the FBI's vaunted Criminal Profiling Unit, could not possibly have made the determination Dr. Roy demanded from a patrol officer in a scant few minutes. Nor is her belief that the GSR established that Mr. Thornhill was not the shooter accurate.[259] These tests are like finger-prints or DNA samples: they must go to a lab and undergo thorough analysis before any conclusions can be drawn.

Blame cannot be laid at the feet of these officers attempting to develop critical information on the first two shootings as quickly as possible. This is particularly true in light of the unprecedented deployment of law enforcement resources in a case of that type. Nor can they be criticized for not being "seasoned" enough to have clairvoyantly devised that Thornhill was innocent and that the GSR test would yield proof that he hadn't fired a weapon within a four hour period[260] – or at least had not done so without wearing gloves. This would be akin to insisting that any "seasoned" college professor would have known upon meeting Cho that he was about to commit the worst shooting mass-murder on an American campus in history and thus prevented it. In both cases such expectations would be grossly unrealistic.

–

At the hospital while writing his report on the WAJ killings, Jersey Dominiczak had continued to monitor both the medical radio channels as well as the police transmissions. As the tactical medic for the Virginia Tech Police Department's ERT he knew the team had already been activated. He had graduated from the CONTOMS course[261] for tactical medics put on by the U.S. Park Service at Bethesda Hospital,

258 Roy, p. 108.
259 Ibid.
260 GSR can only determine whether a person has shot a gun within four hours and can be ineffective if he has changed his clothes or washed his hands.
261 Counter Narcotics and Terrorism Operational Medical Support

and did all the tactical training and deployments with the team. He already expected that this would be a long day for himself and his team. After being part of the hunt for the cop-killer Morva the previous August on the Virginia Tech campus, together with this morning's events, Jason had seen more than his share of trauma as a medic and certainly more than most local law enforcement tactical medics ever did. His depth of experience was soon going to surpass what most law enforcement medics ever see, and even what many of their military counterparts deal with.

Jersey had continued writing his report and monitoring the police radio when the call of, "Activer shooter at Norris Hall" burst from the speakers. He was taken back but reacted like a well-trained veteran. He ran up and told the ER nurses and the single doctor, "We have another shooting. Get ready!" He sped off toward the campus. "I was really thinking mass casualties at that point," he recalled. With that thought in mind he threw all of his gear into his vehicle and headed straight to the building. Though his other medical responders on the VT Rescue Service were capable, he knew that he was the only one that could go into the building with the ERT's "shooters." While en route he was seeing to it that all the rescue squad personnel were prepared for a mass casualty response. "We started alerting other hospitals at that time, even though we had no information that anyone had even been shot." "I just had a feeling," he said.

—

Sometime between 9:40 and 9:41 a.m. Cho began entering rooms and shooting professors and students on the second floor. The second floor hallway was merely seven feet nine inches wide, and 42 yards long from the furthest point to the end. From room 211 to the far end at the front of the building at the furthest southern point was more than 30 yards long.

The classrooms themselves were quite small, with a large number of desks inside which created narrow aisles, leaving little in the way for maneuvering or avenues of escape for those seated.

In some cases there were no real aisles at all, with the desks being jammed so closely together that students would have to enter from behind the chairs. After everyone was seated it would have been impossible for the innermost students to get up without all others getting up and moving, not unlike very tightly packed church pews or being in the window seat of a crowded plane.

On the third floor some of the rooms were even smaller, no more than 10 feet by 12 feet. The official measurements of the rooms on the second floor were:

Room 204	28' x 25'
Room 205	24' x 25'
Room 206	22' x 25'
Room 207	24' x 25'
Room 211	22' x 25'

Thus each room was small and densely packed with desks, and the students had little to no room to move. The tightness was evidenced for instance by room 211 in which were situated 39 desks, in addition to AV equipment, a podium and a teacher's desk with a large amount of space at the front. All doors opened inward on both the second and third floors. On the third floor some classroom doors had small viewing windows made of safety glass with wire mesh. None of the second floor classroom doors had windows. In those rooms where students tried to hold the door shut they could only imagine the rage that was on the other side.

The GPR speculated that the shooting may have begun as early as 9:40 a.m., "based on the time it took for the students and faculty in the room next door to recognize that the sounds being heard were gunshots, and then make the 911 call."[262] However, the attack may have started as much as a minute later. The first room Cho entered was 206 on the east side of the building where a graduate Engineering class in *Advanced Hydrology* was being held.

262 GPR, p. 27, footnote 1.

Cho opened the door, took a fixed position just inside the door, and began shooting from left to right. Students and the professor all scrambled to the floor, pulling desks and chairs over them with their legs. It was a small class and almost everyone was sitting toward the front. Cho couldn't miss. He shot most of one magazine and reloaded. He did not walk up and down the aisles at this point. His shooting was reported as slow and methodical. Though no evidence would ever be evinced of any formal training in firearms or tactics, he would demonstrate some impressive tactical skills. He continued firing into the students at close range.

With students diving to the floor, Cho walked across the room to Prof. Loganathan and killed him with a direct shot to the head. He shot at, but missed, one male student, but fatally shot two others. He shot his second magazine, then reloaded and shot a third, simply dumping magazines on the floor. Cho would return to this room twice more. Before all of his trips to room 206 would be over he would kill nine students and wound three others of the total 12 students in the room, in addition to killing the professor. As he left room 206 the first time a student initiated a 911 call.

That didn't take long at all. And I hardly used any bullets. Lots left. Coming out I see the door to 207 straight across the hall is open. People are looking at me through that door. They see death, they see me for what I am. Maybe they heard the shots, can see the gun smoke. Need to kill them next. I see those two bastards running for the stairs. They think they can get away from me. I think I hit at least one of them.

Next door in room 204, Professor Liviu Librescu immediately recognized the sounds for what they were, and told the students to begin pulling out the windows and screens at the back of the room and start jumping. As a result of his years barely surviving in the hell that was a Nazi concentration camp he would be the only one who knew what gunfire really sounded like. He told his students that he would attempt to hold the door shut. Attempt to buy them some time.

Years of atrocities left him with no illusions about the deadly nature of those sounds. Yang Kim and Jamal Carver, students in the class, decided to make a break for it. They raced out of the room, turning left toward the nearby southern Drillfield stairs. Only room 200 was between them and the safety of the staircase. As Cho exited room 206 he saw Kim and Carver leaving room 204 and fired at least one round at them, wounding Carver in the back of his arm. The two students raced down the stairs and attempted to escape through the southern entrance, but found the doors chained. Trapped inside, they hid in a lab on the west side of the first floor and fashioned a sign from paper and a marker that read "WOUNDED," which they placed in the window in the hopes that arriving police would rescue them.

Hearing the sounds of gunfire, teacher Haiyan Cheng and student Theresa Walsh looked out of room 205, across and down the hall to the left (north) toward room 206. Cho had just left that room and shot Jamal Carver. He saw the faces of the two women peering at him and fired, hitting neither. They leapt back into their room where the young Chinese grad student, who on short notice had been asked to teach the *Scientific Computing* class for the professor that morning, told the students that they needed to start barricading the door.

In 207 they all fall to the floor; cowering chickenshits. This is going too fast. I thought they might fight, that I'd have to use more ammo but they just lay there and let me shoot them. I've hardly missed at all. How can I with them making it this easy? What room next? Oh no, there's two professors at the door! Shot that one right in the head. The other's running. Just need to pop a few rounds at him. I think I hit him but he didn't go down. The cops'll be coming for sure now. Gotta work faster. Saw the teacher looking at me out of 211. She dies next. Not that it matters, they're all gonna get their turn.

After shooting at Carver, Kim, Cheng and Walsh, Cho crossed the hall from 206 directly to room 207 on the west side where an *Elementary German* class was being conducted by teacher Christopher James

Bishop. The doors matched up across the hall from each other exactly, and Cho was there in a second. Upon entering room 207 he repeated his attack tactics from 206: he shot left to right across the front of the room. He reloaded and killed Prof. Bishop. He paced across the front of the room firing. Again, he did not move up and down the aisles. This rampage resulted in the deaths of six students and the teacher: Lauren McCain, Michael Pohle, Maxine Turner, Nicole White and Prof. Bishop. In all, six were wounded. Eighteen 9mm rounds and one expended magazine were later recovered from the room.

At approximately 9:42 a.m., the same time Cho was assaulting room 207, student Tiffany Otey was completing a test she was taking for Professor James Yardley in room 306 on the third floor. She turned her exam in and walked southward down the hall and began descending the stairs toward the ground floor exit fronting the Drillfield. When she reached the second floor landing she heard what sounded like gunshots. She opened the doors and saw and smelled the cordite haze that was hanging in the hallway from Cho's weapons. She raced back up the steps to her classroom and informed her professor. She told him that the second floor hallway was full of smoke. Prof. Yardley crossed the hall to Professor Kevin Granata's office, room 307, and told him what the frightened student had reported. At Prof. Granata's insistence, Yardley and his students locked themselves in Granata's office. Prof. Granata then proceeded northward up the hall and down the western staircase to investigate.

At the same time, Professor Wally Grant was in his office in room 222 on the second floor of the west-east wing of Norris Hall. He had been hearing what at first sounded to him like metal scraping on metal. Notwithstanding the constant construction noise he had been enduring all year he thought the sound odd, particularly as it was continuing. He left his office, walking west toward the western staircase at the elbow of the two wings of Norris Hall. As Prof. Grant approached the corner where he would turn south into the wing Cho was then assailing, he encountered Prof. Granata coming out of the staircase. The odd sounds were continuing, though they no longer sounded like metal scraping. The two academics moved together southward along the north-south wing to investigate. Cho had just about finished his first effort to murder everyone in room 207 and was then advancing on the door to re-enter the hall.

Just as the two professors walked up to the door of room 207 Cho yanked it open. His first reaction was to raise the 9mm handgun and shoot Prof. Granata in the head. They weren't more than a couple of feet apart. Kevin Granata hit the floor, though he was not dead. Prof. Grant fled northward up the hall, back in the direction they had come from. As he was running Cho began shooting at him, hitting him with a single round in the upper right portion of his back. The impact staggered him, but he did not go down. On the right hand side, just before turning the corner into the west-east wing, was a men's room, next to the water fountain where Cho had left his backpack. Grant took refuge inside. At the time another student was inside, though he had no idea what had been taking place just a short distance down the hall. Prof. Grant made a 911 call. It was only at this point that he realized he'd been shot. With Grant bleeding all over the floor, together they tried to find something with which to barricade the door, but nothing was available. They looked at the possibility of prying the window panes out and leaping, but they were too small, each narrow pane bound by metal. Bloody handprints on the glass and frames told of the desperation of their efforts at escape. They decided to simply attempt to hold the door shut in the event the murderer tried to enter.

After exiting room 207 and shooting Professors Granata and Grant, Cho made a left turn and went to the very next room. This was 211 and the northernmost classroom on the west side of the second floor wing. Madame Jocelyne Couture-Nowak had been teaching her French class. While Cho had been in rooms 206 and 207 she and her students had heard shots, but weren't entirely sure what they were. Student Heidi Miller, tall, redheaded and possessing a smile that could light up a building, recalled that the professor had even stopped teaching and said to the class, "That's not what I think it is, is it?" With that Professor Couture-Nowak peered out the door in time to see Cho shoot Prof. Granata. Cho saw her, along with janitor Gene Cole who had been sent upstairs to find his co-worker Pam after the bomb scare note had been found on the breezeway door and reports had been received of shots fired somewhere in the building. Mr. Cole had just reached the second floor landing and stepped out of the stairwell, at first seeing Cho reloading one of his guns. Cho fired rounds in the direction of both of them. The janitor fled back downstairs, later reporting that Cho fired at him.

I'm in 211. They actually thought those little desks would keep me out. Just inside, that one girl hadn't even gotten out of her chair. It's so easy. The teacher and that kid next. If he thought that because he's Asian I wouldn't kill him he was kidding himself. What the hell?! This guy is rushing me! In a damn cadet uniform! Who does he think he is, Rambo?! Can't miss from this distance though. I keep hitting him but he keeps coming. He's almost at me. I'm scared. What if he gets to me? How many bullets can he take?! He finally dropped. Had to shoot him enough times though. If any of those others had gotten up and jumped me they'd a had me for sure. Now they're all gonna die.

Professor Couture-Nowak leapt back into the classroom and immediately communicated to the class that they should get on the floor, and some should help her barricade the door with desks. She didn't tell them to do this, however. Heidi Miller said that when she jumped back into the room her face had gone ghostly white. Her look of terror was evident to all of the students, and the teacher was too frightened to even speak. All she could do was gesture to everyone what she wanted them to do. But Heidi said that they all understood immediately. The professor managed to communicate to student Colin Goddard to call 911. This was at 9:41 in the morning. Cho's entire attack was barely a minute old.

Colin Goddard's call was actually the first 911 call received by Virginia Tech police dispatch, but it initially went directly to the

Blacksburg operator. Due to the phone system configuration in the area all 911 calls made on cell phones from the university campus were routed to either BPD or the MCSO. The Blacksburg operator had difficulty understanding what was being said and the location of the shooting. When she realized that it was a call from campus she immediately re-routed it to VTPD dispatch. The call was logged by VTPD at 9:42 a.m. April Blankenship, the VTPD dispatch, asked but three quick questions before realizing the nature and magnitude of the attack she was being told about. A message was immediately sent to all county EMS and area police to respond.[263] At exactly 9:42, as the first 911 call was being processed, the Montgomery County Communications Center also paged out an "all call" alert advising every unit to respond to the scene at Norris Hall.[264]

At 9:42 a.m., this first telephone call had come into April's station on the administrative line. It was a male saying that someone was shooting on the second floor of Norris Hall. She didn't know that his 911 cell phone call had been rerouted to VT dispatch by Blacksburg. April could hear shots over the phone line. At that moment the phones went crazy, and by April's own admission she doesn't remember a lot of what happened afterward. From there calls flooded into the dispatch center about the shooting. April broadcast the message, "Active shooter on the second floor of Norris Hall." As other calls would start coming in she would broadcast "Shots fired at Norris Hall."

Tech police Lieutenant Deborah Morgan could not believe her ears. "What was going on at Virginia Tech?" she wondered. "Suddenly everything became chaotic and crazy," according to Morgan. Phone calls were coming in non-stop and rescue units were being dispatched. Morgan quickly took over the phone call to allow April to handle the radio transmissions.

The culture and area of southwest Virginia, particularly the Blacksburg area, was a far cry from the suburban Philadelphia and northern New Jersey areas where Deborah Morgan had spent

263 The GPR only references EMS, p. 27.
264 GPR, 102.

the early years of her life. A Rutgers University graduate, she moved to Virginia and took a job in security at the Radford Army Arsenal. After a cutback at the arsenal, Debbie took a job with the security department at Roanoke University and attended the police academy where she met an instructor by the name of Wendell Flinchum. Fifteen years later she would be working for that same man who had recruited her early on, and thought that the job she took in 1992 was a "good fit." During her time at Rutgers she had worked on the Rescue Squad and became familiar with – and learned to love - the culture of campus police. "It's a great atmosphere to work in," she told Joe Bail. Morgan felt that all school police had the same basic type of problems to deal with; some on a bigger scale than others. "Most kids just make stupid decisions," was how she described her philosophy on the population that university cops served, demonstrating that she was as much understanding protector as law enforcer. On April 16, 2007 one of those young people, Seung-Hui Cho, made not a stupid decision but a deadly one, and Lt. Deborah Morgan would have a pivotal role in its wake.

–

In room 211 student Henry Lee was seated at one of the desks in the front row of the classroom. Charles "Clay" Violand suddenly couldn't even think of what his teacher's name was, but said that he told her to start pushing desks against the door.[265] Lee and Mme. Couture-Nowak began shoving desks against the door. But the student desks were light and they had little time. Having seen the panicked teacher staring at him as he shot Prof. Grant, Cho had headed straight toward her and her classroom, barely 25 feet away. She and Henry Lee had only managed to push a couple of the small desks in front of the door when Cho forced his way into the room. It had all happened so fast that student Rachel Hill was still sitting at the second desk of the first column just inside the door. She hadn't had time to react and was the first person Cho saw as the door was shoved open. She was shot first,

265 Amanda Ripley, *The Unthinkable: Who Survives When Disaster Strikes – And Why* (New York: Crown Publishers, 2008), p. 163.

struck in the head. She collapsed onto the desktop, her head turned to the left. Shannon Combs later said that it looked as though she were just asleep. Anthony Wilson said the same thing. Their minds had blocked out her sightless eyes staring into eternity.

Lee and Couture-Nowak were still just inside the door. Each was shot and killed instantly. Cho then began sweeping the front of the room with gunshots from left to right. Goddard was shot in the leg at the back of the room and dropped his cell phone. Pretty, blonde Emily Haas picked it up and dove into a pile of students in the middle of the back of the room that included Heidi Miller. Violand had quickly gone to the back of the room and simply laid down. He had first headed toward the windows thinking he could jump out, but Cho was inside too fast. "…as soon as I saw the gun come in, I just froze," he said. He later said that he had just laid down on his side under a desk, thinking that it was important not to move. He recognized that the killer would focus on those students in motion.[266]

Seated at the back of the room in the second to the last chair of the second column of desks, was 23-year old Air Force Cadet Matthew LaPorte. LaPorte was part of the VT military cadet program, with his scholarship being administered by the ROTC. He was in uniform and had recently completed the Air Force's special operations introduction course. Though handsome, bright, personable and popular, he was still a commando in the making. One who wanted to ultimately spend his career in military intelligence. As Cho continued firing from the front of the room, the students thought LaPorte had jumped into the pile in the back of the room with them. Instead, Cadet LaPorte did what he had been trained to do, what his character and personal desire to serve the nation in uniform compelled him to do: fight to protect those who could not fight for themselves.

Under heavy fire from Cho, using both semi-automatic handguns from a range of no more than fifteen feet, LaPorte fought his way to the left across the back of the classroom, pushing his way through overturned desks and leaping over other students in the far

266 Ibid.

corner. He turned right, racing along the windows up the side of the classroom. When he reached the front, he turned to the right and raced straight at Cho, running along the blackboard. Cho was pumping rounds into him as LaPorte charged. Arriving police would report that he received what they believed to be eight bullet wounds, all to the front, including a finger and thumb shot, before Cho finally dropped him scant feet short of reaching the enemy. There Cadet LaPorte lay facing the door, his arms reaching out before him, straining to get to Cho in the attack position he had assumed just before getting to the killer. His face was buried in the carpet of the floor, his military high and tight haircut all that could be seen, the telltale military stripe of his uniform trousers stretched out behind him. Former Air Force Vietnam jet fighter pilot Ed Beakley, in attempting to describe Cadet LaPorte's heroic actions that day for an article written for the fighter pilot association publication, *MiG Sweep*, quoted German Ace Adolf Garland: 'the spirit of attack born of a brave heart.'"

With his only threat eliminated, Cho proceeded to walk down the narrow aisles separating closely packed desks, shooting students on both sides. Most of the students attempted to hide under their desks.[267] Violand said that Cho's rate of fire was "rhythmic" as though he were taking his time between students. He could hear the girls moaning and crying.[268] This time Cho was moving up and down aisles shooting students. He even shot under some of the desks trying to get at those that had pulled the furniture over on top of them.

Throughout Cho's first rampage into room 211, his attacks on other rooms, and his second assault on this very same room, with students being shot over and over again, Emily Haas would never relinquish the cell phone. Nor would she stop feeding critical information to the police. Lt. Deborah Morgan was on the other end of the line with her, passing what Emily was telling her to April Blankenship who was in turn relaying it to arriving police over the radio. To the

267 Crime scene photos indicate that several of the shots appear to be direct head shots.
268 Ripley, p. 164.

lieutenant, the sounds of gunfire were so loud it seemed that someone was shooting right into the phone on the other end.[269]

VT: Where are you?

Haas: Two-Eleven Norris Hall.

VT: Are you still there?

Silence

Pop. Pop.

Haas: I can't talk.

VT: Keep yourself safe. We're sending people.

Haas: (whispering) Please hurry.

VT: Try to stay calm. Ease your breathing.

–

Upon Cho leaving room 211 the surviving students played dead, hoping that he would not return. They only wanted the police to come make them safe. Violand said that he just knew Cho would come back.[270]

After Cho had departed the room Morgan, hearing the gunshots become fainter over the phone, continued to talk to Emily:

VT: Stay under the desk. Keep talking to me. We're hurrying. They'll be there in a minute.

Haas: Thank you.

Silence

VT: Are you there?

269 Sari Horwitz, "Revisiting Va. Tech: 8 minutes after 911 call, a rescue from madness," *The Washington Post*, June 22, 2007, www.washingtonpost.com.
270 Ripley, p. 164.

Haas: Yeah, I'm here. We need an ambulance.

Moaning coming over the phone.

VT: Is the door locked?

Haas: It doesn't lock.

Diagram of Second Floor Norris Hall, Depicting Cho's Initial Movements Once Inside.

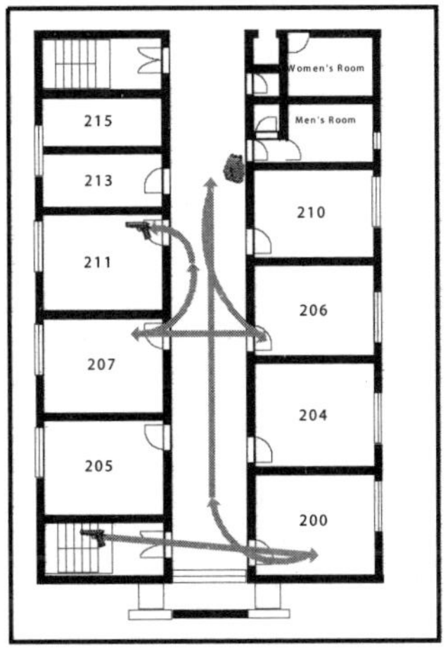

Cho exits southern/Drillfield side stairs on second floor and enters Rm. 200 where he prepares for his attack. He walks northward up the hall, looking into the classrooms. He leaves his backpack outside men's room (top of diagram), then proceeds to Rm. 206 where his attacks begin. After leaving 206 he crosses the hall to Rm. 207, and then turns left (north) and attacks Rm. 211 for the first time.

Geoffrey Allen had actually first met Prof. Lucinda Roy in 2002. At the time she was concerned that a former student, who had been attacking her in blogs and websites, might return to disrupt graduation. At 7:25 in the morning of April 16 Allen's was one of several cars patrolling the campus. He saw a VT rescue vehicle slide sideways through an intersection ahead of him. He got on the radio and was informed about the initial loft bed report and all of the blood in the room. He raced to WAJ where he learned that two students had been shot. By 9:40 a.m. he had climbed into his SWAT gear. The only pieces of kit he was not yet equipped with were his high velocity-round armored vest and helmet, although he did have his assault rifle with him. He had been providing perimeter security around the dormitory, but at 8:15 a.m. had left to join those staging at BPD headquarters. When the call came out of shooting at Norris Hall he was standing at the back of the tactical van with his teammate Tom Gallemore.

Allen came from a family in which everyone either graduated from, or worked at, Virginia Tech. Allen was tough. He had hiked the entire Appalachian Trail from Florida to Maine in 1993, and then immediately returned home and enlisted in the Navy. A former juvenile boot camp drill instructor, he joined the VTPD in October 1999 and worked as a crime prevention specialist. He joined the ERT along with Gallemore at his first opportunity. At the time of the attack he had been married for twelve years.

When that radio call came at 9:42 a.m. both Allen and Gallemore were checking, double-checking and even triple-checking their equipment. They didn't know what was happening that morning, but after the shootings at WAJ they recognized that they just might be called into a gunfight. Like their military brothers before an operation, they couldn't ensure their weapons' functionality enough. Their teammate Larry Wooddell was inside the building. They were rolling the minute the radio call blasted over their commo sets. They traveled the mile and a quarter to Norris Hall in three minutes, arriving at 9:44 with six or seven other officers, all of whom had leapt into vehicles from different points and gone tearing toward the building sitting atop a hill. Gallemore, Wooddell and Allen came up the Old Turner Street side to the north of the building and stopped their car on the back side of Holden Hall, the building that was connected to Norris to the east by the breezeway. This put them more than 100 yards away from the closest door into Norris. Upon arriving Gallemore leapt from the truck and donned body armor. The attack "was active," which meant that shooting was occurring at that moment and so they did not take the time to grab other gear, including entry or breaching tools, or even shields for their own protection. They only knew that they had to get to the threat as fast as possible. They believed that the best protection for themselves and the victims inside was bullets down range at the bad guys.

—

Blacksburg's Chief Crannis, Captain Goodman and Sgt. Anthony Wilson raced out of West AJ. Crannis and Goodman got into Chief Flinchum's car with him at the wheel. Blacksburg Officers Greg Evans, Fred Carlson, Gary Green, Mike Czernicki, Erin Purdy, Chad Horne, Jeff CiChocki, Eric Harris and Steve Workman had been on perimeter at the dormitory. Lieutenants John Glass and Bruce Bradbery, along with Det. Johnny Self, Sgt. Steve Taylor and Officers Scott Craig and Brian Roe came racing from the traffic stop of Karl Thornhill out on Prices Fork Road. Those Blacksburg cops who had staged at the police headquarters there, and who jumped into the closest vehicles to speed to Norris Hall, were Sgt. Gary Thomas, and Officers Jeff Robinson, Brian Cross, Sedrick Hayes, Todd Rutledge, Nathan O'Dell, Shannon Combs, Mark Mitchell and Ben Machingo.

Norris Hall was an obscure building and not readily identifiable to many responding officers. It appeared on the map to be incorporated into the Drillfield series of buildings, but technically the main entrance was also the most obscure, located inside the breezeway from the Old Turner Street side, on the opposite side from the Drillfield.[271] Officers from VTPD and BPD responded from WAJ and BPD headquarters. Multiple routes were taken to reach Norris Hall with officers arriving on different sides of the building. Most BPD officers interviewed advised that they relied on following Virginia Tech units to arrive in the proximity of Norris Hall as their familiarity

271 Though the front of the building naturally appears to be the end of the north-south wing ending at the doors facing Drillfield Driver, it is actually considered to be on the other, northern, end fronting Old Turner Street leading into the breezeway

with the campus buildings was not great. Some ended up following VTPD units into outlying parking lots and had to navigate their way to the building following the sounds of gunshots.

Sgt. Wilson and Officer Dean Lucas departed from WAJ and with Lucas driving traveled southwest on Washington Street, then north on West Campus Drive, finally driving the wrong way on Drillfield Drive which was a one way road; reducing the distance they traversed to seven-tenths of a mile. The most direct route was 800 yards from the front doors of West Ambler-Johnston to Drillfield Drive in front of the southern exit of Norris Hall, but that would have required police cars to drive down outside stairs and across the entire Drillfield in the snow.

The first units arriving on the Drillfield side of Norris Hall included Wilson and VTPD's Dean Lucas, John Glass, Brian Roe and Scott Craig. Subsequent units arrived at the Cowgill Hall service drive well behind Norris Hall to the northwest, including VT's Sgt. Tom Gallemore, Greg Evans, Curtis Cook, Darrell Sheppard, and Self. The bulk of additional units, including the Tech ERT, arrived at the main entrance from Old Turner Street with a few utilizing sidewalks to the Drillfield side and a few others arriving from the Davidson/Hahn Hall area, several blocks to the southwest, from which they moved in on foot. The first officers on scene were confronted with sounds of gunfire echoing throughout the area. The source appeared to be the second floor of Norris Hall and all indications were that the shooting was confined to the inside of the building, which eliminated concerns of a sniper, though some officers thought they might be under fire due to the sounds of the gunshots and breaking glass.

Tech's Larry Wooddell had been inside the BPD building when the call came over the radio. He had his radio on scan so that he could monitor both the tactical and regular patrol channels. He had leapt into the VTPD tactical van with Allen and Gallemore as it sped away. En route he began shrugging into his tactical equipment, gearing up for battle. As soon as his armored vest was on he pulled his handgun as he knew he was rolling into a truly "active" shooting situation. He checked to make sure it was "hot." Like most cops, for years he had lived with recurring nightmares of being in a shootout with an unloaded gun.

As all of the responding officers were descending on Norris Hall radio calls were saying that the shooters had moved over to Holden Hall, causing them to stop short of Norris. Then April corrected the false 911 reports that they had been receiving, and confirmed that the shots were still coming from Norris and not Holden Hall, forcing cops to traverse the rest of the way on foot, in some cases a considerable distance. Running down Turner Street from the east, they immediately moved to the entrance inside the breezeway. One of the officers tried to pull the door open but it was chained. He said that the door was "locked," not realizing this was the work of Cho fortifying the doors from the inside. They then stepped out of the breezeway back onto the Old Turner Street side of the building to the north. Another cop, far down the building at the northwest corner, yelled that they were making entry there. With that their entire hastily assembled team raced westward along the north side of the building to the western doors.

As they were running along the north side of the building a man popped up out of a manhole in the street. There were two workers down there. "Get the fuck out of here!", Geoff Allen yelled. At this time student Jamal Albarghouti was on the circular plaza approximately twenty yards to the northwest of the outside corner of the building and the western doors. He was standing in the very position behind which Curtis Cook was then racing toward, up 160 yards of hill and stairs. Albarghouti was taking video with his cell phone that would shortly be shown unendingly on CNN. He thought Allen was yelling at him and disappeared, though he would later report that he only left after an officer came from behind him and told him to go. Cook later confirmed that by the time he reached that plaza from the rear there was no student there, much less one taking video, and he never told anyone to move.

Upon arriving, Wilson and Lucas had received a radio call that the shooters had moved from Norris Hall over to Holden Hall to the east. Rather than sprint up the stairs and icy grass slopes from Drillfield Drive, Lucas jumped the curb in his car and forced it up the hill. When he was told to go to Holden Hall, he simply turned his car to the east, bumping across the uneven ground, lights and sirens blasting the snow. But just as they reached that building the dispatcher corrected the misinformation and reconfirmed that the attack was still ongoing in Norris Hall. Lucas spun his car around and headed back across the lawn. He stopped about halfway to get out and assess the situation for himself. Gunfire could be heard coming from Norris. Wilson also realized in that moment that he and Lucas were sitting exposed on an open lawn. Any shooter who looked out the window would see that he had clear fields of fire and an open kill zone and that the cops had no cover. The two made a long sprint across the rest of the lawn toward the southern doors of Norris.

Elements of the BPD tactical team had arrived in one or two minutes from the call. Wilson, the BPD ERT leader, had taken off his heavy body armor during his time at West AJ as he had then assumed a supervisory role in the investigation. The first officers marked on scene by radio call to dispatch at 9:45, merely three minutes from the callout, were Anthony Wilson and Dean Lucas, by radio call from Wilson. Immediately after Blacksburg officers John Glass, Scott Craig and Brian Roe pulled up. However, others were already there and had tried to breach both the breezeway and central western doors. Dispatcher April Blankenship, working the radio calls while her lieutenant Deborah Morgan stayed on the phone with a girl inside the building, was told officers were outside the Burruss Hall side, while others were notifying her they were still "en route to Norris Hall." After the initial call from a male [Colin Goddard] a girl had picked it up. "I can hear the police," the young woman told Morgan.

In a small police department the best people often assumed numerous top-level duties, and Wilson was also a detective. When the call came his assault rifle and body armor were twenty yards in one direction, but the police car was five yards in the other. He ran for the car, abandoning both his offensive weapon and personal protective equipment. He would fight to enter Norris Hall along with others, with no body armor at all and merely a handgun, certain that they were racing hell-bent into a gunfight with heavily armed and likely suicidal murderers. Wilson estimated that it took him fifty seconds driving time to travel the three-quarters of a mile from WAJ to Norris. He and Lucas had raced up the one-way Drillfield Drive in the opposite direction of traffic. The Governor's Report stated that the police response was "prompt and effective" due to the large number of officers that had responded to the WAJ shooting. It certainly could not have been faster. Panting from the sprint, when Wilson and Lucas pulled the southern doors open it was clear they were chained. No one thought anything of it at the time as the construction workers had been doing strange things all year. Anthony Wilson was worried about attempting to breach the doors by shooting the chain, believing that VTPD had already entered the western doors and could be anywhere inside the building. Rather than risk a friendly fire incident, he led the officers with him up the west side of the building, racing the 77 yards around the corner and along the wall to the doors leading into the western stairwell.

—

At that same time, at 9:45 a.m. police alerted Montgomery Regional General Hospital's Emergency Department to expect more gunshot victims from the university. They hadn't waited, but could only imagine that with all the gunfire and the earlier murders that everyone had to be ready for casualties. Hospital Security Director Charlie Smith couldn't believe what he was hearing. Two students had already been shot to death that morning. "What in the world is going on?", he wondered.

—

Curtis Cook had run down the steps and out the door of the WAJ dormitory after hearing "Active shooter at Norris Hall," and headed straight to a car on the sidewalk next to the building. Darrell Sheppard already had it roaring to life. Blacksburg's Greg Evans jumped in with them and they took off. They hadn't spoken at all as the car rocketed across campus and the lieutenant didn't ask his officer what route he was taking or why. Although he doesn't remember in detail exactly where they parked or how long it took him to get there, it would later be revealed that they had driven on West Campus Drive past Drillfield Drive and around Norris Hall to Perry Street some distance to the north. From Perry they turned up the Cowgill Service Drive and then parked at the closest point between Cowgill Hall and Randolph Hall. This had forced the three to run 160 yards up hills and outside staircases to approach the building from the northwest, behind the plaza that student Jamal Albarghouti had been standing taking video with his cell phone. Other officers had been there for one to two minutes already, encountering chains and attempting to breach the building.

An experienced and highly trained SWAT commander, Cook was at the height of alertness as he leapt from the car and ran almost two football fields up banks and stairs toward Norris Hall. Several of the Tech police officers and members of the Blacksburg Police Department were already arriving simultaneously, the sounds of gunshots being fired inside the building hastening their movements. Gunfire echoed and the officers were unable to determine exactly what floor of the classroom building the noise was coming from. Curtis Cook recalled, "I heard several shots, seven or eight, and knew that people were being killed, and that's hard to live with to this day."

As Tech ERT commander Cook arrived at the western doors to Norris Hall, the first person he saw was his own Capt. Albert. Albert had been at Burruss Hall 20 yards to the west of Norris Hall, meeting with the university Policy Group. As he raced up to his captain he heard a dispatcher say, "He's outside." But she had meant that the shooter was then outside a particular classroom, but he hadn't heard that part. Confusion was reigning. He couldn't tell if the shots he heard were coming from the second or third floor. Cook ran southward, halfway down along the west side of the building, his weapon up as he scanned the windows of the upper floors looking for a shooter. He heard Anthony Wilson and the others from Blacksburg down at the southern doors saying that they couldn't get in. He could hear glass breaking but was unsure where it was coming from.

Within an hour or so CNN would broadcast several seconds of video shot on Albarghouti's cell phone while standing at the plaza to the northwest of the western doors of Norris Hall. CNN and other networks used this approximate ten seconds of video, slowed down to approximately one-third its normal speed. It depicted officers arriving along Old Turner Street from the breezeway, stopping just short of the doors as shots rang out from the building. They stop, weapons up, and take a brief moment before moving to the doors. However, by playing those few seconds on a never-ending loop and in slow motion, with the staccato sounds of gunfire exploding from the film, the media created the impression that kids continued to be shot down while police stood outside for a virtually endless period of time. This would only be the first of the media's reporting that falsely portrayed the speed and manner in which the police responded.

All arriving officers immediately broke up into three separate teams, in their efforts to enter Norris Hall, each taking a different public entrance door. The GPR reported that, "Hearing shots, they pause briefly to check whether they are being fired upon, then rush to one entrance, then another, and then a third but find all three chained shut. Attempts to shoot open the locks fail."[272]

The men with Lt. Cook - designated Team Three - stacked outside the west entrance as Sgt. Wilson's Team One had initially attempted to gain entry at the southernmost doors fronting Drillfield Drive. Wilson and his team were right there as Lt. Cook's team attempted to breach. The two teams, and team leaders, linked up. They had been through more than their share of high risk operations together in the past and trusted each other implicitly. Both chiefs

272 GPR, p. 27.

and Capt. Goodman, along with other officers designated Team Two, had not yet arrived though they would attempt to enter through the breezeway. They, too, found doors chained and ordered a pair of bolt-cutters brought to them.

—

Along with Allen and the other cops running along Old Turner Street toward the western corner of the building, Tom Gallemore and Larry Wooddell were pounding down the sidewalk. Wooddell saw some people outside smoking cigarettes. "There's a shooter! Get the fuck out of there!", he screamed. As he ran along Norris he saw a guy in a third floor window about to jump, yelling to the police that there was a shooter. He sped to the far western doors just around the corner. He could hear gunfire. Glass was breaking above him and falling at his feet. The report of the gunfire "did not sound real" to Wooddell.

As the team with Allen, Wooddell and Gallemore reached the distant corner of the building they encountered VTPD's Morgan Millirons who told them that those doors were locked too. Allen yanked the doors open and saw the chain. It was too tight for anyone to squeeze through. Certainly the football lineman-sized Gallemore wasn't getting in that way, and in fact none of the responding officers, especially the ERT operators among them, could slip through such narrow spaces. Allen immediately dispatched a sergeant with the keys to the tactical van to retrieve a set of bolt-cutters. Inexplicably, the sergeant couldn't get into the van, so Allen radioed "Jersey" Dominiczak and told him to bring bolt-cutters with him. Without having to be told, he knew the courageous young tac medic would already be on his way.

Blacksburg Officer Craig told Lucas to fire his patrol shotgun into the chain while one of the officers held the door as far open as it would go. He was the only one who had arrived at the building with one. But between the cacophony of gunfire, exhaustion from running, adrenaline flooding systems and fear, the barrel of the gun was slipping from the chain, discharging buckshot dangerously about.

One sergeant who had tried to hold the chain against the shotgun's barrel almost got his hand shot off. The two .00 buck shots that were fired failed to breach the chain.

Frustrated at their failure to enter the building Tech Captain Joe Albert, who had come across the twenty yards from his meeting with the Policy Group in Burruss Hall, told the team to move to the next set of doors. They were only eleven feet to the left from door frame to door frame. These large wooden doors were secured with a deadbolt lock and led into a packed and noisy mechanical room, though no one knew where they led.

The third round loaded in the shotgun was a slug and it blew the bolt lock out of the shop doors. These were the only shots fired by responding officers until clearing the third floor much later. The GPR stated that this was accomplished at 9:50 a.m. In actuality, the clock was well into the 9:50 minute - almost 9:51 - when the final breaching shot was fired. Inside the doors was a forklift with a large propane tank on it. "If a dynamic entry had been used with a shape charge half of the building would have gone up," thought Cook. Wooddell remembered looking at the doors as they entered and also thinking that, "If that big bar had been on the inside of the door to secure it, we would have never gotten in." Just as they were entering VSP Special Agent Eaton had arrived at Norris from WAJ where he had been conducting tests at the first crime scene.

Due to the mechanical noise, no one in the machine shop had heard anything that alerted them to the presence of a gunman or an attack. They had, however, heard the police outside and were about to open the door for them when the lock was blown into the room. Just inside the doors was a shop worker "with eyes as big as saucers," according to Wooddell, as the frantic police raced past him, attempting to negotiate their way through the maze of machinery and into the hallway, toward the shooters. The lock flying into the room had almost taken his skull out. Other mechanical workers showed the officers how to exit the shop and move into the building's interior and where the nearest staircase was located. It was 20 yards from their entry point to the door at the far end that led into the hall. The stairs they were headed toward were the very same ones on the west side of the building they had been unable to blow the chain off of. They had had to circle completely around to end up at the same point they had started at. Only now they were inside the doors instead of standing impotently outside of them. Immediately upon turning the corner toward the stairs on the first floor the cops concluded that gunfire was coming from the floor above.

—

At 9:50, as Jersey was approaching the building with the bolt-cutters he had been ordered to bring, he heard on the radio that the teams had just breached the western doors. However, by that time they actually were already inside the building and moving toward the stairs leading upward to Cho who was then attacking room 211 for the second time. But they couldn't know that. All they knew was that there were shots being fired on the second floor and that the students and teachers were helpless. The shooters would have the advantage, the high ground, and could fire effortlessly down at the responding officers in the stairwells. Rather than get bogged down on the steps attempting to avoid fire from above they all simply raced up the stairs, taking them two and three at a time in a headlong rush to the top.

—

By 9:45 a.m. officers from both BPD and VTPD were converging on Norris Hall. Capt. Goodman had still been at West Ambler-Johnston and said it took approximately three to four minutes from the radio alert for him, Chief Flinchum and Chief Crannis to arrive. They had all piled into Flinchum's car with Goodman in the back, his diminutive frame readied for battle. They entered from the northeast by driving up Old Turner Street (on the north side of Norris and Holden Halls), coming up to the building through the entrance under the breezeway between the two buildings, retracing the steps that Allen, Gallemore, Wooddell and others had taken ahead of them.

Racing toward Norris Hall with lights and sirens shrieking through the wintry morning, a student still walked right in front of the car carrying the two chiefs and Captain Goodman and was almost hit. As they arrived there was confusion over the radio as to whether the shooters had moved to Holden Hall, or were still in Norris. Parking the car on Old Turner Street on the north side, they raced into the breezeway between the two buildings. This point was the only one that entered almost directly onto the second floor, due to a rise in the ground from west to east. It was also the first entry Cho chained before proceeding west along the hallway on the second floor, then down the western/Burruss side stairs to the first floor. When they pulled the doors open and saw the chain Goodman yelled, "Shit, the doors are chained!" Chief Flinchum decided that they could not attempt to shoot it as there were people inside the building. He ordered the bolt-cutters be brought to the walkway. Another door on the other side of the narrow breezeway would have taken them down a set of steps to an underground tunnel that would have led them back across and inside Norris Hall; however, when the commanders tried this entrance they found it to be locked. People could exit through it, but it was secured from the inside. Some VT employees later told Flinchum that was how they had escaped.

At Norris, Jersey grabbed all of his equipment and ran to the doorway inside the breezeway. His car had been blocked out, forcing him to sprint the final block to the building. When he was halfway there one of the ERT guys called him on his radio and told him to get bolt-cutters. He immediately called a rescue squad ambulance to meet him at the top of the street, as they were all equipped with bolt-cutters. Jersey estimated that this all took place within five to six minutes of him leaving the hospital.

With this critical piece of breaching equipment in hand, Jersey ran to the breezeway door, where he met up with VTPD Chief Flinchum, Blacksburg Chief Crannis, Capt. Goodman, VTPD Sgt. Morgan Millirons, Kenneth Craighead and Joe Shanks. Millirons had raced from the western doors the police were trying to shotgun breach to get the bolt-cutters that were on their way. But as he got to the breezeway he received the radio call that they were already inside the machine shop. With bolt-cutters brought to them by Jersey he decided to move into the building from that point. The mindset of the sergeant at that moment was a universal police thought in such circumstances where innocents were being shot: "Let's kill this guy and go home." They made quick work of the chain and entered the building on the second floor at its easternmost point. Flinchum recalls that at that moment, "Kim [Crannis] said that we were cops again," though he acknowledges that they have been criticized by others for forming an entry team of top level police officials in a dynamic, active shooting situation. Nevertheless, no one can fault the courage under fire of these commanders who showed the nation the meaning of the doctrine to always *lead from the front*. Donnie Goodman said: "Kim is incredibly capable and she was very heroic that day. Wendell was too, truly heroic, both of them. They chose to go down that hall and they could have chosen not to. They demonstrated leadership that day; they were pulling the rope."[273]

From the breezeway door they moved into the far eastern end of the west-east wing of the building. Once in the hall, the *ad hoc* entry team formed a conventional diamond configuration to begin moving toward the gunfire. Chief Flinchum said that he didn't remember what position he took as their entry team formed up and moved down the hall. He knew Jersey was there with them, along with Joe Shanks. But Jersey suffered no such memory lapse. "Chief Flinchum, without any body armor, took the lead position in the diamond we formed. He showed no fear and led us straight down the hall," he said.

Flinchum had clearly taken the point. This is the most dangerous position in a diamond. Jersey was in the middle, behind the chief. Chief Crannis was to his right, with two other officers to

273 In reference to a U.S. Army Special Forces saying with regard to leadership, that you cannot push a rope.

Diagram of Attempted Breach Points for Each of the Three Law Enforcement Entry Teams

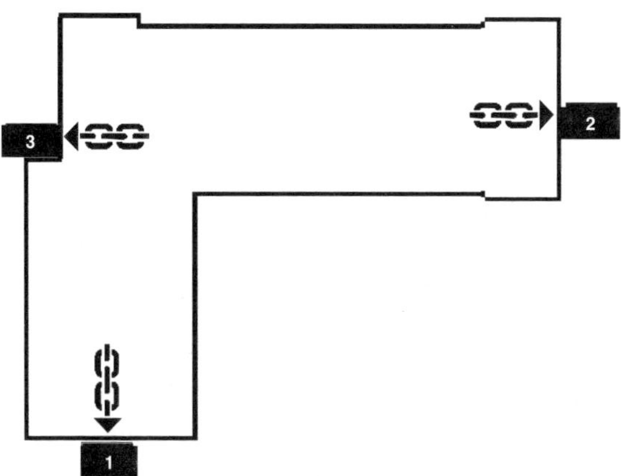

Team One, led by Sgt. Wilson, first attempts entry at the southern /Drillfield side entrance. This is the last entry Cho chained before proceeding up the adjacent staircase onto the second floor. Lt. Cook's Team Three is already attempting to breach the western/central doors. Team Two, led by both police chiefs will attempt to enter the breezeway doors.

his left and two more immediately behind him. He realized that neither Wendell Flinchum nor Kim Crannis had body armor. Flinchum remembers feeling "like a cop again" as he experienced the tunnel vision that many survivors of shooting events report. Lined up directly behind Flinchum, Jersey found himself "thinking that the chief was a large man." "I was running through my mind what I was going to do if he got shot right in front of me," he remembered. He decided that if the chief went down the first thing he would do was grab his weapon and return fire. Jersey, himself, had neither ballistic vest nor gun. They moved westward up the hallway. "People were popping out of their offices to see what was going on," he said. The entry team moved straight to the west stairwell where other officers were already moving about. Flinchum remembers the same thing: "When we got to the far corner [i.e., the elbow at the west corner of the two wings] we linked up with teams of other officers."

Gotta get back to the other rooms. Which ones haven't I hit yet? As I go by I see people moving in 206 still. Gonna finish them off. Piles of them soaked in blood. I love it. Now I know exactly how Eric and Dylan felt. This is awesome.

As police were attempting to enter Norris Hall, Cho left room 211 after his first assault on it, turned to the right and then across the hall, re-entering room 206. Cheng Park, Guillermo Coleman and Nathaniel Krause lay there, playing dead. Cho walked through the room shooting students, some a second and third time. He stood over Krause and fired, wounding him again. Guillermo Colman had pulled the bloody body of fellow student Partahi "Mora" Lumbantoruan on top of him, as he continued to feign death himself. Cho fired several more shots into Mora's body and then exited the room.

What was that? The door to 207 just slammed shut. Do they really think they can keep me out? Fuck! But I can't get in! They must be holding it shut. Fine I'll just shoot the door. Don't know if the bullets'll go through but I'll try. Four should do it. I heard someone scream in there.

With his menacing blank face, Cho crossed the hall to room 207 where the German class had been held, retracing the path that he had used from room 206 to 207 that had begun his onslaught. Two wounded students, and others who had not been injured, were by then holding the door shut with their hands. Among these was Derek O'Dell, bleeding from an earlier wound, Katelyn Carney and Kevin Sterne. Cho forced the door open an inch or two. He uttered not a sound, not a grunt, not a word. The silence of the murderer would have been unnerving, like a robot programmed merely to kill, dispassionately, inhumanly. Those behind the door managed to force it back shut. Enraged at having been denied entry, Cho stepped back and fired four rounds through the closed door. One bullet passed through the loose shirt that Derek O'Dell was wearing, barely missing him. Katelyn

Left: Room 4040 West AJ, showing location of Emily Hilscher across the room under the loft bed, and Ryan Clark just inside the door, when police and paramedics arrived. Note standup closet inside door to left Cho is believed to have been standing behind.

Walter Chi diagram.

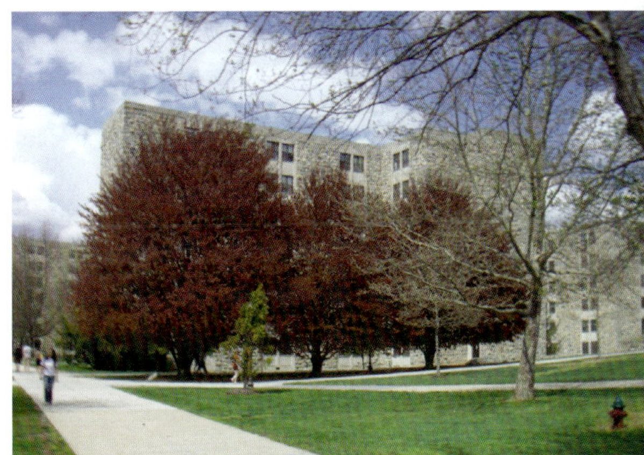

Right: Sidewalk leading up to eastern doors of West AJ (on the right). Many officers had to make the 80 yard run up this sidewalk to their cars when Cho began shooting in Norris Hall.

Bail photo.

Bottom Right: Duck Pond from approximate position where Cho was reported to have been standing between the West AJ and Norris Hall attacks.

Bail photo.

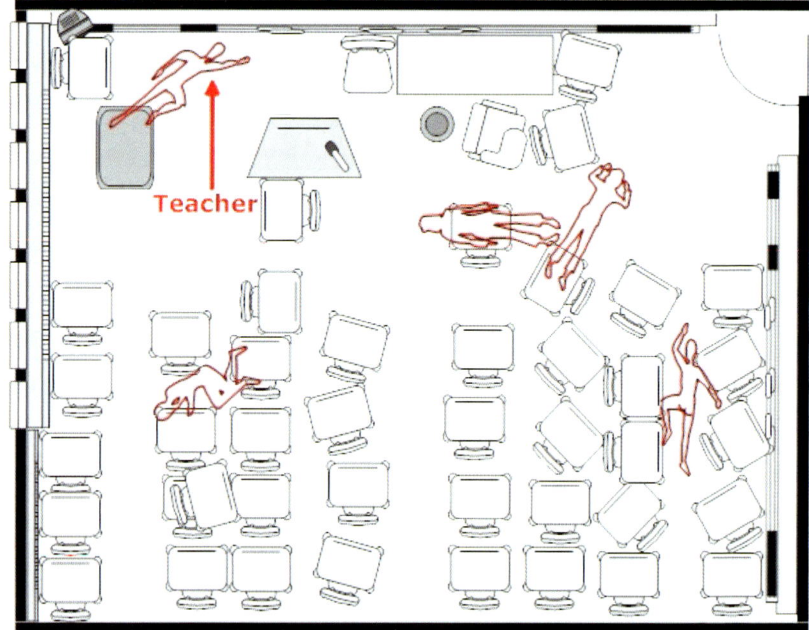

Above: Diagram of room 207 when police entered, including the location of the bodies. Walter Chi diagram.

Below: Diagram of room 204, including the location of the bodies of Professor Librescu and Minal Pinchal. Walter Chi diagram.

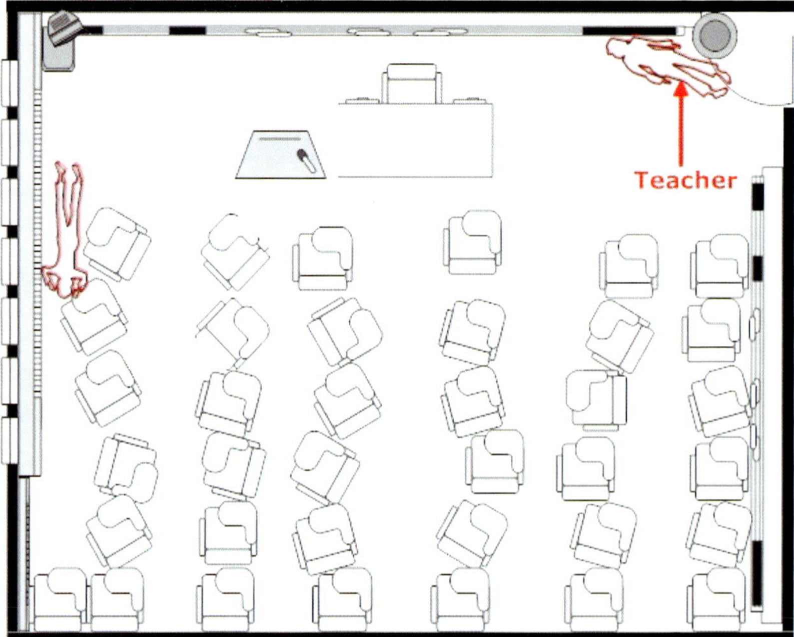

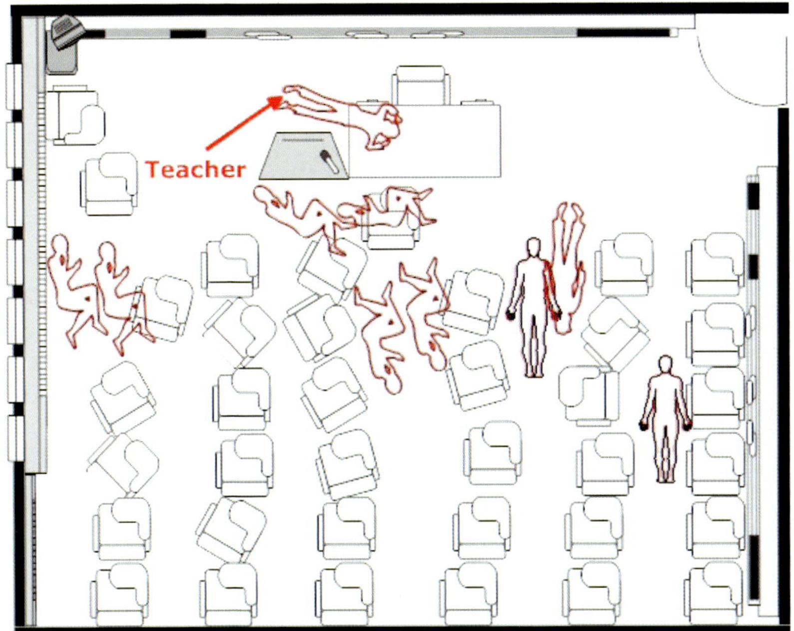

Above: Diagram of room 206 when police entered, including location of the bodies. Walter Chi diagram.

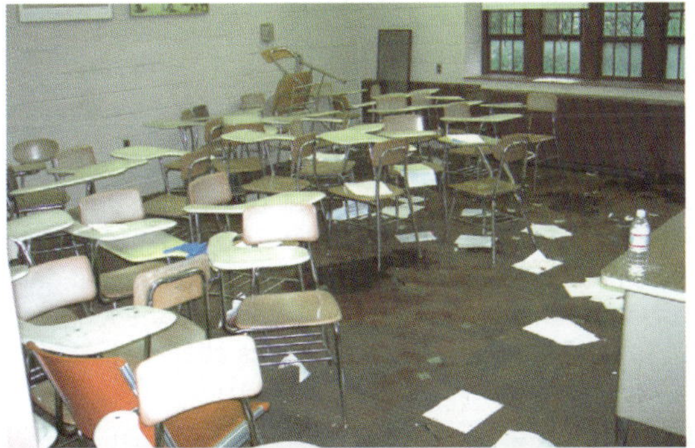

Top Left: Room 206.
Giduck photo.

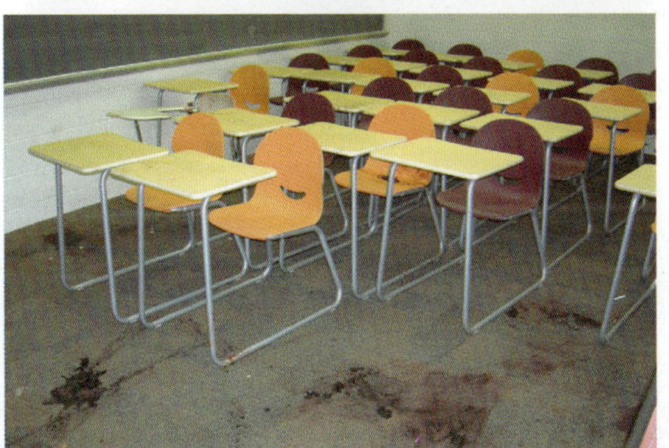

Bottom Left:
Room 211 after desks were rearranged showing tight confines students had to attempt to take cover in.
Giduck photo.

Top Left:
View up from Drillfield Drive of the more than 100 yards to the southern doors of Norris Hall.
Bail photo.

Bottom Left:
View of the mechanical room or machine shop from the hallway. The doors the police entered from the outside are at the far opposite side of the room.
Bail photo.

Below: View from the northwest of Norris Hall of the mechanical room doors (left) and western stairwell doors. Two shotgun blasts did not breach the chains of the stairwell doors, but a slug did gain the police access through the mechanical room. Note the long wing to the right (south) with the rooms Cho was attacking.
Bail photo.

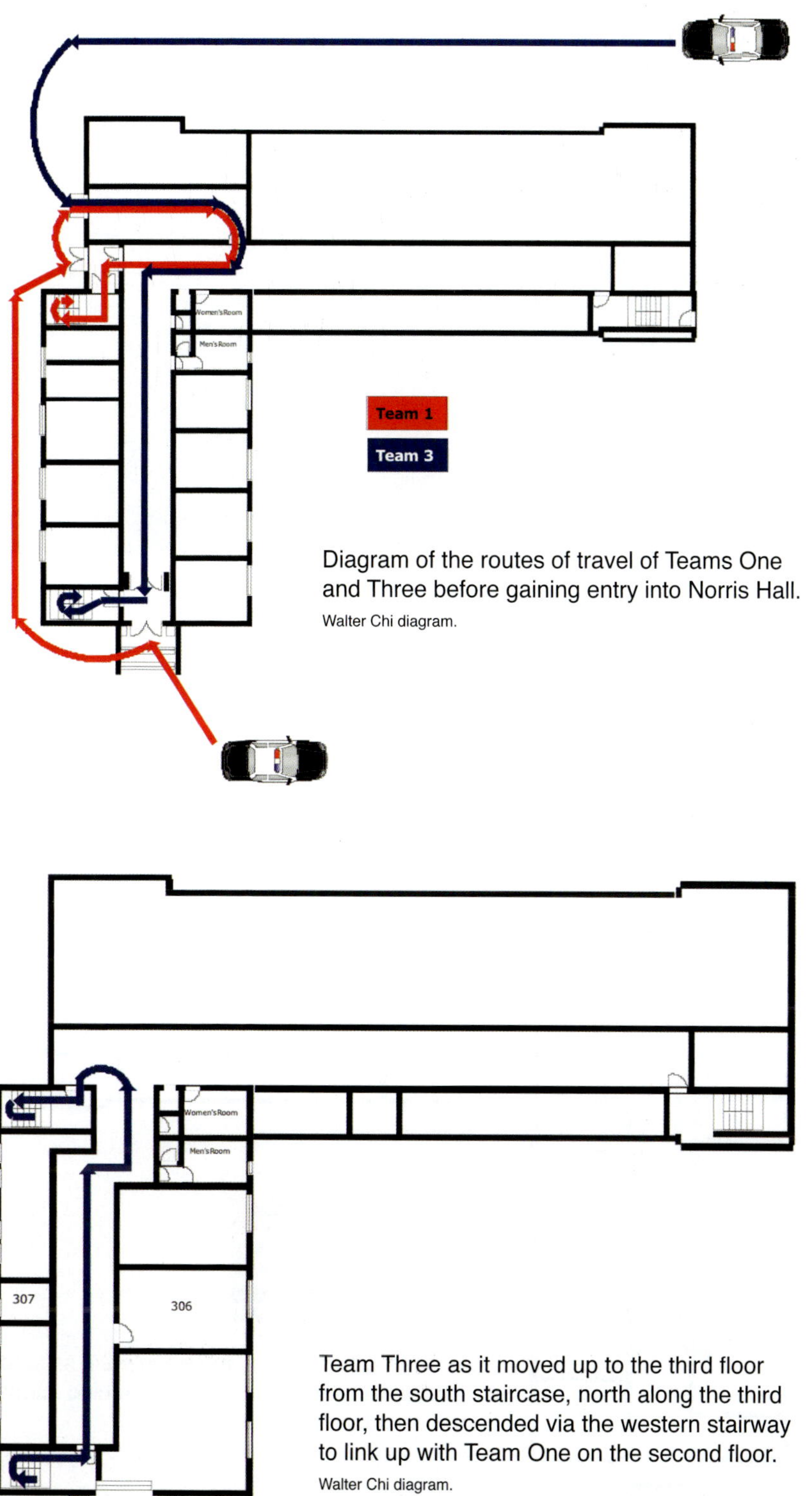

Diagram of the routes of travel of Teams One and Three before gaining entry into Norris Hall.

Walter Chi diagram.

Team Three as it moved up to the third floor from the south staircase, north along the third floor, then descended via the western stairway to link up with Team One on the second floor.

Walter Chi diagram.

Above: View of Norris Hall from the southeast. The north-south wing is to the left, with the bush the students from room 204 were jumping into in the center. The west-east wing is at the top of the photo. Note the rise in the ground to the breezeway at the right end of that wing.

Chris Hays photo.

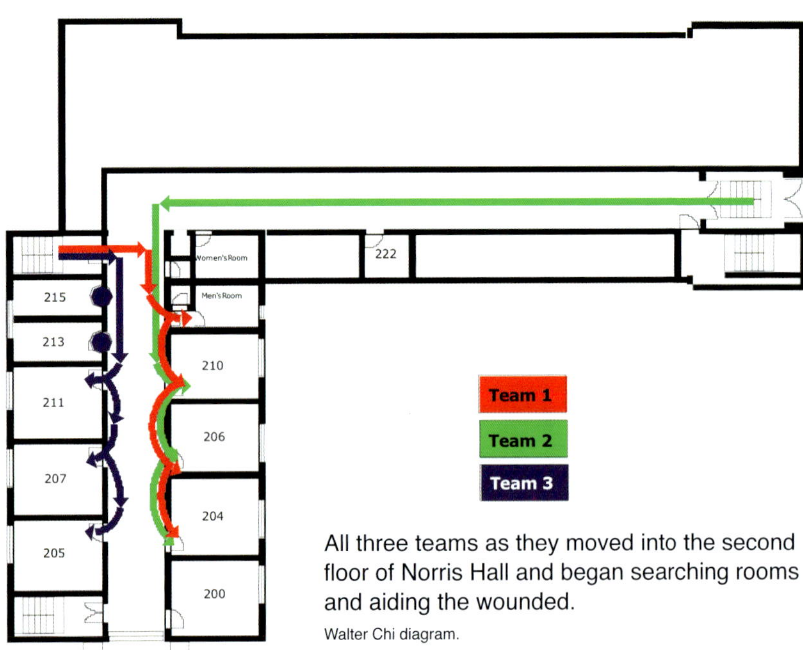

All three teams as they moved into the second floor of Norris Hall and began searching rooms and aiding the wounded.

Walter Chi diagram.

The breezeway door *(above left)* breached by the team led by the police chiefs, the western stairwell doors *(above right)* and mechanical room doors, and the southern doors of Norris Hall *(bottom right)* that were breached from the inside in order to evacuate wounded students.

Bail photos.

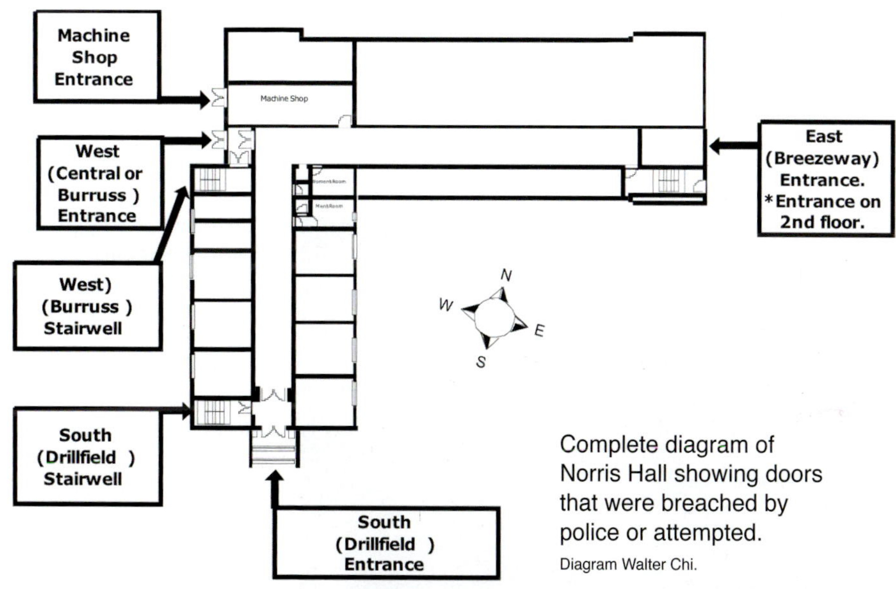

Complete diagram of Norris Hall showing doors that were breached by police or attempted.

Diagram Walter Chi.

Left: Large display honoring the police who responded to Norris Hall erected on the Drillfield by the students.

Bail photo.

Above Left: Virginia Tech Police Chief Wendell Flinchum.

Above Center: Virginia Tech ERT leader Lt. Curtis Cook.

John McMormick photo, reprinted with permission.

Above Right: Blacksburg Police Operations Captain Donnie Goodman. Depicted in photo in his current position as Chief of the Radford Police Department.

Left: VTPD Emergency Response Team.
Top row (L-R)
Detective Daniel Hardy ,
Officer Geof Allen ,
Sgt. Tom Gallemore ,
Sgt. Sean Smith,
Officer Jaret Reece.
Bottom row (L-R)
Lt. Curtis Cook , Ofc. Larry Wooddell ,
Lt. Scott Lau .

Carney was shot. Another struck Kevin Sterne in the femoral artery. He fell to the floor, arterial spray erupting from his leg. He and others began trying to stem the blood flow. Frustrated, Cho abandoned his effort to finish what he had begun in 207 and moved on. The following students in room 207 would be wounded but survive: Katelyn Carney; Jarrett Evans; Elilta Habtu; Sean McQuade; Derek O'Dell; and Kevin Sterne. Lauren McCain, Michael Pohle, Maxine Turner, Nichole White, and Christopher Bishop all died.

Okay where haven't I hit yet? I want some fresh meat. It's getting boring just putting bullets into corpses. Don't worry, I'll soon be joining you all. Difference is I'm not afraid of it. Saw those two girls looking at me out of 205 before. Time for them to meet me. I can't believe it! Somehow they're holding this door shut too! I hear the door hitting something solid, like they've got something heavy pushed up against it. What the hell could that be? Fine I'll just shoot through this door too. Damn! They've kept me out of two rooms now. Never figured on that. Thought they might fight me, but not barricade themselves in. What the hell is in a room to do that with? Fuckers, why don't you just die just like you've killed me all my life?

Cho then turned southward down the hall to 205, the very next room. The students in that room were attending a class on *Issues in Scientific Computing* being taught by graduate assistant Haiyan Cheng who was substituting for the assigned professor. This was the room in which both the teacher and student Theresa Walsh had looked out in the hallway some five minutes earlier and seen Cho, and had been shot at. When this happened, they had ducked back into the classroom and begun figuring out how to barricade the door. Unlike the students in 207 who would bravely stand behind the door merely holding it shut with their hands and getting shot for their courage, those in 205 had had enough time to devise a plan. They pushed the teacher's desk against the door. Each room had a desk or table for the teacher and a podium that was bolted to the floor. The students were lying on the floor, holding their barricade in place with their hands grasping the bottoms of the desk legs, their own toes dug into the carpet to keep from being pushed backward.

Having just been frustrated at room 207, Cho would have been furious and intent upon entering 205, a room he had not yet attacked. It was a room with fresh victims. As before, he attempted to force his way in. But the fortifications held and he could not shove the barricade aside to open the door. Angry, he again stepped back and this time fired two rounds through the door before moving on. He had failed entirely to shoot anyone, so high above the barricading students had his bullets gone. Grad assistant Cheng was huddled behind the podium across the room. Bullets splintered the wood above her. This would be the only room from which everyone emerged unscathed.

Only room left is 204. That old man is in that one. Speaks with an accent. Foreigner like me. Doesn't belong here either. He should have stayed wherever he came from. I can feel someone holding the door shut, but I'm too powerful. I won't let it happen again. Have to get in. A couple bullets through it and I'm in. It's just the old man. Well, he was *just the old man. He went down like a ton of bricks. But where are all the kids?! There's only three. This girl is begging me. She dies. These other two are at the back, just lying there. Easy to hit. Only three though! Where are the others? Oh, I see, the window's out. They're all down there. Jumped into a bush! It's a long way down. I can't believe it.*

Frustrated, Cho proceeded across the hall to room 204 where Prof. Liviu Librescu had been pressing the door closed with his hands and body since the rampage had begun, providing his students time to remove a window and screen so they could leap to safety. This was no mean feat. The windows themselves were not designed to be opened or taken out easily. Almost 40 years old, they were thick casement window sections, with individual panes bound in metal frames that were each only approximately eleven by six inches. To open the window, first the screen had to be pulled out, then the large casement window section – which probably hadn't been opened in years – had to be forced outward. Even after that a lower transom window still had to be climbed up on, adding to the height from which the students would fall. A few lowered themselves to arms length, dangling from the top of the transom window, before dropping to the ground. They were attempting to land in a large bush to the left of the window, but after the first couple of students it was providing no cushion for the rest making the 19 foot drop.[274] By the time Cho arrived at 204 ten students had crashed into the bushes below. Jeffrey Twiggs suffered a compound fracture of his leg. He limped more than 200 yards to a bus stop where he caught the bus to the hospital. Despite having told the driver what was happening, the bus still made two more stops before taking him to where he could receive medical attention.

First Cho fired two rounds through the door to room 204. He was not going to be denied entry to a third room. He hit the door hard and Librescu was overpowered and knocked to the floor. Photos indicated that the teacher may have been struck in the body by one of the bullets that pierced the door.[275] Cho fired a single shot from his right hand pistol, striking the elderly professor in the head. All but three students had already escaped by jumping out the window, or in the case of Carver and Kim fleeing down the nearby stairs. After killing the professor Cho moved across the front of the classroom. There he confronted coed Minal Pinchal. He shot her in the head, mortally wounding her. He then moved down the aisle along the windows on the east side where he reached the remaining students, Nathaniel Webster and Justin Klein lying on the floor. Standing directly over them, firing at point blank range, he shot both.

274 Height reported by VSP Lt. Lyon.
275 Autopsy reports have been sealed.

Diagram of Norris Hall, Second Floor, Depicting Cho's movements from his first attack on Rm. 211, then onto Rooms 206, 207 and 204.

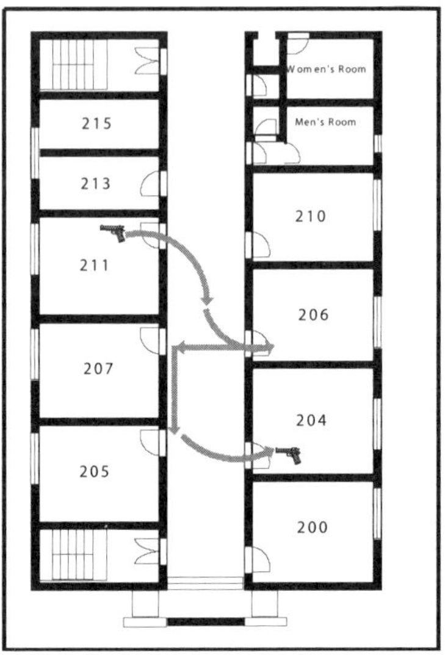

After his first attack on Room 211, Cho returned to 206. He then proceeded across the hall and attempted to assault Room 207 and 205 for the second time, but by then the students were holding the door shut, denying him entry. He then moved to Room 205, where he also failed to gain entry. From there he crossed the hall to 204 where Prof. Librescu was attempting to hold the door shut, allowing his students the opportunity to jump from the windows at the far right (northeast) corner of the room.

In all, 11 9mm bullet casings, and 12 .22 caliber casings would be recovered from this room and the victims he shot in 204. Two expended magazines, one each containing six and eight unexpended rounds were found. Twenty-three total shots were fired in room 204. Two people were killed: Prof. Librescu and Miss Pinchal. Klein and Webster, both wounded, would live. Also wounded or injured were Jamal Carver; Jeffrey Twiggs; Sundeep Patel; Caroline Merrey; and James Calhoun.

The cops're here. Gotta move faster. Need to make sure everyone's dead. Couldn't get into 207 or 205. No point trying again. Can't waste time. I can hear the cops everywhere trying to get in. Didn't think they'd get here this fast. Didn't they see the bomb note I left? That should have slowed them down. Gotta make sure they're all dead in 206 as I go by. They look it. What the hell, put a few more bullets in them.

From room 204 Cho moved next door and attacked room 206 for the third and final time. Those already wounded over and over lay there, quietly absorbing even more bullets. They knew that if they made any noise at all that he would know they were alive and kill them for sure. Ultimately, 34 9mm rounds and 11 .22 caliber rounds would be expended in this room, for a total of 45 bullets fired into a classroom of 24 people.[276] No one emerged from this room without being shot. Wounded were: Guillermo Colman; Nathaniel Krause; and Cheng-Min Park. Deceased were: Brian Bluhm; Matthew Gwaltney; Jeremy Herbstritt; Jarrett Lane; Partahi Lumbantoruan; Juan Ortiz; Julia Pryde; Waleed Shaalan; Daniel O'Neil; and Vasudevan Loganathan.

That leaves 211 where that hero tried to take me out. Shoulda used my Tae Kwon Do on him and kicked him in his jarhead face. They're all in piles just waiting for me. Christ, they haven't even moved, like they want me to do it. I hear someone on a cell phone. Okay, I'll just keep shooting into the pile until I end that conversation. Shit the cops are in! How did they do that so fast? I heard the guns but didn't think they were getting in. I can hear them coming up the steps. There's so many of them. Thought they'd stand off a while longer. How did so many get here so fast?! Thought I might take a couple out, but there's too many. They're all over the place, I can hear them yelling. Okay, gotta do it now. You son of a bitch. You shouldn't've tried to jump me. Make sure you're dead, put one more in your head for good measure. It's time. I gotta do it now. The cops are almost on me.

276 VSP Lt. Lyon says it was 46 rounds total, with 34 9mm and 12 .22 bullets discharged.

Cho then returned to room 211, the French Class, and repeated his steps. Emily Haas had continued to speak to the dispatcher, begging the police to hurry. The only thing that Lt. Debbie Morgan could hear was the hushed voice of Emily and the sounds of gunfire. She relayed the intelligence that she was getting to April Blankenship, who forwarded it on to the ERT members inside Norris Hall. Some of the sounds got fainter, and then suddenly Emily gave a blood-curdling scream. She had just been struck in the back of the head by two rounds.

At the sound of more gunfire Morgan screamed at April Blankenship right beside her, "Still shooting in Norris!" Cho stomped up and down the aisles shooting students, some over and over, just like room 206. He shot Kevin Goddard who had been shot in the initial assault, twice more at this point. Clay Violand continued to lay perfectly still. He said Cho was "unloading what seemed like a second round into everyone again. It had to be the same people. There were way more gunshots than there were people in that room. I think I heard him reload maybe three times."[277]

On the phone, Lt. Debbie Morgan kept hearing gunshots.

Haas: He's in here. Then screaming. I just got hit.

Silence

Haas: He's reloading.

VT: Okay, there's units there. Stay calm. Try to stay calm. Ease your breathing.

VT: What's your name?

Haas: I can't talk.

Emily did not lose consciousness, but continued to lie on the floor amidst her fellow students, feigning death, yet keeping the line open and continuing to pass information to the dispatcher. Lying with her

277 Ripley, p. 170.

face down, her blonde hair and baseball cap were hiding the phone she had pressed to her right ear.

This was the only time that the students all lying in a pile in the back of the room felt themselves getting angry with the police, according to Heidi Miller. She said:

> We were just lying there, not making a sound. The shooter was walking around the room looking for anyone still alive to shoot. Emily told the police dispatcher that he was back in the room so she had to stop talking. But the dispatcher kept telling Emily to not make a sound, to just lie still and not to say anything, to be quiet.

However, according to Heidi, the dispatcher's voice could be heard over the phone alerting Cho to the fact that they were alive and talking to the police. That was the time they were the most scared. Heidi, a soft-spoken young woman, said that she just wanted to scream into the phone to "shut up!"

—

Cho exited Room 204, then returned to attack Room 206 for a third and final time. When he left 206 he closed the door behind him, then turned right (north) and proceeded back to Room 211, which he attacked for the second time.

He would ultimately kill himself in Room 211 (note figure depicting Cho's demise) when Team One reached the second floor landing at the top of the stairs just up the hallway (north), and scarcely ten feet away.

During the attack on Norris Hall, numerous surviving students and teachers reported that Cho fired in a controlled, steady staccato tempo. He was accomplishing high speed reloads of his weapons, simply dumping mags on the floor, with some reporting that it only took him two seconds to change magazines. At times he would walk down the aisles, a gun in each hand, firing at students on

Final Movements of Cho

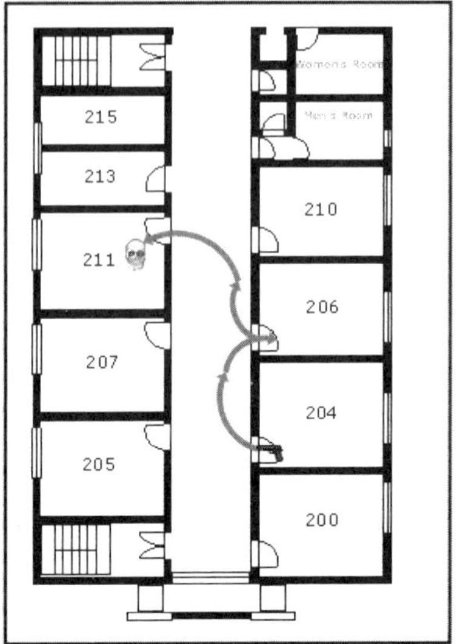

Cho exited Room 204, then returned to attack Room 206 for a third and final time. When he left 206 he closed the door behind him, then turned right (north) and proceeded back to Room 211, which he attacked for the second time.

He would ultimately kill himself in Room 211 (note figure depicting Cho's demise) when Team One reached the second floor landing at the top of the stairs just up the hallway (north), and scarcely ten yards away.

both sides of him, huddled on floors. In "*Lifting Our Eyes*," Derek O'Dell recalled Cho's eyes and described them as "empty." The Norris Hall classrooms did not have interior door locks on the second floor, but the offices did on the third, which did not require keys to secure from inside. All classroom doors were heavy, solid wood. The backpack that Cho had left by the water fountain outside the men's room contained a number of loaded magazines and other loose ammunition. It is likely he intended to fall back to that cache of ammunition to continue his massacre after expending all of the full magazines that his fishing vest held. In all he had fired 62 rounds inside room 211 alone, killing 12 in addition to himself.

Chapter Seven

Saving Lives

"Battle is the most magnificent competition in which a human being can indulge. It brings out all that is best; it removes all that is base. All men are afraid in battle. The coward is the one who lets his fear overcome his sense of duty. Duty is the essence of manhood."

George S. Patton

As the two teams of cops tore out of the machine shop, they had to make a right hand turn which took them to the elbow between the two wings. The shots were still echoing through the building as Wooddell, Cook, Wilson, Gallemore, Hardy, and others made entry and rushed into the sounds of the gunfire. The western stairs – the doors to which they had failed to breach – was just across the intersection of the two hallways. They suddenly couldn't hear any more gunshots though. As they raced toward that corner Curtis and Anthony quickly decided to split the teams. Anthony's Team One – with Craig, Roe, Lucas, Evans and Self - would take the nearby western stairs, a 19 yard sprint from the machine shop door that led into the hallway. Curtis would run his Team Three – which included Robinson, Weaver, Wooddell, Gallemore, Reece, Smith and Hardy - 62 yards down the hall to the far southern end and ascend to the second floor there. It took them but a second and just a few words to formulate this plan. The two leaders had worked together too long, and knew each other too well. They were racing against a speeding clock.

When they reached the second floor, the two teams would have the source of the shooting caught between them. Upon Team One reaching the second floor landing the last two shots were heard.

Diagram of First Floor of Norris Hall.

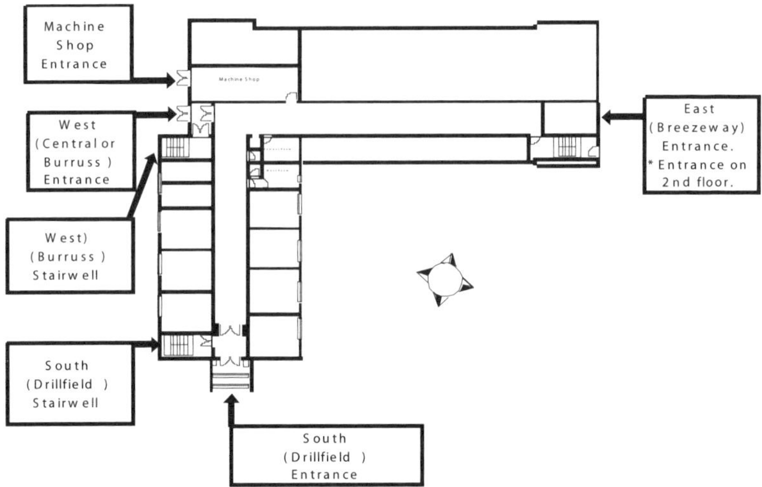

Note points of attempted entry by arriving police officers.

It took the teams merely 28 seconds from the instant the lock was blown on the shop doors for them to enter, negotiate their way through the shop, race toward the staircase at the west corner of the building and assault up to the second floor, forcing Cho to stop his rampage by taking his own life. They could not possibly know that at the time, however.

Carefully turning the corner into the suddenly silent second floor hallway revealed to Team One a single downed victim – Professor Kevin Granata - approximately halfway down the north-south corridor, and the floor littered with shell casings. The only sounds heard were those of the wounded professor whose respirations were accompanied with the heart wrenching rattle of someone in his final minutes.

—

As Team Three had headed down the long hallway toward the southern stairs Larry Wooddell was happy. He had wanted to head in that direction as that was where he thought the last shots had come from before entering the building. He could still hear the pop of Cho's guns as he reached the end of the hall. They stopped just before he and the others hit the southern stairs. Cook remembered hearing several shots and then "no more."

It is certain that Cho's observations of the cops' rapid response threw him off balance and denied him completing his assault plan. Evidence of this can be seen in the additional 203 rounds found on him and in his backpack that he clearly intended to use, but had not yet gotten to. In addition, there were 70 to 80 people on the third floor of Norris Hall alone, with numerous others on the first floor, all of whom were waiting victims. That would have left almost three rounds per person, the identical average number of wounds suffered by those in the classrooms he had attacked. But for the breakneck pace at which the police reached and then breached the building, the carnage could easily have been double what it was. Or worse.

Cho was well aware that law enforcement had arrived. He was reported by survivors in room 211 to have heard the sirens, and to have looked out the windows where he would have seen the police advancing on the building. He heard the shotgun rounds breaching the doors, which were almost directly below the windows of room 211, and just 25 feet to the north. The sounds of the breaching rounds were even audible on the 911 recording of Emily Haas' conversation with the dispatcher. Virginia State Police spokeswoman Corinne Geller later explained that: "You can't just rush into a building. You have to have a game plan. They didn't know what they were up against, whether it was more than one gunman, part of an ambush, if there were hostages. They literally had to get into position."[278] Still, rushing into the building was exactly what they had done.

As Team Three reached the second floor landing the officers with long guns were moved to the front to begin entering the hall. Wooddell merely had a handgun. He noticed that there were two

278 This statement, offered in response to erroneous news reporting and the distorted cell phone video, appeared to restart criticism of the police response as it allowed others to infer the officers took the time to meet and discuss a plan for entry, when in fact they did rush into the building with no time lost.

different types of ammunition clips discarded on the floor, forcing him to speculate, "There must be two shooters." There was complete silence on the second floor when they reached it, and at Lt. Cook's direction Wooddell went up to check the third floor. At that point Cook was thinking that the shooters might have moved up to the next level. After a quick peek into the third floor hallway to ensure that no shooting was going on, no bullet casings were visible, and that there were no wounded, he returned to the second floor. Cook was "horrified" at the sights in that second floor hallway.

Lt. Cook remembered: "As we hit the second floor landing we had kids running toward us. I told Wooddell and Weaver to take the kids down and out the door, where they encountered those [southern] doors chained as well. Wooddell told Weaver to "Shoot the fucking thing!", not knowing that VTPD Detective Sergeant Tony Haga, BPD Officer Nate O'Dell and others were just outside the doors. The cops on the other side didn't appreciate it at the time, but they had to get the kids out. This could have resulted in a horrible "blue on blue" shooting, or what civilians know as friendly fire. Wooddell was thankful that didn't happen and that he was able to assist the students to a safe zone. With the students in good hands, he turned and moved back up the steps into the nightmare that was Norris Hall.

—

When "Active shooter at Norris Hall" had echoed through the department, Shannon Combs and Ben Machingo had grabbed the keys to a patrol vehicle and raced toward the scene, entering the area from Old Turner Street. They ran from the car, running into the breezeway between Holden and Norris halls. They arrived there between the time Gallemore and Wooddell's team had already abandoned that entrance for the far western one, and just before the two chiefs and Captain Goodman got there. The door was chained and they had run down the ice and snow encrusted slope on the south side of the building toward the Drillfield entrance. As Combs and Machingo moved along the outside of the north-south wing he came up to the point where the students had been leaping from the windows of 204. Lying beneath an open second floor window Shannon observed a single shoe and a backpack, which he checked for weapons.

As he approached that area, a shotgun blast breached the heavy wooden southern doors from the inside and students started to flee the building. Machingo clearly saw the wounds and directed the students to a safe area where they could be triaged and shuttled to a hospital for definitive care. There were a half a dozen victims with mostly arm and leg wounds. Ben remembered one student with blood pouring from an arm wound. "What do I do?", the student pleaded. Ben directed him to safety.

Rebecca Hawkins, holding position just outside those same doors thought, "Holy shit they're coming out." She had only begun working in law enforcement in January 2006, and had barely been a cop for a year. The VT police department was the only police job she had had in her life, and her very first career position. Tall, blonde, pretty and lithe, with long willowy limbs she looked as though she should have been gracing the covers of vacation magazines advertising skiing in Aspen or Sun Valley, Idaho, not recounting the horrors of that day. She was no older than the students she was there to save. Her tiny diamond nose stud glittered as she quietly and calmly related her experiences.

She had just finished working the midnight to 7 a.m. shift with Larry Wooddell a couple of hours before it all began. As she was walking out of the police headquarters that morning on her way to home and much needed rest, Emily Hilscher and Ryan Clark lay bleeding in room 4040 of WAJ with gunshot wounds to their heads. Just as she was drifting off to sleep the jangling of her phone shocked her back to full consciousness. She was being called back into work as part of the mobilization of police resources in the investigation of the shooting of the two WAJ residents. She had been assigned to the Blacksburg Police Department staging area when the call had come over the radio of gunfire at Norris. She and the others with her took two vehicles to respond to the call. She was in a Jeep with Mason

Boggess and they had driven their vehicle right up the 100-yard long steep bank, stopping it at the low wall surrounding the porch just outside the southern doors of the building. When they arrived VTPD Sergeant Tony Haga was already there, standing just outside the entrance in an orange coat. He couldn't get in due to the chains, and so had taken cover behind his car. She remembers that they could hear gunshots, but that they did sound a bit like construction noise. Even to a police officer.

Within a couple of minutes of arriving Hawkins and Haga heard the shotgun blast from inside the southern doors they were holding position just beyond, and then those doors flew open. With her weapon aimed, she was just glad that she hadn't shot back in that moment. No one had alerted them to the fact that police were about to blast the chains and open the doors. After hearing gunshots for minutes, with weapons out and pointed at the doors, it was only due to the training and professionalism of Haga, O'Dell and Hawkins that none of them had opened fire on Wooddell and Weaver.

Immediately kids began coming out. One student ran up to the officers covering the southern doors and dove over Hawkins' Jeep to the other side, seeking safety. She and Boggess took as many students as they could behind the Jeep and tended to the wounded. One girl from 207, wounded and bleeding, ran past them. She would continue to run more than a half mile to the tennis courts across the street from Lee Hall before collapsing. Some of the kids were in such shock that they did not realize that they were even injured. Chief Flinchum had made his way down the south stairs where he encountered Emily Haas all alone, bleeding from two grazing bullet wounds to her head. He took her to Lt. Bradbery's car to be transported to the CCP (Casualty Collection Point) that had been established in McBryde Hall along with the Tactical Command Post (TCP) as the EMS teams had not yet entered Norris. Eventually the TCP would be set up outside in the Blacksburg Fire Department's mobile CP vehicle, and then moved over to the Old Security Building where the VTPD headquarters had been years before.

—

As soon as the kids from 207 had been evacuated out the southern doors, Wooddell and Weaver had raced back up the steps to the second floor where they joined the stack of officers searching other rooms. Wooddell related that at no point did he ever go into "first aid" mode. Instead he remained in "tactical search and engage" mode, looking for shooters. As Wooddell looked at bleeding kids, saw and stepped around the twisted and shattered bodies of the dead in the rooms, all he could think of was his own 19-year-old son. With those thoughts in his head desperation drove his efforts to find another threat - any threat. Believing that other killers still stalked the building, he silently swore to himself that no matter who else was still there, or anywhere on campus with evil intentions, that not another kid was going to get shot that day.

Larry Wooddell was likely older than many of the deputies that responded to Norris Hall. Born and raised in Staunton, Virginia he was possessed of a country accent so thick that his co-workers often had to decipher his *Wooddellisms* as they were called at the department. He had worked at the Montgomery County Sheriff's Office with Curtis Cook beginning in 1986. But in 1994 an administration shift had militated in favor of a change in career path. At the time a lot of the older guys at VTPD had been there since it had been merely a security department and were getting ready to retire. Seeing opportunities, Larry became a Virginia Tech police officer at 29. He was a member of the ERT, the Dive Team and was also a bicycle patrolman. Over his years in law enforcement, especially the sheriff's department, he said that he had seen "a lot of dead people, murders, suicides..." but nothing like he was going to experience in Norris Hall.

However, behind the Andy Griffith facade and country vernacular lies a keen intellect and almost encyclopedic memory.

The VTPD tactical team had been started in 1991 and Larry joined it right away. Curtis Cook, along with several other sheriff's deputies who would ultimately enter Norris Hall that day, also moved over to VTPD from the same sheriff's office at Larry's urging, with Cook coming in 1997. When Curtis arrived he and Wooddell started the VTPD Dive Team. However, Wooddell corrected erroneous reports that he was a K9 officer at the time of Cho's attack. Though he later became one, he was a bicycle officer at the time. Keith Weaver, however, was a K9 officer and was at Norris Hall, but at no time did he or anyone else enter with a dog.

—

As the police entered the second floor of Norris Hall from opposite directions the two *ad hoc* team leaders communicated with one another through radio and hand signals. According to Cook, with two groups of cops pointing weapons in each other's direction in a narrow hallway, "Anthony [Wilson] and I were trying to communicate by Nextels held in one hand, with our handguns in the other, while still trying to juggle our patrol radios." As a result they decided that Team Three should relinquish the second floor to Team One by moving up to the third floor, proceeding northward up that corridor checking rooms, and then down the western staircase to join Team One from behind.

Initially Lt. Cook had left Officer Weaver alone to hold position in the second floor landing. As he and the rest of the team reached the third floor in that same stairwell he realized that Weaver was hanging out there on his own. Sending his team down the third floor to quickly clear it and then descend the western stairs to join its sister team led by Anthony Wilson, Cook and Wooddell moved back down the southern stairs to back up Weaver and secure that end of the hall and ensure no shooters moved up the from the first floor or attempted to flee the second floor down that southern staircase. The ground floor had not as yet been searched or secured, and at that moment was completely unguarded.

The majority of Cook's Team Three moved northward along the third floor hallway, clearing rooms as they passed to the extent possible. During this first sweep they did not breach any locked doors, but merely rattled doorknobs and kept moving. Later, county sheriff's deputies would shotgun breach three doors – all on the west side of the corridor – with slugs, which included two classrooms and one storage room. Gallemore attempted to get into the west-east corridor lunch room by smashing the door with a fire extinguisher, then attempting to bash the safety glass out of the door, resulting in a severe gash to his hand that would require six stitches. After moving through the third floor, the team descended the west staircase, linking up with Team One. Team Two's Crannis, Flinchum, Craighead, Dominiczak, Millirons and Shanks had made entry through the breezeway doors and moved westward down the second floor hallway securing rooms as they advanced.

–

This wasn't the first time many of the officers who raced into Norris Hall had dealt with an emergency of sufficient magnitude to capture the attention of the nation together. Among others, both police chiefs, Captain Goodman, both ERTs and team leaders, in addition to Larry Wooddell, Daniel Hardy, Tom Gallemore and Geoffrey Allen had searched for the escaped cop-killer William Morva on campus just eight months before.

In response to that double homicide, as numbers of requested and arriving volunteer officers increased, command and control was essential as the fluidity of the situation required coordinated movements of officers and the ability to secure an enormous area. Integration of commanders, dating back to football game logistics the two departments had developed over the years, allowed for the deployment of cross-jurisdictional teams and management of a dynamic crime event.

BPD Captain Donnie Goodman – now chief of the Radford police department – ticked off just a few of the hard-won lessons from Morva that stood them in good stead immediately upon the ending of Cho's attack on Norris Hall.

> We knew that we would have hundreds of cops in no time again this time. And you have to have people already organized to manage them, to give them jobs to do. Because when all those cops arrive and you don't give them something to do, they're going to *invent* something to do, and that isn't always in everyone's best interest, especially in circumstances like that.

Also the Morva event taught the police that with that level of response they needed to immediately arrange for thousands of bottles of water to be brought in, along with food. Moreover, portable toilets were needed. With that many people arriving, together with thousands of citizens and reporters descending on the area and attempting to contact others, the local cell phone system would be overwhelmed and shut down. The phone companies had to be contacted to bring in portable cells to supplement the existing system and allow the police and university continued communications capability. And something had to be done to deal with the plague of reporters that would arrive. Joe Bail said that events of this magnitude were why the Incident Command System had been mandated by the federal government since 9/11.

9:50 a.m. to 10:08 a.m.

As officers were entering Norris Hall at 9:50 that morning, the VT community was notified of the shooting that took place earlier at WAJ by an email that was drafted, approved and issued by the university Policy Group working out of Burruss Hall just to the west. Capt. Albert had already raced out of the meeting room and across to Norris Hall. The email read:

"Subject: Please stay put."
"A gunman is loose on campus. Stay in buildings until further notice. Stay away from all windows."[279]

At 9:52 a.m. Cho was still in room 211. The entry teams had maneuvered through the Rube Goldberg of intertwined machinery in the shop, out into the hallway and were headed up the western stairway shouting, "Police, Police!" There had been a 28 second period of quiet, with no shots fired by Cho between the last shotgun breaching round that gained the teams entry into the building, and the first of Cho's final two shots. Evidence indicates that the first of Cho's last two shots was made into the right side of the head of Air Force Cadet Matt LaPorte. Ernie Manerchia, a senior investigator with the Chester, Pennsylvania Police Department's Crime Scene Investigation Unit and forensics expert, says that Cho was standing right next to LaPorte when he shot him. "It's clear from the crime scene photos that Cho was standing right next to LaPorte. His feet were probably even touching LaPorte's shoulder, standing directly over him, when he committed suicide," Manerchia contends. "From the very close proximity of the bodies even after Cho fell, and the blood spray against the wall from LaPorte's head wound, it is obvious that Cho had stood right next to him and bent down directly over him, shooting him at point blank range," he said. "Then he shot himself."

However, all indications are that Cadet LaPorte was long since dead. It appears that Cho took that last shot at LaPorte simply because that young man had enraged him. That single act of courage, even as he suffered bullet after bullet entering his body, should have silenced all of the pundits who decried a student body and faculty that did not fight back. Per Lucinda Roy, this misplaced outrage was perhaps most personified by *National Review Online's* conservative talk show host John Derbyshire, who asked why no one had "jumped" Cho, complaining that Cho wasn't some "Rambo, hosing the place down with automatic weapons."[280]

279 Various news media reported this at 9:54 a.m.
280 Roy, p. 237.

The warrior spirit and pride of uniform and service under harrowing conditions demonstrated by the thousands of VT graduates who had seen combat, the more than 300 who died serving America in the military, including Medal of Honor recipients, continued right up to April 16 when a young Air Force cadet moved toward a heavily armed killer in the front of classroom 211 in Norris Hall. Cadet Matthew LaPorte truly lived and died according the Virginia Tech motto, *Ut Prosim*, "That I May Serve." Ryan Clark had done no less inside West Ambler-Johnston Hall.

Still, others in Norris Hall were shot barricading doors, and in the case of an already wounded Derek O'Dell withstood bullets passing through his clothing as he held the door to room 207 closed against a second entry attempt by Cho. Others helped wounded to safety, but no one else actually fought back. Some of the students later reported that when Cho was inside shooting the thought of trying to take him on never occurred to them. They simply didn't think of anything but getting to the floor.

At 9:52 a.m. a radio call went out for all area EMS units. One minute later it was repeated. The entry teams were neither aware that Cho had shot himself, nor aware of the number of shooters in the building. As they reached the second floor and all went quiet, the team leaders immediately suspected that the shooters had taken hostages or were reloading and preparing to ambush them. According to Lt. Morgan, still on the phone with Emily Haas, "there was another extremely loud gunshot and then silence." The teams transitioned to a tactical search of the building. This is different from an active shooter response where officers will race pell mell toward the sound of guns, with the only tactic being to get there fast and eliminate the threat. This was a protocol devised in the aftermath of the Columbine shooting where police were held back while unarmed and helpless students were gunned down. Transitioning to a tactical search meant that everything went slow and quiet.

Outside room 211 Larry Wooddell saw the men's room door fly open and Professor Wally Grant and a male student popped out.

Wooddell, weapon drawn, came close to shooting them. The phrase "being on a hair trigger" could almost literally be applied to the police inside Norris Hall as they worked amidst the blood and bodies, ready to take on other shooters in an instant. Further down the hall was Professor Granata, his moaning was nerve-wracking to the officers poised to react to an ambush. Violating virtually every rule in the book of tactical response in a high-threat environment, Officer Brian Roe risked his life to race down the hall to the stricken professor. No one knew how many shooters there were, or where they were hiding at that point. But he didn't think about that. He certainly didn't talk to anyone about it, or even ask authorization from one of the commanders. He just took off running down the hall, weapon out, scanning the doors on either side of him for threats.

Wooddell saw him start his sprint and, realizing that he had not alerted anyone or asked for back-up, laid down on the floor to cover him with his handgun should any bad guys suddenly leap out of the rooms. Upon reaching the stricken academician, Roe holstered his weapon and grabbed him by his feet and implemented the first rule of the Tactical Combat Casualty Care training that the Delta Force had developed from its experiences in Iraq and Afghanistan: *Get the victim and the rescuer out of the killbox as fast as possible!* With Wooddell covering them, Roe drug the professor down the hall and into the western stairwell.

Upon the chiefs' team reaching the stairwell landing in the northwest corner of the second floor, Jersey had dumped his gear and hastily set up a triage and treatment station for any wounded. On the way down the hall he had not seen any blood or bullet casings, nor had he seen any evidence of casualties in the offices they had passed. No time had passed, however, before he was informed that a casualty was coming in. Professor Granata was dragged to his triage station, and he started to work on the *in extremis* academician with SWAT operators leaping over and racing around him in attempts to clear the building. Geoffery Allen and his team moved past Jersey, heading up to the third floor. "I'll never forget the blood trail where Kevin

Granata was pulled down the hall into the stairwell," Flinchum sadly recalls.

Popular professor Kevin Granata was presenting with involuntary twitching and bad respirations. Jersey "bagged" him with the medic's "ambu bag" which aids in breathing. He was getting no response. The professor had been shot pointblank in the head. Others told him that there were more casualties and he had to move his CCP. His mind raged at the very thought of it, but he had to black tag the Professor and prepare for others. The "black tag" was the medical community's way of saying a person was dead or had no hope of surviving. The officer who had violated important safety rules and raced halfway down a 42-yard long corridor, under threatening and unsecure combat conditions, to drag the wounded and moaning teacher back to the stairwell had not been trained in wound assessment. Two years later Jersey would say, "If I could have, I might have been able to tell him that he 'was a corpse' and wasn't worth the risk to the operator's life."

—

Throughout the second floor not a single victim – no matter how badly wounded or in pain – was making any sound at all. None of the victims, even if being shot over again, made any noise as they were concerned that doing so would have told Cho that they were alive, and would have gotten them shot even more. All those living were pretending to be dead. With the building so quiet, Cho would have heard Team One assaulting up the staircase, and this was substantiated by survivor accounts. One survivor reported that at this time Cho walked to the door of room 211, looked out into the hallway,[281] then walked back into the center of the room toward the front and shot himself in the head. Cho had placed the handgun toward the front left side of his head, blowing brain matter out the rear right

281 This may not be accurate as the bodies of Prof. Couture-Nowak and student Henry Lee were slumped against the door from the inside, unless he positioned them after looking out and closing the door to further retard law enforcement entry; though there is no eyewitness account establishing this.

quadrant of his skull. Though Cho was right-handed, he shot himself in the head with his left hand.

Looking into the second floor hallway, other officers were seeing the two different types of ammunition, causing them to also assume there were at least two shooters. As the teams were beginning to search the building other officers arrived and joined up. VTPD's Allen, Lau and Reece entered and quickly joined Team Three on the second and third floors. Blacksburg PD's Hayes and Cross entered and were directed to link up with Team One on the second floor. They moved up the breezeway stairwell and ultimately arrived on the third floor where they removed barricaded subjects from the dean's office.

When Jersey had arrived at Norris Hall and gone immediately to the tactical medic side of his duties, he knew that he was leaving Medical Incident Command in the hands of his first lieutenant, Colin Whitmore. Whitmore's office was one block from Norris Hall and when the call had come in he had just grabbed his gear and run the distance, saying it was faster. However Jersey knew that the conventional medical rescue units would stay out of the hot zone until it was declared "safe," but that he was needed inside no matter the risk. The police and the wounded had to have a medical professional inside with them, saving lives, even if that meant that shooters could still be lying in wait.

In addition to Professor Granata, police would also complete a rescue of Minal Panchal out of room 204 after the initial clearing of the second floor. Miss Panchal was ultimately moved to the Burruss-side stairwell with Professor Granata, where both would die despite Jersey's efforts. Their bodies would lay there, hands touching as though in silent embrace as police continued to race past them searching the building for additional threats and evacuating students. Long after, swirling smears of blood, scarlet-soaked bandages and ambu bags would litter the landing, a monument to the desperate efforts that one lone young man, a volunteer medic from the university, had made to save their lives. This hit him hard. He'd already lost another beautiful young girl that morning. He had worked frantically to keep her alive inside a rocketing ambulance. But he couldn't take even a minute for himself, or for them. Others were dying and needed his help.

Jersey and Blacksburg Police ERT Medic Brad Previtt were doing fast triage in the hall, giving directions, checking the walking wounded and getting into all the rooms where survivors lay. The two young men worked well together, functioning as efficiently as any combat medic team anywhere in the world. They had to keep reminding themselves, however, that this wasn't a war zone but an American university classroom building.

Lying semiconscious in room 207, student Kevin Sterne had a "textbook femoral artery bleed," according to Jersey. He had been shot in the leg as he braced himself against the door along with Derek O'Dell and others against Cho's second attempt to enter, when frustrated he had fired through it. As Jersey entered the room he saw ERT operators Jaret Reece and Shannon Combs attempting to cut a cord from a projector to use as a tourniquet. In their haste to save the lapsing student they had failed to unplug the cord before slicing it with a combat folder knife. Jersey yelled to pull the cord from the wall first, whereupon they cut it to length and began using the cord as a tourniquet to staunch the blood erupting from Sterne's leg.

But a geyser of blood continued to erupt from the wound. Jersey reached for his tourniquets but they were gone. In the chaos he had dropped his bag of combat tourniquets somewhere, but had no idea where. Even with the electric cord bound to the young man's leg the blood flow was frightful. Sterne had already had a jacket tied around his leg, but to no effect. Jersey saw Blacksburg ERT tac medic Previtt passing by the room in the hall and called for him to deal with the pierced artery. He said that Sterne was barely even conscious. Previtt immediately slapped an Israeli combat tourniquet around the thigh and stopped the bleeding and saved the student's life. Every officer there reported that the Israeli tourniquet "turned the bleeding off like a faucet."

—

Machingo and other officers entered the first floor of Norris Hall from the southern Drillfield entrance and began clearing the building. As he entered the hall Ben observed haze in the hallway and smelled the cordite from the gunfire that a short time before had snuffed out the lives of so many students and faculty. Some doors were unlocked, but others needed to be rammed. Machingo double-checked the rooms on the second floor for another shooter and then helped remove everybody from the building that he could assist with. Shannon Combs had entered the Drillfield doors after they were breached and helped search and secure the first floor. He located three or four people huddled behind a locked door that he forced open. One of them, Jamal Carver who had made the desperate run from room 204 into the stairwell and gotten shot in the arm at the beginning of Cho's attack, was one of them. Later, Machingo and some of the other officers were moved to McBryde Hall to decompress. Taking only a brief respite, they went quickly back into action clearing other buildings of the campus quadrant in which Norris Hall stood. "I'm okay," Ben later told his wife when he had a moment to phone. "What in the hell is going on?" she asked. But he didn't have any answers.

—

At 10:08 a.m. the two teams moved southward along the second floor of Norris Hall, attempting to determine whether any students were alive and the location of the shooter or shooters. The largely Blacksburg-comprised Team One was also joined by VTPD Lt. Scott Lau and Sgt. Jaret Reece. All three teams had been making tactical movements to rescue victims or clear spaces on the second floor. But they had begun this process in the even-numbered classrooms on the west side of the hall. At this time Emily Haas, who was still on Colin Goddard's cell phone, told Lt. Deborah Morgan that the shooter was in room 211 with her. Whispering, she said that she believed he was dead, but did not want to move, lift her head or even open her eyes to find out. She stated that there was only one shooter. The human mind plays tricks on people when they are involved in traumatic critical incidents and Debbie Morgan was no exception. She readily admits that there are "bits and pieces of time" and certain things that she just "doesn't remember."

Eventually Emily must have looked up, though she didn't seem to remember it later. She verified that Cho was in 211 and dead. Her information was immediately relayed to the teams, but only that the shooter was in 211. They weren't told that he had taken his own life. Virginia Tech dispatch merely advised that they had a caller on the line who stated that she was in room 211 and that the "shooter is also in the room." Teams One and Three immediately moved to room 211 in tandem.

While part of Team Three was clearing the third floor, and most of the rest was on the second floor having come in behind Wilson's Team One, Lt. Cook heard the transmission that the shooter was in room 211. "We went straight there from our end of the hall, and the rest of my team came down the western stairs from the third floor." But the door was blocked. Lt. Morgan was still trying to get information from Emily Haas and to see if she could let the team in the door. Morgan said to her: "The police are at your door. Can you get up and open the door?" Emily got up and moved to the door. She tried not to look at Cho. She tried to pull the door open but it just slammed shut on her. It is likely that she was in shock and at first did not notice the bodies of her teacher and classmate propped against it.

Tall and bulky Tom Gallemore was already attempting to push the door to the room open, his gashed hand leaving bloody smears across the wood. But each time he shoved, it slammed back on him. He called for anybody inside who could to come to the door. Emily Haas, bleeding from her head wounds, and Clay Violand – the only person to escape the room unscathed – both walked up to the door, but no one opened it. Morgan heard the rescuers at the classroom door over the phone. She kept trying to convince Emily to open the door for the officers. Emily then told Morgan that she couldn't get the door open because of the two bodies lying in front of it, and Morgan relayed this to the officers. Both of the entry teams stacked outside the door. Gallemore was the point man in the lead stack of VTPD's Team Three outside the classroom door. He was ready to face the shooter he believed was just inside.

Gallemore is a big, strapping country-looking man with a gentle demeanor and boyish smile. He looks like the kind of guy who always loved to hear the "blitz" call in a football game, no matter which side of the ball he was on. Born in Heidelberg, Germany to a military father, he largely grew up along the West Virginia border. He served in both the active duty Army and Reserves, and by 1999 was working for the Virginia Department of Corrections on the DOC Strike Force rapid reaction team. He moved over to VTPD in January 2003, and joined the ERT in April 2004. On April 16 he was an entry team leader and inside Norris Hall assumed that position without having to be told. At the time he was 32 years old.

The silence was deafening and the smell of freshly fired gunpowder still lingered in the hallway as Hardy, along with Curtis Cook, Sean Smith, Geoffrey Allen and Tom Gallemore, stacked on one side of the door that led into room 211. Seeing the evidence and carnage in the second floor hallway Daniel Hardy thought, "there must be a second shooter." The shooting had stopped but there had been so much more for Hardy and the other officers to do. They had needed to secure the area, check for other shooters and get treatment for the kids. Now they were ready to do battle with the perpetrators of the horror they were seeing.

Gallemore tried to push the door open but it slammed shut. Then it opened partially from the inside and closed once more. Cook had glimpsed a blonde-haired girl's face inside the room as the door popped briefly open. He believed this might be Emily Haas, who had been on the phone with the police dispatcher throughout the attack. "He is holding her hostage," Cook thought. "The shooter must be behind the door."

The door banged closed in their faces once again. Per Cook, "It opened and shut several times." Cook yelled to the beefy lineman-sized officer: "Tom, shoulder that door!" Gallemore had already decided that, no matter what, he was forcing himself in the next time. "Oh shit we're going to encounter somebody," the SWAT cop thought as he prepared to make a final attempt to enter the room. Believing that the shooter was just inside the door Cook said, "I was worried that the first two guys to move through that door might be dead meat." But they were top level operators and knew what they were doing. As their commander he had to rely on their skill and training. What they couldn't have known was that Cho had propped the bodies of French professor Jacqueline Couture-Nowak and student Henry Lee against the door and they were jammed under the bottom of it, only allowing it to be opened a few inches before their weight slammed it shut. They could not possibly have fallen in those positions on their own as they had been dead since Cho's first entry into the room.

Gallemore had been hitting the door and announcing himself as a police officer to all inside. Everyone behind him started talking at once and he had to yell at them to "Shut up!" He yelled at the dispatcher to get Emily out of the way if she could move. "Tell her to step back," he said. As he hit the door a third time, sweeping it completely open with one huge arm, he burst into the room. The bodies were swept into the corner behind the door in sitting positions. There they would remain, upright in the corner, leaning against one another in repose. Lt. Cook says simply, "He did it and we got in." But there is obvious pride in the commander's recounting of the Herculean feat of his young sergeant. "We made a textbook dynamic entry, and they did it great," he said. Cook was "proud of the team's performance" but "shocked at the carnage." The cops were pouring inside yelling, "Hands up! Show us your hands!" "This is worse than we thought," Cook said to his friend and counterpart on the Blacksburg ERT, Anthony Wilson. Wilson's blue eyes had gone to ice.

Gallemore had moved in first, matching his speeding entry to the swinging door. Allen was right behind him, then followed by the diminutive Hardy, Sean Smith, and finally Cook. They all burst into the room and immediately took positions covering the entire area with their weapons, ready to fire at the first sign of a threat. One of the female students had been pulled out behind Gallemore as he entered, even as the other cops were sweeping into the room. It was Emily Haas. Cook thought that somehow Gallemore had yanked her out the door even as he exploded into the room. "I think that then the chief [Flinchum] took her out of the building, but I'm not sure," said Cook. Like the others they have large holes in their recollections of specific events. He struggles to remember to this day. But Gallemore doesn't remember doing it, and thinks one of the other cops grabbed her and yanked her out the door past the big SWAT sergeant, believing he was rescuing her from a gunman just inside.

Wendell Flinchum does remember. He didn't take her from the room, but minutes later encountered her all alone on the southern second floor landing bleeding from her neck wound. He led her to Lt. Bradbery's police vehicle outside the Drillfield door to be triaged and transported to the hospital. As the cops were moving into 211 Allison Cook, who had been shot three times in the leg, walked out under her own power. She just managed to squeeze quickly past the hulking Gallemore and into the hall. Charles Violand walked out after her. He doesn't remember seeing his teacher dead or anyone outside the immediate vicinity of the desk he had been hiding under.[282]

Gallemore immediately saw the two guns on the classroom floor, and the black vest-clad Asian male lying at the front of the room. This was consistent with the suspect information that they had received from other students prior to entering the room. The self-inflicted gunshot wound to the left temple had clearly left him dead. Daniel Hardy was at the back of gargantuan Tom Gallemore. Hardy grabbed Cho's 9mm Glock and rendered it safe, then handed it to Allen. Gallemore picked up and cleared the Walther .22 then stuck

282 Ripley, p. 170.

it in his belt. Cho was on his back. Hardy flipped him over onto this stomach and saw gray matter falling out of his skull. Though there was no way Cho could be alive Hardy, with a nod of approval from Cook, cuffed his hands behind his back. Cops – like soldiers – had all seen too many corpses suddenly come back to life and kill innocent people. They were taking no chances. Standing in the midst of the bloodiest crime scene that he had ever seen his mind was processing what Gallemore, the cop, needed to do. He was trying to suppress the horror that Tom, the person, was witnessing.

Though there was no identification on the body, Lt. Cook immediately announced on his police radio: "Shooter Down! Shooter Down!" It was 10:08 a.m. Cho had been dead for 16 minutes. Cho's entire shooting spree, at its greatest estimate, had lasted only 11 minutes.[283] From the point at which the first 911 call was received and officers dispatched to Norris Hall until his suicide, less than nine minutes had elapsed. From the time the officers first arrived at Norris Hall in their vehicles, until gaining entry into a barricaded building took five minutes. From entry until movement toward the shooter forced him to take his own life rather than confront police, took 28 seconds. With regard to Air Force Cadet Matt LaPorte, Lt. Cook said, "What that kid did gave us an edge in what we did and were able to do."

Jersey had moved straight to room 211 when the information was given that the shooter was there. "Daniel Hardy is already in there. He has Cho facedown with handcuffs on," he recalled. Geoff Allen had somehow worked his way to the back of the classroom but could not get back, trapped by the immense tangle of desks and bodies – living and dead - strewn throughout. Jersey saw three other cops also in the back. He yelled at them to start looking for anyone still breathing. "One girl in the rear right of the room had a gunshot wound to the chest." He can't remember who she was or even what she looked like. His eyes and brain were focused only on the students' wounds. Geoff Allen was right by her, and Jersey threw him an

283 GPR, p. 28.

Asherman chest seal. But Geoff had never seen one before and just held it against her wound, still in the package. Jersey had to show him how to tear it open and apply it.

At that point Allen saw movement at the back of the room. Up to that time, with the exception of the two girls and Clay Violand who immediately went through the door after the police rushed in, there had not been any motion. Not a sound was heard, and they had no reason to believe anyone else was alive. Blood, brains and twisted bodies were everywhere. This would be replayed in room after room. The students had no idea that the men then in control of the building were actually police. Anyone could yell "Police!" They had lain there taking bullet after bullet from Cho, not uttering a sound. Not a peep or a moan was made, as the shooter would have known someone was alive and delivered the fatal headshot that took the lives of so many. Most wouldn't even open their eyes to see who was in the room.

This was not what Blacksburg patrolman Shannon Combs had trained for or expected in an active shooter case. He had anticipated mass hysteria and noise. Instead there was not a peep, only "dead silence." Combs remembered the smell of exploded gunpowder, the cloud in the hallway, and the metallic smell of blood everywhere. These were unmistakable sights and smells; ones that you never forgot. Ones that you hoped to never experience again. In the rooms, the first time police would know anyone was alive at all was when a hand would reach out from a tangle of bloodied bodies and grab the pants leg of an officer. As he moved slowly, stepping over and around the bodies, weapon at the ready, Geoff Allen's mind flashed back to a scene from the movie *Titanic*, where after the giant ship had slipped beneath the waves lifesavers were yelling, "Is anybody alive?" He suddenly found himself a part of that very scene being played out in the classrooms throughout the second floor.

The movement Allen had keyed on in the back of 211 was Heidi Miller. Tall and redheaded, she had been shot three times including once from the back of her leg that destroyed her knee cap. Colin Goddard was also toward the back of the room, about two desks up from the rear wall on the right side as you faced the class from the front. He was alone, lying under a desk, Allen recalled. Allen first helped move Heidi out of the room. He then went to help Goddard and others. Pretty and slender Kristina Heeger couldn't move. Though she was wearing a white top the police saw no blood. However, she had a .22 round lodged low in her spine. She couldn't feel anything. As there was little to no bleeding Jersey decided not to put any kind of bandage on it at that point. He didn't want to risk spinal cord damage. At this point Colin Goddard started screaming which set others off, including Heidi. Until then all Heidi could think was how horrible it must be for the police officers to come in there and see them all like that. She pitied them.

Gallemore then began rendering aid to beautiful, raven-haired Hillary Strollo who was lying on the floor next to Rachel Hill. Rachel had been in the first occupied seat just inside the door along the wall to Cho's left when he initially burst into the room. It appeared she was the first to be shot. She knew nothing was happening and died in her chair. Hillary was shot multiple times, including in the head and through the buttocks and liver. She had one bullet lodged in her spine. Gallemore asked her name, but he couldn't hear what she said clearly. He replied, "Okay Katie, you're going to be okay." Despite her wounds and indescribable pain, the strength of her character came through and she corrected him, but he still couldn't understand her. He called her Katie again, and she corrected him once more. Finally the young sergeant said, "Well, today you're going to be Katie."

Jersey triaged and provided immediate treatment to those he was able in room 211, then began moving from room to room doing what else he could. In the rush of trying to be everywhere for everyone, with people bleeding all around him, he admitted that he somehow "lost five minutes of time somewhere." The number of dead and dying was overwhelming. He radioed in and said that he had approximately 40 to 50 patients. He was hoping he was over-estimating, but wanted to err on the side of big numbers to ensure that sufficient resources arrived and that the hospitals would be ready.

The most difficult part for George Jackson doing his job amidst the carnage was the constant vibration of the students' cell phones. He did not want to turn them off because if the parents realized the phone was off, "they would assume the worst." He remembers one cell phone he recovered during the evidence search. The last text that it had received read: "Please call Mom."

Capt. Goodman stated that all of the officers that arrived at Norris Hall during the shootings maneuvered aggressively and either attempted to enter the building or took forward positions. Not a single officer withdrew or attempted to move outside the danger zone. Because of that they were able to save many lives.

10:09 a.m. to 12:00 noon

Cook advised all those listening to their radios that there were multiple casualties inside room 211. As the bodies piled up and strewn about were still restricting the movement of police, medics, and the evacuation of the wounded, Capt. Goodman, who had come in behind the entry team, had the bodies moved.

Police accessing room 211 provided the first suspect description over the radio: Asian male, khaki pants, black vest. When Cho was identified as the shooter in room 211 Cook wondered if it wasn't a whole Asian gang that had attacked the building. As they moved through the room Gallemore told Cook that he found a phone that was on. "We have an open phone line, do you want me to close it?" he queried his commander. Cook told him to shut it off. "I didn't want whoever was on the other end to hear what was going on. I knew it would be ugly," he recalled. Morgan had heard Sgt. Gallemore breach the classroom door. The cell phone was then suddenly turned off. The phone that was on was the one that Emily Haas had been using, though no one could have known that a dispatcher was on the other end. It had "only been somewhere around ten minutes," but according to Deborah Morgan, "it felt like four hours."

At that point he looked over to his friend and counterpart from Blacksburg, ERT leader Anthony Wilson. They locked eyes.

He said, "Anthony, this is a lot worse than we thought it was." "I remember seeing these kids and seeing my own kids in my mind and thinking 'how are we going to tell these parents about this'?" Cook told us later.

In all, a total of 61 shots were fired by Cho in room 211. Thirty-six 9mm bullet casings were found, along with 25 .22 caliber casings. Three magazines which contained a total of eight rounds between them and four empty magazines were recovered. Wounded were: Allison Cook; Colin Goddard; Emily Haas; Kristina Heeger; Heidi Miller; and Hillary Strollo. Ross Alameddine; Austin Cloyd; Caitlin Hammaren; Rachel Hill; Matthew LaPorte; Henry Lee; Daniel Perez; Erin Peterson; Mary Read; Reema Samaha; Leslie Sherman; and Jocelyne Couture-Nowak, all died.

Cook said to everyone: "We need to maintain a dynamic team and start clearing rooms." "We called room 206 the *Death Room*," Cook admitted. This was not the dark humor police were notorious for. They were all in shock. The room was horrific. Simply, they didn't know how else to refer to it. No one who had been in room 206 escaped being shot, and only three would live. Cook told Daniel Hardy and Scott Lau to go in there and check for vital signs. "The room was a mess, a horror," Cook recounts. "I don't think I could have done it myself." Anthony Wilson was yelling, "We've got to get help in here!"

"Police, anybody alive!?" Daniel Hardy yelled as he entered Room 206 along with Joe Shanks and Scott Lau. The carnage was beyond belief. The officers began to move around the classroom and began checking the bodies for a pulse or signs of life. There were 13 bodies strewn across the classroom, some piled on top of each other. Only three of these showed signs of life and were triaged and sent to the hospital for treatment and recovery.

Room 206 was also the first room that Chief Flinchum entered. He, too, was looking at the spent cartridges and different calibers, and the carnage. "It was the first room I went into. All I could think was, 'How in the hell did one person do all this'?" "However, as soon as

I knew there really was only the one gunman and the building was secure, I went from being a cop back to being a commander."

As Hardy moved around the other rooms on the second floor searching for victims and possibly other shooters, he remained mindful of other threats that might be lying in wait. He could not comprehend the amount of damage that he was currently witnessing was the result of one individual's twisted mind. In the midst of frantic efforts to save lives, Lt. Bradbery took a quick minute to phone his wife. He had no idea how the press was reporting this, and didn't want her to worry about him. "I'm okay," he said, "but whatever you've heard, take the worst case and multiply it by 20 and that's what we're standing in."[284]

—

At that point Curtis Cook called for "Rescue Teams!" over the radio to get the civilian paramedics waiting outside to come into the building and start triaging the casualties. The police were overwhelmed and Cook knew he needed more paramedics to help handle this. The wounds were too severe and the number of wounded too great for the two tactical medics they had inside with them, who were racing frantically about trying to treat everyone at once. Kids were bleeding out and there was only so much they could do. Cops – trained to never touch a bleeding person but to stand back and let the medical professionals do it – were working feverishly on anyone they found, doing what they could, their hands and arms sticky with blood.

The phrase Cook had used to get the medics huddled outside into the building created a misunderstanding between the police and the medical services. April Blankenship, the dispatcher he had spoken to had an EMS background. She said that the teams wouldn't come in until the scene was secure. She simply wasn't understanding the terminology that Cook was using. EMS units don't normally enter a hot zone, insisting on remaining outside a building until it has been cleared and secured. Police units rush into those same sites to save

284 Horwitz,"Revisiting Va. Tech."

others in the midst of the very threats the paramedics avoid. None of the units were sure what the command really meant. They didn't know if Cook was calling the tac medics or telling the paramedics outside that it was safe to enter the building. In reality he needed, and was asking for, both. They needed all the help they could get before any more people died. April radioed what she thought Cook wanted: "Virginia Tech to Jersey, Lt. Cook needs rescue." Exasperated at the refusal of critical medical personnel to get their "asses in the building," Cook told Wooddell to "go down there and drag their asses up here." Cook then used his command status to accomplish the one thing quickly he did have control over. Getting back on the radio he demanded "Police rescue teams!" Jim Cornwell then got on the radio to him and replied that the teams were just outside and would be in right away.

Three years later April swore that she would never allow a miscommunication to happen again. Not to her, and not to anyone she ever trained. She recognized that terminology was critically important when involved in emergency services. A caring professional, it was clear that she had beat herself up over that one mishap ever since. "I felt that I could have gotten them there faster," she admitted.

Cook and the other officers secured the rest of the rooms but found no other assailants. Looking at the number of rounds and magazines expended throughout the hall and inside the classrooms it was hard for the cops to accept that it could have been the work of a single shooter. After what they had already had to deal with that morning at West AJ, they simply weren't going to accept it. "What's next?", so many of them wondered. They would stay geared up and ready throughout the day and into the night. It would be almost 24 hours before they would allow themselves to relax at all and be satisfied there had not been other shooters who managed to escape the building. The carnage, the dead and dying, the wounded, were all simply too great for them to accept anything else.

Aftermath

As the building was being swept and secured, and the wounded given life-saving treatment, all other available rescue assets were called for and staged in close proximity to Norris Hall. The tac medics had to move their initial triage and treatment CCP from the western second floor stairwell landing to the southern end of the hallway as that was the established evacuation point for all wounded. They were all being carried down the southern steps, bursting out those doors into the chill wind. The building walls and billowing snow were made eerily red by the lights of the police cars and ambulances parked just outside. If there was one color no one wanted to see any more of, it was red. Even the cops' uniforms and faces appeared awash in blood from the crimson glare. It was hard to tell what was real and what was not.

No matter what the students told them, the officers and commanders inside Norris Hall continued to function under a worst case scenario; that the entire thing could kick off again at any moment. Tactical teams were redeployed to clear all rooms in Norris Hall. Other officers that had been arriving from countless jurisdictions around the region provided support to the rescue effort and otherwise served to form a very large perimeter. As word had spread across police commo networks that a massacre was occurring at VT, and that the police there were desperately engaged, cops came flying in from everywhere. They knew nothing other than that innocent college kids were being shot down. They didn't ask any questions, nor did they question their own motives. They simply came. And they came fast. Three hundred police officers would converge on the campus within an hour.

Police teams continued to locate wounded victims in rooms 204, 206, 207 and 211. At first it appeared that every single student was fatally wounded or dead. Even the few students not shot were covered with blood. On closer examination, viable victims were identified but had to be coaxed by officers into conversation or movement. Some were discovered hiding beneath the bodies of their deceased friends and classmates, playing dead or in shock. Some were unconscious. Several officers made their way into room 205 and were met by the classroom full of students who had successfully held the shooter out. Scott Lau along with Daniel Hardy, who seemed to be everywhere, were the first cops inside 205, bursting into the room yelling, "Show me your hands! Show me your hands!" A male student refused. Lau almost shot him. He later resigned from the ERT, and in August 2009 was assigned as the VTPD's representative on the FBI's Joint Terrorism Task Force.

Upon determining that no threats existed among the students in the room and that no one had been harmed, they were removed to a secure area. Grad student and teaching assistant Haiyan Cheng related this experience in a filmed interview the following morning. Hardy instructed a patrol officer with a shotgun to keep the kids safe.

Hardy and Chief Crannis would then enter and clear room 200 alone, the room in which Cho had dressed for his attack. Chief Crannis had immediately gone to Lt. Cook and said, "Tell me what you need me to do." Despite being the chief of another agency all she could think to do was pitch in and help. "Thank God it's empty," Hardy thought as they entered 200. The young officer never thought about these types of scenes when he was growing up as a law enforcement Explorer back in Pittsylvania County, Virginia. That was the final room. At least the second floor of that wing was secure.

Perimeter and arriving officers were directed to form rescue teams and report to the second floor to remove the victims. Ambulances were staged on Old Turner and Stanger Streets to the northeast as well as in the Alumni Mall area of the campus, to the east of the Drillfield. Still, no helicopters could be put into the air due to the wind and freezing snow and rain. Officers were ordered to continue clearing the building and protect the rescue effort as the possibility of additional shooters had not been ruled out, nor did they discount the possibility of explosive devices. The bomb threats were still fresh in their minds. A number of first floor rooms that were locked were breached with rams and hammers Cook told us.

However, the problem was that this would result in a hole being punched in the wood before the lock mechanism would give way. The GPR noted that the police had their priorities in order in being extremely cautious.[285] Security teams were formed and continued to breach doors and secure the multiple rooms and spaces throughout the three floors and two wings of Norris Hall, and controlled access to the entire Norris-Holden-Burruss area.

—

At 10:00 a.m. the hospital was notified that "multiple gunshot victims were confirmed" at the university and would be on their way. Code Green, the disaster code for all employees, was broadcast throughout the building. At 10:05 Jeffrey Twiggs arrived on the area bus with a compound fracture of his leg, earned when he leapt from the window of room 204. By 10:15 a.m. two gunshot victims had rolled up in an ambulance. Charlie Smith and others met all the arriving units at the door, triaged them and directed them inside for treatment. The female victims presented a particular problem as none of them had identification because they had left their purses in the classrooms, and they couldn't have more than one "Jane Doe" listed in the casualty environment. The medical examiner needed fingerprints to identify a number of the bodies and police had to go to the homes to obtain samples for comparison. With this battlefield environment unfolding in the Emergency Department Charlie said that all the hospital clinical directors were ordered to the Emergency Room to assist in the care and treatment of the arriving wounded. With the word rapidly spreading through the surrounding communities about the Virginia Tech shootings, additional staff started arriving at the hospital without even being called to report for duty.

At 10:30 a.m. four more gunshot victims arrived at the hospital. Smith was outside helping remove the patients from the vehicle. He remembered thinking that this was like the old prank of how "many students can you put in a telephone booth?" He couldn't

285 GPR, p. 98.

figure out how they all fit in the back of that ambulance. The hospital went into lockdown, and all elective surgeries and non-essential procedures were cancelled to free up surgeons and surgical teams, personnel and beds for the "incoming casualties." When your hear Charlie Smith relate these events, followed by descriptions of blood gushing everywhere while teams of medics, nurses and doctors drove their hands and arms into wounded kids, images from the TV series *MASH* force their way into your mind. But there would be no comic relief for anyone that day. Certainly there would be none for the victims.

About six minutes later, the news media arrived at Montgomery Regional. As the security chief at the hospital they would prove to be one of Smith's greatest challenges throughout the coming week. Smith felt that the hospital had the responsibility to provide security to protect the patients and their parents from the press, and their constant attempts to pry into the lives of the grieving families.

—

At the VT Communications Division the phones started ringing and didn't stop. They would never even make it back into their cradles before going off again. News media, parents, psychics, medical units, and other law enforcement agencies were all wanting information. The list of callers was unending. Then the front door of the police department opened and in walked a crew from *FOX News*. They wanted answers, answers that Deborah Morgan didn't have and at that point could not release even if she had them. They handed her a written request for the 911 tapes. The smell of gunpowder and blood hadn't even begun to dissipate inside Norris Hall yet.

—

Once Norris Hall appeared to be somewhat under control, Donnie Goodman wasted no time. He knew that there were plenty of qualified officers dealing with issues inside of the building. Though he had been with the two police chiefs in breaching the breezeway doors, he immediately recognized that he could better serve the wounded kids elsewhere.

At first he went down the first floor at the door into the machine shop. They were evacuating kids out of the external machine shop door the police had breached. They were all walking and Donnie started asking if they were hurt, how many shooters there were, etc. Quickly he heard a call over the radio that they had to "blown the inside south door" and Donnie headed straight there.

Students were being brought out of the Drillfield doors, but cops were carrying and dragging them more than 100 yards to waiting vehicles on Drillfield Drive. Goodman, weapon drawn against the possibility of other shooters suddenly opening up on the wounded and police from windows, sprinted downhill for the Drillfield entrance. As he raced down the embankment between the two building entrances his feet flew out from under him on the ice and snow packed slope, sending him tumbling down the hill. As a police captain he was required to be attired in his formal dress blue uniform, with military-style low quarter dress shoes. Shoes that had no tread on the soles. He had never imagined being called into a virtual combat zone that morning when he had dressed for work. Two days after the event he swore that would never again "wear those damn shiny shoes." He thanked excellent trigger-finger weapon safety training for the fact that he did not end up spraying bullets in all directions, including into himself, as he tumbled down the lawn. He popped to his feet, covered in snow and ice, weapon still in hand and ready, and continued toward the southern entrance.

Outside of the southern doors, together Goodman and Hawkins tried unsuccessfully to convince the EMS rescue units who were holding position some distance from the building to move inside the perimeter that had been quickly established. By then Lt. Bradbery had made four trips carrying multiple wounded all the way down to the street. Goodman ordered the police to start driving their "damn cars up the hill to the doors" rather than force other cops to continue carrying and dragging wounded kids all the way to the street. At Goodman's direction Hawkins assisted the injured students into police vehicles so that they could be driven to medical units for transportation to the hospital.

Rebecca Hawkins, with no sleep in almost 24 hours, held her post outside the southern doors until three o'clock that afternoon. She put "crime scene" tape up around the entire area, from Drillfield Drive up to the building. She was running on nothing but adrenaline, and was starting to feel the stress and tension of the long hours at work and the malignancy of the attack that had just unfolded at the school she was committed to keeping safe. "I couldn't even sleep that night [the 16th]," she later said. "Maybe just one hour." She doesn't even remember whether she worked the following day. As of her interview with us in the fall of 2009 she had been assigned to a drug task force with officers from three counties and the state police.

"When are they going to stop coming out?", Goodman wondered as the stream of students being carried or stumbling out of Norris Hall seemed endless. He kept asking them if they were shot, and one male said, "Yes, I'm shot." But he just kept going. Donnie had to literally put him on the ground to stop him. "I don't know how many times Todd Rutledge kept going back in and bringing wounded out," Donnie said later. "I don't know how many times anyone did. We were covering wounded up with our coats." He remembers Hillary Strollo being so severely wounded. Donnie almost lost control emotionally at that point. "I remember getting choked up when I saw Hillary," he recounted later. "I kept telling her not to die." When he saw her all he could think of was his own young daughter, Jennifer, then a student a Radford University. She had just sent him a text that read: "I love you Daddy, be careful." The day Morva escaped had been his own daughter's first day at Radford. He had insisted on taking her to school that day until the call out came. In the midst of that chaos and fear he had gotten a text from her then too. That one said simply: "Daddy, I love you." He had saved both of them on his phone for years. Press photos of victims being removed from Norris

Hall by officers were actually of the last three living victims removed from Norris Hall: Hillary Strollo, Kristina Heeger and Kevin Sterne. "What is going to happen next?" Donnie wondered.

Goodman told us that a lot of his daughter's friends who she had grown up with were then at Tech. "Please don't make me have to tell parents I know that their daughter has died," he prayed. "As a cop they teach you to kill. They teach you to do first aid," he told us. "But they don't teach you to deal with wounded. Just what do you say to them?" he asked. "What do you say to a beautiful 19-year-old girl who's just shot to shit? I'd know what to say to one of my officers, but not to a young girl whose only crime was that she went to class, who did everything right," he explained. It was clear that right then, in that moment with Hillary Strollo bleeding in front of him, that it was almost more than he could take. It was more than any of them would ever be able to take.

Donnie told us that his father, Richard Goodman, was a seaman first class who served in the Pacific in World War II. His ship had been hit by a kamikaze plane attack during the battle of Iwo Jima. "Like me, my dad was a small guy," Donnie said. Because of that they had tied a rope to him and lowered him into the hold of his ship to retrieve the sailors' bodies. A few months after the VT shootings his father told him that story for the first time. Donnie said, "Dad, I didn't know that. You never told me." Like most World War II veterans, his father never talked about the event that had defined so much of his life. After having heard what Donnie had gone through and dealt with he said, "Well, son, I figured that now you would understand." Donnie wipes his eyes as he tells this story.

Norris Hall may not have been a crippled ship off the coast of Iwo Jima. But the ages of the students were the same as those comrades of Richard Goodman, whose burned corpses he had plunged time and again into cold, oil and blood slicked seawater inside of his ruptured ship to retrieve. And these were Donnie Goodman's kids, people he had felt responsible for. Yes, he could indeed understand what his father had gone through. Seeing the condition of the dying as they were carried from the building, and the courage of the "walking wounded" caused a groundswell of emotion inside of him. He remembered "one Middle Eastern guy completely covered in blood." He had a .22 caliber round in his head, under the skin. He handed Donnie his cell phone and asked if he could please call his wife for him. Another African American man had bullets in each leg, but managed to walk out of the doors saying, "Praise Jesus!"

"It's all really just a blur," Morgan Millirons confessed as he recalled carrying the injured students out of the bloodbath. "There must have been a crazy man in here," he had thought as he surveyed the damage done by Cho. The horror of people looking for their children and trying to get into Norris Hall to find them played over many times in his mind. Many parents, unable to reach their kids by phone since the system had become quickly overloaded had simply headed right there. One father with a picture looking for his child is etched in the stone of Millirons' mind.

As the kids kept coming out of Norris Hall Donnie Goodman was worried that if something else happened he knew he had wounded to protect, and he just didn't know "what was next." As all rooms in Norris Hall were being cleared and secured, and wounded students were being transported to area hospitals, at 10:17 a.m. a third email was sent to the VT community. It read:

> Subject: All Classes Canceled; Stay where you are.
>
> Virginia Tech has canceled all classes. Those on campus are asked to remain where they are, lock their doors and stay away from windows. Persons off campus are asked not to come to campus.
>
> All people in university buildings are required to stay inside until further notice.[286]

Much criticism would be heaped on the Policy Group for these emails as being uninformative and inexcusably delayed.

286 Newsmedia, including the *Collegiate Times*, reported this email being sent at 10:26.

—

With the wounded still coming out, the cops were on a hair trigger. They had all received the description of Cho. They still would not accept that a single shooter had caused all the destruction. The media had been kept well back. Then suddenly an Asian male face was seen peering around the corner of Burruss Hall. Then an optic was put up to his face. Fearing that this was part of a gang attack the police pounced on him, quickly cuffing his hands behind his back. He was a reporter for *The Collegiate Times* who had simply picked the wrong place and moment to assert first amendment press freedoms. One cop said that he almost got his head blown off. By 10:51 a.m. all of the wounded from Norris Hall had been transported to hospitals or to a minor treatment unit. Ultimately, after being treated by the tac medics and police, every single person who was alive when he or she left Norris Hall would survive. Between 10:45 and 10:55 a.m. five more Virginia Tech students arrived in three different ambulances. According to Smith, the hospital was on "critical divert," which meant that it was only accepting patients from the university. Other emergency patients were sent to different area hospitals.

At 10:50 a.m. both chiefs, Flinchum and Crannis, had to go over to Burruss Hall to advise the Policy Group on all that had happened, all that they had seen. After what they had just been through, it was a lot to ask. Wendell Flinchum told them that it was very bad, that they had one shooter in custody but could not yet rule out the possibility of another shooter, or shooters. Nor could they yet link the two different sets of killings that morning. Based on this information the Policy Group immediately issued its final email to the students and campus community at 10:53:

> In addition to an earlier shooting today at West Ambler-Johnston, there has been a multiple shooting with multiple victims in Norris Hall. Police and EMS are on the scene. Police have one shooter in custody and as part of

> routine police procedure, they continue to search for a second shooter.
>
> All people in university buildings are required to stay inside until further notice. All entrances to campus are closed.[287]

At 10:57 a.m. an initial casualty count was taken in Norris Hall. All of the rooms in the building were secured of all but essential personnel, with sentry positions established to keep others out. Per the university, there should have been 148 students inside Norris Hall during that class period, although it was known that at least 31 had been absent. Of the 117 students inside, in addition to the myriad office and lab workers, maintenance staff and teachers, fully 42 had been shot. In the midst of such butchery Goodman had learned that many of the cops who had arrived from remote jurisdictions had been going into the building. This was to have been expected. Police live their lives every day out on an edge that most in society avoid even acknowledging exists. They stare into Nietzsche's abyss. It was important in what they do – and in what they know they may someday be summoned to do – for them to confront the worst humanity could throw at them. They had to know that they had stared into that abyss, and that the abyss had stared back into them. And they had to know that they had been up to that test.

Col. Dave Grossman calls it "psychological inoculation," and insists that it is as important in warriors as medical inoculations are to children, soldiers and even doctors working in diseased areas of the world. However, not all the officers were dealing well with what they were confronting inside. It was beyond imagining, and some were realizing that they were all-too-human after all. Goodman ordered everyone out except those whose presence was absolutely essential. How Wilson, Cook, Wooddell, Hardy, Crannis, Flinchum, Gallemore, Roe and all the others were holding it together he couldn't imagine.

287 *Wikipedia* and GPR claim this was at 10:52.

Even while still on the second floor of Norris Hall Chief Flinchum met the arrival of officers and agents from other departments. He requested the Virginia State Police agent take jurisdiction over the investigation. He knew his department would not be able to handle it under the circumstances. George Jackson was already at Norris trying to figure out how he was going to even begin to process it as a crime scene. He was quickly joined by a member of the Virginia State Police Crime Scene Unit and together they prepared a plan for processing all of various the crime scenes at Norris Hall. This included a roof access which had been unlocked by someone. It was possible that this was to have been a possible escape route for Cho that was foiled by the rapid arrival of the police, or even a planned shooting position.

Throughout Donnie Goodman – among others – was "all over the place." He'd worked the investigation, TCP, was at Blacksburg Police headquarters and all over the campus, including Norris and West Ambler-Johnston halls. "At the end of the day you just don't remember what all you did," he explained in a way that would articulate the experiences of many of the cops there. "Our fire department did a great job, showed up with its mobile CP with cases and cases of water for everyone," he proclaimed. However, it was hours before he would get so much as a sip. When he finally got to actually take a drink he remembered to call his wife Anne, but the phone system was still jammed and he couldn't get through. He thinks he tried again later, but couldn't get a call through then either. He's just not sure. Despite his lapses of memory about some of the things he did, he is full of praise for what he knows others accomplished. "Anthony [Wilson] did a tremendous job of getting all the other agencies in and set up," he says. "Then, on top of all that, we had the president come in." On the 17th the two commanders went together to see some of the kids in the hospitals. "I didn't know what to expect, if they were going to yell at us or what," Donnie recollects. "It was very good for us to see some actual living, breathing college kids."

Ultimately it would be determined that VTPD would keep the investigation of the original WAJ shootings, and the state police would investigate the Norris Hall attack. This continued until the lab confirmed matches between the two shootings. Ballistics tests conducted by the U.S. Bureau of Alcohol, Tobacco, Firearms' explosives lab in Maryland confirmed that the 9mm Glock had been used in both the WAJ and Norris Hall shootings.[288]

In addition to the 9mm Glock 19 semi-automatic handgun and .22 caliber Walther semi-automatic handgun that were recovered near Cho's body, a combat folding knife, fixed blade knife and claw hammer were all found in Cho's backpack left near the water fountain just outside the men's room. In all, Cho expended 174 rounds comprised of 113 9mm and 61 .22 caliber bullets. Seventeen empty – or near empty – magazines[289] were found inside Norris Hall, comprised of eight 9mm magazines and nine .22 caliber magazines. One hundred twenty-two 9mm and 81 .22 caliber live cartridges were found, including two pre-loaded high capacity 9mm 15-round magazines. Most of the additional 203 rounds were found in Cho's backpack. No other ammunition was ever found anywhere outside of Norris Hall, so there was no evidence that Cho intended to attack any other buildings, or escape Norris Hall in a running gunbattle. In addition, Cho had not yet moved to the west-east leg of Norris Hall, or any of the classrooms, labs or offices on the first and third floors.

—

At about 11:15 a.m. Montgomery Regional's hospital staff was getting confusing and sketchy information as to how many victims they would still be receiving. *There's more coming!? How could that be?* Charlie Smith had a Site Liaison Person sent to Norris Hall to provide the information in real time back to the Emergency Department to

288 "Investigation Update," *Virginia Tech: Archived News and Notices,* posted April 30, 2007, www.remembrance.vt.edu/2007/archive.

289 Cho didn't shoot all of his magazines empty, instead utilizing tactical opportunities to reload, a point we are confident will not be lost on law enforcement. Only 7 or 8 magazines of the total 17 were empty, though VSP Lt. Lyon says there 19.

help alleviate the confusion and conflicting reports. By 11:51 a.m. they were told that all patients had been transported to the hospitals.

Suddenly a report of a "shooting at Lee Hall" was received,[290] and numerous officers responded, racing to the dormitory a half mile for Norris Hall. Everyone believed that what they had been fearing for the past hour – that there were other shooters and it was all about to begin again – was happening. However, there were no other threats, and the "shots fired" report was false. The wounded female student who had raced past Donnie Goodman had managed to walk 943 yards to the tennis courts near Cassell Coliseum, where she collapsed. She was treated and survived her wounds.

—

The TV was turned on in the VTPD communications center so that they could put what they were hearing over the police radios in some context. An intern reported in and sat diagramming and highlighting maps for the incoming police who were unfamiliar with the campus. The Nextels went down because the circuits were jammed. Sprint responded immediately to the campus and put in a temporary tower. Deborah Morgan sat in the midst of the chaos and noise, nursing her own shock and wondering about the young girl that she had spoken with inside room 211. Of the more than 3,000 calls that came into her center that morning, that was the one that she remembered. Beyond that she was worried about all the others: the kids and the cops. She was very worried about her former instructor and boss, Wendell Flinchum. She remained on duty until about 3:00 a.m the next morning. After a short stop at home she was back on campus by 7:00 a.m.. These 14 to 16 hour days continued for quite some time. She can't even remember how long.

At 11:30 a.m. the Policy Group alerted faculty and all other employees to a planned evacuation of the university. On the Tech website they wrote:

290 Time based on VSP Salem Division Dispatch.

> Faculty and staff located on the Burruss Hall side of the drill field are asked to leave their office and go home immediately. Faculty and staff located on the War Memorial/Eggleston hall side of the drill field are asked to leave their offices and go home at 12:30 p.m.

One hour later, at 12:30 p.m., they amended the website notification:

> Virginia Tech has closed today Monday, April 16, 2007. On Tuesday, April 17, classes will be cancelled. The university will remain open for administrative operations. There will be an additional university statement presented today at noon.
>
> All students, faculty and staff are required to stay where they are until police execute a planned evacuation. A phased closing will be in effect today; further information will be forthcoming as soon as police secure the campus.
>
> Tomorrow there will be a university convocation/ceremony at noon at Cassell Coliseum. The Inn at Virginia Tech has been designated as the site for parents to gather and obtain information.

—

Over in the halls of the Montgomery County Courthouse, first the rumors had begun. Shortly after, accounts of Cho's rampage on the campus were being broadcast on any device capable of picking up a signal. Sharon Flinchum remembers the news accounts of the number of dead and wounded varying with every report, but never knowing who the victims were. The couple of hours seemed like forever to the terrified wife. "I didn't know what to do," Sharon recalls. By noon the Montgomery County Courthouse cancelled court as every cop there was being sent to Tech. Sharon was a Montgomery

County Prosecutor's Office employee and wife of Wendell Flinchum, the VT chief of police. Yet she had no idea what had been happening. It would all come quickly crashing down on her. They just left the TV on, waiting for reports. "Watching for and hearing the numbers of dead going up on the television was just awful. We didn't know if it was students, officers, teachers or what," she told us. Two hours in front of the TV seemed like forever to her. She didn't call her husband, however. As the wife of the chief she knew that the last thing he needed were distractions from the critical and life-saving tasks he had at hand. Still, not being able to talk to him was killing her.

She left work and headed for The Inn on campus, where the first press conference was to begin. Her husband acknowledged her with a glance. Their eyes met, but she didn't get a chance to actually talk to him. "Until that point I didn't know if he was dead or alive," she said. "But when I saw him, saw the look on his face, he looked like he had died." Sharon went home and glued herself to the TV for more information, and now admits that she foolishly believed the initial accounts from the media. As a concerned spouse, she became "worried about her husband's silence" about the event. She suddenly became very protective of her man. She knew that Wendell needed a supportive wife to help deal with the negativity that neither she nor he had ever confronted before in their lives. It came at them with the speed of a pack of rabid wolves, and hit with the impact of a hurricane. In the midst of that Wendell Flinchum, too, remembers wondering whether "the young girl, Emily" had lived. Clearly, Miss Haas had impressed many with her courage, tenacity and calm under fire, doing what many could not have done even as she was wounded.

—

At the same time Command Posts (CPs) were established in Norris and Burruss Halls. Then the noon press conference was held in the Holtzman Alumni Center at The Inn at Virginia Tech. The news reports were, as is typical, contradicting at first. Eyewitnesses had students jumping from windows of Norris Hall, though the local television stations reported such accounts with skepticism, seemingly convinced that they were the product of youthful exaggeration.[291] VT Police Chief Wendell Flinchum "wasn't the first to say the number twenty [dead], just the first to confirm it," lamented Lucinda Roy. "Hearing it from him was what made it real."[292] Dr. Roy, along with the rest of the nation, watched Chief Flinchum as he tried to withstand barrages of questions at that first press conference "hurled at him from reporters." Roy wrote, "I had no doubt that this tragedy would haunt him because it had happened on his watch. Some of those with guardianship responsibilities are able to shake these things off, move on. I felt instinctively that Chief Flinchum was not one of those men. The horror of this day would never really leave him. Like many others in the VTPD, he would have died to protect the students."[293]

I had watched Chief Flinchum try to hold it all together at that conference from my home in Colorado. In that instant he reminded me of Park County Sheriff Fred Wegener in the aftermath of the Platte Canyon High School hostage siege and death of 16-year-old Emily Keyes just seven months before. In both, the men trying to deal with the public presentation side of their respective atrocities were drawn, ashen, shaken and understandably guilt-ridden. Not that they had done anything wrong in either case, but no warrior – especially warrior-leaders – can confront such outcomes without feeling the soul-wrenching remorse of not having been able to save everyone. In fact Lucinda Roy's words had echoed that of John-Michael Keyes, father of Emily, as Fred Wegener, with trembling voice had announced that she had died. Rather than run for attorneys, John-Michael had embraced Fred before all of the assembled people and cameras, and clearly stated that he knew if Fred could, that he would in that instant give his life to bring Emily back. No one who had ever known Wendell Flinchum doubted the same about him. It wouldn't be until I communicated with Fred while at VT that I would learn that he and Wendell had actually been classmates at the FBI National

291 Roy, p. 20
292 Ibid.
293 Ibid.

Academy just two years before. Sadly, at that point they had far more in common than just police work and high level training by the nation's top law enforcement agency.

At the press conference at VT, the Associate Vice President of University Relations confirmed 22 dead and 15 wounded. According to the *Collegiate Times*:

> The number of casualties and fatalities escalated over the remainder of the afternoon to 32 dead and 29 wounded at the subsequent press conference at 4:30 p.m. Classes were cancelled, campus traffic was restricted and Gov. Tim Kaine declared Virginia to be in a state of emergency.[294]

At 12:42 p.m. VT President Charles Steger announced that police were releasing people from buildings they had been held in for medical observation and questioning, and that counseling centers were being established for everyone. Just after 1:00 p.m. two more patients arrived at Montgomery General from the rampage. These patients had transported themselves to the hospital. They would be the last to arrive at the hospital. At 1:30 p.m. Montgomery Regional Hospital was able to rescind its critical care divert status and terminated its disaster code. However, the last patient would not leave the operating room until 7:45 that night.

Then at 1:35 p.m. a 911 call came in reporting possible gunshots fired near the Duck Pond. The police, exhausted from all that they had been through, their nerves frayed and adrenaline levels continuing to suffer from the roller coaster effect of the day, went racing there. The report proved to be false.[295]

George Jackson recalls: "Most police officers can make sense of a domestic related homicide, but they just can't rationalize this type of event." The officers involved in anything that results in the death

294 Kevin Anderson and CT Staff, "Week of strength follows day of horros on campus," *Collegiate Times*, Special Edition, Monday, April 23, 2007, p. 1.
295 Time based on VSP Salem Division Dispatch.

of innocent people start to question themselves. Did we do the right thing? Did I get there quickly enough? The questions can be endless, and they were already starting to go through George's mind like a videotape on a loop, never-ending. April 16th became a very long day for the members of the Crime Scene Investigation unit, comprised of local, state, and federal law enforcement agencies. Jackson fingerprinted Cho at the scene. His identity still had not been made positively. In the backpack a receipt was found which ultimately helped them.

The victims' bodies had to be moved out of Norris Hall and Jackson knew that this had to be done quickly, efficiently and with the respect that was due them. Norris Hall had already become the center of national and international news reports. Jackson did not want the victims' families to be further victimized by media depictions of their loved ones. He decided to have the bodies removed surreptitiously in black bags through the breezeway that connected Norris Hall and Holden Hall.

The first corpse was not removed from Norris Hall and transported to the medical examiner's office until 5:00 p.m. however. The last deceased victim would not be moved until 8:45 that night. Someone gave the ambulances transporting the dead the order to go "lights and sirens" to the morgue. With the media having been kept at bay outside a perimeter that was established with a radius of hundreds of yards, all they had seen for hours was police standing their posts on that outer cordon. Standing there with their weapons drawn. Suddenly ambulances were racing out of the campus with lights and sirens blaring. They immediately speculated that shooting had been continuing on campus all this time while law enforcement officers had stood outside allowing kids to be shot down.

As soon as it was determined that at least one shooter – and the only one believed to be in Norris Hall – had been neutralized as a threat, all agencies immediately began transitioning into casualty care and evacuation mode, and campus security phases. Command staff set up a TCP in McBryde Hall immediately upon the commencement of the rescue effort at Norris Hall. At the same time, a 42-man outer perimeter was established,[296] and by 5:30 p.m. five surrounding-area SWAT teams with bomb dogs had completed clearing all buildings in that entire quadrant of the campus - approximately 20 in all.

Within a few hours Virginia Tech was already being called the largest mass killing in an American school, until research reminded the press that the explosives-based attack in Bath, Michigan in 1927 had yielded a bigger bodycount. Still, Virginia Tech was quickly labeled as the biggest mass shooting-murder at a U.S. school in history.[297] It took the *New York Times* only until early that afternoon to contact Professor Roy and ask her to write an op-ed on how the tragedy affected the VT community. It would run in the following morning's paper.[298] Yet how she, or anyone, could have been expected to articulate how the community was affected by a tragedy of such horrific proportions that no one yet knew the full magnitude of, or how it would affect the university in the future, is a mystery. One thing she knew for sure, however, was that Virginia Tech president, Charles W. Steger, was "visibly shaken," when he called the attack "a tragedy of monumental proportions."[299]

This was understandable, for Norris Hall was a mess and President Steger was trying to deal with the fact that a slaughter had taken place on his campus. By the time I first got into Norris Hall the bodies had been removed, but little else had been disturbed. Placing the positions of the dead and severely wounded was easy. Large pools of blood and spray from head wounds formed a gruesome kaleidoscope, and brain matter fouled the thin carpets. The desks were mostly still just where they had been found, where students had attempted to pull them over themselves for shelter. Or where the police had flung them as they tried to get to kids before they bled out on them. It was easy to find the few rounds of Cho's that had missed his intended

296 Many of the officers from various agencies standing post on the security perimeters would be the subject of news photos as long as two hours later, which were then reported as proof that police were doing nothing while children continued to be killed.

297 Roy, p. 22.

298 Roy, p. 23.

299 Roy, p. 21.

victims, though a number had clearly gone through someone before becoming embedded in a wall. The blood trail from Prof. Granata being drug down the hall by a brave Brian Rowe was evident, as were the telltale signs of a desperate medic frantically trying to save lives in a tiny stairwell landing. The officers didn't want to go back into the rooms with me as I walked about, measuring, assessing, trying to picture in my mind all that had gone on. No one could blame them. The rooms smelled of death and evil permeated the walls, hung in the air. Furtive glances into some of the rooms through haunted eyes were all that some of the cops were capable of. I could tell that in their minds the kids were all still lying there, crying out to them for help … others silenced forever. I knew that they didn't want to be there, would never again want to walk into either Norris Hall or West AJ. They had already seen enough.

—

By that evening a search warrant had been served at the home of Karl Thornhill, Emily Hilscher's boyfriend. Investigation would go on for some time as to whether there was any possible way that he could have been linked to the first crime. The two attacks would not be definitively tied together until the following day, Tuesday, April 17, 2007. When the police revealed that the shooter had been an Asian English major, Professor Roy received a call from a colleague suggesting that it might have been Seung-Hui Cho. She said that couldn't be true. Having lost contact with him during the sabbatical she had taken to Africa since resigning her position as head of the department she believed that Cho had already graduated.[300] Then on the morning of April 17 the university released his name. Dr. Roy would lament it was only then that she understood the depth of her own ignorance and "felt the excruciating pain" which came "with that realization" when she was forced to accept the fact that it was her own "brooding young English major … who wanted to be a writer and whose presence seemed to mimic absence," that had murdered 32 innocent

300 Roy, p. 23

people that day.[301] Finally everyone knew that Karl Thornhill had nothing to do with the death of his beautiful girlfriend, or of the young man who had died trying to protect her.

On Wednesday morning, April 18, Burruss Hall was evacuated in response to "an unfounded threat."[302] There would be numerous other threats and bomb scares in the coming days. Then at 4:30 p.m. that same day news broke that *NBC News'* New York office had received Cho's multi-media package that he had mailed between his two attacks. Cho had written a zip code that was erroneous by one digit in addressing the package, which had delayed its delivery. Cho's long, ranting and profanity-laced written diatribe was sent along with dozens of photographs and videos. In his videos he blamed the world, seemingly everyone from his own tortured past, and certainly the bright and beautiful young VT students and their dedicated professors, for his suffering:

> You sadistic snobs. I may be nothing but a piece of shit. You have vandalized my heart, raped my soul, and torched my conscience. You thought it was one pathetic boy's life you were extinguishing. Thanks to you, I die like Jesus Christ, to inspire generations of the weak and defenseless people. Do you know what it feels like to be spit on your face and to have trash shoved down your throat? Do you know what it feels like to dig your own grave? Do you know what it feels like to have your throat slashed from ear to ear? Do you know what it feels like to be torched alive? Do you know what it feels like to be humiliated and be impaled upon a cross? And left to bleed to death for your amusement? You have never felt a single ounce of pain your whole life. Yet you want to inject as much misery in our lives as you can just because you can? You had everything you

301 Roy, p. 24.

302 Kevin Anderson and CT Staff, "Week of Strength Follows Days of Horror on Campus", *Collegiate Times,* April 24, 2007, p. 2.

wanted. Your Mercedes wasn't enough, you brats. Your golden necklaces weren't enough, you snobs. Your trust fund wasn't enough. Your vodka and cognac weren't enough. All your debaucheries weren't enough. Those weren't enough to fulfill your hedonistic needs. You had everything.

When the time came, I did it. I had to... You had a hundred billion chances and ways to have avoided today, but you decided to spill my blood. You forced me into a corner and gave me only one option. The decision was yours. Now you have blood on your hands that will never wash off.

You just loved crucifying me. You loved inducing cancer into my head, terrorizing my heart, and raping my soul all of this time. ... I didn't have to do this. I could have left. I could have fled. But no, I will no longer run. If not for me, for my children, for my brothers and sisters that you fucked; I did it for them....

Oh the happiness I could have mingling among you hedonists, being counted as one of you, only if you didn't fuck the living shit out of me. You could have been great. I could have been great. Ask yourself what you did to me to have made me clean the slate. Are you happy now that you destroyed my life? Now that you've stolen everything you could from me? Now that you have gone on a 911 on my life like fucking Osama. Now you have fucked your own people like fucking Kim Jong Il. Now that you have gone on a hummer safari on my life like fucking Bush? Are you happy now?

> All the shit you've given me, right back at you with hollowpoints.[303] Don't you just wish you finished me off when you had the chance? Don't you just wish you killed me?
>
> You wanna rape us John Mark Karrs?[304] You wanna rape us Debra LaFaves?[305] Fuck you. Let the revolution begin!

The statement, "Don't you just wish you killed me?" was accompanied by two photos of drawings: one of a heart encompassing a cross with eyes over each of the arms; and the other of two interlaced number 8s, with the caption *Number of the Anti-Terrorist*. According to the Anti-Defamation League the eighth letter of the alphabet is "H", and double "8s" signify "HH." This is shorthand for the Nazi greeting "Heil Hitler." Eighty-eight is often found on hate group flyers, in both the greetings and closing comments of letters written by Neo Nazis, and in email addresses.[306]

Lucinda Roy would point out, however, that many of the students he killed had overcome financial woes and "economic hardship" themselves, to attend Virginia Tech. "Many were about as likely to have trust funds as he was," she wrote.[307]

—

As of noon on Monday, April 23, a full week after the attacks the local office of the FBI had not yet made any effort to interview the BPD tactical team. Reportedly, the Bureau had spent the interim days interviewing students, professors, parents, security and law enforcement officers who had been on the perimeter, or assisted in the recovery phase of the incident. No one seemed to want to talk to the cops who had actually dealt with it all. Also that day Cho's family was secluded

303 This statement was accompanied by a photo of a box of hollow point bullets.
304 One of the suspects in the murder of Jon Benet Ramsey in Boulder, Colorado.
305 A Florida school teacher who pled guilty to statutory rape in 2005 for having sex with one of her male students in a high profile case.
306 Database of Anti-Defamation League, www.adl.org/hate_symbols.
307 Roy, pp. 86-87.

under protection by the Virginia State Police and the FBI, according to Consul General Taemyon Kwon at the South Korean Embassy in Washington.

On Tuesday, April 24 VSP tac team members heard that VT students were circulating a petition stating that they believed the police had done nothing wrong, and had, in fact, performed well in responding to the shootings. Sitting in the bar at the top of a long, steep staircase on the main street of town called Big Al's every single night, reviewing our notes, working on our findings and drafting our AAR, everyone from Archangel got to spend a lot of time talking with the students. We didn't solicit it; they would just come by and say that they knew we weren't professors, that we didn't look like parents or reporters, and they knew we weren't students. So they would ask just who were we and what were we doing there? One young lady looked straight at Joe Bail and Chris Hays and said, "You've just got to be cops." To a person they were an impressive group of young men and women.

Also, to a person they told us that they didn't like it when the police wrote them speeding or parking tickets, or told them their parties were too loud, or they got in trouble for drinking on campus or in town. But the universal statement we heard was that despite all that they thought their cops were good people, were great at their jobs, and made them all feel safe. And that they believed the police *kept* them all safe. But at the time, with the news media eviscerating the brave men and women who had raced to Norris Hall, they weren't hearing too much in the way of compliments. Daily the two departments were receiving hundreds of letters and emails saying that they should kill themselves, blow their own brains out, that they were cowards and hid outside while innocent kids were shot down. We were informed by students on campus just a week and a half after the shootings that the petition already had more than 3,000 signatures.

Critical Incident Stress Management and support services were made available to all officers as this incident had affected them greatly. Whether they voluntarily took advantage of these counseling services or not, every single officer who had responded to either WAJ or Norris had to undergo one mandatory counseling session. The commanders we spoke with all said that they believed these services were very important, certainly to the officers. However, as was typical for cops not a single one of them corroborated this. Despite the availability of the counseling the officers had limited down time as the incident was ongoing. We saw scores of cops who had been at Norris in uniform, patrolling the campus, or stationed at the TOC at the top of the football stadium virtually around-the-clock, for days and weeks after the shootings. Various SWAT teams remained "tac'ed" up and ready to move at the first call signaling trouble. And those calls kept coming in, virtually all of them false alarms.

We wouldn't see Anthony Wilson out of his SWAT uniform for two weeks. Nor did we ever see him leave the campus, except perhaps to go to the Blacksburg headquarters. When he finally showed up one evening in Captain Goodman's office in civilian attire on his way to an investigation as a plainclothes detective we were all shocked. Suddenly he looked like a regular person; a normal guy. Without his military-style tactical gear and uniform he suddenly seemed somehow less formidable. It also appeared that with the shedding of his special operations attire – the same uniform and gear he had raced to Norris Hall and worked desperately to save students' lives in – that he had also shed a bit of the stress and horror of that day. He seemed somehow lighter, as though a weight had been lifted from his broad shoulders. As we chatted he even allowed a small, quick smile to play across his mouth. None of us had ever seen him smile before.

Roving patrols of two and three man SWAT teams scoured the campus day and night. Cops were everywhere, and they would remain so throughout the university until after graduation. I spent time driving through the campus with Curtis Cook, round and round, just letting the kids see his car. He was tense; ready for anything. The end of the semester couldn't come quickly enough. The police wanted the kids to know that there was no way any further harm was going to come to them. Many departments – including the Division

3 Virginia State Police SWAT team from Virginia Beach – contributed mightily to this effort and worked long shifts. Being mostly young males, the patrol teams delighted in returning to the TOC, proudly displaying cell phone photos of themselves with groups of beautiful young VT coeds. It was clear that the students were happy that they were there. It became almost a competition among the young officers: each trying to best the others with the most photos, or by having the prettiest girls in pictures with them. During short breaks they would gather in small groups at the TOC, comparing pictures like boys flipping baseball cards at recess. It was an endearing and innocent twist finally put to the tragedy that had brought so many cops and students all together.

Many officers refused to take any time off and were working double and sometimes triple shifts. One cop we spoke to summed it up for everyone when we asked him why he hadn't taken a single day off since the 16th. He said, "What am I going to do, go sit at home for days, lying on my couch watching daytime TV and drinking scotch alone? I'd rather be here where I can be a part of what's going on, doing some good, keeping the kids safe." Perhaps he was right, and being on duty with comrades, protecting those they were pledged to keep safe, was the best therapy of all.

The university also provided a family assistance center at The Inn at Virginia Tech.[308] A great number of counselors were brought in to assist with the students and professors, including the use of therapy dogs. The Governor's Report concluded this did not help the families much, however, due to lack of leadership and poor organization among the service providers. In addition, The Inn was also where the university chose to house much of the news media that was arriving. Putting the two groups together wasn't anticipated to be a poor idea.

308 GPR, p. 3.

Chapter Eight

Post Attack Operations and Politics

"We sleep safe in our beds because rough men stand ready in the night to visit violence on those who would do us harm."

George Orwell

Ultimately, Sgt. Jason Haga, of the Virginia State Police's (VSP) Division 6 tactical team, assumed command at Norris Hall. On April 17, VSP First Sergeant Haygood took over command from him. He would remain in command throughout VSP SWAT's presence on campus until the end of the spring semester.

Haygood should have been the poster boy for the state police. He was tall, handsome, muscular and extremely fit, known as an accomplished tri-athlete. His razor sharp flattop haircut and creased uniform with pants bloused into gleaming tactical boots like a paratrooper only lent to his overall appearance of physical perfection within the Virginia State Police. The presence of the VSP SWAT team lent an air of state authority and control to all that was going on.[309] Also on the 16th, the VSP Division 3 SWAT Team commanded by Sgt. Robert Hafley had arrived and served as the VSP "Day Group" team in the days and weeks that followed. Despite the arrival and presence of the VSP in force, all of the responding departments created and conducted a joint operation center, which was manned

309 Sadly 1SGT Haygood developed a rare form of brain cancer shortly after his service at VT. He died before year end.

by SWAT commanders and teams from VTPD, BPD, MCSO, VSP and Christiansburg PD.

They jointly set up a tactical command post on the fourth floor of the stadium, and handled all violent calls in the county for at least the next two weeks. The SWAT teams from all of these departments split day and night shifts in the weeks to come, with MCSO even handling all night shift calls in Montgomery County from the TOC. Capt. Goodman had notified the local FBI office in Roanoke approximately 30 miles away immediately after the second shooting, and agents were on scene within 30 minutes. Goodman reported that the relationship between the FBI local office and BPD was excellent and that they worked very well together and had handled a number of matters jointly. He said that one of the special agents "had just transferred out of HRT[310] and showed up 'strapped up' in all his SWAT gear."

VSP SWAT Sergeant Bob Hafley was the first cop I had run into on campus whom I knew. He and his entire team had gone tearing up the highways at more than 100 miles per hour all the way from their headquarters in Virginia Beach the moment they got word of the attack on Norris Hall. They covered the 322 mile distance in under three hours. As our Archangel team was walking through the campus, observing and assessing the police presence, security positions, behavior and reaction of the students and the university, we approached a large group of police standing just outside West AJ. Walking up with our team members I heard a voice say, "Hey John, what are you doing here?"

Bob Hafley had attended a SWAT school that I had had the privilege of helping run with famed Delta Force plankowner and Command Sergeant Major (CSM) Mel Wick. Mel was a legend in the military special operations community. He had been one of the original, hand-picked team of NCOs tasked with creating Delta from the ground up. In more than 30 years of Special Forces service he spent 16 of them with Delta, rising to the positions of both Command Sergeant

310 The FBI's elite Hostage Rescue Team.

Major of Delta and CSM of all of SOCOM.[311] One of the purposes of the SWAT school we had run in Conshohocken, Pennsylvania just outside of Philadelphia, was to prepare police to operate with units such as Delta should it ever be deployed on U.S. soil in response to a terrorist takeover, particularly of a school along the lines of Beslan in Russia. Units like Delta had serious concerns about having to operate in tandem with American police SWAT teams, and even greater concerns about working with teams comprised of regular patrol officers. According to CSM Wick, to Delta's way of thinking "police were too deliberate, too slow, too pedantically tied to doctrine, tactics and whatever plan got developed, and too concerned for their own safety and liability exposure." These things would make them a liability for their much faster, deadlier, innovative and risk-taking counterparts in Delta and SEAL Team Six, the Navy's version of Delta.

That was the third such training program I had been a part of, and the class had also included two of the Pennsylvania State Police SRT unit members who had responded to the Nickel Mines takeover. It was, indeed, a very small community throughout the country. Bob had remembered me from that school, and I him. He had proven himself to be a capable, hardworking and dedicated SWAT leader.

Bob was of average height, but possessed of the tough, lean but muscular frame seen on special operators the world over, as well as top level wrestlers, boxers and mixed martial artists. His dark hair shorn into a military-style haircut and chiseled features were easy to pick out of the crowd. He introduced us around to his team. His assistant, Trooper Andrew Jordan was a VT alumnus, and we were standing just outside his former dormitory: West-Ambler Johnston Hall. In answer to Bob's question I explained that we were there doing much the same thing I had done in Beslan: attempting to gain a factual understanding of the event and make an assessment in order to get critical information to law enforcement around the country. To my way of thinking, what Cho had just accomplished was a perfect example of a prolific means of terror attack: an Active Shooter Decimation

311 United States Special Operations Command.

Assault, where heavily armed terrorists enter crowded civilian areas and simply keep shooting everyone down until someone comes and shoots them down. Israel and especially Egypt had already seen its share of these This type of assault would be incorporated into the terrorists' overall attack plan in Mumbai, India in November 2008, and both Russia and Afghanistan had experienced them. Hundreds of these very attacks had already happened in Afghanistan, Pakistan, Thailand and Indonesia, all at the hands of jihadist terrorists.

Between the similarities to potential terror attacks, the unending targeting of schools by America's own socially produced predators, and the already-rampant rumors that Cho had been part of some type of Islamist terror group, there were many reasons to invest time and money trying to learn about what had just happened at Virginia Tech. For those reasons it was important to assess the specifics of Cho's attack and the manner in which the police had responded. Based on everything we had heard from the news media, however, none of us was hopeful that we would learn anything positive about the way the cops had handled it. Time and effort would teach us that we should have never paid attention to what the media reported, and that we could not have been more wrong.

Bob explained all that had happened since his team's arrival, and what he understood about Cho's tactics and weapons. He attempted to correct some of the things that had been disseminated by the press already. He took us up to the TOC and introduced us around, including making sure we got to meet Blacksburg SWAT leader Sgt. Anthony Wilson and operations commander Capt. Donnie Goodman, one of whom had just finished reading my Beslan book and the other then in the process. Between the book and Bob Hafley's willingness to vouch for us, they understood that we weren't there to do a news media-type hatchet job on anyone. That wasn't our purpose there. Our job was to gather information, then analzye that information. Our assessment would then be disseminated to other police agencies that needed to be better prepared for the next attack. We believed that our job was not to point fingers at people, but to point fingers at opportunities in future incidents. For if this effort wasn't being made then those victims had truly died in vain.

They knew that we would be objective and fair, but critical. We would report the event as we saw it, but generally believed that there was always some way any operation could be improved on in the future. Nevertheless they were willing to help us get important information; to the extent they could. Already pressure and blamism from the media and a paranoiac fear of litigation had descended upon the university and the departments that had raced to Norris Hall to save innocent lives. Everyone was afraid to talk, and at first all of the VT cops were told not to speak with us at all. But then they weren't supposed to speak to anyone. Learning what really happened and how the police had responded was not going to be easy; and it was going to take a long time, requiring many trips back to Blacksburg and the university that would forever be branded by Cho's hatred.

Medical Attention of the Wounded at Norris Hall in Restrospect

Per the GPR, at 9:52 a.m. - the time Cho shot himself and Team One had ascended to the top of the western stairwell - tac medics from VTRS and BVRS entered Norris Hall on the heels of the entry teams. This, however, wasn't exactly true. While the two tac medics, Jersey and Previtt, assigned to their respective SWAT teams had entered immediately and begun triaging and treating patients, it would be some time before the others could be coaxed into the building. As wounded were being evacuated they were loaded into police SUVs and transported to local EMS treatment areas. The medics were identifying and tallying total numbers of wounded and dead, and moving the most ambulatory victims to a safe area where further triage and treatment could be administered. Per the GPR, the tactical medics employed the START triage system (Simple Triage And Rapid Treatment) to assess victims quickly.[312] Victims were evaluated on the severity of their injuries and likelihood of survival. Treatment

312 GPR, p. 104.

priorities were then developed. This was done with a color code system in which red was "immediate need," yellow was "delayed," green was "minor," and black was "deceased or about to expire despite medical treatment" whereupon no further efforts would be made in lieu of using limited medical resources on others who could be saved. The victims were evacuated based on this same system of priority. It was a necessary but horrible thing to ask of anyone, much less young medics. To be forced to choose between life and death for victims is the sort of thing that tears at the soul. To be made to do it for kids no older than themselves was heart wrenching.

The patients with red tags who were severely wounded were first taken to a critical treatment unit set up on Old Turner Street. The patients with yellow tags, less critical, were taken to the delayed treatment staging area at Stanger and Barger Streets. The victims with green tags, minor injuries, were moved to a minor treatment area set up on the Drillfield.[313] Medics Previtt and Dominiczak operated in heroic fashion throughout this ordeal and their intervention resulted in the survival of several of the victims. Only after a preliminary clearance of the building was completed were traditional rescue units moved to the forward triage point on the Drillfield end. All viable victims – 17 in all - were removed and arrived at area hospitals. Twenty-four victims total would end up at four different hospitals. Due to the rapid and expert treatment of them by the young tac medics, every one of them would live.

VT had an all-volunteer student rescue squad. All of those who responded to Norris Hall were emotionally overcome by the carnage they witnessed, and most became physically sick. Both of the tactical medics were volunteers as well, and full time students at Tech. Neither was trained or sworn as a police officer and did not carry firearms.[314]

Evacuation of the wounded from Norris Hall was difficult as it was too windy for helicopters to be used. "We had to pull

313 GPR, p. 107.

314 Although Jersey would later become a certified police officer and ERT member, Previtt graduated and enlisted in the army

ambulances from all over," said Captain Goodman. At one point, a passenger bus reportedly transported several injured students directly to the hospital in Christiansburg, though Archangel's investigation could not verify this beyond the one student with a compound fracture of his leg having simply gotten on a regularly scheduled bus when he saw the word "Hospital" on the bus marquis. Montgomery General Hospital was exactly 4.2 miles from Norris Hall. Capt. Goodman had immediately arranged for the convoy of ambulances and wounded evacuation vehicles to enter the pickup zone, driving west up Drillfield Drive, stopping at the front walkway leading up to Norris Hall, being loaded with wounded, and continuing to exit south then southwest down Drillfield Drive to West Campus Drive. This was a very good, efficient system and allowed for the rapid movement of wounded evac vehicles to load up wounded and move out of the shooting site and off campus toward the hospitals quickly. At one point, with vehicles considered to be too far away to carry some of the wounded, Capt. Goodman ordered the vehicles to drive up the hill, right up to the building. He estimates that another ten victims were transported to the hospital in police patrol vehicles.

Of those shot, the majority had two to three bullet wounds, all at close range. All of the entry wounds on the students were from direct fire. Virtually none were from ricochets, and no one died from any ricochets. A number of the students were "stitched" up their bodies with bullets. For example, one round in the low chest, a second round in the upper chest or throat, with a third round in the face. One coed was shot three times with one round entering just below her mouth, a second round entering through the bridge of her nose, and the third through her forehead.

The majority of students who died were shot in the head. Immediately, Sgt. Wilson and others had stated that Cho had used both of his firearms and that there were a great number of both 9mm and .22 caliber shell casings everywhere. In the rooms that were assaulted on the second floor there was evidence of missed shots in the walls, though not a great number. There was also evidence of rounds in the walls of the second floor corridor. Officers reported their belief that the evidence of shots in the walls of the corridor were consistent with rabbit rounds (rounds skipping along walls). Some of the students that were wounded, but survived, had defensive wounds from putting their arms up to protect themselves, then rolling or diving to the floor. Some pulled dead students on top of them to hide and simulate death themselves. Some of the students who were killed had not had time to react at all. Sergeant Wilson and others detailed their experiences of moving carefully through the classrooms, stepping among the carnage of blood, tissue, brains and bodies, believing everyone was dead, only to feel students reaching out and grabbing their ankles and feet, pleading for help.

VSP SWAT team leader, Sgt. Hafley, reported to Archangel that 70 students had been evacuated from the third floor alone by the first arriving police departments. All of the third floor people evacuated were uninjured. Sgt. Wilson stated that all the uninjured and unwounded were evacuated on foot northwest approximately two blocks to Perry Street where they were picked up and transported by buses. Originally they were told to move west 20 yards to Burruss Hall, but many fled in all directions. The uninjured were moved by bus according to standard off-campus routing. Also, the police used the Blacksburg Transit System buses to move officers to the perimeter and the command post.

In the race to determine the number of shooters, their location and types of weapons, Goodman was asking students for this information as they were exiting the building under their own power. In some cases the students would answer all of his questions, and only later tell him that they, too, had been shot. While Capt. Goodman did this out of the press of the circumstances, it was both appropriate and necessary. Though victims may be wounded, for those who are mentally and physically capable of providing necessary intelligence in an ongoing threatening and hostile situation, they must be exploited for all available information with little consideration at that moment for pain or injuries. To attend to the injuries first – particularly in a still evolving tactical situation – may result in the complete loss of that critical information and cause further injury and death to others.

Though initial reports indicated that fully 28 or 29 students were wounded or injured,[315] that was downgraded to 25 in most reports. The GPR stated that 17 were wounded by gunshots, six injured jumping from the second floor, and four injured by other causes,[316] for a total of 27 wounded or injured.

The wounded and injured were taken to three primary area hospitals. The first victims were taken to Montgomery Regional General Hospital which received the largest number, at 17.[317] Montgomery Regional was the second largest hospital in the area; however, many of the seriously injured victims were stabilized and taken to other hospitals.[318] Carilion Roanoke Memorial Hospital in Roanoke some 36 miles and a 43 minute drive away, took the most severe cases. It was the region's Level I trauma center. A handful of patients were sent to New River Valley Medical Center in Radford, Virginia 12 miles away. A fourth hospital, Lewis-Gale Medical Center in Salem, took some students as well.

The Governor's Report concluded that the emergency medical care was very effective and timely; both on-site and at the hospitals. It did, however, report that the Virginia Tech emergency operations center could have increased communication of accurate information to the hospitals. It further stated that the Office of the Chief Medical Examiner properly discharged the technical aspect of his responsibility, but had poor communication with the victims' families. While noteworthy, these are non-law enforcement and non-tactical aspects of the post-operation phase of the VT shootings and beyond what the purpose was for our efforts there.

The majority of students were treated and released from the hospitals by April 24. There were, however, exceptions. Among those were the following:

315 Tim Thornton,"Another Victim Out of Hospital," *The Roanoke Times*, April 24, 2007, p. 4; and , Kevin Anderson and CT Staff, "Week of Strength Follows day of Horror on Campus," *Collegiate Times*, April 23, 2007, p. 1, reports fully 29 wounded.

316 GPR, p. 98.

317 Tim Thornton, "Another Victim Out of Hospital", *The Roanoke Times*, April 24, 2007, p. 4.

318 Lueders, p. 30.

Sean McQuade, a 21-year old Mathematics major from Mullica Hill, New Jersey, who was still hospitalized in serious condition at Carilion Roanoke Memorial Hospital as of that date. McQuade had been shot five times;[319] and,

Kevin Sterne, 22, of Cumberland, Maryland, who was scheduled to graduate in May with degrees in Electrical Engineering and Media Communications.[320] Shot twice in the right leg in room 207, BPD Lt. Glass and Officer Combs, and VTPD Reece had attempted to fashion a tourniquet from an electrical cord. A tac medic then applied a life-saving Israeli combat tourniquet that stopped the blood loss. Sterne was also the student depicted in the famous photo of four law enforcement officers, including Virginia State Police Sergeant Matthew Brannock,[321] carrying him from the building by his arms and legs. On April 24 he was the only student who remained in Montgomery Regional Hospital, and was in stable condition at that time.

"Awesome," was how Shannon Combs described the two medics' performance as he had watched them inside room 207, working on Sterne's leg along with so many others. "The medics did a hell of a job that day," he said.

Law Enforcement Operations in the Aftermath.

Approximately 400 officers total responded to Norris Hall. They had not previously been called in to assist with the shootings at WAJ. From the attack on Norris Hall on Monday, April 16 until Wednesday evening April 19, they were put on perimeter security duty. On Wednesday evening the VSP tac team was redeployed to provide tactical support to VT and BPDs' tactical operations center. A command post was initially set up in McBryde Hall, which was directly to the northeast of Holden Hall. As all of the buildings were being searched in that quadrant of the campus, Christiansburg PD was also put on

319 Thornton, p. 4.
320 Ibid.
321 *The Roanoke Times,* April 23, 2007, p. 7.

alert and was standing by. The media was kept outside a designated radius from Norris Hall. Though initially quite close, they were later moved back to the upper quad on campus.

Upon Norris Hall transitioning from an active/tactical shooting situation to a recovery phase, still more Blacksburg Police resources were provided to, again, bolster not only the entire VT police department, but other arriving agencies as well. The BPD officers were assigned and staged as follows: Captain Sam Bishop was command staff; Lt. Ken Gray, Sgt. Jerry Bowyer patrol supervisor; Lt. Marty Hauschildt for Montgomery Regional Hospital (MRH)/ Security; Lt. Greg Frazier, Officers Charlie Eades, Carla Cross and Ian Buckley at MRH and The Inn as part of VT/Security; Lt. Joe Davis, Sgt. Kit Cummings, Officer Jennifer Cease, Ambler Johnston/Scene Security; Sgt. Anthony Wilson security; Sgt. Casey Jones, Officers Tommy Sarver, Brandy Self and Det. Glen Richardson on Norris Hall/ Scene Security; Officers Marc Haynie, John Goad, Jason Blackburn, Mike Mickey all Blacksburg patrol; and Officer Todd Brewster at McBryde Hall and as staging officer.

The various local, state and federal law enforcement agencies had a long list of things that had to be accomplished, seemingly all at once. First the crime scene at Norris Hall had to be secured, and it would remain so for three days. That alone took a large number of police resources. VSP agents attended all 30 autopsies. A large number of interviews had to be conducted of students, faculty, businesses… the list seemed endless. Evidence collection had to begin immediately, all of which would be initially stored in a 40 foot long trailer. Six hundred pieces of evidence had to be logged immediately. Evidence was still being collected as the Governor's Panel began its investigation, a move that many thought was premature. Certainly the media had to be dealt with, and that alone required platoons of police and public information officers. The logistics challenges of dealing with all this and the thousands of people, police, government agents, journalists, parents, alumni and others descending on the campus and the town was a daunting task. Personnel were needed to staff all of the teams and commands trying to perform all of these functions. This included the coordination of overwhelming law enforcement assets that were still incoming. Families needed to be notified of deceased and wounded, more analysis was needed and incident command had to be set up and everyone had to know what the chains of command were. The demands on the police were massive.

And search warrants had to be obtained and executed. That night, April 16 at 7:30 p.m. ATF, FBI, and state police knocked on the door of Cho's suite. The police, still cautious, moved inside with guns drawn. They had no idea what they would find, who was part of this plan, or what they were about to walk into. After all that they had been through that day they were taking no chances. Karan Grewal and two of his suitemates were taken out and handcuffed. Grewal remembered that he and his roommates were separated and questioned. He was asked about Cho. They wanted to know what he looked like, and Grewal was informed that he was the suspect in the murders that day. Karan explained to the police that he did not know Cho that well, but he was shocked to hear that his suitemate committed the murders. He did not think that Cho was capable of that. He explained that Cho was not an aggressive person.[322]

The following day, Tuesday, April 17 there was a bomb threat to the County Government Building in Blacksburg. After the shootings BPD, VTPD and VSP SWAT officers were paired up in two man units with regular patrol officers for all violent calls. On Tuesday, April 24, one week later, other bomb threats caused the teams at the TOC to respond. Both the town and university continued to be on edge, and the police were tensed and ready to respond day and night.

Although the warrant had been executed and Cho's entire suite thoroughly searched on several occasions, it would be many weeks before his bloody clothes were found. Residence Life staff had finally contacted the police department to find out what they should do with Cho's belongings so they could assign the room for summer

322 Lazenby, pp. 96, 97.

activities. When VTPD sent officers to inventory and collect everything that was still there they found the bloodstained clothing and shoes from his first murders at WAJ in his clothes hamper. Somehow they had been missed.

From the time Cho was dead inside Norris they were trying to tie him to the WAJ murders. VT's newly minted forensic expert, Lt. George Jackson, had taken photos of the shoes that Cho was wearing when he died, but they didn't match the pattern of the tread from the one bloody footprint that was leading out of Emily Hilscher's room. If they had checked Cho's clothes hamper when they first executed their search warrant that evening "we could have tied him to the first killings right away," Jackson said. Supposedly Cho had also left a note in his room in which he criticized "rich kids, debauchery and deceitful charlatans" and also said that "you caused me to do this."[323]

Cho Reaches Out From the Grave

The videos that NBC received two days after the shootings were later determined to have been made prior to April 16 at two locations: the hotel in Roanoke and inside the Kia Sedona van Cho rented while sitting outside the shooting range. As is now widely known, Cho's "manifesto" was sent with the wrong zip code, which delayed its delivery to NBC by one day. On the sender receipt Cho wrote the name "A. Ishmael" which raised many questions. In the book *Lifting Our Eyes*, Beth J. Lueders wrote "...Cho lists himself as 'A. Ishmael,' perhaps in reference to Abraham's firstborn son through Sarah's concubine. The Bible's Genesis 16:12 declares this about the ancient Ishmael: 'He will be a wild donkey of a man; his hand will be against everyone and everyone's hand against him, and he will live in hostility toward all his brothers.'" The GPR noted that "A Ishmael" was similar to "AX Ishmael," which was written on Cho's arm when he committed suicide and was also the name he used to sign some emails.[324]

323 "Killer's Note: You Caused Me To Do This," *ABC News*, September 16, 2008, cited in *Wikipedia*.
324 GPR, p. 86.

All manner of theorists, conspiracists and Islamophobes have speculated, variously, that Cho had converted to Islam; that Cho had gone to a mosque in the Student Union on campus and conducted ritual suicide-martyrdom prayers, including shaving all the hair from his body, before committing his attacks; had become conscripted into or obsessed with al Qaeda, and so forth; all of which was the reason for what was seen as the biblical references. However, there is no definitive evidence of any of this, though clearly Cho was influenced by something or someone to use these names. As well, there was no mosque in the Student Union. Nor was there any evidence of Cho having contact with any radical Islamist groups or individuals, although, again, the hard drive to his computer remains missing and would likely provide a great deal of information about him.

Dr. William Massello, assistant state medical examiner based in Roanoke, Virginia stated on Sunday, April 22, after concluding Cho's autopsy that he died of a self-inflicted gunshot wound to his temple. No evidence of chemicals or drugs was found in his body, nor were there any brain tumors that would have provided a physiological reason for his behavior, as had been found with Charles Whitman, the 1966 University of Texas-Austin tower shooter who had a glioblastoma, and whose suicide note had asked that an autopsy attempt to determine why he was suffering from homicidal thoughts.[325] Nothing else of any real significance was revealed in Cho's autopsy. Massello also said that many of the victims exhibited defensive wounds consistent with victims trying to shield themselves from gunfire. He confirmed that Cho "hit many of his victims several times. Several of the victims had gunshot wounds to the head."[326] Dr. Massello was also reported in *USA Today* as saying that "autopsies showed Cho fired more than 100 shots into his victims...." "Cho was not especially accurate with his shots, but hit many of his victims several times,"[327] he was quoted as saying. Nothing could have been further from the truth, as out of the 174 rounds Cho fired, few missed his intended victims.

325 Roy, p. 233.
326 Kristen Gelineau, "Nothing Unusual Found in Cho's Autopsy," *The Roanoke Times*, Monday, April 23, 2007, p. 6.
327 Andrea Stone, Roger Yu and Martin Kasindorf, "Law Would Focus on Gun Buyers' History of Mental Illness," *USA Today*, Monday, April 23, 2007, p. 5A.

Between the two attacks a total of 32 people lost their lives: 18 under-graduate students were killed, nine graduate students, and five professors.

The Politics of a School Massacre

Three days after the two shooting incidents at Virginia Tech, at the request of university president Steger, the Governor of Virginia, the Honorable Timothy Michael Kaine, commissioned a panel of "experts" to investigate the attacks and produce an in-depth report to be called the Governor's Panel Report.

The Governor's Panel was composed of: Panel Chair, Col. Gerald Massengill, a retired Virginia State Police Superintendent; Panel Vice Chair, Dr. Marcus L. Martin, Professor of Emergency Medicine; Gordon Davies, former Director of the State Council of Higher Education; Dr. Roger L. Depue, twenty year veteran of the FBI; Carroll Ann Ellis, MS, Director of Fairfax County Police Department's Victim Services Division; the Honorable Tom Ridge, former Governor of Pennsylvania and the first Secretary of the Department of Homeland Security; Dr. Aradhana A "Bella" Sood, Professor of Psychiatry and Pediatrics; and the Honorable Diane Strickland, former Judge of the 23rd Judicial Circuit Court. The panel also included the expertise and assistance of TriData, a division of System Planning Corporation, led by Phil Schaenman and Hollis Stambaugh; and legal counsel by the Washington, D.C., office of the law firm Skadden, Arps, Slate, Meagher & Flom, L.L.P., led by partners Richard Brusca and Amy Sabrin.

In the foreword, Governor Kaine stated: "In the days immediately after the shooting, I knew it was critical to seek answers to the many questions that would arise from the tragedy. I also felt that the questions should be addressed by people who possessed both the expertise and autonomy necessary to do a comprehensive review."[328] However, based on the panel selected by Gov. Kaine it was

328 GPR, p. vii.

immediately certain that the GPR would take a particular direction and focus on specific issues important to both universities and society, but not necessarily provide the detailed analysis of the tactical response that police throughout America,who would be called upon to respond to attacks in the future, most wanted to know.

Nevertheless, the Governor's report and the executive order he issued did direct the panel to answer the following questions:

1. Conduct a review of how Seung-Hui Cho committed these 32 murders and multiple additional woundings, including with out limitation how he obtained his firearms and ammunition, and to learn what can be learned about what caused him to commit these acts of violence.

2. Conduct a review of Seung-Hui Cho's psychological condition and behavioral issues prior to and at the time of the shootings, what behavioral aberrations or potential warning signs were observed by students, faculty and/or staff at West Field High School and Virginia Tech.

3. Conduct a review of the timeline of events from the time that Seung-Hui Cho entered West Ambler-Johnston dormitory until his death in Norris Hall. Such review shall include an assessment of the response to the first murders and efforts to stop the Norris Hall murders once they began.

4. Conduct a review of the response of the Commonwealth, all of its agencies, and relevant local and private providers following the death of Seung-Hui Cho for the purpose of providing recommendations for the improvement of the Commonwealth's response in similar emergency situations.

5. Conduct other inquiries as may be appropriate in the Panel's discretion otherwise consistent with its mission and authority as provided herein.

6. Based on these inquiries, make recommendations on appropriate measures that can be taken to improve the laws, policies, procedures, systems and institutions of the Commonwealth and the operations of public safety agencies, medical facilities, local agencies, private providers, universities, and mental health services delivery system.

In summary, the panel was tasked to review the events, assess actions taken and not taken, identify lessons learned, and propose alternatives for the future. Its assessment included a review of Cho's history and interaction with the mental health and legal systems, and of his gun purchases. The panel was also asked to review the emergency response by all parties: law enforcement officials, university officials, medical responders and hospital care providers, and the medical examiner. Finally, it reviewed the aftermath; that was, the university's approach to helping families, survivors, students, and staff as they dealt with the mental trauma and the approach to helping the university itself heal and function again.[329]

We at Archangel didn't care about most of these issues. Though of tremendous importance, they were best left to others: professionals more expert in addressing grand social and political matters. What we cared about, and what we believed was the biggest question before the public at the time, was whether the cops had blown it. Everyone wanted to know whether the police had inadequately handled the first shootings in the West AJ dormitory, and whether – as had been consistently depicted in the media – they had stood outside as at Columbine High School for minutes if not hours, holding position, doing nothing while defenseless people were gunned down. But with really only the one exception of Col. Massengill, no one on the Governor's Panel had the experience and expertise to make that determination. Nor would any real effort be made to answer those questions. The GPR did state in several short sections that the police had moved quickly and responded well, and we have referenced those

329 GPR, p. 6.

statements throughout this book. However, with the news media evisceration they had suffered, this answer necessitated considerably more than that. As a result, the police continued to endure the torture, pain and humiliation of the wrongfully accused, the bane of an American nation that had no idea just what they done.

The Governor's Panel conducted over 200 interviews, but the vast majority of them were of top level FBI agents, national experts, consultants, and other parties not directly involved in the attacks. Very few responders to the incident were interviewed, and those who were expressed disappointment at the brevity and superficial nature of the questions posed to them. Captain Donnie Goodman – the Blacksburg Operations Division Commander, under whom the ERT's overall command fell, and who had a critical role in both shootings - was not asked to be interviewed or appear before the panel at all.[330] Only three of the surviving students and teachers from Norris Hall were met with. The Governor's Panel scarcely talked to Jersey Dominiczak, the tac medic who had saved so many lives. He said they only interviewed him for five to ten minutes. He tried to give them additional information, "but they shut me down." "All they wanted to know was 'what's the general picture of things,'" he chided. He said that they weren't even interested enough to report the proper units that handled the first shooting at West Ambler-Johnston. The men and women who were involved in every aspect of the events of that day either were never called at all, or were asked few, and to them insignificant, questions before being ushered out.

When Lucinda Roy was called in by investigators, she was surprised that they had no questions of her. She turned over all of the written materials she had amassed that pertained to her time with Cho, and emphasized that she would be willing to help with anything at all, and that they shouldn't hesitate to contact her. Other than her own later telephone calls to the FBI to express concerns about the case, she never heard from anyone with any investigative or law

330 The direct commander of BPD ERT was Lt. Glass.

enforcement agency. Simply there was nothing that they wanted to know from her.[331]

The panel was not authorized to issue subpoenas, but with most of the police and other first responders virtually dying for a chance to be heard, to tell their story, to let someone in authority know what they had done and why, they would have shown up voluntarily. They would have shown up on their own time. Many would have taken vacation leave to explain to someone – anyone – what had really happened that day. No subpoenas would have been necessary, if only the governor's appointees would have listened to them. Still, several of the officers reminded us that the governor could have given the commission subpoena power if he had wanted. They said he didn't because he didn't want certain things coming out. "It was ass covering," we were told.

Nevertheless, of the interviews that were conducted no recordings or written transcripts were made. From the work it did do, the panel made over 70 recommendations to colleges, universities, mental health providers, law enforcement officials, emergency service providers, law makers, and other public officials.

Before that investigation could be completed and the Governor's Panel issued its findings, however, another report was made to the President of the United States on the Virginia Tech shootings. Dated June 13, 2007, it was authored by Michael O. Leavitt, Secretary of the Department of Health and Human Services; Margaret Spellings, Secretary of the Department of Education; and Alberto R. Gonzales, Attorney General Department of Justice. That report identified five key themes:

A. Critical Information Sharing Faces Substantial Obstacles;

B. Accurate and Complete Information on Individuals Prohibited from Possessing Firearms is Essential to Keep Guns Out of the Wrong Hands;

331 Roy, p. 27

C. Improved Awareness and Communication are Key to Prevention;

D. It is Critical to Get People with Mental Illness the Services They Need; and,

E. Where We Know What to Do, We Have to be Better at Doing It.

This report was only 22 pages long and also failed entirely to address the law enforcement response to the shootings, the professional way the police committed all available resources to finding the killer of Emily Hilscher and Ryan Clark, and the courage under fire they demonstrated in racing to Norris Hall and breaching sophisticated fortifications to save innocent lives. The police continued to fall prey to a vicious media which had long before decided to hang the blame for one social misfit on the only men and women who had actually tried to stop him.

The Governor's Panel Report was distributed two months later in August 2007,[332] just in time for the start of the following fall semester. While it provided important and detailed information surrounding many aspects of the attack, its treatment of the law enforcement response was minimal relative to many other issues addressed in depth. Still, numerous errors would necessitate a second version in December 2009 and then a third on January 6, 2010. The continued publication of mistakes drew the ire of both the university and the families of the victims.[333]

Among the many societal, security, statutory and psychological issues the Governor's Panel focused on were the warning/alert system employed by VT, and the university's emergency response planning. In addition to its assessment of the sufficiency of the sys-

332 The report itself, entitled *Mass Shootings at Virginia Tech, Report of the Review Panel,* did not provide a specific date for its release and publication.

333 "Third Version of Va. Tech massacre report released," *Associated Press,* January 7, 2010, www.policeone.com/school-violence/articles/1986581-Third-version-of-Va-Tech-massacre-report-released

tems then in place, the panel critiqued the decisions made by the university Policy Group convened in the morning of April 16, the decisions and recommendation of the VTPD, and in particular, Chief Flinchum.

The timing of emails that were issued, information actually conveyed to the VT community, and the decision to not lock down the campus after the first shootings were all criticized by the panel. Due to the fact that certain aspects of the warning/alert system and the decision to not lock down the campus are relevant to appreciating the overall tactical response of law enforcement, some aspects of them are deserving of discussion.

Warning/Alert System

The first floor of Norris Hall was comprised of administrative offices, a machine shop, and resource labs. Certain of these were occupied at the time of the shooting, including the machine shop. A number of the classrooms in this building were considered extra or surplus. Staff offices usually had locks, but the classrooms had none.[334] Some universities have locks on classroom doors, but as they are intended to keep students and strangers out when not in use, they usually lock with a key from the outside and can't be locked from the inside.[335]

In order for VT to lock the doors in all of the buildings they had to call people in the Buildings Department and have someone go to each building and manually lock the doors, with the exception of dormitory external doors which automatically locked from 8:00 p.m. to 10:00 a.m.[336] There were no guards at campus buildings or cameras at the entrances or hallways, but some buildings did have a loud speaker system that could be accessed from a panel in the building.[337] This loudspeaker system was intended for firemen - not for police - and could not be utilized for a campus-wide broadcast.[338]

334 GPR, p. 13.
335 Ibid.
336 Ibid.
337 Ibid.
338 Ibid.

The GPR stated: "This level of security is quite typical of many campuses across the nation in rural areas with low crime rates."[339] Virginia Tech was in the process of upgrading its campus-wide alert capability in spring 2007 when the attacks came.[340]

The GPR also stated that VTPD erred by prematurely identifying a sole suspect in the double homicide at WAJ, and in not requesting that the Policy Group issue a campus-wide notification that there was a double homicide at WAJ and to remain alert and cautious. However, the Virginia Tech Police Department merely reported *to* the Policy Group. The Policy Group – the "law of the land" so to speak at the university during emergencies - was there to make its own decisions concerning notifications on campus. The GPR reported, "Virginia Tech had the capability on April 16 to send messages to the student body, faculty, and other staff via a broadcast email system. The associate vice president for University Relations had the authority and capability to send a message from anywhere that was connected to the web." The report also stated that the Policy Group failed to issue an all-campus notification for almost two hours.

Contradictorily, the GPR also stated that the VTPD erred by not sending the message. Even more confusingly it stated, "While the Virginia Tech campus police had the authority to send a message, they did not have the technical means to do so."[341] How the VTPD police chief was to have circumvented his superiors and sent a message – even if he had wanted to - when they were unwilling to do so was not explained. It is important to point out, however, that this is of importance only in examining the GPR, as Chief Flinchum never said that he desired to send any such message.

The timing and content of the messages sent on April 16 remains one of the major controversies surrounding this incident.[342] The GPR reported that sending a message on that day was "cumbersome, untimely, and problematic" as the police had to wait for the

339 Ibid.
340 GPR, p. 14.
341 GPR, p. 16.
342 Ibid.

deliberation of the Policy Group to convene and decide whether a message was to be sent and its content.[343] This email system had 36,000 registered addresses and the distribution rate was 10,000 per minute.[344] The university also had a web site where users could post emergency information and on April 16 the VT website was experiencing 148,000 visits per hour.[345]

The university also had contacts with every local radio and TV station.[346] "The Virginia Tech associate vice president for University Relations has a code by which he can send emergency messages to the stations that could be played immediately. This process could take 20 minutes or so because each station has its own code to validate the sender," it stated. However, this system was usually only used for weather alerts and the campus community was supposedly trained to stay tuned for further details.[347]

The GPR estimated 96 percent of students carried cell phones and suggested that this would have been a faster way of sending messages. The Report further stated the university was still in the process of installing a text message system and had no way to send texts on April 16. The university also had a phone-mail system but students and faculty had to register their numbers. In addition, it required 11 separate actions to send a broadcast.[348]

A university switchboard with four operators was functional during normal business hours and could handle up to 100 calls.[349] The university was in the process of installing six outdoor loudspeakers to extend its messaging system.[350] Some would be mounted on buildings and some on poles. Four had been installed by April 16 but did not play a significant role in the response to the attacks, or the university's handling of them.[351]

343 GPR, p. 17.
344 GPR, p. 14.
345 Ibid.
346 Ibid.
347 Ibid
348 GPR, p. 15.
349 Ibid.
350 Ibid.
351 Ibid.

As a last resort, the warning system contemplated using resident advisors in dorms, and floor wardens in some older classrooms and office buildings to personally spread warnings.[352] In Norris Hall, Ishwar Puri, the chairman of the Engineering and Mechanics Department, whose office was on the second floor, said he had been issued a bullhorn to make announcements and was instructed to go to classroom and office doors to notify people if the emergency system failed.[353] In the book *April 16th: Virginia Tech Remembers*, he described how they were supposed to run up and down the hallways with an air horn and yell "fire" or "evacuate."[354] This system guaranteed the university a low tech solution, as technology was not always dependable. However, in instituting it as an alert option it was clear no one recognized that in a tactical situation, in which someone was shooting innocent victims in the Columbine model of attack, that either no one would attempt to accomplish that task, or would be quickly killed themselves. With Cho on the same floor as Chairman Puri, if he had run down the hall announcing an attack the chances of him having lived beyond a few seconds would have been remote. Events had proven that in active shooting situations would-be victims invariably went into hiding or ran away from the threat. Few ever ran toward it.

In the spring of 2007 the university was in the process of installing a unified multimedia messaging system that was to be completed before the next semester.[355] It was to allow for messaging to be issued through computers, cell phones, PDAs, and telephones. Messages could be sent by anyone registered with the authority to do so.[356] Students would have to be registered in the system to receive messages, rather then making it a mandatory requirement. Parents could also be included on the list. The GPR reported: "All students and staff were encouraged, but not required, to register with the new system. Each user can set the priority order in which their devices are called." For a community of 36,000, this system would

352 Ibdi.
353 Ibid.
354 Lazenby, p. 21.
355 GPR, p. 15.
356 Ibid.

cost $33,000.00.[357] Virginia Tech was planning to use this system for emergencies only; however, it was found that some universities that had implemented it had ended up using it for routine messages,[358] increasing the likelihood that over time its messages would be ignored by most of the recipients. As well, the GPR reported that some universities had experienced problems with the system.[359]

Still, the efficacy in the university alerting everyone in the VT community immediately upon the first two deaths in WAJ must be examined from a realistic perspective. All too often in the aftermath of a critical incident those in investigative roles who enjoy the benefits of hindsight engage in wanton blamism. Assuming, *arguendo,* that the VT Policy Group had sent out an email to everyone in the university immediately upon convening and being notified of the killings at WAJ, the reaction would not likely have resulted in any significant difference in the tactical situation the police confronted, their initial investigation, or Cho's ultimate attack.

By the time the Policy Group convened at 8:35 on the morning of April 16, the majority of students were already in class. Just as with Cho having used his cell phone to take pictures, the use of cell phones for calls, texts and instant messages during class was a clear disruption and tolerated by few teachers. It would have taken some time for the Policy Group to be sufficiently informed of the incident, discuss and agree on what message and by what medium to transmit the alert, and what actions were to be taken in response to the situation. This would not have been able to be handled in the 30 minutes between the Group convening and the second class period – during which Cho began his attack on Norris Hall - beginning at 9:05 a.m. Even if some hastily drafted message had gone out, it would likely have either gone unnoticed by many of the students moving quickly between classes, or may have been read and ignored.

As well, experience with the university student population had taught law enforcement that the very reaction they hope for

357 GPR, p. 16.
358 Ibid.
359 GPR, p. 18.

– and sometimes implore – from the students in emergency situations is not only never forthcoming, but the young adults comprising the university student base will do just the opposite. This was the experience all police agencies responding to the Morva manhunt the previous August had learned when alerting students to stay in their dorm rooms, and for anyone off campus to remain off campus and in their homes. Few heeded this warning, and many were intentionally outside in a show of juvenile bravado. Some were even holding parties with signs and firearms inviting criminals to *bring it on!*

The final point to be considered was just what an earlier message would have said that could possibly have made a difference. Non-tactical professionals, including those of political and academic orientations, parents and the news media, seem to believe that there exists a one-size-fits-all tactic that could be employed and that serves as a panacea against any and all threats to schools. This is not only unrealistic, but naïve. The remedy that appeared to garner the greatest support for the illusion that if one particular step had only been taken (or is taken in the future) everyone would have been safe was the lockdown.

While lockdowns are an important first step in responding to active shooter situations in primary schools (elementary, middle and high schools), they are merely that: a *first* step. Even then lockdowns are not a complete answer. At VT the ability to lockdown an entire campus was non-existent. With 2,600 acres of open ground fronting numerous roads that could be accessed anywhere and everywhere, 16 unguarded road entrances, 150 total buildings and more than 30,000 people on campus, a complete lockdown was impossible. To effectively lock down the university, law enforcement would have had to stage a tight perimeter around the entire campus. At over four square miles, and with officers maintaining a ten yard spread between them, this would have required 1,105 police officers just to maintain the outer perimeter.

Even with virtually all of the BPD and VTPD forces deployed in response to the initial killings, the total force did not constitute even ten percent of that number. And more than an hour after the Norris Hall shootings, with several hundred cops having descended on VT, they still would have lacked the numbers of police necessary to cordon off the entire university. While conducting the investigation into the WAJ shootings the police could not begin to even contemplate locking down the entire campus, as the numbers necessary for that would have had to be added to all of the forces already being used to secure a perimeter around WAJ, and maintain roving patrols on campus looking for the suspect's vehicle on the 19.6 miles of road on campus and in the 14,369 parking spaces. Topping this inconceivable level of law enforcement manpower resources would, by necessity, have requuired tactical teams, other police to continue routine law enforcement operations, command staff, additional investigators to conduct interviews, and more.

And what if the campus had been locked down? Knowledge of emergency response procedures by student-shooters gives them perfect intelligence on how their target will react. If trapped inside any building due to a lockdown, it would have been all the easier for Cho to hunt and kill his quarry. Moreover, if Cho had accomplices the bodycount would likely have been far greater under lockdown conditions in a single building. Or a series of simultaneous attacks would have occurred at buildings across campus. Then the numerous attackers would have been inside their respective targets with the victims, rendering it impossible for law enforcement to respond sufficiently, and certainly not quickly, to any of them much less all of them.

The reality is that with perfect hindsight in assessing the situation with which VT and the two police departments were faced on April 16, 2007, everyone on campus would likely have been safer if an alert had been disseminated instructing them to leave buildings and flee out into the common areas of that enormous campus, and remain there until any potential threat had either been eliminated or determined to not exist. Major Malik Nidal Hasan's alleged attack on Ft. Hood in November 5, 2009 would prove that as a number of the soldiers fleeing across common areas were not hit, even at relatively close distances.

Unfortunately, on April 16, 2007 Cho was going to attack students somewhere. If denied Norris Hall he would have simply launched his attack in whatever building he was in. If he was "locked down" in a cafeteria, for instance, students densely packed into close confines would have been shot in large numbers. If in a dormitory, or even his own dorm, it would have been easy to move through hallways killing people as he had already done in West AJ. Simply, people were going to die that day, and if the university had attempted to lock everyone in it was just as likely that even more would have been shot than were at Norris Hall. But as Lori Haas, mother of courageous Emily Haas told me, "At least then it wouldn't have been my daughter." Mrs. Haas' anger stems from the fact that the university didn't disseminate the information that it did have as soon as it was known, and allow the students to make their own choices that day. In the case of her daughter, Lori says that if the information had been sent that Emily would have called her parents, who would have told her to not leave her home just as they had done during the Morva manhunt.

Emergency Response Plan

While shootings at universities are rare, out of 4,000 institutions America sees an average of about 16 a year. Thus, emergency planning is an important part of any institution. Virginia Tech's Emergency Response Plan addressed many emergencies, but did not have specific SOPs[360] for shootings. On April 16, 2007, the then-current version of its emergency response plan had been in effect for two years.[361] The emergencies were categorized by levels 0, I, II, and III.[362] The plan called for an official to be designated as the Emergency Response Coordinator (ERC), to direct the response and for an Emergency Operations Center (EOC) to be established.[363]

360 Standard Operating Procedures
361 GPR, p. 16.
362 GPR, p. 17.
363 Ibid.

At the time of the shootings at VT there were multiple ERCs and EOCs but not one central EOC.[364] Moreover, the critical ones were implemented by responding law enforcement and medics, highlighting the fact that one of the weaknesses for elaborate committee-type response planning is that any actions the committee takes will be limited to the recovery or aftermath phases of a true emergency. In the case of shootings, the threat will typically begin and end long before a policy and decision-making group can even be convened, much less take any effective steps. In the interim, when lives are in immediate danger, it will be police who will take the most important steps. If Cho hadn't needed to ensure that he could kill and thereby ended up murdering two students in WAJ, the Policy Group would have never been convened at all until long after the attack at Norris Hall had ended and all the wounded were in hosptials.

Two key decision groups were identified in VT's plan: the Policy Group and the Emergency Response Resources Group (ERRG).[365] The Policy Group was comprised of nine vice presidents and support staff, chaired by the university president. The Policy Group handled the procedures to support emergency operations and to determine recovery priorities. It was above the emergency coordinator for incidents, and usually asked campus police to have a representative at its meetings.[366] The ERRG included a vice president designated to be in charge of the incident, police officials, and others depending on the nature of the event. This group ensured the resources needed to support the Policy Group and the emergency.[367]

Although a number of people we spoke with believed that VT's extensive and management-layered emergency response and incident command model looked to only be capable of existing in the artificial world of training exercises and theory-laden tabletop discussions, after the attack on Norris Hall it had to try to deal with all of the various issues surrounding the arrival of 1,500 responders

364 Ibid.
365 Ibid.
366 Ibid.
367 Ibid.

from 27 agencies, with 11 command and control stations, and four hospitals. Ultimately 84 agencies helped manage the crisis. However, all of these seemed to work well together; a success that could only be attributed to that prior planning. This proved that incident command systems only work with planning and training.

The GPR did, at least, acknowledge that locking down the campus of Virginia Tech would have been virtually impossible due to the size of the police force, the absence of security, the fact that the doors of most buildings did not have electronic controls, and the number of unguarded roadways into the campus. In addition, it had vast tracts of open land that could be traversed anywhere.

The VT Emergency Response Plan, however, did not address the prevention of events.[368] For example, the Governor's Panel made note of the fact that on two other campuses in Virginia the chief operating officer received daily reports on all incidents to which law enforcement responded, and shared them with offices that were responsible for the safety and health of the campus.[369] However, this system, even if in place, would not have prevented the attacks at VT. The GPR stated that the VT plan was deficient in several respects, including its failure to place police high enough on the decision-making hierarchy, and did not include a threat assessment team. The GPR also noted that the VTPD's expressed primary purpose in the Emergency Response Plan was not law enforcement.[370]

The limitations experienced by the Virginia Tech Police Department in the response to the first shootings at WAJ do not appear to be isolated problems in academia across the state, and very likely across the nation. The GPR stated that several leaders of campus police chiefs in Virginia commented that they did not feel that they always had adequate input in security planning and threat assessment.

One of the other criticisms laid at the feet of university officials was that the university did not implement a telephone number

368 Ibid.
369 GPR, p. 17.
370 GPR, p. 19..

that families could phone to check on their children.[371] The influx of calls soon overwhelmed the service capability of the area, and many worried parents simply got in their cars and drove to the campus, many from several states away. Parents, of course, found campus roads blocked off by that point, so many made their way to the local hospitals which caused security issues there. Blacksburg Police Chaplain Tommy McDearis described the Montgomery Hospital as "controlled chaos."[372]

Thus, in critiquing the decisions of law enforcement and the university itself, in response to the events of April 16, 2007, everyone must be realistic in assessing the propriety of those decisions in terms of the information possessed at each moment in time; the experiential basis of police, the university and America upon which situations must be gauged in response to any incident; and whether any particular decision, procedure or tactic would really have prevented the second attack by Cho.

But the conduct and decisions of the university and its police department were not only relevant during the day of, and between the attacks on, April 16. The conduct of those same institutions was just as scrutinized in the aftermath of the events of that day. According to Lucinda Roy, by "the end of that first week following the tragedy, President Steger and his key advisers had 'battened down the hatches,'" a phrase she had often heard applied by his own team in depicting the university administration's approach to the media.[373] Dr. Roy lamented that "the hatches were battened down internally also."[374]

In the weeks after the attacks, every single day all of the VT police seemed to be stumbling about, certain that they were all going to be fired at any minute. This never went away. We were told that Wendell Flinchum arrived at work every morning expecting to be terminated. For Lucinda Roy, who was certain that for a man like Charles Steger "who abhorred scrutiny," the investigation

371 Lazenby, p. 75.
372 Ibid, p. 77.
373 Roy, p. 68.
374 Ibid.

and media attention "must have been mortifying."[375] She would agree with Teresa Cook that all "lines of communication were being shut down." Not only did they believe this occurred between the president and the victims' families,[376] but between the president and his entire administration and their own police officers, who were left adrift, living with the daily – if not hourly – fear of being both blamed and fired. Resultantly, in our AAR we had written, "This does not seem to have prevented Virginia Tech, itself, from placing much of the blame for its actions on VTPD and Chief Flinchum in particular." As we learned more since the AAR was distributed, however, this may not have been either a fair or accurate assessment. In his letter of October 3, 2008 to us responding to that section in our AAR, President Steger wrote:

> Neither I nor anyone speaking on behalf of the university administration has ever made statements attempting to blame law enforcement for anything. Their service has been extraordinary. I recall vigorously defending Chief Flinchum when there were many calls for me to remove him from office.
>
> Thank you for taking the time to consider my opinion in this matter.

Perhaps much of this misunderstanding was a matter of perception. Certainly Dr. Steger and others in top administrative levels of the VT hierarchy had to be reeling not only from the horror and magnitude of the event itself, but the enormity of the media response and reporting. And while the university had issued its official statement that it supported what the police had done – and we have no doubt that he staunchly defended the police department and Chief Flinchum to outside critics - that did not seem to have been well communicated to the men and women of the department.

375 Roy, p. 76.
376 Ibid.

Perhaps one lesson to be taken from the aftermath of this event and applied to future incidents of this magnitude, is for those in corporate leadership positions to realize that no matter what they are suffering or dealing with, that it is quite a bit less than the strain and agony that their officers who handled the horror are enduring. And while the officers may hold it together while at work, their families continue to endure the backlash, and need both support and training to give them the tools needed to deal with it.

Despite this, the university administration did deal quickly and decisively with its students, attempting to do whatever was necessary to ease the pain of their experience. Classes were cancelled for a week after the attack, and students were then given the option of simply ending their spring semester at that time, accepting the grade they had earned at that point and avoiding final exams, or completing the course work. The kids were, in many cases, just too overcome by the enormity of what had happened at their school, in their home, and to their friends to function. Many of the female students told us that all the girls were sleeping together, piling as many as three, four or five into a bed, just for comfort through the nights. At the major memorial service held on April 17, televised throughout the nation and the world, President George W. Bush said:

> Yesterday began like any other day. Students woke up, and they grabbed their backpacks and they headed for class. And soon the day took a dark turn, with students and faculty barricading themselves in classrooms and dormitories – confused, terrified, and deeply worried. By the end of the morning, it was the worst day of violence on a college campus in American history – and for many of you here today, it was the worst day of your lives.
>
> It's impossible to make sense of such violence and suffering. Those whose lives were taken did nothing to

> deserve their fate. They were simply in the wrong place at the wrong time. Now they're gone, and they leave behind grieving families, and grieving classmates, and a grieving nation.[377]

A petition was quickly put on a website expressing support of President Steger and Chief Wendell Flinchum, and ultimately delivered to Governor Kaine. Reportedly signed by 37,371 people, it included some 18,000 messages.[378] Whether this was the same petition the students had told us about within a few days of the attacks, wherein they said that more than 3,000 students had already appended their names to its expression of support and confidence in the police, we cannot know. No other petition was ever provided to us.

Classes were scheduled to recommence on Monday, April 23, but at that time it was still not certain that Cho had acted alone.[379] Police had matched the 9mm rounds used in the first two murders of Ryan Clark and Emily Hilscher to the weapon that had been used in Norris Hall, but that did not definitively establish that it had been the same shooter in both attacks, or that he didn't have help. Professor Carl Bean – the target of Cho's venom in his letter to the English Department – cancelled his four classes, concerned that his students could still be in danger if accomplices of Cho decided to complete his final act of revenge against all those who had wronged him.[380] Lucinda Roy herself had even received an email that she forwarded to the FBI, warning that the English professors "needed to read things carefully" if they "wanted to avoid tragedy in the future." It was signed: "One for all and all for one."[381]

As was expected, the VT massacre ignited a firestorm of debate over gun control, political debate over the so-called "trade-show loophole" for unregistered firearms purchases, and the issue of firearms on campuses. VT had already seen the latter issue rear its

377 President George W. Bush, http://www.whitehouse.gov/news/releases/2007/04/20070417l.html.
378 Roy, p. 78.
379 Roy, p. 80.
380 Roy, p. 80
381 Ibid.

head two years before Cho's rampage when a student with a valid concealed carry permit was found in possession of a firearm. This resulted in the university officially banning all firearms in the face of a tidal wave of protestation by gun rights advocates. Lucinda Roy would point out that the Panel Report recommended the state attorney general issue a clarifying policy due to the fact that state statutes were not clear on the issue of weapons on college campuses where the bearers had proper permits. Apparently two pieces of proposed legislation that would have given individual universities the power to regulate weapons on their own campuses died during the 2005 state legislative session.[382] Since the shootings Virginia has passed legislation that denies anyone involuntarily committed for psychiatric reasons to purchase a firearm from a registered vendor. The tradeshow loophole still exists though.[383]

Certainly, America had already seen instances in which gun-possessing students and administrators had prevented the taking of further human life. Though the Governor's Panel found that no such instances had ever occurred,[384] history dictates that its research was flawed. In 1997, Pearl, Mississippi student Luke Woodham's shooting rampage at his school was quickly stopped by armed assistant principal Joel Myrick who held the student-shooter at gunpoint until police arrived. Then in 2002, Appalachian School of Law student Peter Odighizuwa killed three and wounded three others in an attack at his college in Grundy, Virginia, a short distance from VT. The murderer was stopped and captured by two students who retrieved firearms from their nearby cars.[385]

Early on in our investigation we met a young man, fresh out of the Navy SEALs. More than a week after the attacks, during the VSP SWAT team's first night off duty we were having drinks with them in the Top of the Stairs bar in Blacksburg. The place was packed with students, all talking about the attacks. Some clearly had

382 Roy, p. 217.
383 Roy, p. 224.
384 GPR, p. 75.
385 Roy, p. 218; facts of incidents confirmed.

continued going to classes, seemingly more out of habit than anything else. Their friends could be overheard telling them how crazy they were, that the semester was over and that they didn't need to be going to class. Trying to squeeze through the crowd at the three-deep bar we found ourselves talking to a young man with a military haircut sitting on a stool, muscles straining his t-shirt. He was 27-years old and after eight years in the Teams had decided to leave the Navy and finish the degree he'd been working on at Tech. Talking to him all night – and on subsequent visits – we were left to wonder just how different April 16 might have turned out if that student, or any like him, had been in the building and armed. We had no doubt that this man, one of the world's elite commandos, would have moved quickly to the enemy and eliminated the threat. Just as we had no doubt that if Matt LaPorte had only been armed, that the entire rampage would have ended right then. We were left to wonder whether Cho – or any of the others who had attacked schools – would have made their horrific decisions if they knew that trained and qualified students and teachers might be armed inside.

Citizens, school officials and pundits alike speculated whether the arriving police would have shot an armed student or professor they encountered, even if he had just stopped the massacre. Most seemed to believe that in the chaos and horror that the police were thrust suddenly into, that there was no way that an armed person they confronted would not have been immediately riddled with bullets by panicked cops. But the officers we spoke to disagreed. They said that at no time were they panicked. Certainly, they were shocked and on edge by what they were seeing, but they never lost their professionalism or acted outside their training. Captain Goodman said simply, "the police inside were all too good. They were too well trained. It might have been tense for a bit, but no one would have pulled the trigger on an innocent person just because he was armed, who didn't make a threatening move."

Frustration over the perceived lack of security at VT, coupled with the university's hand-wringing over a policy to prohibit law-abiding students from possessing firearms, leaving them helpless against other Cho's who might want to exceed his record of death and destruction, saw the formation of the Students for Concealed Carry on Campus (SCCC) group, with the help of the NRA.[386] This resulted in a silent protest by countless students at VT on the one year anniversary of the killings, when students wore empty holsters on campus in solidarity of their belief in their right to be able to defend themselves. More controversial was a visit that day by Eric Thompson, owner of TGSCOM Inc., in Illinois from which store Cho purchased the first .22 Walther P22 handgun. In a tragic irony it was also the same store from which subsequent Northern Illinois University shooter Steven Kazmierczak bought two 9mm magazines and a holster in anticipation of his rampage on February 14, 2008 which resulted in five dead and 18 wounded. Brought to VT by SCCC as part of what it called "Firearms Education Week," Mr. Thompson offered to sell guns to all VT students to help prevent future attacks.[387]

Since April 16 other American schools and colleges have been attacked. Delaware State University was shot up in September 2007. One month later a high school in Cleveland, Ohio was struck. In February 2008 alone Northern Illinois University, a technical school in Baton Rouge, Louisiana, a high school in Memphis, Tennessee, and a middle school in Oxnard, California were all the victims of shootings. In addition, a school in San Mateo, California fell victim on August 24, 2009.[388] Littleton, Colorado saw yet another school attacked by a gunwielding assailant, who was tackled and subdued by a middle school math teacher on February 25, 2010. Additionally, schools were attacked in Stuttgart, Bonn and Ansbach, Germany in 2009, and two schools struck in Finland, one being Jokela High School in Tuusula in November 2007 and the other in Kauhajoki in September 2008.[389] As of the printing of this book the list in America and the world is incomplete. And it will continue to grow.

386 Roy, p. 219.
387 Roy, p. 220.
388 Roy, p. 295.
389 Ibid.

Chapter Nine
Tactical Post Mortem

"Those of us who maintain a dangerous lifestyle will experience fear and anxiety. But, to do so, allows us to join a fraternity of those who have, since the beginning of man's time, endured... They endured. We endured. It is the cost of the privilege of such company."

Paul Whitesell 1998

Dissecting Law Enforcement Decisions

In order to properly assess the overall handling of both shooting incidents at VT, a detailed analysis must be made of each critical decision point throughout the day of the attacks, as well as the preparations of the relevant law enforcement agencies in developing the capability of adequately responding to an extreme tactical threat. The following are the decision points which proved crucial in the police response to the first murders at WAJ, its investigation of those killings, the overall tactical and security response, and the subsequent attack on Norris Hall.

1. Had the relevant law enforcement agencies obtained adequate training, improved their capability based on prior experience, and developed SOPs sufficient to allow them to adequately respond to a major incident?

The fact that both departments had worked so closely together, and that both ERTs rarely functioned without the other, created a model of almost complete inter-agency operability. This allowed officers from each department to not only respond with tactics and movement that had been well prepared and synchronized in past callouts, but gave them the confidence to operate quickly and decisively with their counterparts on the other agency.

Mark Baganz, Esq., one of the nation's preeminent legal experts on police training, preparedness and negligence, concluded that both of these departments were adequately trained under federal legal standards.[390] Moreover, Captain Goodman indicated that the scene at Norris Hall resembled training exercises both departments had run in the past. This was evidence that their training was realistic. In addition, VT students had also participated in mass casualty drills. The active shooter training at the Blacksburg middle school just two months prior, where Thornhill was contacted, was real enough that when officers arrived on scene at Norris Hall they were able to quickly and competently devise a plan to assault the building and develop an appropriate attack plan once inside. In helping prepare other officers and departments for future attacks Captain Goodman opined: "This clearly shows that the mindset of all officers needs to be tactical."

It would be difficult to imagine any two agencies – particularly small ones – that could have been better prepared through training, SOPs, experience and joint-operational capability, than VT and Blacksburg demonstrated on April 16, 2007.

2. What information did police actually receive, and how well did they respond to that information, with regard to the first call alerting officials to any type of problem at WAJ?

The first indication of any problem was a generic call alerting VTPD to a possible injury due to accident in room 4040 of WAJ, which was delivered via the department's administrative line. Many departments might not dispatch one of only a very few on-duty police officers to assist paramedics in a dormitory accident as a matter of policy. In this instance, the presence of a trained law enforcement officer allowed the VTPD to quickly assess the situation, make a determination of

390 See complete legal opinion of Mark Baganz, Esq., Addendum B.

who should be immediately alerted, begin the callout of the relevant and necessary law enforcement officials and experts, and secure the crime scene and prevent contamination of it.

It was Archangel's assessment in our original AAR that this policy – and its implementation – allowed the VTPD to begin making important and critical decisions, and accelerated its investigation into the first two shootings. This was not only a policy that was prescient in its existence, but any law enforcement expert would be hard-pressed to improve on it.

3. How quickly did the agencies commit law enforcement resources in response to the first shootings at WAJ, and were those resources sufficient under the circumstances?

Considering that the first call, reporting a possible accidental injury in WAJ, came into the VTPD at 7:20 a.m., it is clear that even this report received high priority. The Virginia Tech Rescue Squad (VTRS) and a police officer were dispatched at 7:21 a.m. Many departments would have assessed this as a much lower priority, or not been so quick to respond, if at all. A lower prioritization and response by law enforcement – under the circumstances of the call and initial information conveyed - would not have been a failure to meet its duty to the university and its students. At that point there was no indication of any type of a crime, nor was there any objective, discernible need for law enforcement involvement at all. Moreover, there was not even a report of severe injury from the accident.

Despite this, both VTPD and VTRS arrived at WAJ and entered room 4040 within three minutes of receiving the call. Given the size of the campus, distances traveled, lack of any direct route from origin to destination, and the thousands of students and employees walking and driving about at that time of the morning, this was remarkably fast. Another factor in assessing the police response to, both, this first call and later police movement to Norris Hall from WAJ and the BPD headquarters when the call was received of shooting at Norris Hall, was the fact that on campus pedestrians had the right of way. During all of the time we spent on the VT campus since the incident proved that large groups of students consistently walked straight into oncoming traffic without a glance to ensure that cars would stop for them. This made rapid law enforcement movement across campus all the more dangerous to the very population they were sworn to protect, and in fact Chief Flinchum almost struck several students who walked right in front of his car even though he was speeding across campus toward Norris Hall with lights and sirens blaring. The speed with which the VTPD officers and VTRS medical personnel accessed room 4040 after arrival at the building also demonstrated clear concern on the part of both services in not delaying their entry into WAJ and movement toward the reported accident site.

4. How quickly were the night shifts of the two departments recalled to duty, and was that reasonable and necessary under the circumstances at the time?

All aspects of the police response to the first two shootings at WAJ must be viewed and critiqued in light of a very broad spectrum of similar crimes experienced by the law enforcement community across the nation, which created a standard of what was ordinary and reasonable behavior.

Many jurisdictions experience many crimes that, by all initial appearances and taken in the totality of the circumstances of the first two shootings at WAJ, would have been initially concluded to have been a domestic shooting. To criticize the response and handling of this initial crime by the two law enforcement agencies, one would first have to be able to reasonably contend that any police department that encountered a young woman and young man, both shot in the head in her room – and he in his underwear – just minutes after being dropped off by her boyfriend, should have anticipated that the worst mass murder shooting rampage ever seen at an American school was about to take place. Such a conclusion would have been ludicrous. And it would still be ludicrous the next time it was encountered.

The overwhelming majority of murders are committed by those individuals who already hold a position in the victim's closest circle of intimates. Those individuals must be examined first. The next, further-out circle or ring of likely suspects, are those who are not as intimate, but who have a motive for such an attack. Those more distant than that are individuals who have no discernible motive, or certainly no quickly discernible motive, such as for-hire killers and random murderers. For police to initially commit enormous resources in attempting to examine whether a victim was killed by a random murderer (extremely rare) or a for-hire killer (even rarer), would be to waste both resources and time in determining a strong suspect and being able to contact that individual.

In accepting these realities that police must face and work with, not only did VTPD act quickly and decisively in summoning tremendous resources, but in few jurisdictions would that magnitude of resources have been activated based on the crime scene and evidence. Many departments – particularly larger, urban metropolitan areas – see this type of crime on a regular basis. Rarely does it ever engender the massing and commitment of law enforcement resources seen as a result of the shootings of Emily Hilscher and Ryan Clark. Despite the fact that two relatively small departments were responsible for handling the investigation into those shootings and apprehension of a suspect, more police officers were quickly tasked to that effort than would typically have been seen with their big city counterparts confronting the identical circumstances.

Thus, the fact that the first officer arrived at 7:24 a.m. and called out additional resources immediately, with additional officers from VTPD arriving at 7:30 a.m., was indicative of their proper and rapid response to the crime scene. A mutual aid request was made 21 minutes later at 7:51 a.m., and both BPD officers and some ERT members had arrived by 8:15 that morning. Both police chiefs were on scene by 8:11 a.m., which would be rare in any jurisdiction. They quickly elected to recall their night shifts that had just gone off duty at 8:13, just two minutes later. This unequivocally demonstrated a rapid decision-making paradigm under difficult circumstances and two chiefs of police who immediately elected to err on the side of over-committing law enforcement resources, rather than leave anything to chance even if the statistical probabilities of the shooter being a danger to other citizens were extremely remote at the time.

5. How quickly were the two departments' tactical teams assembled and deployed, and was that reasonable and necessary under the known circumstances?

Again, one must examine the standard set by law enforcement across the nation. The overwhelming majority of ERT or SWAT teams are reserve or part-time teams, as were the ERTs for both BPD and VTPD. With most departments, this sees an average delay of 30 minutes to two hours between SWAT being called out, officers returned to police headquarters, vehicles, equipment and weapons readied, teams briefed and transported to a deployment point. An anecdotal average seen by the Archangel Team members was 45 minutes to an hour. This reality has seen many departments modifying SOPs, and training patrol officers to take a faster and more tactical role in responding to immediate threat situations. This is based on the recognition that in many instances a criminal attack can be resolved long before SWAT can be mobilized if patrol is properly trained. Active shooter training, since the Columbine attack on April 20, 1999, is an example of this modification in police response training, TTPs[391] and SOPs.

With that in mind, the quick decision to mobilize both departments' ERTs early on in the investigation not only met the highest standard and duty that could be applied to the police handling of the WAJ shootings, but could hardly have been accomplished faster.

391 Tactics, Techniques and Procdures

With BPD Chief Crannis arriving at WAJ by 8:11 a.m. (less than an hour after the shootings), and elements of both agencies' ERTs arriving by 8:15, it is clear that she had already decided to commit important resources to the investigation by another department, even before her arrival and personal assessment. This demonstrated confidence in the abilities of each chief's counterpart. Moreover, both full ERT units were mobilized at 8:15 a.m. and were assembled, organized, tasked and in position by 9:15 a.m., with the VTPD ERT having been assembled prior to that. While it was possible that this could have been accomplished in less time, it was clearly a rapid response and mobilization of substantial forces: virtually all officers from both departments.

6. How did the commanders of the two agencies decide to deploy and array the tactical teams, and was this sufficient?

As discussed above, in response to what would be considered – in the totality of circumstances – to have most likely been a domestic double homicide, the rapid arrival of two chiefs of police was significant. The speed with which this decision was made was indicative of the close working relationship between the two departments and the two chiefs. The joint decision to immediately activate substantial police resources could hardly have been made faster, nor could either agency have drawn on more officers.

Even then, other area departments were notified and conscripted into the investigation and anticipated apprehension of, first, a primary suspect or person of interest. If any criticism is to be made over their response, both departments likely over-committed their available resources as they exhausted the complete assets of their departments, potentially leaving little available for other possible emergencies demanding law enforcement response or intervention, or even protracted law enforcement presence.

7. Was it necessary under the circumstances of the information and evidence possessed by law enforcement commanders at the time to have committed so many resources in terms of police officers to arrest a single person? Would this same decision have been made by other – perhaps even better – departments under the identical circumstances?

The simple answer to this question, is "no." Most departments throughout the country would not have committed such great assets to the investigation of a double shooting, and the apprehension of a single young male adult college student. This point is best understood when considering what the liability would have been to those departments if a separate and completely unrelated emergency had occurred, and the police response was delayed due to the over-commitment of their assets. Even then, the placement of the police teams was done in such a way as to prevent any delay in law enforcement response should such a second, unrelated incident have occurred. In short, it is very difficult to find any weakness in the manner in which law enforcement was deployed, organized and placed in a very short period of time in the morning of April 16, 2007.

8. Was there sufficient evidence up to the questioning of Karl Thornhill, for law enforcement to pursue any other possible suspects? If not, did police meet their duty in solely focusing on that one individual, or did they, in fact, continue to conduct a thorough investigation that might have uncovered other possible suspects?

To answer this, one must review the information available to police and gleaned from the investigation into the first shooting at WAJ, with the benefit of the acuity of hindsight. Even with that perfect understanding of events there is still nothing that would have indicated that the attack would, or likely could, have been perpetrated by anyone other than a close intimate of at least one of the two victims. While most evidence dictated Miss Hilscher's boyfriend as a most likely suspect, the murders could have been committed by a jealous girlfriend of Mr. Clark's, or some other person (likely a student) who killed in a fit of jealousy over some perceived infidelity. This person would have most likely been a resident of WAJ or a guest of one. This made the securing of the building, and the containment and questioning of everyone inside critical. Then leads from those interviews had to be followed up. This, in and of itself, was a long and painstaking process.

Thus, the prioritization of steps in the investigation was without flaw. Though substantial resources were committed to finding Karl Thornhill as a priority, the departments jointly continued to conduct a complete investigation, including forensic examination of the crime scene, locating and interviewing a multitude of witnesses, and roving patrols of officers throughout the campus. Any one of those efforts could have provided information that would have led police in a different direction in the investigation. It was during this time that trash collection was cancelled to ensure that any evidence that had been disposed of would be contained and preserved. In short, the two agencies were "covering all the bases," and did not pursue merely a single avenue of investigation at any time during the short period between arriving at WAJ and the shootings at Norris Hall.

9. Once contacted, did the police move quickly to eliminate Thornhill as a possible suspect or "person of interest?" Even if they did, should law enforcement have continued to investigate him, or should those resources have been committed elsewhere?

When Thornhill was contacted on Prices Fork Road he was immediately questioned. Police did not waste time in first transporting him to either police headquarters before beginning the questioning process. Through that questioning, police began to suspect that Mr. Thornhill might not be the shooter. His willingness to submit to a GSR test went a bit further to cast doubt on the likelihood of him having committed the first two murders. Nevertheless, police continued in their investigation of him, including the execution of a search warrant of his home that evening, hours after the shootings at Norris Hall had ended. In all, the police followed standard and expected protocols in conducting a complete and thorough investigation into the two shootings that occurred that day, and did not cease those efforts until absolutely certain they had reached final conclusions based on well developed facts and evidence.

10. Did law enforcement move at adequate speed to search the campus and ensure Thornhill, or whoever the killer was, was not present at VT, and thus not a further threat to the VT community?

In light of the fact that the VT campus had 16 road entrances, 19.6 miles of roadway and 14,369 parking spaces, the police moved at remarkable speed to, not only, obtain a description and identifying information on Mr. Thornhill's vehicle, but committed enormous resources to searching the entire campus. This included patrolling every mile of road and inspecting every one of the parking spaces, to be able to provide some assurance to the university that the most likely suspect was no longer on campus. If any other person had been acting suspiciously it is almost certain that with so many police searching the campus that he would have been noticed and questioned.

11. Did responding law enforcement officers alert VTPD Chief Flinchum in a reasonable period of time under the circumstances of the scene they encountered?

The first officer was on scene at WAJ room 4040 at 7:24 a.m. Additional police and rescue assets were requested and on scene between 7:26 and 7:30 a.m. The first priority for all of those responders was saving the lives of the two victims, both shot but still alive. The officers were first focused on rendering first aid, requesting and securing transportation to the hospital, and then reporting the situation, with that information going up through channels to the VTPD chief of police. All of this took place between 7:30 and 7:40. This constituted a rapid assessment and reaction to the crime scene, prioritization and communication of it as a major criminal event, which was reported to the chief of police in a very short period of time.

12. Did VTPD alert BPD and request mutual aid in a reasonable period of time? Should they have done so at all under the circumstances?

As discussed above, the mutual aid request made by VTPD to BPD was done very quickly and possibly much faster than might have been the case with many departments across the country. Not only was it quickly made, but given the relative inexperience of VTPD in investigating murder scenes, that decision reflected the professionalism and objectivity of Chief Flinchum and the VTPD command staff.

13. Assuming it was reasonable and necessary for VTPD to request BPD resources, did VTPD request the appropriate resources from BPD?

Clearly, with BPD recalling night shift officers who had gone off duty, alerting its ERT, and committing virtually every other officer to this effort in some form, it would have been impossible for VTPD to request more resources, or for BPD to have provided them. Notwithstanding this, both departments still quickly involved other area departments, including MCSO and VSP.

14. Upon receiving this request from VTPD, did BPD respond in a reasonable period of time and manner?

BPD did not delay at all in responding to the request from VTPD The presence of BPD Chief Crannis at WAJ by 8:11 a.m., and deployment of substantial BPD assets even prior to that, was evidence of this.

15. Did both departments commit all resources necessary to the investigation into the WAJ killings under the circumstances?

Again, with the vast majority of officers from both departments deployed in response to the initial shooting at WAJ, it would have been virtually impossible to commit more.

16. Did the responding agencies alert and involve VSP and other agencies in a reasonable period of time?

Other agencies were rapidly notified and their assistance requested to an appropriate degree with all due alacrity. By 8:00 a.m. VSP, MCSO and other area departments had been conscripted into the effort to locate Mr. Thornhill, and VSP had dispatched an agent to assist in the investigation at WAJ. In fact, it was a MCSO deputy sergeant who located and stopped Mr. Thornhill. At no time did VTPD or BPD hesitate to request assistance or demonstrate any level of territoriality, conflict, or competition with their sister agencies.

17. Should the two responding departments have seen, identified and detained Cho as he walked across campus between the two attacks?

During our investigation into the law enforcement response to the VT shootings, both Capt. Goodman and Sgt. Wilson readily admitted that they could have driven past Cho several times as he walked across campus into the town of Blacksburg and back again to Norris Hall. However, with no single witness having seen, described or identified Cho, he would simply have been just one of more than 20,000 students walking on campus that morning. In fact, with nothing connecting Cho to either Emily Hilscher or Ryan Clark, and no single witness having seen him, if he had not committed the second attack on Norris Hall it is likely that he would never have been apprehended for the first two murders at all. There was simply no evidence tying him to those two shootings.

18. Subsequent to the shootings at WAJ, did law enforcement do a sufficient job of securing that building and establishing a demonstrable presence of police throughout the campus?

Yes. Not only was WAJ put under lockdown immediately upon the arrival of police (though Cho had long since exited, walked the two to three hundred yards back to Harper Hall and entered it at 7:17 a.m.), but dozens of patrol and ERT officers were teamed up and in position securing a tight perimeter around the building. This continued up to and through Cho's attack on Norris Hall.

19. Upon detaining Thornhill, did police stand down the two ERT units and additional officers from the two departments? Would it have been reasonable to do so?

Thornhill was the only immediate, identified possible suspect. It was their search for him and anticipation that he might resist arrest violently that dictated the decision to deploy both ERTs. However, the outcome would have likely been the same no matter who had killed the two WAJ students. Once Thornhill was contacted without incident, it would not have been unreasonable for the teams to have been stood down. However, this was not done. Secondarily, as it was appearing less likely that Thornhill was a suspect, and with no other immediate suspect whose arrest was imminent, it would not have been unreasonable for the teams to have been stood down. This was not done, either. The decision by the two chiefs of police and their respective command staffs to maintain the strongest possible police presence, including the visible presence of fully equipped and uniformed SWAT-type officers, in both the town and on campus, was evidence of the highest priority the first two murders were given, and commitment of those individuals to ensure the safety of their citizen populations.

20. Should the campus have been locked down immediately upon police concluding that the shootings at WAJ constituted a double homicide?

The desire of schools, the American public, politicians and the news media to believe that there is a single response to any attack that will serve as a panacea - eliminating the need to better prepare, plan and train for future attacks - has almost become an obsession. Those who do not wish to deal with the harsh realities of these horrific attacks want to believe that if police (or in this case the university) would only implement this one reaction immediately, that no one would ever have to worry about being injured or killed.

This smacks of the worst kind of constructive ignorance and vicious and baseless finger-pointing. No one tactic will ever be completely effective against attacks on schools. Lockdown can be - under certain circumstances - an effective first reaction. But it is only that: a first or initial response. Moreover, lockdowns are not always possible and can be ineffective depending upon the area under threat, numbers of potential victims, building dynamics, numbers of assailants and their knowledge of the school's response plan.

With the case of VT, the sheer size of the campus, ability for anyone to access it from any point on foot along its approximate 11,088 yard perimeter, almost 20 miles of road and 16 unguarded roadway entrances made an actual lockdown physically impossible. Even if VT's emergency plan to any violent episode called for immediate lockdown, the students and faculty would all know it. That could easily be integrated into any attacker's plans. That would allow the next person to first commit a diversionary crime designed to incite the lockdown response. With the attacker already in the actual target-building, his prey would be trapped. If Cho had accomplices, they could have caused far greater devastation in a single building, or split their attacks among a number of buildings, which would have seen the effective law enforcement response to Norris Hall not only delayed, but diluted. Even poet and English professor Dr. Roy recognized that even if a warning had been issued early on to the entire campus, "it would have resulted in a similarly tragic outcome. Seung-Hui Cho was determined to kill as many people as he could that morning."[392]

The tactical reality is that under the circumstances seen at VT on April 16, 2007, the students and teachers on campus would have been far safer if told to leave their buildings and flee into open areas.

392 Roy, p. 109.

Thus, locking down might have saved some lives at Norris Hall, but would have likely resulted in at least that same number of lives being taken at another building. It would have been no more difficult, and perhaps easier, for Cho to have followed the attack plan of Klebold and Harris (with whom he was so enamored) and assaulted students in a cafeteria, where he would have had large numbers in a confined space. As well, just walking through any dormitory and attacking individuals in their rooms could well have netted him a greater body count, with no one barricading themselves in their rooms, and no one recognizing that others were being attacked in the hallways. The lack of sufficient sound from the discharge of the first two rounds from Cho's 9mm Glock in Emily Hilscher's room, to alert anyone that shooting was taking place in WAJ, was proof positive of this reality. In fact, Molly Donohue – the nextdoor neighbor of Emily Hilscher – was certain that she heard yelling, but no one on the floor heard any gunshots.

21. Did police do an adequate investigative job of locating and questioning Emily Hilscher's next door neighbor, Molly Donohue?

From Archangel's investigation, it appeared that police were searching for Miss Donohue on campus, at her assigned class, in the cafeteria, calling her cell phone and contacting other friends of hers, all with no success. From Miss Donohue's statements it appeared that she was so overwhelmed by the shootings and deaths of Miss Hilscher and Mr. Clark that she couldn't remain in class, and was simply walking around campus in a daze. If she was not answering her phone, was not present in any anticipatable location, and not in contact with friends who knew police were looking for her, there was little else that could have been done. On a 2,600 acre campus with thousands of students walking about, bundled up on a very cold and windy day, the ability of law enforcement to locate this one young lady, while being so focused on finding a murder suspect and protecting the community, was like looking for a needle in a haystack.

22. How well were law enforcement forces positioned when the 9:42 a.m. 911 call came in from Norris Hall?

It would be difficult to imagine how police could have been better situated to respond to any emergency call from VT. In reaching that conclusion, it is relevant that the police had no reason to know, suspect or even anticipate that: (1) suspect Karl Thornhill would actually commit some other violent criminal act; (2) whoever the murderer of Hilscher and Clark actually was, would be a threat to anyone else; (3) any other emergency call to respond to violent crime would occur; (4) any crime would take place in Norris Hall; or (5) any attack would take place on the VT campus again that day.

Despite all of those factors, law enforcement forces were patrolling the town of Blacksburg and its surrounding environs, including all the way out to Radford. All police departments in a large area had been contacted and alerted. All roads and parking lots on the VT campus had been swept. Police had been to Thornhill's scheduled class at Radford University and his home. Both patrol officers and ERT were teamed up and positioned at the Blacksburg Police Department and WAJ, ready to respond on a moment's notice. With this arrangement of available police officers, they were as ready for any emergency as they could have been.

23. How well and sufficiently did law enforcement move to Norris Hall upon receiving the radio call of shooting taking place at Norris Hall?

Due to the first shooting having occurred at WAJ, the tactical teams of both VT and Blacksburg police departments were assembled and on-site. Capt. Goodman stated that if the first shooting at WAJ had not taken place the normal complement of officers would have been merely five BPD and four VTPD. In a meeting with Captain Goodman in July 2007, he estimated that if the Norris Hall shooting had been the first, or only, assault of Cho it likely would have taken even more time for VTPD to respond, request the assistance of BPD, and for sufficient officers to have arrived on scene, formed a team and begun to attempt entry into the building. With Cho's rate of fire this would have resulted in many more people being shot.

As it was, within a minute of the radio alert of shooting at Norris Hall, police had raced to vehicles and begun to drive to Norris Hall. Anthony Wilson had to make a short sprint from the front of WAJ to his car. He had removed his heavy vest while assisting at WAJ in an investigative capacity, and when he heard the "Active shooter," call at Norris come over VTPD Officer Lucas' radio they quickly ran to the car. By the time he realized he did not have his vest, it was too late to backtrack to get it, his M4 assault rifle or any of his other kit, as their only thought was of getting to Norris Hall as quickly as possible. Sgt. Wilson would breach Norris Hall and enter room 211 without any personal protective equipment.

The two shortest routes to Norris from WAJ were either .7 or 1.0 mile. Lt. Cook and others took a less direct route traveling approximately 1.3 miles north up roads to the west of Norris before turning east. This allowed them to come in behind (to the northwest) of the building after a 160-yard sprint, mostly up a hill and external stairs, from the closest position they could exit their vehicles. The two chiefs and Captain Goodman took the most circuitous route, nearly two miles. Officers quickly dispersed and traveled each of the available routes, effectively allowing them to come at Norris from all sides, eliminating any egress from escaping assailants, and allowing them the ability to approach the building from all points, quickly attempting entry from the three public entrances. All of this was accomplished in three minutes, with some officers arriving in less time than that. As stated, this all had to be accomplished on a campus with thousands of students walking about and crossing streets with no effort to monitor traffic for their own safety.

Initial arriving officers were grouped into two entry teams in seconds, with a third formed within another minute or two. Three teams would attempt to breach four different points (including the use of two shotgun efforts at one door and a third at another), under the sounds of gunfire, while attempting to provide cover for each other while outside the building. This would take five minutes, including Sgt. Wilson and Officer Lucas and others initially receiving a report on arrival that the shooter had moved from Norris to Holden Hall, effectively traversing the breezeway between the two buildings. When this information was communicated Wilson and Lucas had already begun driving Lucas' car up the lawn to the southern doorway facing Drillfield Drive, a 70 yard distance. Halfway up, dispatch relayed 911 reports that the shooter was in the more distant Holden Hall. He and other officers changed direction and continued to drive across grass and concrete sidewalks toward Holden Hall.

As they were approaching Holden, the dispatcher related that the earlier report was incorrect, that the shooter was still in Norris, forcing them to retrace their steps back toward Norris Hall only on foot at that time; a distance of approximately 120 total yards run by the officers. It was at this point that they also realized they had an untenable tactical position, sitting outside in the open under the view of all east side windows. They then moved quickly to the southern doors. Only at that point did they learn those doors were chained, and then moved an additional 77 yards up to the west (or Burruss) side entryway. Thus, from the time they had arrived, Sgt. Wilson and Officer Lucas had run close to 200 yards, and driven still more, before even reaching the western doors and joining up with Lt. Cook, who himself had run 160 yards uphill.

After failing to breach the public entrance doors, they moved 11 feet to the left (north) and breached the machine shop doors. From the recorded sound of the breaching round gaining them entry into the machine shop, until they had maneuvered through the shop, out into the hall, back down and around the corner into the stairwell, and had reached the second floor landing at which point Cho shot himself, was a mere 28 second period. It is hard to imagine any police department – and few elite military units – that could have done it better or faster.

24. Did law enforcement arrive at Norris Hall in a reasonable amount of time?

Without question, and in fact they managed to organize different approaches and teams in a very short period of time.

25. Did law enforcement wait an unreasonable amount of time before attempting to enter Norris Hall?

Contrary to grossly erroneous and arguably malfeasant news media reports, they did not wait at all. One cell phone video clip from a student standing to the northwest of the western entryway, appeared to show police standing outside the building with handguns drawn and pointed at the building, while gunshots could be heard from inside. The timing of the video was at the moment Wooddell, Gallemore and others were racing along Old Turner Street on the north side of Norris Hall toward the western doors, and prior to Lt. Cook arriving on scene, even though the student reported that officers came up from behind him and ordered him out of the area. This seconds-long video depicted officers arriving at the west entrance from Old Turner Street and stopping momentarily to assess the situation and maneuver toward the doors while possibly under fire. There was never a period where police simply stood outside the building and waited.

26. Did law enforcement address the fortifications and obstacles encountered upon attempting entry into Norris Hall in a reasonable manner and amount of time? Could and should entry have been accomplished faster?

With the benefits of the perfection of hindsight, arriving law enforcement officers could possibly have breached Norris Hall in less time. First, better training on the use of shotgun breaching rounds could have gained them entry into the west doors faster. This might have saved them some time, though less than a minute. Though Cho's rate of discharge was one bullet fired every 3.79 to 4.14 seconds depending on when his attack actually began. However, upon the audible sounds of law enforcement arriving at the building, he had slowed down his gunfire considerably. Still, the ability of police to quickly breach any building is critical, as every second an entry can be reduced by, may represent a bullet that did not go into an innocent victim.

As well, questions have been raised as to why the arriving officers did not drive their vehicles into the doors, gaining them immediate penetration into Norris Hall. Certainly, Archangel Group has been a proponent of this for years, and has trained police departments and SWAT teams around the country in tactics that involve vehicle breaching ever since the Beslan school siege in Russia in September 2004. However, this is a tactic that is most valuable in either (1) initially, seemingly stable barricade situations, or (2) those situations where intel has been received that doors are fortified. Clearly, there was no time for police to assess the situation and prepare immediate entry. This is the case in most domestic hostage-taking and barricade scenarios. This opportunity was also seen at the Nickel Mines Amish School in Pennsylvania, when Charles Carl Roberts nailed lumber up over windows and secured doors. But without training in this tactic, it was unrealistic to expect police to think it up, plan it and implement it in the seconds they had while gunfire was heard from inside.

Under the circumstances of Norris Hall, the police arrived and attempted entry. They had no time to assess the situation as gunfire could be heard. They also had no reason to anticipate that the doors would be fortified. Most police cars were at least 100 yards away. No car could have entered the breezeway and maneuvered to breach the eastern doors inside the covered portico. The Drillfield side entrance to the south would have necessitated a car driving up a fairly steep bank, maneuvering around a low wall and up a set of short, but steep steps before making contact with the doors. Just getting back over to Wilson's car parked on the grass outside Holden Hall and returning in it, would have required someone to run more than 100 yards, and then drive back. This would have taken more time than ultimately needed to breach the machine shop doors.

And if a car had been brought up to ram the western (central) doors, it would have entered a very tiny, confined space which would have blocked the steps, necessitating it then be withdrawn before officers could gain entry. Here as well, it would likely have taken more time to accomplish this than the officers needed to breach the machine shop doors.

Should this experience alert departments across the country to develop superior breaching tactics that guarantee entry in seconds upon responding to an active shooter, or even seemingly stable barricade situation? The answer is: Absolutely. Between the recent experiences at Nickel Mines, Pennsylvania and Virginia Tech, alone, it is clear that these techniques must be developed and included in response protocols. Did the police responding to Norris Hall fail to perform adequately in the face of the unanticipated and unanticipatable fortifications they confronted? Absolutely not. The officers that first reached Norris Hall confronted effective fortifications. They moved quickly to devise a series of methods to neutralize those fortifications and enter the building to eliminate the threat to innocent victims. They did not hesitate, but moved at the greatest possible speed. Breaching windows on the ground floor would not have been the most efficacious approach, as they were very small-paned glass sections, each held in place by thick metal bands. Clearly, these officers reacted to the obstacles they confronted, and ultimately overcame those obstacles, in a short period of time.

27. Once inside Norris Hall, did the police entry teams organize and formulate a tactical plan in a reasonable manner and amount of time? Did they execute that plan sufficiently?

According to tactical expert, and Delta Force Command Sergeant Major (ret.) and plankowner Mel Wick, upon gaining entry Teams One and Three addressed the three factors which were the most critical in an instant:

1. Move to the shooter(s) and eliminate the threat as quickly as possible;

2. Surround the shooter(s), which they accomplished by immediately sending Team Three down the first floor hallway, then up the steps to the second floor where the shooter(s) would be trapped between them; and,

3. Avoid friendly fire casualties in implementing the attack plan.[393]

These were the most critically important aspects of the assault plan that was being developed "on the fly," and they implemented tactics to address all three in a more than expeditious fashion. As well, they did not make the mistake of treating their plan as something that was to be followed without exception. This is a mistake of many law enforcement agencies: they view an OPLAN[394] as a fixed set of steps, rather than as a general guideline that must be fluid and flexible, allowing the officers the ability to modify the plan and adapt to circumstances that had been unexpected.

28. Upon reaching the second floor stairwell landings, did law enforcement respond appropriately to the cessation of shooting by the assailant? What did they do and could they have done it better?

Upon Team One reaching the second floor landing, Cho took his own life. The police, however, did not know that, nor could they have. They immediately accepted the tactical likelihood that the shooter or shooters had taken hostages, gone silent to reload, prepare battle positions, arrange human shields, and set up an ambush of officers as they moved down a long corridor that was merely 7 ft. 9 in. wide with 11 doorways on the sides of them.

393 See Expert Tactical Opinion, Addendum A.
394 Operations Plan

With Team Three initially attempting to penetrate up the second floor hallway from the south, and Team One doing the same from the opposite direction, the team leaders quickly realized the threat of a blue-on-blue, or friendly fire, incident and casualties. This, however, took some time. It was decided, communicated and implemented that Team Three would leave three officers inside the southern stairwell to prevent anyone from escaping down those steps from the second floor, or anyone on the first floor assaulting the second floor from below. The rest of the team moved up the stairs to the third floor, swept and cleared the rooms on that floor that were unlocked, before proceeding down the western steps to come in behind and link up with Team One, so that they could begin a complete search of the second floor rooms. This was as tactically effective a plan as anyone could have devised, communicated and executed in the short time they had been inside the building.

29. Did the entry teams address all of the possible escape routes of the shooter(s), as part of their plan?

Yes, and instantly. Every escape route was controlled or defended by law enforcement from the time they entered Norris Hall, with the possible exception of someone on the inside breaching windows. With windows throughout the building, they could not all be under the direct supervision of an assigned officer. However, with more and more police arriving every minute the likelihood of someone escaping at that point was small.

30. Did law enforcement inside Norris Hall follow appropriate protocols in moving throughout the second and third floors?

Yes, with the exception of the rescue of Prof. Granata. Despite the fact that he was severely wounded and respirating noisily in a manner that gave the police reason to believe he might die if not quickly treated, the entry teams violated what would be considered standard protocols or combat tactics by allowing an officer to run more than 60 ft.

down an unsecured corridor, with doors on both sides and the belief that shooters were establishing ambush positions for police, to drag the professor back up the hall so he could receive immediate medical care. No one can fault the courage of the officer who did this, or the humanitarian nature of the decision he made, but under the circumstances the better approach would have been to allow Prof. Granata to remain where he was in the hallway until all rooms between the entry team to the north and him (outside room 207) had been cleared and secured. The steadfast rule under such circumstances is not to make a bad situation worse by sending rescuers into an unsecured and extremely vulnerable area, only to end up with three, four or five severely wounded or dead people (including critically necessary members of the rescue team), rather than a single victim who has already been shot.

31. How unreasonable was the almost 16 minute period of time, during which law enforcement was on the second floor, before finally moving to room 211 in which Cho had shot himself? What were they doing during the interim and what should they have been doing?

As the police began their systematic search of the second floor in tactical mode – including silent movement and a thorough inspection of each room to ensure shooters were not present among the victims and the beginning of first aid for those victims - some officers had to provide cover to those moving down the hallway. With people down, bleeding and dying in each room they approached, they did not know which one might be a shooter. They had to carefully move through each room, rendering first aid to those in immediate need, move those most critical out of rooms and into the second floor landing to receive immediate treatment from the tac medics.

The police were following a well-prepared, combat effective, and proven tactical plan of systematically entering each room, providing sufficient cover for the entry teams and the hallways. It was due to the large number of dead and dying in room 206, which was the first classroom they came to on the east side with people in it, that they began on that side of the corridor. This was the opposite side of room 211, the door to which was closed as were the two other small offices between it and the staircase on the west side. It was while implementing this approach that they were alerted the shooter was alone, in room 211, and most likely dead. Even then, with the bodies of student Henry Lee and Prof. Couture-Nowak jammed behind and against the door, it took officers some time to attempt to encourage students to get up and help, and ultimately to blast the door open through sheer physical force. They then had to quickly assess the room, identify the shooter, and secure his weapons before Lt. Cook could send the radio message of, "Shooter down." From the time Cho shot himself until that moment took 16 minutes. And while this may seem like a long period of time, just attempting to walk through the same movements, searches and assessments made by those teams on the second floor of Norris Hall during the Archangel investigation yielded the intensely time consuming nature of all that they accomplished.

Another tactic that could have been used and that former Navy Chief John Mason says may be better, is to simultaneously enter all of the rooms using two and three man teams. Mason is a plank-owner of SEAL Team Six, now known as Dev Group,[395] the Navy's version of the Delta Force and its most elite counter-terror and hostage rescue unit. In this way any ambushing "bad guys" cannot hear the police coming as they move from room to room, clearing and securing each on the way toward an ambush. Any police teams that enter empty rooms immediately move back into the hall where they provide cover and stand by as a ready reserve in the event another team makes contact or needs assistance. Another advantage of this approach is that it allows police to contact the wounded all quickly – and simultaneously – for triage and treatment purposes, rather than have victims in the furthest rooms die in the time it takes to reach them, as happened to a school teacher in Columbine High School.

395 Combat Development Group

32. Upon determining that Cho was dead, was law enforcement negligent in continuing to search for other shooters (despite being told that he was alone) and possible explosive devices, or should those resources have been dedicated elsewhere, such as the care and transportation of the wounded?

No, and in fact they would have been grossly, legally and morally negligent if they had accepted a single unverified statement by an unknown individual that Cho was the only shooter. In fact, Emily Haas herself could not have known for certain that Cho was the only shooter. He was merely the only shooter she had seen. Moreover, they could not assume at the time she made that statement that she was not being made to do so at gunpoint.

33. Did the first responding agencies perform adequately in dealing with the numbers of other police arriving from other departments in the aftermath of the Norris Hall shootings?

If there was one aspect of the entire series of events that unfolded on April 16, 2007 that both BPD and VTPD were well prepared for, had experience in, and not only anticipated but managed almost perfectly, it was the invasion of hundreds of police officers from surrounding areas. This was anticipated by both departments, mechanisms put in place to deal with them, assignments made, resources secured and made available to provide for those officers, and the entire post-tactical phase handled without any substantial problems.

34. Did the relevant agencies meet their duties in committing substantial resources to searching and clearing numerous buildings in an entire quadrant of the campus, or could those resources have been better utilized?

Again, it would have been negligent of the departments to satisfy themselves that there were no other threats, stand the existing teams down, and not conduct an immediate search of area buildings.

Coupled with the recent bomb scares the university had suffered – including the one that day at Norris Hall – no one could afford to assume explosives devices had not been planted elsewhere, or that other accomplices were not still present on campus and a threat to the community.

35. Was it reasonable for the police departments to remain unwilling to accept that all involved in the shootings had been eliminated, and continue to investigate and search for others?

The police – and the community – could have ill afforded to simply assume Cho was acting alone until a complete and thorough investigation had been conducted. Also, Cho was incorrectly identified at first, so it was not until the following morning, April 17, that police knew for certain who the shooter was, and had a reasonable degree of confidence that he had acted alone. At first officials believed him to be a Chinese immigrant who had recently arrived in the U.S. through the San Francisco airport.

36. Was the police response to the presence of dead and dying victims adequate under the circumstances? Could it have been done better?

Many tactical teams with police departments across the country do not have assigned tactical medics. The presence of these medics – and their training, integration and experience with their assigned ERTs – allowed them to save many lives. The fact that every single victim that left Norris Hall alive would ultimately live is a testament to not only those medics but other officers in Norris Hall rendering crucial first aid. With 174 rounds having been expended into 47 victims (number of dead plus wounded, but not including those injured from other than gunshots), the average number of wounds was three per victim. Many were head shots or other critical areas.

It is impossible to suggest many ways the medical response could have been better – including the arrangement of transportation to hospitals, triage and treatment areas – under the circumstances with which law enforcement was confronted that day. One of the very few things would have been getting other "civilian side" paramedics and medical first responders into the building faster. This delay was due to a misunderstanding of terminology, and the nationwide proclivity for such professionals to refuse to go into a situation that has not been rendered completely safe. Even with more rapid entry of all medically trained personnel at such scenes it remains important that law enforcement in America recognize the need for all officers to undergo newly developed Tactical Combat Casualty Care training, which focuses on the differences between most severe and life-threatening injuries in the civilian world, and those wounds and injuries confronted in tactical situations.

An Analysis of Mass Murder Attacks

If, indeed, Cho was involved in the perpetration of the bomb scares in the weeks leading up to the shooting attack, this ultimately was counterproductive. Not only did that put both Blacksburg and VT police on high alert, but his initial shootings of the two students that morning had the affect of mobilizing and assembling all tactical and patrol teams so that the law enforcement response to the Norris Hall assault was much faster and larger than it otherwise would have been. Whether or not he was involved in the bomb scares, it is certain that with all tac teams having been mobilized for each one, penetrating the subject buildings and conducting exhaustive hours-long searches, he would have had an opportunity to observe them operate. This may have been a significant factor in the tactic he devised to chain and lock the doors to Norris Hall.

It must be assumed that terror groups and even America's own homegrown terrorists monitored and studied Cho's attack and the police response, just as American law enforcement agencies have been doing. One of the likely conclusions drawn by these terror groups would be that the general composition of American police SWAT teams may actually reveal an unexpected weakness in standard al Qaeda assault and mass-hostage siege planning. Al Qaeda planning doctrine includes the use of diversionary assaults to draw off responding forces. This is often important in the planning of *Decimation Assaults*, but may be absolutely critical in Mass-Hostage Sieges. This reality would be all the greater in the United States where police patrol response times are very short and police arrive on scene quickly. Anecdotally, this is seen frequently with the rapid response of police to bank and convenience store robberies, which results in hostage barricade situations completely unintended by would-be robbers. In al Qaeda planning, due to these rapid response times, law enforcement would most likely need to be drawn off, far away from the actual, primary assault or siege site. The other factor in this is the fact that of the 1,892 police departments in the U.S. with tactical or SWAT teams, only 165 are full time teams. The remaining 1,530 are part-time and require a significant amount of time to assemble, kit up, and deploy.[396]

At VT, due to the first shooting the part-time ERTs of both Blacksburg and VT police departments had been assembled and were present at the site of that double murder and the Blacksburg Police headquarters. In part this decision was taken due to the fact that BPD headquarters is actually closer to the central campus area than VTPD's. Though WAJ was across the campus, it was 0.7 or 1.0 miles driving distance at the shortest depending on the route taken, or approximately 1.3 miles from the headquarters in Blacksburg. When the call was received at 9:42 a.m. signaling the beginning of the second attack at Norris Hall, this readiness allowed the ERTs to arrive within two to three minutes. Had Cho not committed the first attack, none of these tactical teams would have been assembled and deployed, and response times would have been much longer. Cho had begun the second attack with 377 rounds, most of which were preset in magazines for his two weapons. Only due to the very short response time was he able to fire only 174 of those rounds. Immediately upon the entry teams breaching Norris Hall and assaulting up the staircases, he was forced to break off his attack on the students and teachers and

396 Data provided by the National Tactical Officers Association, which indicated that the status of 197 of the teams was unknown.

take his own life before the teams reached him. In all likelihood, if he had not committed the first double murder two hours earlier he would have had sufficient time to discharge all of his ammunition prior to the arrival of the tactical teams, or even a sufficient team of then on-duty officers from the two departments.

He began firing sometime between 9:40 and 9:41 a.m. This is based on an estimate that it took one to two full minutes from the first rounds being fired for a 911 call to be made, to have dispatch take the information, forward it to VTPD dispatch, for that operator to obtain sufficient information, and then make a radio call to the responding officers. The 911 call was received at 9:42, and then transferred from Blacksburg to VTPD dispatch, with the radio call being made at 9:43. The first radio call reporting arrival at Norris Hall came at 9:45, though other officers had arrived already. They had breached and entered the building well into the minute of 9:50. They had moved to the top of the western staircase leading to the second floor classrooms merely 28 seconds from entry. Thus, Cho had managed to fire 174 rounds in at most an eleven minute time span, or was firing at a rate of 14.5 to 15.82 rounds per minute, or one round every 3.79 to 4.14 seconds throughout the attack. This ratio does not take into account time for his movement between classrooms, crossing the hall or attempting to breach some of the classroom doors, during which he was not shooting.

If this had been his first attack of the day, and assuming he had used the same defensive tactics (the chaining and locking of external doors), it is not unreasonable to estimate that the first responding officer may have arrived within several minutes, but in many jurisdictions it could have been as long as ten minutes from the beginning of the attack before sufficient patrol resources from two departments could have arrived on scene, organized their teams and begun to even attempt entry. Recognizing an active shooter situation, VTPD doctrine dictated that a Hasty Team would have been formed by the first three officers to arrive. Estimating an additional two minutes for the next two officers to arrive and establish an entry team, they would have still confronted the chained and secured doors. As happened, the patrol officers would have lost valuable time breaching the doors. This would have resulted in repeated efforts to use shotgun rounds to eliminate the chains. Forty-year police veteran, Major Joseph M. Bail, Jr. estimated that this would have taken at least three to four rounds to eliminate the first chain and enter the building. If not successful in this endeavor, or if no shotguns were present in vehicles, the responding officers would have had three remaining options available; all time consuming:

(1) Return to patrol vehicles and drive them through the doors, if thought of;
(2) Return to patrol vehicles and retrieve bolt-cutters if available; and,
(3) Breach side windows in the first floor labs and offices and enter through them.

At a minimum, each of these options would have taken an additional minute, and most likely three minutes or longer. In fact it took the entry teams at VT, including trained and equipped ERT veterans with top level commanders present, five minutes from the radio report of their arrival to ultimately gain entry. If an alternative breach plan had been pursued by officers who had had no advanced warning of such an event, it could have taken ten to 12 full minutes from receiving the call before officers would have been inside the ground floor of the building. The entry teams at Norris Hall moved quickly through the ground floor, but this still took an additional 28 seconds. Even at that speed, this could have allowed Cho an additional 13 minutes. Depending on the shooter, this time could actually have been greater as it cannot be discounted that part of Cho's impetus to take his own life was the overwhelming law enforcement response and large numbers of police at Norris Hall. If that number had been merely three, he (or any shooter) might not have made the decision to end the attack by taking his own life so quickly. In fact, he may have chosen to ambush and engage police at such low numbers.

Applying the fire rate of Cho, this would have resulted in an additional 188.5 to 205.66 rounds having been fired at the very least; though Cho only had an additional 203 rounds with him. If any, or all, of these factored times were actually longer (as they might be depending on the geographical size of any jurisdiction and patrol area vis-à-vis the number of officers present and distances to be traveled), this number would, of course, increase. Of 174 rounds, Cho managed to strike (i.e., wound or kill) 47 victims, or affect a casualty ratio of 3.702 rounds per victim. This supports the tac team commanders' observations that most students had been shot two or three times, with some as many as five times.

Applying the range of additional rounds Cho would have discharged to the rounds-per-victim, this delay in law enforcement response could have yielded an additional 55.28 to 59.53 victims, for a total count of wounded and dead of 106.28 to 110.53. Applying as well his ratio of 59 percent killed and 41 percent wounded, the casualty numbers would have increased by at least 32.65 deaths and 24.41 more wounded. For him to have expended the 203 rounds he was not able to fire, would have taken only 12.83 to 14 minutes more than the time he was actually attacking the students on April 16. Thus, we come dangerously close to the complete expenditure of his complement of ammunition, and a maximum casualty number of 111 victims, comprised of 63 deaths and 46 wounded. This would have been more than double the 30 dead and 17 wounded actually suffered at Norris Hall.

Juxtaposing this with al Qaeda teaching, it will be realized by terrorists that what would ordinarily be a vulnerability in U.S. law enforcement response capability – i.e., the need to assemble part-time SWAT teams – will actually work to the advantage of police if terrorists, in fact, use diversionary attacks well preceding the primary attack. Recognizing that within terrorists' paradigmatic thought and planning, the first attack at WAJ was, for them, a tactical diversion. Yet this diversion only resulted in superior law enforcement presence, preparation and reaction time. This may result in any future terrorist assault plans either not including the use of diversionary attacks, or planning such attacks much closer in time to the primary assault.

For this reason, it must be part of standard police response TTPs in the event of any major attack – particularly any attack on an educational institution – that all departments' tactical teams within a broad area be assembled and ready to deploy. It would not be efficacious to deploy all such teams to the site of that first attack, as it must be considered that terrorists could plan to ambush those rescuers before moving onto the primary attack. Or, they could simply use that opportunity to increase the bodycount of that first attack with more police officer deaths, even if it is the only one. Moving these teams to positions from which they can quickly deploy to the attack site, without placing themselves in a danger zone, would be the optimal approach. From those positions they could quickly move to the initial attack site if additional support was needed, or move to any secondary, tertiary or quaternary attack sites in the area. This approaches the military model of always keeping a ready reserve unit behind to use in just such exigencies and was fundamentally the way law enforcement forces were staged between the WAJ and Norris Hall assaults.

With an attack of this type, both administration and police are confronted with a dilemma. To not attempt to limit large numbers of students moving about outside could be both dangerous to the students and render it impossible for police to identify and isolate an assailant. However, not knowing how many attackers are part of the plan to shoot and kill innocent victims inside buildings, ordering everyone to remain in their current locations could create better mass killing conditions for the assailant(s), particularly in buildings like Norris Hall where the classrooms could not be locked from the inside. Ordering large numbers to thus remain inside rooms that cannot be locked and secured merely ensures large numbers of confined victims without the ability to move, secure themselves or even defend themselves.

There must be a way for everyone to secure themselves inside of classrooms and offices, yet still allow police to breach those rooms quickly in an emergency. Master keys distributed to all police patrol and SWAT officers is, perhaps, the simplest and cheapest. Or all rooms could have keypad locks inside and out, with emergency responders having a single code to access all rooms and buildings. But even technological solutions like this have inherent problems. The GWOT (Global War On Terror) has taught us, as did America's experience in Vietnam, that there are always low tech solutions to high tech security and obstacles. A single gunshot to a keypad could render it impossible for arriving police to open the doors from the outside.

It is clear, as the VT experience and others have shown, that there is no single, one-size-fits-all solution to the preparation of law enforcement or schools, emergency response procedures of schools, or response tactics of police that will serve as a panacea for all attacks. One of the most important things that any school and law enforcement agency can do first, is recognize that America's school are under siege. Every school in America is under threat. In every elementary, middle and high school, there is a Klebold or Harris who has a plan to attack that school, as they did at Columbine and so many others have done across the nation, before and since. Every town in America has a Charles Carl Roberts, IV from Nickel Mines, Pennsylvania or a Duane Morrison from Bailey, Colorado, and those two murderers have just empowered the others, giving them confidence they can achieve the revenge they crave. Every college and university in the country has a Cho, and they are all putting plans together to defeat law enforcement and surpass Cho's tally of wounded and killed. And in every state in America there is an al Qaeda or related terror group cell, and they are all gathering intelligence on our schools in anticipation of a possible Beslan-style assault.

Every one of these groups studies the attacks that came before. They examine what has worked and improve on the tactics and fortifications from those earlier attacks. Just as Cho studied the attack on Columbine and had an opportunity to learn about the fortifications used in Bailey and Nickel Mines a short half-year before his rampage. Thus, police must be studying them as well, and recognize that the next one will be worse. The attackers will have a plan designed to be impossible for police, for they must delay police response and entry into a building to give them sufficient time to kill as many people as possible. This is the value in police forever preparing for the worst possible things they can imagine. They must push themselves in training and in their FTXs to constantly confront newer and ever more difficult tactics. This is where they should fail: in training. Only then can they learn from their training efforts, and improve their capabilities. Gone are the days when FTXs can or should go smoothly, with the police tactics working perfectly and all of the victims or hostages being saved, with no officers lost. For the enemy – in whatever form that enemy takes – is not going to make things that easy on our police officers.

Thus, we must look at the degree to which the primary departments of VTPD and BPD had prepared for, and responded to, the circumstances they confronted on April 16, 2007. The police response to those events can be broken down into several general categories:

1. Law Enforcement (LE) preparation and training for extreme tactical events;

2. LE response to the first shooting at WAJ;

3. LE and VT response to ensure the security of the university community;

4. LE positioning prior to the assault on Norris Hall;

5. LE response to the assault on Norris Hall;

6. LE and medical first responder performance in the post-assault phase at Norris Hall.

Taking all aspects of that horrific day into consideration, the police performed competently in the administration of their duties, and admirably in the speed and commitment demonstrated in moving quickly to and into a fortified building with an active shooter.

For two small departments in a remote, rural region of the mountains of southwestern Virginia, it would have been impossible for anyone to have imagined the magnitude of the attack experienced on the campus that morning. In fact, no one anywhere in the country, even in our biggest and most crime-ridden urban areas, could have imagined it. It was, after all, unprecedented. Still, the command staff of these departments ensured that their officers were well equipped, well armed, well trained and had prepared for every possible major threat scenario from Columbine-type active shooter attacks to terror assaults. They had learned well the lessons from the Morva murders and manhunt the prior August, and they brought those lessons quickly to bear at Norris Hall. More than even that, due to the intensely close relationship between the two departments and their respective chiefs and command staffs, the Blacksburg and Virginia Tech police departments were an almost perfect model of law enforcement interagency operability.

From interviews it became clear early on that the mentality of such critical command personnel at VTPD as Chief Wendell Flinchum, ERT commander Lt. Curtis Cook, BPD ERT Operations Commander Capt. Donnie Goodman and ERT leader Sgt. Anthony Wilson, was that every officer must be trained and ready to fight to protect the innocent. Their mentality was that "if it could happen anywhere, it could happen here." And they were ready. Certainly they were as ready as they could be. Also, from time spent with those professionals it was clear that they were all saddened to have been proven right.

The law enforcement response to the first two victims at WAJ could scarcely have been better, and with virtually all resources of both departments committed it is difficult to imagine how it could be improved on in the future. From the initial response, to the investigation, call out of all available resources, deployment of the ERTs, to the search of the campus, presence of security patrols and staging of officers and ERT to respond to a possible hostile situation with the one potential suspect, both departments demonstrated a deep commitment to both the resolution of that first criminal episode, and the protection of the citizens of Virginia Tech and Blacksburg. Even detractors who may argue that these agencies were too focused on the one potential suspect, could not contend that the deployment of such a vast array of law enforcement resources and the manner in which they were positioned placed them in a weaker position to respond to any other unanticipated emergency.

With regard to the decisions of the university Policy Group and VTPD in not immediately closing campus, going into lockdown, or better alerting the university community with more specific information on the first shooting at WAJ, their propriety and efficacy can be debated endlessly. Many of the issues surrounding that debate have little relevance to the tactical aspects of the police response, which is the sole focus of this book. Still, it should be noted – as discussed in this chapter – that a large school, comprised of 131 buildings on campus (153 in all), and with all of its various 26,000 students locked in, could have posed an even greater problem for both police and the victims than was seen at Norris Hall. It would have been impossible to secure the entire campus.

Just assembling the minimal number of police necessary to cordon the campus would have taken far more time than the two hours between the two shootings. Even if a police perimeter could have been established around the entire university in an impossibly short amount of time, Cho would have been locked off campus, as he was returning to VT from Blacksburg by 9:02 that morning. Not only could police, in all practicality, not have maintained this campus-wide lockdown for long, but Cho would have simply waited to re-enter and then launch his assault, even if that meant attacking Norris Hall the following day, or he would have launched his attack the day after that, after things had settled down. In short, such efforts would have been a horrendous waste of time, effort and law enforcement resources, and yielded no benefit to either the police or the VT community.

In future attacks, quickly notifying the community via radio, television, email, cell phone message, instant message, and website, may be the best way of communicating in-depth information. Whether officials should attempt to meet a duty to fully inform that community of the reality of a major crime, or protect them from that information due to concerns over inciting fear and panic or alerting the attackers, is another issue that can be validly debated, and over which reasonable people may disagree. Certainly, Virginia Tech could have made the decision to attempt to notify everyone at the university of the first shootings immediately, allowing each student to make his or her own decision about venturing out that morning.

The sad reality is that no matter which a university and police department chooses to do in a future attack, they will be subject to liability exposure for the decision they do make. And despite the benefit of hi-tech systems to communicate crucial information, it must be recognized that many members of the targeted audience – particularly on a college campus – will not be in a position to receive that communication. A far lower technology solution in the form of a campus-wide loudspeaker system for emergency use only, may be a more efficacious – and cheaper - solution. If utilized, however, that system could only ever be used to communicate information in true emergencies, as to use it for more mundane purposes would, over time, have the likely effect of students ignoring it.

Notwithstanding the sufficiency of the information VT communicated to its students and employees, the reaction of police to the WAJ shooting was exceptional. The presence of law enforcement investigating the shooting of Emily Hilscher and Ryan Clark was demonstrative. The police presence securing the area around WAJ was more than sufficient. Locking down WAJ was a necessary and appropriate decision until all possible witnesses had been interviewed and it had been determined that the assailant was not still in the building. Roving patrols of police on campus, searching for any indication of the attacker in addition to searching for Mr. Thornhill's pickup truck was handled quickly and sufficiently. The recall of the night shifts from both departments was an extra step that ensured adequate police resources for, not only, the investigation into WAJ and apprehension of Mr. Thornhill, but to be able to handle standard law enforcement duties on both the campus and in Blacksburg. Calling in the MCSO only added another layer to this, and demonstrated both professionalism and foresight. The callout of both ERTs in full force, and their deployment and use both on campus and at the BPD headquarters and elsewhere, was as good a pre-tactical plan as could have been devised under the circumstances.

The law enforcement response to the radio alert of shots fired at Norris Hall was as rapid as could have been accomplished. The pre-positioning of all police assets not only ensured a substantial and rapid response, but resulted in police approaching Norris Hall from all points, a necessary tactic (intended or otherwise) in advancing quickly toward either a Mass-Hostage Siege or Active Shooter scenario. The police wasted no time in advancing on the building and attempting to enter. It must be realized that upon approaching the building police immediately attempted to enter – without delay – and only then learned that doors had been chained. This bespoke the tactical mindset, courage, professionalism and commitment of the officers.

Upon encountering the chained doors, decisions were made quickly to defeat the fortifications. When one effort was unsuccessful, they defaulted to an alternate plan in seconds. This was done repeatedly. This is one of the most important skills to develop in police when responding to such scenarios: the ability to abandon any aspect of a plan – or an entire plan – when circumstances dictate a different approach. Attack plans, no matter how carefully and perfectly prepared, must be recognized as mere guidelines. They must always remain fluid and adaptive. And while breaching capability of the two departments at Norris Hall could, arguably, have been better, in the end they gained entry into Norris Hall in an expeditious manner and moved quickly to the sound of the guns. The lesson there was that all departments must be developing superior breaching capability in both its patrol and tactical officers. In the three most recent, major school attacks – Bailey, Nickel Mines and VT – the attackers used fortifications. Each attack improved on the fortifications of the one that came before. Police must anticipate that the fortifications used in the next school attack – or assault on any building – will be superior to those used by Cho, and have the capability to eliminate them quickly.

The medical response – including the aid provided by tac medics, paramedics and police officers – was rapid, competent and life saving, although the "civilian-side" medic assets should have entered the building more quickly. They do not have to be trained to operate "with" police in a high-threat environment, but they should follow law enforcement instructions on when to enter. Triaging of patients and the rendering of care was virtually textbook, especially by the two tac medics. But even this was only possible due to the SOP of both ERTs having a tac medic deploy with them. Every victim who was alive when transported from Norris Hall ultimately lived. Despite the inability to put helicopters in the air to aid in the transport, convoys of vehicles to definitive care facilities was competently and expeditiously arranged. Even if wind conditions had allowed the use of helicopters, the large number of severely wounded would have quickly exhausted those assets and any benefit therefrom, and ground transportation would still have been needed. Those victims suffering from lesser wounds were moved and treated at first aid stations established a short distance from Norris Hall.

There are two important realizations to be taken from the post-tactical phase of Norris Hall. One is that all police need to be trained in Tactical Combat Casualty Care. This is the best training to be made available for law enforcement and military alike in decades. The second comes from Sgt. Anthony Wilson. In the aftermath of the horror that was Norris Hall, he said that all police needed to realize that when dealing with young victims, children and even young adults, all the rules change. He acknowledged that police are taught to not touch wounded victims, to not get bloody, to wait for the medical professionals to arrive. But, he said:

> When it's just kids, and in the case of Norris Hall when there are so many of them that the medics can't deal with them all, you're going to get bloody. If you have to put your bare hands into the body of a child to pinch off an artery, you're going to do it. If you have to put your mouth on the mouth of a child or young girl to save that life, you're going to do it, and you're not going to hesitate. You're not going to look for gloves, or a screen to keep your mouth off of their mouth. After all, you're a police officer and an adult. You've had your chance at life. You're trained and capable. Those kids haven't had their chance yet.

Nothing could better articulate the mindset and commitment necessary in all of America's police in preparing for the next attack.

Wendell Flinchum adds a couple of things of his own that he believes are important for all police to realize. First, that it is important to have already established relationships with other police departments and agencies, and to be able to call on them for help when the time comes. Col. W. Steven Flaherty, Superintendent of the Virginia State Police – the chief executive officer of the entire VSP – agreed saying, "You don't build those [relationships] in a foxhole, you build those before it happens." Chief Flinchum also thinks that shotguns remain an important and viable law enforcement weapon. "I know some PDs think shotguns are obsolete," he said. "But if you can have both [shotguns and carbines], then carry both. Shotguns are cheap insurance." Finally, he has come to believe that on arrival at a critical, active shooting situation that the first cop needs to go in. He points out that most of these shootings – especially those in our schools – are ending by suicide as soon as the first cop gets in the door. With regard to his own behavior at Norris Hall that day he says, "Talking with Kim [Crannis] there was never any thought of 'should we or shouldn't we', it's that we were cops and that's what we had to do."

Within two hours of the attack at Norris Hall news media "experts" on major cable and network channels were condemning the police response. Some supposed experts, even claiming affiliation with the largest and most prestigious law enforcement associations, were making such statements as: "They do not deserve to call themselves a police department," and "They do not deserve to call themselves a SWAT team." Within a few days of the attacks I received an email from a reporter with an eastern newspaper. It contained the complete article he had written on the police response, including a page and a-half of his conclusions of all the things they had done wrong. He was merely looking for some supposed "expert" whose name he could hang on the article, who was willing to be attributed with saying all of those things, of criticizing what the police had done. I wrote back, telling him that his entire article was inappropriate. I stated, "At this point in any event of this magnitude no one knows exactly what happened. The only thing that is certain is that what happened is not what you in the media have been reporting." The reporter found someone else to hang his claims against the cops on and still ran his article. To his credit, however, he did include my objections.

All of these erudite dilettantes were willing to roundly criticize the actions of a group of dedicated men and women, reacting quickly and decisively to the worst mass shooting ever seen by any department in our nation. These media hounds, more desirous of their own celebrity than the truth, were not there, and at the time they were rendering their vexacious opinions they knew virtually nothing of the facts, truth, or actual conduct of those agencies. That evening, with the university Inn being used as an assembly point for the parents and families of the victims, Chief Flinchum was making death notifications inside. When he was speaking to one of the victim's parents at The Inn they were watching the national news, and they were announcing how badly the police departments' performance was. He didn't know how to even respond. But then just how do brave yet humble men and women even begin to defend themselves, especially in the midst of so much death? He said that making the death notifications was particularly horrendous. In another instance,

Donnie Goodman appeared to tell a family that their child had died, only to learn that it was a mistake. "That's how screwed up things were for a while," he said. The stress and anxiety for Flinchum and the others would only continue in the days and weeks ahead.

As of the writing of this book, almost four years after the shootings, and with the benefit of months spent at VT and Blacksburg over a dozen trips, countless hours interviewing police, command staff, students and first responders, plus additional days spent with Sgt. Wilson doing joint training at a regional SWAT conference in Colorado, the assessment of every aspect of the police response and operations, including discussions with those who survived, it is hard to imagine how any department could have performed better. Delta Force plankowner and Command Sergeant Major Wick, in his expert analysis and in our conversations, said of the law enforcement response to the Norris Hall shootings that no other unit, even the military's most elite counter-terror teams, could have done it better or faster. And that the police at Virginia Tech probably moved too fast. This is high praise coming from one of the creators of the world's most elite special operations and hostage rescue units, whose concern in ever operating with police has been that they typically move too slowly and carefully. The training, preparation, interagency operability and conduct of these departments and their officers should serve as a model for all police throughout America. Still, as one officer explained, the trauma from the event itself is one thing. But the trauma created by the media is truly devastating. Irresponsible media reporting has devastated the families of the victims, the families of the officers, and the cops themselves.

However, whether inexcusable or meeting the highest standards of journalistic ethics, the Virginia Tech shootings were a big story. Even good, factual reporting was affecting people and relationships, so great was its magnitude. No one was prepared for such an onslaught. The problems with the media on the VT campus, and throughout the town of Blacksburg, were overwhelming. Within a day of the attacks, with a veritable blight of reporters having descended on the grieving community, like a swarm of locusts feeding on the crops of human suffering, every door on every building on university grounds had a sign posted. It read:

> NOTICE TO THE MEDIA
> We ask that you respect our grieving and recovery.
> Please no media beyond this point.
> For interview requests, call 540-231-5396.
> The Virginia Tech Community.

For weeks, enormous news vehicles with their satellite antennae thrusting toward the sky, consumed every parking space in the area, legal or otherwise. Instantly 125 of those behemoth vehicles seemed to have materialized on campus, and police had to find places to stick them. Guests in hotels could scarcely find room for a single family car. The entrance doors of virtually every bar and restaurant in the town had signs – some of them handwritten – that said, either, "Media not welcome," or "If you are a reporter you can enter to eat and drink, but keep your cameras in your car and your mouths shut." Horror stories of journalists' behavior circulated through the area at the speed of sound. Among the worst was the story of one reporter who dressed as a priest to sneak into the hospital rooms of wounded and suffering students to extract any scandalous statement he could use for a headline. Other reporters paid students for their IDs to get into the hospital with. Even to this day, the names of several national news media anchors and reporters are spat from the mouths of cops there as though they are the foulest of curses.

Lucinda Roy observed that "reporters were blamed … for their reckless, insensitive pursuit of the story, and for the ways in which the tragedy was being sensationalized."[397] In all of this, the town of Blacksburg – in its singular and united hatred of the media – would bring a flood of memories from Beslan racing back to me. Roy wrote, "If you were a member of the media, you were despised. And if you spoke to the media, you were complicit in wounding the community."[398] At Beslan, the only thing that kept you from being

397 Roy, p. 87.

lynched by the people of the town was the ability to quickly convince them that you were not a reporter.

Dr. Roy has been critical of what she considered to be the university's ostrich-like reactions in dealing with the media tidal wave. In comparing it to Cho's diagnosis of selective mutism while in middle school, she wrote:

> After the tragedy it seemed to me that his condition was contagious. It was as if a collective selective mutism had descended upon an administration determined to keep silent in the face of harsh criticism. Terrified of litigation, embroiled in a controversy about the infamous 'two-hour delay' in notifying a campus, a president and his advisory team circled the wagons.[399]

However, even Professor Roy admitted that some improvements have been made in the wake of Cho's rage. She acknowledged that there was a "very efficient emergency notification system (e-mail, phones – cell and landlines) and a siren warning." Moreover, new people have been hired in important positions within, both, the VTPD and student support. No doors can be chained shut in any building on campus. An announcement screen informs all what to do in the event of an emergency.[400] Perhaps in an effort at tying the strengths of academia to the healing process, two new programs were being instituted. A Center for Peace Studies and Violence Prevention is chaired by Professor Jerzy Nowak, widower of slain French professor Jocelyne Couture-Nowak, and students would soon be able to earn a minor in Peace Studies through the College of Liberal Arts and Human Sciences. A Center for Student Engagement and Community Partnerships was also slated to begin. As of the publication of her book, both were to be headquartered on the second floor of Norris Hall. [401]

398 Ibid.
399 Roy, p. 5.
400 Roy, p. 293.
401 Ibid.

Conclusion

"Oh God said to Abraham, 'Kill me a son...'
Well Abe says, 'Where do you want this killin' done?'
God says, 'Out on Highway 61'."
Bob Dylan

Despite the intense media scrutiny, and daily – if not hourly – desire of reporters to invent new spins on the story, reliable information on Seung-Hui Cho was not in abundance from media sources after the attacks. As neither BPD nor VTPD took the lead role in the investigation of the shootings or Cho himself subsequent to the massacre, even their information on him was not in-depth.[402] A significant amount of information was later provided by the Governor's Panel in its report, including what the GPR stated was, "one of the most significant" sources of information having been a three-hour interview its investigators conducted with Cho's parents and sister.[403] "The family stated that they were willing to help in any way with the Panel's work, and felt incapable of redressing the loss for other families," the GPR stated.[404]

Concerning the incident on April 16, 2007, Cho's sister expressed remorse and disbelief on behalf of herself and her family. On April 20, 2007, Sun-Kyung discussed her feelings and those of her family in a prepared statement:

> On behalf of our family, we are so deeply sorry for the devastation my brother has caused. No words can express our sadness that 32 innocent people lost their

402 There was an investigative task force and VTPD was part of it, but it was the VSP's investigation.
403 GPR, p. 31.
404 Ibid.

> lives this week in such a terrible, senseless tragedy. We are heartbroken.
>
> We grieve alongside the families, the Virginia Tech community, our State of Virginia, and the rest of the nation. And the world….
>
> We are humbled by this darkness. We feel hopeless, helpless, and lost. This is someone that I grew up with and loved. Now I feel like I didn't know this person. We have always been a close, peaceful, and loving family. My brother was quiet and reserved, yet struggled to fit in. We never could have envisioned that he was capable of so much violence. We pray for the families and loved ones who are experiencing so much excruciating grief. And we pray for those who were injured and for those whose lives are changed forever because of what they witnessed and experienced. Each of these people had so much love, talent, and gifts to offer, and their lives were cut short by a horrible and senseless act. He has made the world weep.[405]

Cho's sister and family ended with the statement: "We will do whatever we can to help authorities understand why these senseless acts happened. We have many unanswered questions as well."

Despite this heartfelt expression of despair and willingness to assist in the investigation by Cho's family members, the information obtained must be viewed with a certain amount of circumspection, as the Governor's Panel appeared to have failed to follow minimal protocols in conducting such an interview. Cho's parents were apparently uncomfortable communicating in English (or were simply incapable of it), and the panel investigators did not arrange to have a professional, objective interpreter translate the questions and answers

405 "Cho family statement, *CNN.com*, " http//:www.cnn.com/2007/US/04/20/shooting.family.statement/index.html..

between English and Korean. Instead, they relied on Cho's sister, Sun, to perform this function. Thus, it is possible that important information was lost, filtered, modified, not communicated, otherwise paraphrased or euphemized, or simply not conveyed, based upon filial loyalties and emotional stresses. This is in no way an indictment of Sun, or intimation that she would have done anything intentionally to limit the exchange of information. However, for a young woman who was suddenly thrust into the role of being the sole conduit of intimate and sensitive information about her brother, whom she loved, and officials investigating the worst mass shooting murder at a U.S. school in history, committed by that very brother, it would be impossible to expect that she would be capable of performing that task to the degree of a qualified professional with no personal ties to the subject or his family.

She was not just being asked to translate words. She was being asked to serve as a channel for information, a portal between two worlds and cultures, and a prism for interpreting all that had ever gone on in her brother's and her family's life together. At once she was interpreter, translator, culture expert, witness, grieving family member, loving sister, family representative, wounded victim and protective daughter. How could she possibly have been asked to do this?

It is unlikely that anyone will ever know much of the information that might have been gleaned about Cho's behavior, motivations, preparations or prior behavior, that would have served as *indicia* that an attack was in the offing. Or even know the myriad tiny details of his life that might assist experts understand such behavior, and create some type of profile that could be of benefit in the future. Had the interview been conducted according to standard procedures used in even the most minor judicial proceedings, all law enforcement interviews and advisements, and intelligence-gathering operations, information developed would likely not only have been more complete, but could have aided in efforts to develop recognition of predictive behavior of others in the future. At the very least, much more might have been understood about Cho and his life.

Much of this would also have centered on Cho's last years. A great deal of speculation was incited by Cho's writing "Ismail AX" on his forearm in red ink prior to his attack, and his choice of "A. Ishmael" as the name he put on the return address of the package he mailed to NBC between the two sets of shootings. "Ismail" is the spelling preferred by Muslims, and "Ishmael" the Judeo-Christian spelling of this name. Both refer to the son of Abraham and Agar, the concubine of Sarai, Abraham's wife when she could not conceive a child. The name meant "may God hear." According to history Ishmael's father, Abraham, was the son of a wealthy idol manufacturer. He grew up in present day Iraq. He eventually came to believe that there was only one true god and, according to legend, took up his axe and smashed his father's idols. He later moved to present day Israel where he was confronted with a barren wife who could not produce a child. Only after the bastard son Ishmael had been born did he have a son by his wife, whom he named Isaac.

God ultimately came to Abraham and instructed him to kill his son Isaac as a test of his devotion. Abraham took up his knife and was about to murder Isaac when God stopped him. Isaac lived and ultimately inherited all that Abraham had and became a man of great wealth, and the progenitor of the Jews. Ishmael and his wife were then disinherited and cast out into modern day Saudi Arabia. Then in the 7th century the founder of Islam, Muhammed, altered the story to say that it was Ishmael who was the true, faithful descendant of Abraham, not Isaac. He claimed that Ishamel was the one God ordered killed, making him the "Son of Sacrifice," even altering the tool of Abraham's murder to an axe rather than a knife. Many Muslim groups trace their origins to Ishmael and his founding of the 12 Arabic tribes.

Barely had blood begun to cool when all manner of would-be experts, conspiracy theorists and Islamophobes began disseminating their certainty that Cho had converted to Islam, that he had become a radical jihadist.[406] Rumors even abounded that he had prayed in the mosque located inside the Student Union building, shaved his body

406 Others speculated that it was a reference to Herman Melville's *Moby Dick*, the famous opening line of which was, "Call me Ishmael."

of all hair and performed other martyrdom rituals in anticipation of the killings and his ultimate death. Not only was none of this true, but there was no mosque in the Student Union at all. Even people we met at VT immediately after the attacks, including a psychologist, were convinced of these fantasies. Still, the fact that Cho selected Holocaust Memorial Day to launch his attack, together with other evidence, have given rise to not unreasonable suspicions that he was a member – or wanted to become one – of a Korean Islamist or other jihadist group.

"Ismail" was also quickly connected by experts, pundits and bloggers to a "Virginia jihad network," which was also known as the "Paintball Jihad Network." Two of its more notorious members were South Korean-born Yong Ki Kwon, also from northern Virginia (in the Fairfax area) and an Engineering alumnus of VT, and one Randall Todd Royer. Yong was convicted of conspiracy to commit acts of terrorism in November 2003, when Cho was in the fall semester of his freshman year at VT. Sentenced to 11-and-a-half years in prison, Kwon ultimately testified against others involved in the Virginia jihad, including Ali Al-Timimi, an Islamic scholar sentenced to life in prison in April 2005. This was during spring semester of Cho's sophomore year. Khwaja Hasan, another partner in their terrorism effort, also pled guilty.

At a meeting on September 16, 2001 they had all agreed to travel to a Lashkar-e-Tayyiba (LeT) camp where they intended to obtain combat training, from whence they intended to engage in violent jihad in Afghanistan against the American troops that they expected to soon invade the country. LeT would be the group that launched the terror attacks on Mumbai, India in November 2008. Occidental, American Royer was known under the alias "Ismail" and convicted of conspiracy to conduct jihadist acts in 2004. Kwon graduated before Cho arrived at VT, and there has not been any information released from the investigation of the Governor's Panel to establish that Cho ever met or corresponded with any of the convicted terrorists, or any member of the Virginia Jihad Network, as it was dubbed by federal officials.[407] Then again, the panel may not have looked into this at all. Still, the high profile indictments, pleas of Kwon and his partners and subsequent northern Virginia media-focused trial of Al-Timimi himself, likely did not go unnoticed by Cho. These cases received blanket news coverage throughout Virginia, and the VT connection with Kwon was well known.

For many, the fact that Cho, Kwon, Al-Timimi and the entire Virginia Jihad Network were all based in the same general area of northern Virginia, together with the commonality of Cho and Kwon being South Koreans and both having enrolled at VT, was enough information to incite suspicion. All of that, together with Cho's use of the pseudonym "A. Ishmael" on his NBC package and writing the name "Ismail AX" on his forearm in advance of his massacre, was enough to allow many to conclude that if he had not actually become conscripted into an Islamist group, he was likely inspired by them in planning and launching his attack. Certainly, the nature of his video-taped rants against other students for alcohol consumption, immoral sexual relations and excessive Western decadence could have been written by Usama bin Laden himself, a person he even referenced in his diatribe.

Indeed, this conclusion was not only drawn by those seeking to project Cho's attack onto a larger, global screen, but Islamist terrorist groups themselves. Their websites quickly used the same information to adopt Cho as one of their own, touting his self-generated attack as exactly the type of commitment to jihad and deaths of infidels, and those attacking Islam, that all Muslims must strive toward. The town of Blacksburg did have two mosques and a large Muslim population that, according to officials, largely maintained itself quite separate from the community-at-large. No information has ever been released addressing whether Cho had ever attended or even visited either.

407 Roy, pp. 262-263; see generally, Milton Viorst, "The Education of Ali Al-Timimi," *Atlantic Monthly,* June 2006, http://www.theatlantic.com/doc/200606/viorst-terrorist.

April 16 and its conspiracy-fueled aftermath was not the end of the tragedy that the two police departments would endure, however. It merely put a spotlight on them, a laser beam of infamy on their heretofore sleepy town and idyllic college setting. Since Cho's massacre, not only have they continued to suffer a seemingly never-ending series of devastating events, but each one that had the name "Virginia Tech" appended to it in any contrived or tenuous way succeeded merely in refocusing that spotlight on them. Thus, four years after Cho's rampage things for the VT police had still not returned to normal.

The ominous cloud that brought both Morva and Cho to Virginia Tech and gentle, quiet Blacksburg continued to blot out the light of hope that they may someday get beyond the image of Cho, get beyond the dead. Within a year after Cho's attack South Korean student Daniel Kim committed suicide by shooting himself in the head in the Target parking lot in nearby Christiansburg, saying that he felt he looked like Cho and was hated. In the aftermath of Cho's horror he supposedly was unable to take how he perceived others saw him. His parents sued the university.

But for the police officers from the two departments it was not destined to end even there. More than a year after the attacks they were still receiving more than 100 letters and emails a week from people who called them murderers, who said that they should blow their brains out for having been such cowards, for having stood outside for hours while innocent kids were gunned down. Wendell Flinchum told us, "You wouldn't believe the hate mail and emails I got and still get to this day." At one point he had received more than 800 addressed just to him in a single day. Though many were positive, there were many "hate emails" as well. The stress continued. And so did the incidents that served to forever remind the world of what had taken place there in April 2007.

As late as November 17, 2008, even VT's local paper *The Roanoke Times* ran an article with a photo of a horde of police officers frantically racing toward one of their staff photographers with the caption: "Blacksburg police officers run **from** Norris Hall on the Virginia Tech campus on April 16, 2007." (emphasis added)[408] The paper just couldn't help but twist yet another knife into the back of the police, even in an article that was about nothing more than Russians from the Beslan school siege coming together with those who had provided assistance in the aftermath of the Virginia Tech tragedy. However, the caption was clearly misleading as the *Times* had given one of the major weekly news magazines authorization to use the very same picture for its issue that dealt with the attacks. On the front cover of the April 30, 2007 *U.S. News & World Report "Special Report"* that very same photo carried the caption, "Police respond to the second shooting incident at Virginia Tech, April 16, 2007." In four years of investigation and research we were yet to find a single instance when any of the police on the Tech campus that day ran "from" anything.

Then on January 23, 2009 death came to another Asian student. Xin Yang, a first semester coed from China was murdered by her Chinese doctoral student boyfriend, Haiyang Zhu, in a café in the lobby of a graduate student dormitory. Though she had barely just arrived at VT, and he was listed as her emergency contact, he seemed to believe that she was cheating on him. While sitting at a table in the café arguing, he drew a steak knife and stabbed her in the throat. She fell to the floor. He jumped on top of her and began stabbing her. Witnesses said that he flipped her over and slowly sawed her head off. She was decapitated while seven onlookers did nothing.

When one of the witnesses called 911 the VT police, once again, went racing to one of the most grisly scenes imaginable. Nicole Irvine was the first officer on scene and witnessed a man carrying a woman's severed head around inside, holding it by the hair with one hand. She quickly drew her weapon, made him release the sickening result of his mayhem, and got handcuffs on him. Shortly behind her was studious Geoffrey Allen. Rebecca Hawkins would be there as well. She would attend the victim's autopsy along with Detective Stephanie Henley.

408 Greg Esposito, "Two communities separated by thousands of miles come together to talk about healing," *The Roanoke Times*, November 17, 2008, www.roanoke.com/news/nrv/vtnews/wb/184533, accessed November 21, 2008.

Jersey was also there. He was yet one more young officer who had been there in the swamp of blood that had become Norris Hall, and had worked the Morva manhunt eight months before even that. He, too, had seen the worst, and attended to the worst. Yet he still managed to handle it all with a modest smile and positive outlook. Despite being inundated by vexatious and slanderous news reports, hateful verbal attacks by the public, and plaintiffs' attorney tearing at their very hearts, the officers of the Virginia Tech Police Department – though bowed – remained unbroken. An alert was sent out to everyone; however, the VT campus was not closed, nor were classes cancelled in the aftermath of this grisly murder. No one stopped to think that this might have been the beginning of a major attack launched by a group of Chinese students intent on showing Cho and the other jihadist network which included Koreans just how it could be done. Nor did they think of the myriad other possibilities that could have seen April 16, 2007 repeated suddenly. If they did, they certainly did not act on those concerns and close the school. Today, neither VT nor any other university can ever afford to not think such macabre, endgame scenarios.

Then on July 14, 2009 the Virginia Tech Airport suffered another plane crash. The police responded along with other agencies, as they must. However, it was just one more opportunity for the media and the nation to resurrect the specter that was Cho and the destructions he had wreaked on that small community.

One month later on August 26, 2009 a young couple, both students at VT, were brutally murdered in the national forest just outside the campus. David Metzler, age 19, and Heidi Childs, 18, had gone there to watch the sunset and play the guitar. She was the daughter of a Virginia State Police helicopter pilot. The police have no suspects.

Then on October 17, 2009, when VT coed Morgan Harrington disappeared at a Metallica concert at the nearby University of Virginia at Charlottesville, Tech and its police were once again thrust into the media spotlight. She was the daughter of the associate dean of the Virginia Tech Carilion School of Medicine. Moreover, she lived in the same apartment complex as the slain couple, in the building right next door. In January 2010 her body was found in a field on a farm ten miles south of the John Paul Jones arena from where she disappeared. According to Teresa Cook, her husband had not been back into either WAJ or Norris Hall in the more than two-and-a-half years since Cho's attack, but had to go into both to investigate Miss Harrington's disappearance. Even several years later it was still not easy for him. The media once again descended on the school and headlines resurrected the specter that was Cho and his horror.

Then suspected Ft. Hood jihadist killer Dr. and Major Nidal Malik Hasan was quickly recognized as a VT alumnus after a rampage during which he allegedly murdered 13 people, wounded 32, and discharged 214 rounds of ammunition. He, too, allegedly managed to amass a substantial bodycount with nothing more than a semi-automatic firearm, an FN 5.7mm with high capacity magazines. Cho's legacy lived on through the emulation of his tactics and the media made sure the world knew it. It was more than any school, and any group of police officers, should ever be asked to endure.

Finally, on March 18, 2010 Internet postings from Italy warned of another attack that was to take place on the VT campus. FBI, VT and Blacksburg police departments were all alerted. Other area law enforcement agencies had to be advised. No one could afford to take a chance again.

With all this to continually contend with, Curtis Cook admits, "It's been difficult to work here." "In the aftermath we have no room for error; we're constantly under the microscope." Cook said, "People have no idea. Every week seems to be like this anymore. We've got nuts coming out of the woodwork, and they all seem to have a connection to VT. No matter what, the media seems to find a link and that becomes the headline." Rebecca Hawkins put it even more succinctly. "It sucks," she said.

Perhaps the *coup de grace* delivered to the wounded animal that had become Virginia Tech in the years after the massacre came at 10:30 in the morning on Thursday, December 9, 2010 when the U.S. Department of Education (DOE) issued its letter and final report on allegations that the university had violated the emergency notifications provisions of the federal Clery Act on April 16, 2007. Against the strong opposition of Tech officials, the DOE found Tech had committed two violations in failing "to issue adequate warnings in a timely manner in response to the tragic events of April 16, 2007." And when the warnings were finally issued, they "were not prepared or disseminated in a manner to give clear and timely notice of the threat to the health and safety of campus community members," it went on to state.[409] It was later reported that the university might be fined $55,000.00 for its transgressions. This was due, in part, to the fact that while the general population was not given sufficient information promptly, that a continuing education center and the university's veterinary college were locked down, one school official locked his own office, and even campus trash pickup was cancelled. "...all of these actions took place before e-mails were sent to students, faculty, and staff on campus," a *Homeland Security Newswire* report said. Suzanne Grimes, mother of Kevin Sterne, was quoted as saying: "They couldn't fine enough money for what happened that day and how it altered our lives. It's more about the truth of what happened. That's what I sought for all these years."[410]

However, in an op-ed written by VT Professor Clifford W. Randall in *The Roanoke Times*, the findings of the DOE were put in question. Prof. Randall argued that either "those responsible for the report had very incomplete information regarding the events of that day, or they lacked the ability to correctly interpret the details that were given them." He also questioned whether they "genuinely understood the Clery Act." Randall pointed out that the very

409 Tonia Moxley, "Report: Virginia Tech violated federal Clery Act on April 16, 2007 [with documents], *The Roanoke Times*, December 9, 2010, www.roanoke.com/news/nrv/breaking/wb/270250.

410 "U.S. rules that Virginia Tech violated Clery Act during 16 April 2007 massacre," *Homeland Security Newswire*, December 17, 2010, www.homelandsecuritynewswire.com/us-rules-virginia-tech-violated-clery-act-during-16-april-2007-massacre.

violations the DOE found only came about in an amendment to the act in the aftermath of the Virginia Tech shootings, "i.e., after the event rather than before." He further argued that any conclusion that Tech violated the act "rests on a very narrow interpretation of what happened" rather than the timing of the actual events. Despite the fact that 11 of his friends were killed that day, and three others wounded, he defended the actions of the university. He pointed out that at the time the Clery Act did not specify a time period for making crimes public, nor does it now. Its purpose was solely to ensure that crimes and crime statistics got made public "so parents and students could use the crime rate as a factor when selecting a college...." Within that context, he believed that the timing of the university's announcements were not in violation of the act. He concluded his piece with questions and confusion that he was left with:

> This knowledge makes it impossible to understand why some of the parents are still trying to sue the university and its top officials. Is it for misguided revenge, or a misguided hope that somehow their actions will save student lives in the future? Or is it the product of aggressive lawyers who want to build a reputation? One hates to think it might be opportunistic greed. Regardless, it is inexplicable to me.[411]

The lawsuits Professor Randall referenced were tearing at the hearts of all of the officers that had been involved in the attacks that day in April 2007. As of the publication of this book 46 victims or families of victims had either sued the university and the town of Blacksburg, or had threatened litigation against everyone to include both police departments. Of those, all but two had settled their cases. Nevertheless, in terms of any accusations against the police and how they were trained, how they handled the first two shootings at WAJ, and ultimately how they responded to the attack on Norris Hall,

411 Clifford W. Randall, "Virginia Tech did not violate the Clery Act," *The Roanoke Times*, December 26, 2010, www.roanoke.com/editorials/commentary/wb/271880.

national legal expert on law enforcement liability issues Mark Baganz, Esq., after thorough analysis of all that happened determined that the police did nothing wrong. In a detailed legal opinion (see Addendum B) he explained exactly why no one could blame them for the manner in which they had investigated the WAJ crime, nor for the speed or competence with which they responded to the Norris Hall attack.

However, on June 17, 2008 an aggregate settlement of $11 million with 28 of the families of those killed, and 18 of the wounded and injured, was approved by a court. Two families did not sue or express any intention to do so,[412] and two other families said they would never settle. In a January 2009 hours-long telephone conversation with Lori Haas, mother of Emily Haas, who had bravely stayed on the phone with police throughout both of Cho's attacks on room 211, I was told that those families wanted a trial and would not rest until they got one. They seemed to believe that only a trial would provide them with "complete information and total truth." "They have said that they have nothing else to live for, and that they want a trial. They feel that the university and police have not been forthcoming with all the facts and they want complete truth," she said.

As part of the settlements, families were given access to information that they had been requesting, and the university set up a passcode website archive of every piece of information and documentation that anyone associated with Cho at VT had ever generated.[413] As well, certain officials and police officers were made to appear at a meeting with the families. Eager to tell the families and students what they had done that day, how they had responded and why, it took mere minutes before family members were calling them "murderers." Chief Flinchum would tell Joe Bail and me that he did not blame them, however. He said that he knew he could never comprehend the loss and pain they were suffering. When he said that, he looked like the saddest man I had ever seen in my life. The weight of

412 Roy, p. 296, and as confirmed by police sources.

413 Today all of the information placed in the archive is supposedly now available on the Internet. However, since the documents are not organized in any particular way it would be very difficult to confirm that everything was provided publicly.

so much suffering bore down on his broad shoulders. As of the printing of this book a trial had been set to begin in the two remaining cases for September 26, 2011.

Heidi Miller and Allison Cook were the only two students who immediately went to the police departments upon being released from the hospital. They had wanted to thank all of the officers for what they done for them. Heidi told me, "As the police were trying to get into our room [211] I looked around at all of us. I had been kind of on top of a pile of us at the back of the room. Emily was under me. It was so bloody. We were all torn up, just piles of us, and all I could think was, 'Those poor men.' I felt so sorry for them to have to come into the room and see us all like that." It would be a long time before Heidi would even be able to walk normally again. Emily Haas also showed up at the dispatch center with her mother. She wanted to meet Lt. Deborah Morgan who had stayed on the phone with her through Cho's relentless attacks on her room. Deborah had wondered if the girl she'd been speaking with had "made it." She didn't even know her name. She had never gone back and listened to the tapes and didn't want to. Not ever. Then this "petite young girl walked into police headquarters with her mother," Morgan said. "Awesome," was the way she described knowing Emily was alive and getting to actually meet her.

Curtis Cook arrived at his home at about nine o'clock the night of April 16. The look on his face left an indelible mark on his wife Teresa's mind. It was empty and pale. She had never seen him look like that before and instinctively knew that the event had affected him deeply. Her mind raced, thinking about the families of the 32 dead. "They would never see their Curtis's again," she said. She understood that she was luckier than so many. She still hadn't realized the horrible sights, smells and feelings that Curtis experienced that day, or that he would relive that night and continue to for a long time. Kids that he was responsible for had died, on his watch. He was inconsolable. It was the first of many uneasy and sleepless nights for the Cooks. It is unlikely that a single officer who was there that day has been living any different of a nightmare. But no one one seems to care.

Sharon Flinchum agreed: "The wives seem to be doing okay, but we've all been worried about our husbands." She was particularly concerned about all that their husbands wouldn't talk about and kept to themselves, trying to protect the wives from what they had seen.

For weeks after that day, on his way to work Donnie Goodman had to pull over on Prices Fork Road and give himself "at least a minute to just let tears fall out of my eyes," he admitted. Getting over the worst day of his life would take a very long time.

Indeed, April 16, 2007 became the worst day in the 24 years that Wendell Flinchum had spent on the Virginia Tech campus. He instantly became the official face of the massacre, at least the face of a grieving Virginia Tech. It was a position that he was not comfortable with but understood that was what leaders were required to do: put themselves out front to protect those who served under them. He still bristles at the negative way the national press hurt the members of his department.

Wendell was certainly not unaccustomed to tragic events occurring in his police career at VT. There had been a airplane crash at the Virginia Tech Airport on July 27, 2006, and the tragic Morva manhunt the previous August. But those were all events you got past, that you could put behind you. However, the 16th would never be the type of event that you filed away in your subconscious and only resurrected as a talking point when the need arose. In that, Lucinda Roy had been correct in her assessment of the VT police chief. To Wendell Flinchum and his family that day would become a truly life altering and everlasting event.

Understanding all that his officers and those from Blacksburg endured inside Norris Hall that day, Chief Flinchum expresses concern that the pressure from the event, the never-ending media coverage and extreme criticism aimed at the two departments, together with the stress from the lawsuits and microscope under which they have all had to function, has had the potential to cause problems between the two agencies. Friends for years, he says "Kim [Crannis] and I have worked hard to keep that from festering." The devastation that Cho dealt on April 16, 2007 did not stop with the police entry and final shot. It still continues for everyone that lived and survived that horrible 11 minutes. Wendell Flinchum will never be the same man that left for work that cold morning to investigate the death of two students at West Ambler-Johnston dormitory, and ended his day standing alone before the glare of news cameras, the blinding flash of camera bulbs, and the world press.

With all that was going on and being said about the Virginia Tech Police Department in the early part of the events surrounding the shootings that were quickly spiraling out of control, Teresa Cook reached out to the wives of her husband's coworkers and offered her help. Little did she know that she was one of the few people who truly cared about the police families:

> Very quickly the focus shifted entirely to the victims, their families, and all of the students. Not that they weren't deserving of all the consideration, help and compassion that they could get. But no one cared about the officers at all. I mean no one cared one little bit. After everything they had just been through, not to mention the incredible guilt that anyone who was a human being would feel if in their place, not a single person in power at the university seemed the slightest bit concerned about them. I never got a phone call, an email, a letter or a card from anyone at VT.

Not that the officers and their families had no support at all. According to Teresa, "When this happened, at the beginning the community really reached out to the officers. People from churches brought us food, and we were treated very well." "The neighbors were so good," Sharon Flinchum acknowledges. She admits that the acts of kindness, gifts and cards from friends and neighbors helped her survive those days. She ironically describes it as having been "like a funeral," with so many people coming by or calling, sending cards. "The support of family and friends got us through this time." It was almost six months before she and Wendell even ventured out as a couple for dinner. Before that, "for weeks he was getting up in the dark and coming home in the middle of the night," Sharon said of her husband. She wouldn't see him for days at a time. She and Wendell had just moved into a new house. As of our interview with her three years later she still hadn't unpacked many of the boxes. "It is like life just stopped on that day," she explains. Shortly after the attacks their teenage son was going to his prom. When she and Wendell saw "all those beautiful kids just about the same age as at Tech, we just started crying," she said. "They weren't going to have any more proms."

"But it was the support from inside the university that wasn't there," Teresa Cook insists. While that may have been the impression for some, others insist the university was very concerned for its officers and their families, and did everything it could under the circumstances. For instance, VT established a single person through the Employee Assistance Program whom employees could contact directly without having to not go through the normal process. She also went to the PD and met with numerous people, went on ride alongs, etc., so that the officers would feel comfortable with her. Certainly, President Steger – as he pointed out to us – expressed his support publicly numerous times.

The Virginia State Police also brought in counselors for the wives and families of the Virginia Tech Police Department that next day. They were spoken to by the counselors and given a card for making further contact if needed. Teresa knew that the victims' families were a priority, and rightfully so. But she was grateful that someone cared about what they were living with. And unlike everyone else, the cops, their wives and families were living with the overwhelming shame of the blame that everyone in the nation was heaping on them, as hour-by-hour and minute-by-minute a relentless media continued to publicly and baselessly humiliate them. What they had been through was difficult enough. But now they were the subject of national and worldwide ridicule. It was too much for anyone. Rebecca Hawkins once again put it most profoundly. Her answer to those who laid blame at their feet was simply, "You can criticize me if you were standing beside me."

Several of the officers left their respective departments shortly thereafter. Dispatcher April Blankenship didn't see her three-year-old daughter until Friday, at the end of a long week. She just "didn't want to be home," she said. She quit her position with VTPD one year later. However, in September 2009 she returned to the Communications Division of the Tech PD where she remains to this day, though she says the job is now ten times harder. There are always two dispatchers on duty and they receive calls for everything now, not just the routine calls that used to come into the center. She does remember with a grateful heart the outpouring of support that came from all over the nation, when teddy bears, candy, blankets and food came into the center daily. However she well recognizes the reality that exists in the country today. "You never know when it is going to happen again," she says. "It's gonna happen somewhere." The 16th changed April Blankenship. She hasn't watched the news on television ever since. That cold Monday morning "opened my eyes to what I have at home and that it can be taken away," she said.

Like many of the other officers that responded to Norris Hall, Morgan Millirons did not want to go home that night either. His wife and children stopped by police headquarters to check on him. He wanted to talk to them but didn't know what to say. What could he say? He finally went home shortly after midnight, 24 long hours after he had gone on duty on the quiet campus the night before. By the next morning that campus was international news, with scenes being played over and over again on every television in America. W. Morgan Millirons would have memories of his own, scenes that would play in his mind which time could never wash away. He knows from studies of horrific events of this magnitude that on average the stress takes six years off the lives of the cops that respond to them. "Laying in bed at night thinking about it," makes the former K9 officer wonder if not going to the mandatory debrief was the right move. "I didn't need it," was the typical response that is often told to Critical Incident Stress Management Teams when talking about the terrible things that our first responders live with daily.

Lt. George Jackson now understands what a massacre is. He, too, lived it for many months. His "department suffered," he said. They needed to decompress after this tragic event, "But we couldn't," he told us. He has seen many people suffer. His assignment to take the families that requested to go through the crime scene was one of the hardest things he ever did.

However, the officers and their families were not the only other ones at VT who were devastated by both the attack and its aftermath. "The way the shooting affected the professors, … it was heartbreaking," Teresa Cook said. She also saw that the Asian students were devastated. She says that they didn't feel that they were being mistreated, but that "they were afraid that they might be seen as being like Cho." As well she confirmed something we had been told over and over, that "the girls on campus and in town were all sleeping together." Everyone was in a state of shock.

"I think the smell of death in the rooms, the bodies and blood, and the cell phones ringing incessantly in the rooms with parents trying to get a hold of their kids,… these are the things Curtis remembers, that his mind won't let go of," she says of her husband. But she might just as well have been describing the ghosts that every single cop who was in Norris Hall lives with every day. These are the ghosts that visit them when they lie awake at night. "It goes home with the officers and it affects the families, the children, the wives," she explains. For others who may someday suffer a similar experience, she offers this advice to those in command: "The officers need to hear from their top commanders who are like their fathers, that they did a good job. They need to hear from the highest people in the administration. That's what allows them to do it the next time." Teresa Cook knows that her husband and his officers need to go on and work with a sense of confidence. “Those officers who were at Norris Hall needed to hear that they did a good job,” she says.

The day after was a blur. Curtis Cook was back at work. The news media were crawling over everyone and anyone that would talk to them. The news anchors were especially disgusting. “Despise” was not a term that one would expect to come out of mouth of a comely, vivacious southern belle, but Teresa Cook used it freely when referring to the reporters that plagued the town and university in the aftermath. “I knew I had to go right back in [to work] but I didn’t really want to,” Curtis told us. “Just because of the negative publicity. It had already started.” He explained his frustration that, “They had it wrong but we had to go deal with it. I hated it for the university; I hated it for the department. I got up and told myself that it had all been a terrible dream. But then the reality of it smacks you in the head and I went in and we had to go and start running operations again.”

–

The chaos continued at Montgomery Regional General Hospital for seven days, while the hospital maintained its status of controlled access by the press and other onlookers. All the media were referred to the hospital’s public information officer, and under the watchful eyes of people like Security Director Charlie Smith the reporters started referring to Montgomery Regional Hospital as a place that was, “Locked up like Fort Knox.” That is one statement that Smith was proud of. To him it meant that in the midst of all that chaos and horror, that he had done his job and protected the patients, their families, and the hospital staff. The media continued its relentless hounding even as Smith took his family out to dinner during the week following the Norris Hall rampage. Smith said that he had a “gratifying feeling” when he was approached by some of the victims’ family members and thanked for protecting them from the media.

Smith described the days following the massacre as “hectic.” But the outreach of the Blacksburg and Virginia Tech communities was overwhelming. Because the news media had taken over most of the available hotel rooms, some of the hospital workers took the families of the wounded to their homes so that they would have a place to stay while their children recuperated. Again Smith realized - just as he had after the Morva incident – that "Blacksburg was no longer a sleepy little town."

–

In the perennial dissection of the university and police response to the killings, including the first two at WAJ that morning, some discrepancies have surfaced. In her book, *No Right To Remain Silent*, Lucinda Roy emphasized that the information the police developed from Emily Hilscher's roommate Heather Haugh about then person-of-interest Karl Thornhill, may not have been received until 46 minutes after initially reported; and that the Policy Group may not have known of that lead at all until 9:25 that morning. The Governor's Panel Report had indicated that Chief Flinchum had begun giving the Policy Group information, including the search for a possible suspect, at 8:10 a.m. This is relevant to critics as, if true, the police would not have had anyone they were looking for actually identified until much later, yet the campus was not closed and classes cancelled.[414] However, the GPR was inaccurate, as the Policy Group did not even meet until 8:35 a.m., and the police did not even know anything about Thornhill until 8:16 a.m. when the detectives started interviewing Heather Haugh. How it could be possible that Karl Thornhill had been stopped at 9:24 a.m. if the police did not even know who he was until one minute later is not explained however. Nor is it explained how – even if not identified until 9:25 a.m. – there could have been so many officers at his roadside stop at 9:42 a.m. when the "Active shooter at Norris Hall" call was broadcast.

–

Despite their own knowledge of how they had performed, the police continued to live under the cloud of national, if not global, scorn.

414 Roy, p. 297.

The world simply didn't know what had really gone on that day. In light of the circumstances as they were known to them at the time, many officers risked their lives in heroic fashion to save innocent people. Certainly those who fought to get into Norris Hall with no body armor, or with only a handgun, or who were the first through doors into bloody rooms where shooters likely laid in ambush, had risked mightily. And was it not due to their courageous battle to get into the building as quickly as possible that caused the killer to break off his attack and end his own life, thereby sparing countless people? Didn't others work tirelessly to keep wounded kids alive, all the while soaked in their blood; blood that they may forever see staining their hands when they look in the mirror?

As a result, on December 12, 2007 an awards ceremony was held to recognize those very officers from the Virginia Tech Police Department. Those who were directly responsible for providing life-saving first aid or assistance to the victims were presented with the Life Saving Award. They were officers Mason Boggess, Rebecca Hawkins and Jason "Jersey" Dominiczak. The Meritorious Service Award for those who entered Norris Hall and placed their lives in danger went to officers John Berry, Kenneth Craighead, Joe Shanks, Kristi Wilson, as well as Lt. Scott Lau (VT ERT's assistant team leader that day). Chief Flinchum was also presented with this award but refused it. Finally, the Medal of Valor was given to those brave men who had actually entered Norris Hall while shots were still being fired and who placed their lives in extreme danger. They were: Officer Geoff Allen; Sgt. Tom Gallemore; Det. Daniel Hardy; Officer Jaret Reece; Sgt. Sean Smith; Officer Larry Wooddell; Officer Keith Weaver; Officer Dean Lucas; and Lt. Curtis Cook.[415] Perhaps not surprisingly, all but Weaver and Lucas were members of the ERT. They all also received the 2008 Award for Valor from the International Association of Campus Law Enforcement Administrators (IACLEA).

However, the VT officers' awards ceremony was held quietly. There was no public recognition, no media present, and certainly

415 Boggess, Berry, Craighead, Shanks and Wilson left the department.

none of the fanfare usually associated with honoring such heroism. Although the Executive Vice President of the university presented the awards, the VT photographer took photos and other university members attended along with family members, it was as though everyone just wanted to get it over with before someone noticed and the world was, once again, reminded of that day. Chief Flinchum had made the decision to not invite the media as he was concerned that their stories would merely have detracted from the officers being recognized as heroes. All of the officers we spoke with agreed. Not a single one of them would have wanted any reporters there. Cook later said that in the days, weeks and months after April 16, 2007 that they had received letters from schools around the country telling them how well they did, and how proud everyone was of them. "Those letters meant more than any awards for valor," he said.

–

Against substantial pressure to raze Norris Hall and erect yet another memorial to a terrorist-type attack on innocents, the students and faculty insisted that the building was their home, their place, and that it should not be surrendered to such an atrocity. To do so would mean that Cho had won. For some time the classrooms on the second floor were sealed off behind new, heavy doors with deadbolt locks. Today that entire wing of the second floor has been reconfigured and now houses the Center for Peace Studies and Violence Prevention. Another good thing that came out of the event was that the Virginia Tech Rescue Squad received a much needed boost in equipment for serving the university community.

–

Professor Lucinda Roy's efforts to communicate her concerns about Cho to various units throughout the VT community, of letting them know he seemed depressed and angry, and her own struggles to work with him when no other viable alternatives presented themselves, and to convince him to seek counseling, all came to nothing. Nothing she did stopped her sulking student from planning and executing the biggest shooting mass murder on a school in U.S. history. It didn't make "a scrap of difference in the end," she wrote.[416]

Nevertheless, in the end Cho did not win. In the end the police had done it right, and many lives were saved by their rapid and courageous actions. None could have done better. That July, at the orientation for all the new incoming students, the VT police department had a booth, as it always did. Scores of parents came up and thanked the officers for what they did. Clearly they were confident in the department's ability to keep their sons and daughters as safe as they could be anywhere. That fall Virginia Tech saw the largest influx of new students it had ever experienced in its history. This included the siblings of a number of the victims of the attack. The year after was even greater.

–

Within a couple of days of the shootings students at Tech had erected memorials and monuments all over the campus. There were notes written in chalk on sidewalks, enormous albums with messages to dead friends and loved ones penned everywhere, candles burning and banners all over the Drillfield. They had even erected a large display honoring all the police who had responded, thanking them for what they had done. On the Drillfield just across the street from Burruss Hall was the War Memorial. Suddenly there was an arc of 32 Hokie stones arrayed before it, each decorated with flowers, a U.S. flag and other mementos. They were there, one each for every person who had died that day. Then quickly the students added a 33rd Hokie stone and decorated it just as the others. When asked what that one was for we were told that if not for Cho himself, that it was there for his family.

For the families of the dead, and the families of all those who have died in school shootings in America, including the families of those students who have perpetrated such atrocities, their grief may never end.

416 Roy, p. 24.

Epilogue

"History teaches that when you become indifferent and lose the will to fight, someone who has the will to fight, will take over."

Green Beret Col. Arthur D. "Bull" Simons

In the aftermath of the VT shootings everyone became convinced that Cho had disposed of his computer hard drive and cell phone, most likely together. Then in the early morning hours of April 17, at 1:17 a.m. a "ping" came up at the Blacksburg cell phone company. Someone had just turned Cho's phone on. The police had made the phone company put a track on it in the immediate aftermath of the shootings at Norris Hall, as soon as he had been tentatively identified. The phone company's system registered the signal from a cell tower on Washington Street about a block-and-a-half from the southeast boundary of the campus, near the Blacksburg police station. The police were alerted immediately. *Someone was working with Cho and he's out there!*, they all thought. Cops went racing to the area. Through the dark hours of the night they scoured the ground, but found no one. Whoever it was had quickly turned the phone off and disappeared.

Then the pinging started again. Police tried to call the number, but no one would answer. A horde of officers, investigators and police cadets were immediately assembled. They descended on the spot and conducted a shoulder-to-shoulder search of a several square block area of the Virginia Tech campus. Trash cans, dumpsters, rooftops, ground and abandoned property were all thoroughly inspected, but nothing was found. Nor was *anyone* found. The pinging continued for two days, all from the same tower which sat atop a dormitory building. Whoever turned Cho's cell on was making sure he or they were not going to be found by the cops. But who was it? And who were they waiting to hear from?

Cho was believed by everyone to have worked alone, to have plotted and executed his murder spree all by himself. No one even knew of a single friend or associate that he had in his life. But with neither the hard drive to Cho's computer nor his cell phone having been found much information about him and his plot remained a mystery. But someone was out there with at least one of them.

Then on April 20, 2007, merely four days after Cho's killing spree, 18-year-old VT Engineering major Jeff Santodomingo Soriano died in Virginia Beach under mysterious circumstances. He had reportedly been inside Norris Hall during the attack and managed to survive. The media said that he had been racing another car when his own vehicle crashed, killing him, with the other car fleeing the scene, never to be found.[417] Other sources, including some seeming conspiracy theorists, however, claimed that he was being chased at high speed by the other car when he crashed. They reported that he had claimed to have seen another shooter inside Norris Hall, this one six feet tall. In one article entitled "VA Tech Massacre Witness Killed in Mysterious Car Crash" an accompanying photograph showed Cho in a U.S. Marine camouflage uniform along with an identically clad associate, who appeared to be taller.[418] Though both of their faces were partially clad by balaclavas, it was clear that one was Cho and the other Caucasian. The photo was posted on *Wikipedia* immediately after the shootings. Then on April 19 someone removed the image and replaced it with a version that cropped out the other man, as well as the "U.S. Marines" breast tape on Cho's uniform. Who posted it and who substituted it for a doctored photo is also not known.

Yet who was this person, especially since Cho was not believed to have had any friends? And how did the seething would-be

417 "Virginia Tech Student Survives Shooting Dies in Crash," *TheDenverChannel.com*, with contribution by the *Associated Press,* April 23, 2007.

418 "VA Tech Massacre Witness Killed in Mysterious Car Crash," *Total Information Analysis*, May 11, 2007, www.total411.info, also found at legitgov.org.

murderer come into possession of a military uniform? We know Cho was neither in the Marines nor was he a Marine cadet at VT. Whoever the other man was, his identity has certainly never been released. Nor did any supposed eyewitness accounts of an accomplice get mentioned in the Governor's Panel Report.

Interestingly, a police handwriting expert established conclusively that the series of bomb threat notes found on various Engineering buildings on the Tech campus before April 16, 2007 were not written by Cho. Only the one put up at Norris Hall that morning was his. However, the first bomb scare came on April 2. After the police responded *en masse* and searched the building completely, the following day Cho purchased four packs of padlocks, his black baseball cap, targets and the Dremel tool. Two days after returning his van on April 10, he somehow got a ride to Christiansburg and bought his 26-pocket fishing vest. That would be the last of his equipment purchases for his attack. The very next day, April 13, with Cho fully outfitted and armed, three more Engineering buildings suddenly had bomb threat notes posted on them. Again Cho would have seen the police response. So, just who was writing the notes then? And how interesting that they coincided so perfectly with Cho's preparations.

Whatever the truth, it is certain that many of the records and information that would answer questions about Cho and his plot are not publicly available. Even the police can't get them. This includes his cell phone records, which have never been released. It appears that no one is ever to know who he was talking to in the final months of his life. Nor has any information been released on the residents of the dorm that held the cell that his mobile phone was activating from. As well, someone has done an admirable job of keeping NBC from ever releasing all of the photos, the complete videos and even the entire 1,800 word written manifesto that Cho sent between his attacks. The question is "why?"

Glossary

AAR – After Action Review

After Action Review – A 144 page report on the Virginia Tech shootings published by Archangel Group that was intended to be used as a tool for law enforcement and school security for both tactical planning and response, and school emergency planning purposes.

AJ – Ambler-Johnston, refers to the two-building complex that includes West and East Ambler-Johnston dormitories.

Archangel Team – the group of employees and consultants from Archangel Group, Ltd. which traveled to Virginia Tech in the aftermath of the shootings and conducted a detailed investigation and assessment of those attacks and the law enforcement response which culminated in Archangel's 144 page AAR.

BPD – Blacksburg Police Department

Carilion-St. Albans – psychiatric hospital Cho first sent to after TDO was issued.

Casualty Collection Point - a specific location where casualties are assembled to be triaged, provided initial, immediate life sustaining medical treatment, then transported to a medical treatment facility for further care.

CCC – Cook Counseling Center (see below)

CCP – Casualty Collection Point (see above)

Commission on the Accreditation of Law Enforcement Agencies (CALEA) – was created in 1979 as a credentialing authority through the joint efforts of law enforcement's major executive associations with the purpose of improving the delivery of public safety services, primarily by: maintaining a body of standards, developed by public safety practitioners, covering a wide range of up-to-date public safety initiatives; establishing and administering an accreditation process; and recognizing professional excellence.

Command Sergeant Major – highest rank among the enlisted or non-commissioned officer corps in the U.S. military. In the Navy, referred to as Command Master Chief.

Commo – communications

Cook Counseling Center – Virginia Tech's psychological counseling facility

CP – Command Post, the location where the command and control functions are performed through an arrangement of personnel, equipment, communications, facilities, and procedures employed by an Incident Commander in planning, directing, coordinating, and controlling forces in the accomplishment of the mission.

Critical Incident Stress Management – (CISM) is an adaptive short term helping process that focuses solely on an immediate and identifiable problem. It spans pre-incident preparedness to acute crisis to post-crisis follow up. Its stated purpose is to enable people to return to their daily routine more quickly and with less likelihood of experiencing post-traumatic stress disorder.

Emergency Operation Center - (EOC) An emergency operations center is a central command and control facility responsible for carrying out the principles of emergency preparedness and emergency management, or disaster management functions at a strategic level in an emergency situation, and ensuring the continuity of operation of a company, political subdivision or other organization.

ERT – Emergency Response Team, one of the numerous names for police SWAT teams.

Flashbang – A Flash Sound Diversion device that is a canister which is thrown and creates a large flash and deafening sound which is meant to disorient those in close proximity for about five to ten seconds.

FTX - Field Training Exercise

Governor's Panel Report – the report on the Virginia Tech shootings issued by Virginia Governor Timothy Kaine's select commission.

GPR – Governor's Panel Report (see above)

Hollowpoint - A hollowpoint is an expanding bullet the tip of which is pitted or hollowed out, generally intended to cause the bullet to expand upon entering a person in order to decrease penetration and disrupt more tissue as it travels through the body.

IC or ICP – Incident Command or Incident Command Post

IEP - Individual Education Program

LE – Law Enforcement

OPLAN – Operations Plan

Policy Group – A group of senior administrators convened by the University President to determine the university's response to an event. The Chief of the VT Police was not a member of the group on April 16, 2007.

RA – Resident Advisor or Resident Assistant

SERT – Special Emergency Response Team, one of the numerous names for police SWAT teams.

SORT – Special Operations Response Team, one of the numerous names for police SWAT teams.

SWAT – Special Weapons and Tactics, a law enforcement special operations unit that typically handles violent callouts, barricade situations and high risk search and arrest warrants.

Tactical Combat Casualty Care - Tactical Combat Casualty Care is a set of guidelines developed by USSOCOM (United States Special Operations Command) to properly train non-medics to deal with the preventable causes of death that they may encounter on special operations. The guidelines deal with care under fire, care in the field and evacuation of the injured.

Tac Medic - Tactical Medics, those medical professionals who are trained to operate with military and law enforcement special operations teams.

Tailgating – The university term for students gaining unauthorized entry to a building behind an authorized person.

TCP - Tactical Command Post

TOC - Tactical Operations Center

Virginia Tech Policy Group – see Policy Group

VTPG – Virginia Tech Policy Group (see Policy Group)

VTPD – Virginia Tech Police Department

WAJ or West AJ - West Ambler-Johnston Hall

Bibliography

Books

Agger, Ben and Luke, Timothy W., editors. *There is a Gunman on Campus: Terror and Tragedy at Virginia Tech.* Lanham, Maryland: Rowman & Littlefield Publishers Inc., 2008.

Giduck, John. *Terror at Beslan: A Russian Tragedy With Lessons for America's Schools.* Golden, Colorado: Archangel Publishing, Ltd., 2005.

Kellner, Douglas. *Guys and Guns Amok: Domestic Terrorism and School Shootings from the Oklahoma City Bombing to the Virginia Tech Massacre.* Boulder: Paradigm Publishers, 2008.

Lazenby, Roland, et al., editors. *April 16th: Virginia Tech Remembers.* London: Penguin Group, 2007.

Lieberman, Joseph A. *School Shootings: What Every Parent and Educator Needs to Know to Protect Our Children.* New York: Citadel Press, 2006, 2008.

Lueders, Beth J. *Lifting Our Eyes: Finding God's Grace Through the Virginia Tech Tragedy.* New York: Penguin Group, 2007.

Morgan, Robert. *Boone: A Biography.* Chapel Hill, North Carolina: Algonquin Books, 2008.

Ripley, Amanda. *The Unthinkable: Who Survives When Disaster Strikes - And Why.* New York: Crown Publishers, 2008,

Roy, Lucinda. *No Right To Remain Silent: The Tragedy at Virginia Tech.* New York: Harmony Books, 2009.

Magazine and Journal Articles

Newspaper Articles

Anderson, Kevin and CT Staff. "Week of Follows Day of Horror on Campus." *Collegiate Times,* p. 2.

Armellino, Rick. "Revisiting the Amish Schoolhouse Massacre." *Outside the Box.* August 22, 2007.

Gangloff, Mike. "Finding Comfort in Front of Camera." *The Roanoke Times.* April 24, 2007, p. 4.

Gelineau, Kristen. "Nothing Unusual Found in Cho's Autopsy." *The Roanoke Times.* Monday, April 23, 2007, p. 6.

Stone, Andrea; Yu, Roger and Kasindorf, Martin. "Law Would Focus on Gun Buyers' History of Mental Illness." *USA Today.* Monday, April 23, 2007, p. 5A.

Hammack, Lawrence. "Focus Shifts to Gun Laws." *The Roanoke Times.* April 24, 2007, p. 1.

"Law Would Focus On Gun Buyers' History of Mental Illness." *USA Today.* April 23, 2007, p. 5A.

Morrison, Shawna. "Tech police chief studying up on his job." *The Roanoke Times.* December 21, 2006.

Thornton, Tim. "Another Victim Out of Hospital." *The Roanoke Times.* April 24, 2007, p. 4.

Television News Reports

ABC News. "Killer's Note: You Caused Me To Do This." September 16, 2008.

Unpublished Government Documents

Mass Shootings at Virginia Tech, Report of the Review Panel, August 2007.

Report to the President on Issues Raised by the Virginia Tech Tragedy, June 13, 2007.

Internet Sources

Anti-Defamation League, www.adl.org/hate_symbols.

"Cho family statement." *CNN.com,* http//:www.cnn.com/2007/US/04/20/shooting.family.statement/index.html.

"Family friend: Amish girl asked to be shot to save others." *CNN.com.* 2006-10-06. Archived from the original on October 9, 2006.

Courogen, Chris A. (2006-10-03). "AMISH SCHOOL SHOOTINGS: 'ANGRY AT GOD." *The Patriot-News.* http://www.pennlive.com/news/patriotnews/index.ssf?/base/news/1159845919211960.xml&coll=1. Retrieved October 3, 2006.

Esposito, Greg. "Two communities separated by thousands of miles come together to talk about healing." *The Roanoke Times.* November 17, 2008, www.roanoke.com/news/nrv/vtnews/wb/184533, accessed November 21, 2008.

Horwitz, Sari. "Revisiting Va. Tech: 8 minutes after 911 call, a rescue from madness." *The Washington Post.* June 22, 2007. www.washingtonpost.com.

Jones, Tamara; Partlow, Joshua (2006-10-04). "Pa. Killer Had Prepared for 'Long Siege." *The Washington Post.* http://www.washingtonpost.com/wp-dyn/content/article/2006/10/04/AR2006100400331.html. Retrieved 2010-04-23.

Kleinfield, N.R. "Before Deadly Rage, A Life Consumed by Troubling Silence." *New York Times.* April 22, 2007, www.nytimes.com.

McCaffrey, Raymond, Duggan, Paul, and Wilgoren, Debbi (2006-10-03). "Five Killed at Pa. Amish School." *The Washington Post.* http://www.washingtonpost.com/wp-dyn/content/article/2006/10/03/AR2006100300229.html. Retrieved October 3, 2006.

Moxley, Tonia. "Report: Virginia Tech violated federal Clery Act on April 16, 2007." *The Roanoke Times.* December 9, 2010, www.roanoke.com/news/nrv/breaking/wb/270250.

"High school classmates say gunman was bullied," *MSNBC.com*. April 19, 2007, http://ww.msnbc.com/id/18169776/.

President George W. Bush. http://www.whitehouse.gov/news/releases/2007/04/20070417I.html.

Randall, Clifford W. "Virginia Tech did not violate the Clery Act." *The Roanoke Times.* December 26, 2010, www.roanoke.com/editorials/commentary/wb/271880.

www.socialanxietyinstitute.org/dsm.html

"Third Version of Va. Tech massacre report released." *Associated Press.* January 7, 2010. www.policeone.com/school-violence/articles/1986581-Third-version-of-Va-Tech-massacre-report-released.

"U.S. rules that Virginia Tech violated Clery Act during 16 April 2007 massacre." *Homeland Security Newswire.* December 17, 2010, www.homelandsecuritynewswire.com/us-rules-virginia-tech-violated-clery-act-during-16-april-2007-massacre.

Viorst, Milton. "The Education of Ali Al-Timimi." *Atlantic Monthly.* June 2006, http://www.theatlantic.com/doc/200606/viorst-terrorist.

Virginia Tech: Archived News and Notices. "Investigation Update." Posted April 30, 2007, www.remembrance.vt.edu/2007/archive.

"VA Tech Massacre Witness Killed in Mysterious Car Crash." *Total Information Analysis.* May 11, 2007, www.total411.info, also found at legitgov.org.

"Virginia Tech Student Survives Shooting Dies in Crash." *TheDenverChannel.com*, with contribution by the Associated Press. April 23, 2007.

"Amish School Shooting." *Wikipedia.com* http://web.archive.org/web/20061009002325/http://www.cnn.com/2006/US/10/06/amish.girls.reut/index.html. Retrieved 2006-10-06.

"Virginia Tech Massacre Timeline." *Wikipedia.com.*

Acknowledgements

From Author Joe Bail

During my forty years in law enforcement I have often thought about and even made a couple of attempts at putting my experiences and training into book format. For a variety of reasons, some valid and some not, I was never able to complete a manuscript. Although ultimately it was not my own experiences that laid the foundation for this book about the police response to the shootings at Virginia Tech, still it has been the fulfillment of a long sought goal.

With that in mind I must first acknowledge my co-author John Giduck. Without John's mentoring, support and friendship I would never had the opportunity to partake in this venture and present the information that is important to law enforcement and the citizens of America that recognize, unfortunately, we will see this type of event again. John has opened for me a variety opportunities in the many areas of the world that have experienced both school and terrorist events, and allowed me to bring that information back to my counterparts here in the United States. John, through his mentoring, has truly enhanced my literary skills.

I want to thank my loving and understanding wife, Jean, for her unquestioning support of my many trips to Virginia, including the trip that John and I made the day after our marriage. She provided me with information that I might have missed as to where and when Virginia Tech-related presentations were taking place, and took the time out of her busy schedule at Philadelphia University to accompany me on those journeys. Her academic skills in assisting John and I with the many edits cannot go without praise. Her understanding helped me get through some of the emotional times when I was reviewing what the heroes of Norris Hall endured and still live with today.

A special thank you goes to retired Chester Chief of Police John Finnegan, who enabled me to work my police schedule in such a way that the many investigative trips to VT did not overly compromise my command.

My gratitude goes out to all the members of the Virginia Tech Police Department, the Blacksburg Police Department and the Virginia State Police SWAT team that assisted us during the research of this book and their confidence in our team that we would provide an unbiased accounting of the "16th."

Special consideration to my lovely daughter, Jennifer, who on many occasions has made both her "Uncle John" and I realize that the work we do, and the people we work with, are helping America prepare for the horrors that may be seen in our future.

From Author John Giduck

First and foremost I always have to thank Melissa. For without her peerless management of our small company, which often sees her juggling high level people and military officers from countries all over the world with a style and charisma no one could match, in addition to the training schedules of a number of others, none of us could have continued to make a living at what we do. If we have enjoyed any success at all, it is overwhelmingly due to her. Only through her shouldering so many of my responsibilities at our company was I able to focus on this project.

Special thanks to my co-author Joe Bail. He has been a tireless companion and steadfast partner in this endeavor, and so many others. Tremendous gratitude to my mother, Ruth, who once again jumped in at the last minute to do final editing and proofreading in record time. I don't think I could generate a book without her. And once again, thank you to the police officers, commanders, medics, dispatchers, students and others who lent their time and their voices to the information that has been presented on the pages of this book. For this was their experience, and no matter how hard it was at times to share, without their contributions there would have been no story to tell. A big "thank you" to Lt. Col. Dave Grossman who continues to be a wonderful and supportive friend, and one of the greatest assets

American law enforcement and military possess. In addition, I am blessed by so many wonderful friends in so many fields critical to the very survival of our nation. I am forever grateful for your friendship, support and understanding. This includes my son Walter Chi who co-authored the initial AAR on Virginia Tech with me, and Chris Hays who gave up much at his job to assist us.

Special thanks to Shari Nicoletti and Elena Dean for contributing so much of their time, expertise, and academic skill and knowledge to the editing of what started out as a very rough manuscript. If this book managed to paint a picture of this terrible day in America's history at all, it was largely due to them. Part of that accomplishment was also due to the group of people who were regularly asked to review draft chapters as they came off the printer for their reactions and thoughts as a sort of ongoing litmus test of what we were producing. Among that group Lisa Miller was wonderfully giving of her time, and I am grateful for her encouragement. If we failed in that endeavor it was our fault, and in spite of all of their wonderful help. Thank you Shari and Brittany Bragdon for jumping in and doing all the painstaking work to create an index for the readers at the last moment.

I am also grateful to Fred Wegener, Glenn Hardey, Donn Kraemer, Ron Camacho and Bob Hafley: I am in your debt for all of your help. As well, the words and expertise of two top professionals in what would seem to be unrelated fields, Command Sergeant Major Mel Wick and attorney Mark Baganz, added a quality and depth to this book that it benefitted from greatly. Thank you. Again special thanks to Brad Thor. Few people of his accomplishments in the publishing world would ever find the time to lend so much assistance to those of us who function at a much smaller level. Thank you Michel Hogan for your design and help. It is hard work that is too unappreciated. And to Madge and Rick Parks, without your daily support, assistance and generosity I could not do my job at all. Extra thanks to Chris Hays and SF SGT Joe Yohanna both for your friendship and your contribution to the wonderful quotes at the start of each chapter. And to Mike Rich, Ron "So Solid" Lousberg, Shawn Gregory, SF SGM Andy Anderson, SF CSM Mitch Conway, Rick Parks, John Mason, Igor Livits, Joe Bail, Ernie Manerchia, Yuri Ferdigalov and Walter Chi: my team to go through life with. You are all special; I hope you know why. To my nephew Mikey: Hurry up and get out of Penn State, the Green Berets need you. Finally, to all of the wonderful Americans – law enforcement, government agents and officials, military, fire/rescue and just everyday citizens – who I hear from daily. I am forever grateful for all of the kind words and support you give me, and hope I can live up to your expectations.

About the Authors

Joseph M. Bail, Jr.

He studied Criminology at Indiana University of Pennsylvania and graduated from Widener University's Paralegal Studies Program. He was an Adjunct Professor of Criminal Justice Studies at Delaware County Community College.

He is the retired SWAT Commander for the City of Chester Police Department where he was employed for 39 years and held the rank of Major. He is a CALEA certified Instructor in several fields and has lectured to national and international Special Operations personnel. He has also presented at several educational institutions focusing on school violence and preparations for terrorist events.

As a Senior Consultant and Trainer for the Archangel Group, an organization specializing in training police and military units in anti-terror operations, he traveled to Russia after the Beslan school crisis on a fact finding trip for the book "Terror at Beslan" with the author John Giduck. Major Bail is currently the only active American Law Enforcement Officer to interview the Russian Special Forces personnel that responded to the Beslan massacre.

He has traveled to Park County Colorado and debriefed officers involved in the Platte Canyon High School incident. After the tragedy, he traveled to Virginia Tech five times including once during the week of the massacre, with Mr. Giduck, to prepare a fact finding report on the police tactical response in that incident

In his capacity with Archangel he has travelled to the war torn Georgia-Russia border, and the terrorist sites on the Israel border with Syria, Lebanon and Jordan. Major Bail along with John Giduck did an after action survey of the 2008 terrorist attack in Mumbai, India

John Giduck

John Giduck is currently the president of the Archangel Group, Ltd. He has a Bachelor's Degree from Penn State and a law degree from the University of Denver. He also earned a Master's of Social Science degree, specializing in Russian studies, from the University of Colorado, which included completion of the Russian Culture and Language Program at St. Petersburg State University in Russia. In 2011 he completed his Ph.D. in Middle East Studies at King's College London. His dissertation was on the evolution of jihadist terrorist mass-hostage siege tactics throughout the world.

He is a current member of the Advisory Board of the College of Disaster Medicine and Management of Philadelphia University. In addition to other published materials and articles on terrorism, Russian organized crime and close quarters tactics, he finished his book, *Terror at Beslan: A Russian Tragedy With Lessons for America's Schools*, in 2005. His second book, co-authored with Green Beret Sergeant Major John Anderson, entitled *The Green Beret In You: Living With Total Commitment To Family, Career, Sports and Life*, was published in 2007. He is currently working on two other books, including one on the terrorist attacks on Mumbai, India in November 2008.

Addendum A

Expert Tactical Opinion of Law Enforcement Response to Shootings

By Delta Force Command Sergeant Major Mel Wick (Ret.)

The following opinion as to the sufficiency, tactical proficiency of, and decisions made by the two involved police departments has been provided by Command Sergeant Major Mel Wick (ret.). CSM Wick spent more than 30 years in Army Special Forces and Special Operations, including 16 years with Delta, or what is commonly known to the American public as the Delta Force (officially 1st Special Forces Operational Detachment - Delta or 1SFOD-D). He was one of the original cadre members selected by the Delta founder, Col. Charles Beckwith, to create that unit from scratch. He is without question one of America's leading experts in small unit tactics, tactical/combat operations and hostage rescue. CSM Wick was not involved in the actual investigation into the shootings at VT, nor the law enforcement response thereto. His expert opinion was based on the information contained in Archangel's original AAR. CSM Wick's complete bio can be found at the end of this Addendum A.

Conducting a detailed and brutally honest after action review/debriefing after every training event or live operation is a routine part of law enforcement - especially for ERT/SWAT teams. The men and women involved in high risk operations with lives at stake (theirs and the victims) understand the consequences of making mistakes and are normally harder on themselves and their teammates than any outsider could ever be.

In an emotionally charged high profile action like the Virginia Tech University shootings; the media, political leaders, and other so called "experts" have a tendency to try to find someone to "BLAME" instead of doing an in depth analysis and capturing lessons learned to incorporate in future operations and to improve future training. At the political and policy level it is easier to point the finger and say "it is his fault" than to address the training, equipment, communications, and jurisdictional infighting issues that often hamper effective and efficient law enforcement efforts in this country.

Unfortunately this is real life – not a TV show or the movies where the first officer on the scene finds a clue and suddenly understands the whole plot and can anticipate every move the criminal is about to make - In the real world the officers have to follow established procedures, rely on experience, follow their instincts, and use common sense. The Archangel Team report lays out in great detail the time line and actions of the agencies and departments involved. I am not going to rehash their report – I will only comment on the tactical aspects of the Norris Hall activities.

Whether you call it Tactical Intervention, Active Shooter Response, or use some other terminology, when you have opposing forces facing each other with weapons and the intent to kill it has all the elements of combat. When you boil it down to the basics, the critical elements of room combat are:

1. Gain Entry;
2. Eliminate the Threat;
3. Search;
4. Control the Hostages; and,
5. Evacuate.

Arriving from different locations and directions the police from various jurisdictions rapidly organized into teams and within approximately 4-5 minutes from first notification the teams were attempting to gain entry into Norris Hall using multiple entry/breaching points. When they found the primary breaching points blocked they immediately moved to alternate points and gained entry. From a tactical perspective they followed the principles of multiple breaching points: after one attempt at the primary point if entry is unsuccessful move to the alternate entry point.

Once they gained entry they moved rapidly to the area where the threat (shooting) was. Again they used sound tactics of multiple approach routes and entry points. Once they arrived on the second floor the shooting had stopped, the tactical situation had changed and they rapidly analyzed the situation, formulated a plan and began to execute it. Not knowing how many or where the shooters were it would have been reckless to rush about from room to room – instead they started a methodical but rapid process clearing the rooms. Once they received information on the location of the shooter they reacted immediately to that location. Once the second floor was secured they began the treatment and evacuation of the wounded. While maintaining security for the treatment and evacuation process they continued to search the rest of the building to ensure no other threats were present. From a tactical perspective it is hard to find fault with their actions inside Norris Hall.

It is worthy to note here that the "teams" that entered Norris Hall were not pure standing teams that routinely trained and operated together in tactical situations. It was a combination of VTPD and BPD, including ERT, SWAT, patrol, and command staff. From a tactical perspective this type of mix of personnel significantly increases the risk to all involved. VTPD Chief Flinchum and BPD Chief Kim Crannis maintained an active ongoing program of integrated training and mutual support during tactical operations so the integrated teams in Norris Hall had a common frame of reference and previous experience together which was a significant factor in the timely response and sound tactical procedures used in Norris Hall.

From a strictly tactical perspective it might not have been the best decision to rescue Prof. Granata from the hallway, but I would never question that decision – that is what cops do – they risk their lives to protect others. The officers involved should be commended for their bravery.

At the team and individual level, for the officers in Norris Hall, I am sure there are some important tactical lessons learned when they conducted their detailed and brutally honest after action review. Things like additional breaching tools to carry in their vehicles; tactical movement in stairways and hallways; individual equipment carried; stealthy movement vs. shouting "police;" when to put on body armor and leave it on until the action is over; communications between different units; and many others. Although critically important, this level of tactical detail has no impact on the overall assessment and outcome of the actions by the police forces involved that day.

From the initial response to the shooting at Ambler-Johnston Hall to the evacuation of the last body from Norris Hall, VTPD Chief Flinchum and BPD Chief Kim Crannis were faced with a complex, dynamic, emotionally charged incident. Keeping in mind what information they knew at the beginning and the timeline and sequence of events as it unfolded (not looking at what was known weeks after the fact and faulting them for not reacting to what was unknown at the time) they handled it in a very professional manner. Their long standing approach of cooperation instead of competition, mutual training and support instead of jurisdictional bickering, was a significant factor in the resolution of the incident without additional loss of life. The leadership and officers involved demonstrated a high level of training, dedication, and professionalism. No significant tactical principles were violated and none of the officers involved moved away from the sound of gunfire. It was a tragic situation that would have had a much worse outcome without the dedication and efforts of the VTPD and BPD police officers.

Biography SF/Delta CSM Mel Wick (Ret.)

Mr. Wick has more than 32 years experience in the Special Operations community including 16 plus years in Delta Force. He served as the Command Sergeant Major for Delta, the Joint Special Operations Command (JSOC), the US Army Special Operations Command (USASOC), and the United States Special Operations Command (USSOCOM). He has on the ground combat experience in Vietnam, Desert One in Iran, Grenada, Panama, Somalia, Bosnia, Kosovo, and several other classified operations. He has conducted personal security for US Ambassadors during high threat periods, conducted numerous threat/vulnerability assessments of high-risk facilities and has planned and conducted security operations around the world. His diversified career in Special Operations has built a broad base of experience and expertise in leadership, operations planning, managing complex projects in high threat environments and building positive working relationships with indigenous personnel. He has planned, designed, and supervised the implementation of advanced special operations training courses from 1 week to 6 months in duration, planned and conducted joint exercises up to National level as well as designing, planning and conducting operational tests of special operations unique equipment. He was involved in the initial tactical training for the original FBI HRT and has been conducting tactical training for law enforcement personnel ever since.

As the Director and Program Manager for the Center for National Response, Mr. Wick turned an abandoned highway tunnel into a unique one-of-a-kind, national level, Weapons of Mass Destruction and Counter Terrorism training center, training over 10,000 DOD, Federal, State and local first responders to include numerous tactical scenarios for law enforcement teams.

Mr. Wick had the leading role in the site selection, design, construction, stand up, and operation of a Security Training Center in Iraq. He was instrumental in the POI development, recruiting and hiring of the instructors and support staff, pre-mission training, instructor evaluations, and on site monitoring and program evaluation. Mr. Wick has supervised the conduct of threat/vulnerability assessments of critical infrastructure in the US and Iraq, security and training operations in Iraq, employee travel through high risk areas and other security related activities. Mel continues to conduct seminars, training, and realistic scenario based training for law enforcement personnel.

Mel has a Bachelor of Science degree from Liberty University, Lynchburg, Virginia and is currently the President of Quick Services LLC, a Service Disabled Veteran Owned Small Business specializing in providing counter terrorism training and exercises for law enforcement, focusing on the tactics, techniques, and procedures for dealing with trained and dedicated terrorists. From focused classroom presentations, to hands on tactical training (shooting, room clearing, planning, movement, etc) to scenario based training, to full scale exercises – QSL sends the instructors to you, to train where you will fight. You can contact Mel at (703) 491-1790 or Mel.wick@quickservicesllc.com

Addendum B

Federal Legal Standards for Law Enforcement in the U.S. in Similar Situations

By Mark Baganz, ESQ.

A. Introduction

This article is not to be construed as legal advice and each reader should consult with an attorney in their jurisdiction for legal advice on any specific issue.[419]

Furthermore, this article is limited solely to a discussion of a potential federal civil rights claim of failure to train and of a federal substantive due process claim under 42 U.S.C. §1983 against law enforcement and an overview of federal legal standards for law enforcement in the United States in similar active shooter situations.[420]

419 This article is presented with the express understanding that no legal or other service is rendered thereby. Furthermore, the cases, materials, comments, interpretations, and analysis are limited in applicability solely to the facts and circumstances of the particular situation and/or jurisdiction and should not be interpreted as legal advice - the same being expressly denied. Increasing litigation, differences in the substantive law and case decisions in the different states and federal jurisdictions, (coupled with the rapidly developing technological and substantive Changes in legal decision-making and reporting), impact upon current issues and therefore information contained in this article may become outdated. Therefore, the author strongly urges that legal counsel, and such other professionals as may be necessary, be retained to research, consult and update the original sources, as well as to specifically identify any and all legal precedents and issues which are applicable or otherwise relevant to any given fact situation in any particular jurisdiction. Furthermore, the author writes and speaks as an individual and not as an employee of Milwaukee Area Technical College.

420 Accordingly, such incidents as barricaded subjects, excessive use of force, snipers, accidental shooting of a hostage are not involved in this article.

This article does not address or involve any discussion of potential state law claims (whether in tort or otherwise) nor any other type of potential federal claim against law enforcement officers. Federal claims against law enforcement can take many different forms, ranging from claims of excessive use of force by an officer[421] to claims against a municipality for failing to train (or inadequately training) its officers[422] to establishing police policies which are inconsistent with the law.[423] This article also does not address any school or university liability issues.

Since law enforcement faces a myriad of scenarios, the result is that a federal claim against law enforcement can also take on different forms. Accordingly, a brief overview of some points of clarification will be made, followed by a brief synopsis of some concepts concerning federal civil claims against law enforcement.

B. Some Points of Clarification

First of all, probably the most frequently used federal civil claim is called a "1983" action.[424] There are other bases for claims against law enforcement which will not be discussed as noted above.[425]

Secondly, the author frequently hears the phrase "vicarious liability" in discussions about law enforcement liability. This concept

421 See, for example, *Graham v. Connor* 490 US 386, 109 S Ct 1865, 104 L Ed 2d 443 (1989).

422 See, for example, *Zuchel v. City & County of Denver*, Colo. 997 F 2d 730 (10th Cir. 1993).

423 See, for example, *O'Brien v. City of Grand Rapids* 23 F 3d 990 (6th Cir. 1994).

424 "42 U.S.C. §1983
Sec. 1983. – Civil action for deprivation of rights.
"Every person who, under color of any statute, ordinance, regulation, custom, or usage of any State or Territory or the District of Columbia, subjects, or causes to be subjected, any citizen of the United States or other person within the jurisdiction thereof to the deprivation of any rights, privileges, or immunities secured by the Constitution and laws, shall be liable to the party injured in an action at law, suit in equity, or other proper proceeding for redress, except that in any action brought against a judicial officer for an act or omission taken in such officer's judicial capacity, injunctive relief shall not be granted unless a declaratory decree was violated or declaratory relief was unavailable. For the purposes of this section, any Act of Congress applicable exclusively to the District of Columbia shall be considered to be a statute of the District of Columbia."

425 For example, 42 U.S.C. §1985 may also under certain circumstances be the basis for a claim against law enforcement officers. Also, there is what is known as a "Bivens" action which is usually brought against federal law enforcement officials. See, *Bivens v.Six Unknown Named Agents of Federal Bureau of Narcotics* 403 US 388, 91 S Ct 1999, 29 L Ed 2d 619 (1971).

called "vicarious liability"[426] is also referred to from time to time as "respondeat superior." [427]

However, embracing the concept of "vicarious liability" causes confusion, if not outright misunderstanding, when comprehending the federal basis for claims against police. The reason this causes confusion and misunderstanding is that the concept of "vicarious liability" is not a basis of liability for law enforcement on the federal level. It has nothing to do, federally, with attaching liability.

As stated by the United States Supreme Court in *City of Canton Ohio v. Geraldine Harris* 448 U.S. 378, 109 S.Ct. 1197, 103 L.ED. 2d 412 (1989):

> "In *Monell v. New York City Department of Social Services*, 436 U.S. 658 (1978), we decided that a municipality can be found liable under §1983 only where the municipality itself causes the constitutional violation at issue. Respondeat superior or vicarious liability will not attach under §1983." *City of Canton Ohio v. Geraldine Harris* 448 U.S. at page 385.

Thirdly, since there is no "vicarious liability" on the federal level, claims and defenses must be analyzed based upon the focal point of the litigation. Generally, there are potentially three focal points of this type of litigation: The municipality; the supervisor; the line officer. The claims against each of these are based on different concepts.

A 1983 claim against a municipality is based upon a "policy, custom or usage."[428] A claim against a supervisor is based upon that supervisor having participated in the alleged wrongful act, or ordered a subordinate to do the alleged wrongful act, or acquiesced in

426 "Vicarious liability" is defined in Black's Law Dictionary as: "Liability that a supervisory party (such as an employer) bears for the actionable conduct of a subordinate or associate (such as an employee) because of the relationship between the two parties. See RESPONDEAT SUPERIOR." Black's Law Dictionary, 7th Edition, Bryan A. Garner, Editor in Chief, West Group, St. Paul Minn. 1999 at page 927.

427 "Respondeat superior" is defined in Black's Law Dictionary as: "The doctrine holding an employer or principal liable for the employee's or agent's wrongful acts committed within the scope of employment." Black's Law Dictionary, 7th Edition, Bryan A. Garner, Editor in Chief, West Group, St. Paul Minn. 1999 at page 1313.

428 See *Monell v. New York City Department of Social Services*, 436 US 658, 98 S Ct 2018, 56 L Ed 2d 611 (1978).

the wrongful actions of the subordinate.[429] A claim against a line officer is normally based upon the officer actually doing the alleged wrongful act.[430]

C. The Concept of "Qualified Immunity"

In addition to some of the above points of clarification, even if a potential plaintiff sets out allegations sufficient to meet the legal requirements for a cause of action under §1983, the plaintiff is also confronted with the concept of "qualified immunity." Qualified immunity is available to individual officers but it is not available for a municipality.[431] Qualified immunity is determined by the court – not by a jury.

The United States Supreme Court has explained the concept of qualified immunity as follows:

> "Qualified immunity is 'an entitlement not to stand trial or face the other burdens of litigation.' … The privilege is 'an immunity from suit rather than a mere defense to liability; and like an absolute immunity, it is effectively lost if a case is erroneously permitted to go to trial.' … As a result, 'we repeatedly have stressed the importance of resolving immunity questions at the earliest possible stage in litigation.' … " Saucier v. Katz 533 U.S. 194, 200-201, 121 S. Ct. 2151, 150 L. Ed. 2d 272 (2001). (Citations omitted; italics in the original.)[432]

The protocol to be followed by a judge in determining whether or not an officer is entitled to qualified immunity (and therefore dismissal of the lawsuit) was also set forth in Saucier v. Katz 533 U.S. 194, 121 S.

429 See, for example, *Bisbal-Ramos v. City of Mayaguez*, 467 F 3d 16 (1st Cir. 2006); *Randall v. Prince George's County*, Md. 302 F 3d 188 (4th Cir. 2002); *Atteberry v. Nocona General Hospital* 430 F 3d 245 (5th Cir. 2005).

430 See, for example, *Zuchel v. Spinharney* 890 F 2d 273 (10th Cir. 1989).

431 See, for example, *Owen v. City of Independence*, MO 445 US 622, 100 S Ct 1398, 63 L Ed 2d 673 (1980).

432 *Informational note:* On March 24, 2008 the Supreme Court granted an appeal from the 10th Circuit and, when doing so, the Supreme Court expressly stated: "… the parties are directed to brief and argue the following question: 'Whether the Court's decision in *Saucier v. Katz* should be overruled?' " The case on appeal from the 10th Circuit is: *Callahan v. Millard County* 494 F 3d 891 (10th Cir. 2007). It is docketed in the Supreme Court as: *Pearson v. Callahan;* No-07-751.

Ct. 2151, 150 L. Ed. 2d 272 (2001). Basically, the judge is to address two questions and in the following sequence:[433]

1. "Taken in the light most favorable to the party asserting the injury, do the facts alleged show the officer's conduct violated a constitutional right? This must be the initial inquiry."[434]

In essence, if the answer to this first question is "no" – the officer did not violate a constitutional right – then "there is no necessity for further inquiries concerning qualified immunity."[435] The result is the officer is entitled to qualified immunity and the case is to be dismissed as to that officer.

On the other hand, if the answer to the first question is "yes" – the officer did violate a constitutional right – then the judge is to address the second question.

2. "... the next sequential step is to ask whether the right was clearly established."[436]

If the right was not clearly established, then and in that event the officer is still entitled to qualified immunity and the case should be dismissed as to that officer.

If the right was clearly established, then and in that event the officer is not entitled to qualified immunity and the case should go to

433 *Informational note:* On March 24, 2008 the Supreme Court granted an appeal from the 10th Circuit and, when doing so, the Supreme Court expressly stated: "... the parties are directed to brief and argue the following question: 'Whether the Court's decision in *Saucier v. Katz* should be overruled?' " The case on appeal from the 10th Circuit is: *Callahan v. Millard County* 494 F 3d 891 (10th Cir. 2007). It is docketed in the Supreme Court as: *Pearson v. Callahan*; No-07-751. It appears that, concerning the viability of Saucier, the issue is whether the required chronological order of the two questions should be overruled; which would allow courts to address either question first. Right now, under *Saucier,* the courts are required to address the first question before even going to the second question. This case involved the "consent once removed" doctrine. In short, an informant entered a dealer's house at the "invitation" of the drug dealer; when the buy was made the informant gave the prearranged signal; the officers entered without a warrant. The 10th Circuit ruled warrantless entry based upon informant violated 4th Amendment. It is suggested that this case be monitored since at least two potential issues are involved: Does the consent once removed doctrine apply to an informant? What will happen to the "qualified immunity" protocol established by Saucier?

434 *Saucier v. Katz* 533 U.S. 194, 201, 121 S. Ct. 2151, 150 L. Ed. 2d 272 (2001).

435 *Saucier v. Katz* 533 U.S. 194, 201, 121 S. Ct. 2151, 150 L. Ed. 2d 272 (2001).

436 *Saucier v. Katz* 533 U.S. 194, 201, 121 S. Ct. 2151, 150 L. Ed. 2d 272 (2001).

trial. Just because an officer is not entitled to qualified immunity does not mean that that officer loses the case – it means that the plaintiff is entitled to move forward with the lawsuit and proceed to trial.

D. The Concept of "Clearly Established"

Also germane to the issues of law enforcement liability is the concept of "clearly established" – which, as discussed above, is one of the questions the court must answer for purposes of deciding whether or not an officer is entitled to dismissal of the case based upon qualified immunity. Therefore, it is important to recognize how the courts view this particular issue.

Donovan v. City of Milwaukee 17 F. 3d 944 (7th Cir. 1994) involved a §1983 federal civil rights lawsuit against the City of Milwaukee and certain of its police officers. The officers had been involved in a high speed chase of a motorcycle which ended when one of the officers, (according to plaintiff's claims), intentionally backed his squad car into the path of the motorcycle resulting in a collision and the death of the cyclist. The trial court dismissed the lawsuit on the grounds of qualified immunity. The estate appealed to the 7th Circuit Court of Appeals. In affirming the trial court's dismissal, the 7th Circuit addressed, among others, the issue of qualified immunity. In doing so, the 7th Circuit explained the concept of what the courts look for when determining whether or not the right which was allegedly violated was clearly established, stating:

> "In ascertaining whether a particular right has been 'clearly established' within the meaning of [*Harlow v. Fitzgerald* 457 U.S. 800 (1982)], this court has not required binding precedent from the Supreme Court or the Seventh Circuit. … In the absence of controlling authority on point, 'we seek to determine whether there was such a clear trend in the caselaw that we can say with fair assurance that the recognition of the right by a controlling precedent was merely a question of time.'

> … In identifying the relevant trends, plaintiffs need not direct the court to cases 'on all fours' with the case at bar; however, 'case law in a closely analogous area is crucial to permit us to conclude that reasonably diligent government officials would have known of the case law, related it to the situation at hand, and molded their conduct accordingly.' …" *Donovan v. City of Milwaukee* 17 F. 3d at page 952.

Therefore, it is extremely important that even the trends in the case law be identified by law enforcement officials since the courts will actually look not only to binding precedent - but also to the trends in the case law to conclude that a right was clearly established.[437]

E. The Tendency for 20/20 Hindsight

When terrible and tragic events happen, they seem to intensify the tendency to express outrage about those events through the lens of hindsight. Such incidents invite a proclivity to review the incident itself, and the actions of law enforcement officers, with facts and circumstances only discoverable after the incident is over. Such information also tends to be blended into potential criticism or critique of officers' actions with the information which was not available at the moment of the officer's conduct. Such 20/20 hindsight perspective does a disservice to those involved, tends to cloud the issues, and implies that officers should know the future before it happens. The United States Supreme Court and other federal courts have clearly indicated that this 20/20 hindsight is simply an unacceptable means by which to judge law enforcement officers' actions. Those courts have also set legal standards for judging officers' actions.

In *Graham v. Connor,* 490 U.S. 386, 109 S. Ct. 1865, 104 L. Ed. 2d 443 (1989) the United States Supreme Court set out the standard to be used by courts to determine whether or not a law enforcement

437 See also, for example, *Anderson v. Creighton* 483 US 635, 107 S Ct 3034, 97 L Ed 2d 523 (1987).

officer has used excessive force under the 4th Amendment in effectuating the seizure of a "free citizen."

Although *Graham* was an excessive use of force claim, the reasoning of the Supreme Court and the premises upon which its ruling relied, are relevant in evaluations.

In *Graham* the Supreme Court identified some of the factors which are to be considered in an excessive force case, stating:

> "... [The] proper application [of the 4th Amendment's 'reasonableness' test] requires careful attention to the facts and circumstances of each particular case, including the severity of the crime at issue, whether the suspect poses an immediate threat to the safety of the officers or others, and whether he is actively resisting arrest or attempting to evade arrest by flight. ... (... [T]he question is 'whether the totality of the circumstances justifie[s] a particular sort of ... seizure'.)" *Graham*, 490 U.S. at page 396.

> "The 'reasonableness' of a particular use of force must be judged from the perspective of a reasonable officer on the scene, *rather than with the 20/20 vision of hindsight.* ...." *Graham* 490 U.S. at page 396. (Italics and underlining added.)

> "With respect to a claim of excessive force, the same standard of reasonableness *at the moment* applies: 'Not every push or shove, even if it may later seem unnecessary in the peace of judge's chambers,' ... violates the Fourth Amendment. ..." *Graham* 490 U.S. at page 396. (Italics and underlining added.)

> "The calculus of reasonableness must embody allowance for the fact that police officers are often forced to make split-second judgments – in circumstances that are tense, uncertain, and rapidly evolving – about

> the amount of force that is necessary in a particular situation." *Graham* 490 U.S. at page 396, 397. (Citation omitted.)

In Bell v. Irwin 321 F. 3d 637, 640 (7th Cir. 2003) the 7th Circuit had this to say about the legal standard for judging officers' conduct:

> "Under the Constitution, the right question is how things appeared to objectively reasonable officers at the time of the events, not how they appear in the courtroom to a cross-section of the civilian community." (Citation omitted; italics in the original.)

Therefore the actions of particular law enforcements officers need to be judged from the legal standard of an "objectively reasonable officer at the time of the events."

Other courts have added their comments about not using 20/20 hindsight to judge officers' actions.[438]

F. The Necessity for Rational Inferences

Law enforcement officers in the United States are trained in legal and constitutional matters in accordance with what this author calls the "principles of democratic policing." In other words, there are legal and constitutional rules and requirements which law enforcement officers must follow to do things properly and legally.

One of these rules is that an officer must establish some level of objective justification for the officer's actions. This requires

438 See, for example, Jiron v. City of Lakewood 392 F. 3d 410 (10th Cir. 2004): "Perhaps the situation might have been more peacefully resolved had Officer Halpin waited for backup to arrive. We cannot answer that question, nor is this kind of retrospective inquiry relevant. We evaluate the officer's reasonableness from the on-scene perspective, not with the advantage of 20/20 hindsight."; Saucier v. Katz 533 U.S. 194, 121 S. Ct. 2151, 150 L. Ed. 2d 272 (2001): "Excessive force claims, like most other Fourth Amendment issues, are evaluated for objective reasonableness based upon the information the officers had when the conduct occurred."; Plakas v. Drinski 19 F. 3d 1143 (7th Cir. 1994): This case involved a lawsuit brought by the estate of a person who had been shot by the police. The trial court dismissed the lawsuit and the estate appealed. In affirming the dismissal, the 7th Circuit commented as follows concerning the concept of "hindsight" and "other alternatives:" "We do not return to the prior segments of the event and, in light of hindsight, reconsider whether the prior police decisions were correct. Reconsideration will nearly always reveal that something different could have been done if the officer knew the future before it occurred. This is what we mean when we say we refuse to second-guess the officer." Plakas 19 F. 3d at 1150.

utilizing permissible "inferences." In essence, a permissible "inference" is a conclusion based logically from facts.[439] Officers are legitimately trained, and legally required, to justify their actions – not on speculation and hunches – but rather upon rational inferences from the facts available to those officers at the moment they act.

For example, law enforcement officers are constitutionally required to have "probable cause" before they can arrest someone. The facts establishing probable cause are "to be viewed from the standpoint of a reasonable police officer." *Maryland v. Pringle* 540 U.S. 366, 124 S. Ct. 795, 157 L. Ed. 2d 769 (2003). In *Pringle* the United States Supreme Court defined probable cause as follows:

> "On many occasions, we have reiterated that the probable-cause standard is a 'practical, nontechnical conception' that deals with 'the factual and practical considerations of everyday life on which reasonable and prudent men, not legal technicians act.' … '[P]robable cause is a fluid concept – turning on the assessment of probabilities in particular factual contexts – not readily, or even usefully, reduced to a neat set of legal rules.'"

> "The probable-cause standard is incapable of precise definition or qualification into percentages because it deals with probabilities and depends on the totality of the circumstances. … We have stated, however, that '[t]he substance of all the definitions of probable cause is a reasonable ground for belief of guilt' … and that the belief of guilt must be particularized with respect to the person to be searched or seized."

> "To determine whether an officer had probable cause to arrest an individual, we examine the events leading up to the arrest, and then decide 'whether these historical

439 See, for example, the definition of "inference" - Black's Law Dictionary, 7th Edition, Bryan A. Garner, Editor in Chief, West Group, St. Paul Minn. 1999 at page 781; see also definition of "infer" – Merriam-Webster's Collegiate Dictionary, 11th Edition, Merriam-Webster, Springfield, Massachusetts, 2004, at page 639.

> facts, viewed from the standpoint of an objectively reasonable police officer, amount to' probable cause ...."

As another example, law enforcement officers also are constitutionally required to have "reasonable suspicion" before they can make a Terry stop of an individual. Officers must be prepared to point out "... specific and articulable facts which, taken together with rational inferences from those facts, ..." justify their actions. *Terry v. Ohio* 392 U.S. 1, 88 S. Ct. 1868, 20 L. Ed. 2d 889 (1968). Officers cannot legally or reasonably rely on speculation or remote possibilities. Rather, the courts give due weight in determining reasonable suspicion not on an officer's " ... inchoate and unparticularized suspicion or 'hunch,' but to the specific reasonable inferences which he is entitled to draw from the facts in light of his experience." *Terry v. Ohio* 392 U.S. 1, 88 S. Ct. 1868, 20 L. Ed. 2d 889 (1968).

G. Failure to Train Claims

Failure to train, or inadequacy of a training program, is a claim leveled against the municipality and the legal standard which a plaintiff must meet is "deliberate indifference." *City of Canton Ohio v. Geraldine Harris* 489 U.S. 378, 109 S. Ct. 1197, 103 L.Ed. 2d 412 (1989). In *Harris* the Supreme Court ruled that in certain circumstances a municipality can be held liable for failing to train its officers, stating:

> "We hold today that the inadequacy of police training may serve as the basis for §1983 liability only where the failure to train amounts to deliberate indifference to the rights of persons with whom the police come into contact." (Footnote omitted.)
>
> "... '[M]unicipal liability under §1983 attaches where – and only where – a deliberate choice to follow a course of action is made from among various alternatives' by city policymakers. ... Only where a failure to train reflects a 'deliberate' or 'conscious' choice by a municipality – a

> 'policy' as defined by our prior cases – can a city be liable for such a failure under §1983."
>
> . . .
>
> "Only where a municipality's failure to train its employees in a relevant respect evidences a 'deliberate indifference' to the rights of its inhabitants can such a shortcoming be properly thought of as a city 'policy or custom' that is actionable under §1983." *Harris* 489 US at pages 388-389.

The Supreme Court has indicated that the "deliberate indifference" standard is a difficult standard to meet.

The Supreme Court pointed out additional focuses in evaluating a deliberate indifference in training claim:

1. "… focus … on the adequacy of the training program in relation to the tasks the particular officers must perform." …

and

2. "… the identified deficiency in a city's training program must be closely related to the ultimate injury."[440]

Although the deliberate indifference standard is very difficult for a plaintiff to meet, there have been instances where municipalities have been liable for failing to train or for inadequately training its officers.[441]

H. Duty to Protect Arguments

As are most claims against law enforcement agencies and officers, "active shooter" litigation is fact specific. "Active shooter" litigation involves complicated and difficult issues. Often overshadowed is that officers who are caught in an active shooter situation are also victims of an active shooter. They put their lives on the line yet we do not even know their names or recognize their faces.

440 *Harris* 489 US at pages 390-391.

441 See, for example, *Zuchel v. City & County of Denver, Colo.* 997 F. 2d 730 (10th Cir. 1993).

On the federal level, there have been attempts to hold officers accountable for the acts of an active shooter by claiming that the officers had a "duty to protect" under the due process clause of the 14th Amendment. However, the courts have basically rejected that argument holding that as a general rule law enforcement officers have no constitutional duty to protect people from harm caused by a private, third-person's actions. *DeShaney v. Winnebago County Department of Social Services* 489 US 189, 109 S Ct 998, 103 L Ed 2d 249 (1989).[442]

In *DeShaney*, the Supreme Court rejected plaintiffs' 14th Amendment Due Process "duty to protect" claim and affirmed the dismissal of the case. The Court explained:

> "But nothing in the language of the Due Process Clause itself requires the State to protect the life, liberty, and property of its citizens against invasion by private actors. The Clause is phrased as a limitation on the State's power to act, not as a guarantee of certain minimal levels of safety and security. It forbids the State itself to deprive individuals of life, liberty, or property without 'due process of law,' but its language cannot fairly be extended to impose an affirmative obligation on the State to ensure that those interests do not come to harm through other means." *DeShaney* 489 at 495.

> " … Its [the Due Process Clause] purpose was to protect the people from the State, not to ensure that the State protected them from each other. …." *DeShaney* 489 at 196.

442 In the *DeShaney* case, a divorced father severely beat his 4-year old son causing severe and permanent brain damage. The boy and his natural mother sued the County and certain employees of the Department of Social Services (DSS) for failing to protect the boy from the father's abuse. The facts revealed that there had been previous complaints of child abuse to DSS and that DSS had at one time removed the child from the father's home but later returned him to the father after which the DSS still received complaints of child abuse. The boy and his mother claimed that the state (County) and its agents and its DSS agency had violated the boy's 14th Amendment rights by failing to protect the child from the violence of his father. *DeShaney* 489 US at 193.

> "... As a general matter, then, we conclude that a State's failure to protect an individual against private violence simply does not constitute a violation of the Due Process Clause." *DeShaney* 489 at 196, 197.

However, from certain language found in the *DeShaney* case, the federal courts have carved out two exceptions which are known as the "special relationship" doctrine and the "state created danger" doctrine.

These doctrines will be briefly discussed in the following sections.

I. The Special Relationship Doctrine

In DeShaney the Supreme Court did recognize that: "... in certain limited circumstances the Constitution imposes upon the State affirmative duties of care and protection with respect to particular individuals."[443]

One of these "limited circumstances" is the "special relationship" doctrine. In explaining this doctrine the Court stated:

> "In the substantive due process analysis, it is the State's affirmative act of restraining the individual's freedom to act on his own behalf – through incarceration, institutionalization, or *other similar restraint of personal liberty* – which is the 'deprivation of liberty' triggering the protections of the Due Process Clause, not its failure to act to protect his liberty interests against harms inflicted by other means."[444]

The Supreme Court noted that "... [t]he affirmative duty to protect arises not from the State's knowledge of the individual's predicament ... but from the limitation it has imposed on his freedom to act on his own behalf."[445]

443 *DeShaney* 489 US at 198.
444 *DeShaney* 489 US at 200. (Italics added.)
445 *DeShaney* 489 US at 200.

Therefore a special relationship would exist based upon the state's arresting, imprisoning, involuntarily institutionalizing, or otherwise placing a person in some type of custodial situation.[446] In such an event, the state places limitations upon such person's "freedom to act on his own behalf."[447]

The troublesome issue which courts have struggled with is the language from the DeShaney Court - "other similar restraint of personal liberty" – and what constitutes such restraint.

J. State-Created Danger Doctrine

The second exception to the general rule that there is no duty to protect is the "state-created danger" theory (from which has developed an ancillary theory referred to as the "state-enhanced danger" theory). For purposes of this article, this doctrine will be referred to as the "state created danger" theory.

This theory has developed in the federal courts from the following comments of the DeShaney Court:

> "While the State may have been aware of the dangers that Joshua faced in the free world, *it played no part in their creation, nor did it do anything to render him any more vulnerable to them.* That the State once took temporary custody of Joshua does not alter the analysis, for when it returned him to his father's custody, it placed him in no worse position than that in which he would have been had it not acted at all; the State does not become the permanent guarantor of an individual's safety by having once offered him shelter. Under these circumstances, the State had no constitutional duty to protect Joshua."[448]
> *DeShaney* 489 at 204. (Italics added.)

446 See, for example, *City of Revere v. Massachusetts General Hospital* 463 US 239, 103 S Ct 2979, 77 L Ed 2d 605 (1983); *Youngberg v. Romero* 457 US 307, 102 S Ct 2452, 73 L Ed 2d 28 (1982); *Waybright v. Frederick County, Maryland* 528 F 3d 199 (4th Cir. 2008);

447 DeShaney 489 US at 200.

448 DeShaney 489 US at 204. (Italics added.)

The "stated created danger" theory has been recognized by numerous federal courts.[449]

In *King v. East St. Louis School District* 189, 496 F 3d 812 (7th Cir. 2007), the 7th Circuit recognized three requirements for establishing a "state created danger" cause of action:

1. "... in order for the Due Process Clause to impose upon a state the duty to protect its citizens, the state, by its affirmative acts, must create or increase a danger faced by an individual."[450]

2. "... the failure on the part of the state to protect an individual from such a danger must be the proximate cause of the injury to the individual." [451]

3. "... because the right to protection against state-created dangers is derived from the substantive component of the Due Process Clause, the state's failure to protect the individual must shock the conscience."[452]

In doing so, the 7th Circuit recognized that although there are variations among the different federal circuits as to the number of elements needed to establish a claim of a state created danger claim[453], it

> "... did not believe that these variations reflect fundamental differences. Each of the various approaches limits liability under the state-created danger doctrine to conduct that violates an individual's substantive due process rights because it is arbitrary in the constitutional sense, i.e. shocks the conscience. We believe that the multi-part tests employed by the various circuits simply reflect

449 See, for example, *Monfils v. Taylor* 165 F 3d 511 (7th Cir. 1998); *Pena v. DePrisco* 432 F 3d 98 (2nd Cir. 2005); *Lombardi v. Whitman* 485 F 3d 73 (2nd Cir. 2007); *Bright v. Westmoreland County* 443 F 3d 276 (3rd Cir. 2006); Uhlrig v. Harder 64 F 3d 567 (10th Cir. 1995).
450 *King v. East St. Louis School District* 189, 496 F 3d 812 at pages 817, 818.
451 *King v. East St. Louis School District* 189, 496 F 3d 812 at pages 817, 818.
452 *King v. East St. Louis School District* 189, 496 F 3d 812 at pages 817, 818.
453 Such as a 4-part test; a 3-part test; a 5-part test; and a 6-part test: See *King v. East St. Louis School District* 189, 496 F 3d 812 at page 818, footnote 3 and cases cited therein.

> an effort to guide the necessarily fact-bound inquiry into whether official conduct shocks the conscience. See *County of Sacramento v. Lewis* 523 US 833, 118 S Ct 1708, 140 L Ed 2d 1043 (1998) …."[454]

Regardless of the number of requirements for establishing a "state created danger" cause of action, it is necessary that all of those requirements be met.

Furthermore, the bottom line is that in the end the plaintiff must also meet "shock the conscience" standard.

In this regard, there are two basic time-line components: one is when there is an emergency and there is the need to act … and the other is when there is time for reflection or as it is sometimes referred to as an opportunity to deliberate.[455]

When dealing with an emergency situation, there is considerable deference which the courts give to law enforcement in dealing with that emergency.

When dealing with a situation in which there is time to reflect and deliberate – the courts have a tendency to impose a more strict standard on law enforcement.

This concept of "emergency response" verses "time for deliberation" stems from the United States Supreme Court's decision in *County of Sacramento v. Lewis* 523 US 833, 118 S Ct 1708, 140 L Ed 2d 1043 (1998). In Lewis the Supreme Court distinguished between:

> "… decisions necessarily made in haste, under pressure, and frequently without the luxury of a second chance … [P]olice officers are often forced to make split-second judgments – in circumstances which are tense, uncertain, and rapidly evolving …"

and those situations where officials have the

> "…luxury… to make unhurried judgments, upon the chance for repeated reflection, largely uncomplicated by

454 *King v. East St. Louis School District* 189, 496 F 3d 812 at page 818, footnote 3.
455 *County of Sacramento v. Lewis* 523 US 833, 853, 118 S Ct 1708, 140 L Ed 2d 1043 (1998)

> the pulls of competing obligations. When such extended opportunities to do better are teamed with protracted failure even to care, indifference is truly shocking. But when unforeseen circumstances demand an officer's instant judgment, even precipitate recklessness fails to inch close enough to harmful purpose to spark the shock that implicates 'the large concerns of the governors and the governed.' "[456]

Therefore, when evaluating the actions, for example of law enforcement officers, under the concept of shock the conscience, it is important to look at a time line and determine whether or not the officers acted in an emergency situation or whether they had time for "unhurried judgments" and "repeated reflection."

K. Active Shooter Case Example: Columbine

The tragedy at Columbine High School on April 20, 1999, from a legal standpoint, gives some guidance on the lawsuits and claims which may follow this type of catastrophe. Several lawsuits were filed but were ultimately dismissed based on some of the different legal standards outlined above.[457]

However, in Sanders v. Board of County Commissioners of County of Jefferson, Colorado 192 F Supp 2d 1094 (D. Colo. 2001), the trial court refused to dismiss the claims against law enforcement command officers in that case. In denying the defendants' motion to dismiss the claims of Angela Sanders, the personal representative of teacher William Sanders killed in the attack, the trial court ruled that the plaintiff had sufficiently alleged "special relationship" and "stated-created/enhanced danger" theories of liability.

456 *County of Sacramento v. Lewis* 523 US 833, 853, 118 S Ct 1708, 140 L Ed 2d 1043 (1998)

457 See, for example, *Castaldo v. Stone* 192 F Supp 2d 1124 (D. Colo. 2001); *Ireland v. Jefferson County Sheriff's Department* 193 F. Supp. 2d 1201 (D. Colo. 2002); *Rohrbough v. Stone* 189 F. Supp. 2d 1088 (D. Colo. 2002); *Rohrbough v. Stone* 189 F. Supp. 2d 1144 (D. Colo. 2002); *Ruegsegger v. Jefferson County Board of Commissioners* 197 F. Supp. 2d 1247 (D. Colo. 2001); *Schnurr v. Board of County Commissioners of Jefferson County* 189 F. Supp. 2d 1105 (D. Colo. 2001); *Schnurr v. Board of County Commissioners of Jefferson County* not reported in F. Supp. 2d (D. Colo. 2001).

In Sanders the trial court denied the defendants' motions to dismiss finding that there were sufficient factual allegations to establish a due process violation under the "special relationship" doctrine. The court stated:

> "... [T]he affirmative duty to protect arises not from the State's knowledge of the individual's predicament, but from the limitation which it has imposed on his freedom to act on his own behalf."[458]
>
> "... if the state restrains an individual's liberty, the state may thereby enter into a 'special relationship' during such restraint to protect that individual from violent acts inflicted by others." [459]
>
> The trial court concluded that there was a special relationship in this case:
> "Plaintiff's Complaint contains a wealth of factual allegations setting forth the Command Defendants' conduct resulting in the prolonged involuntary confinement of Dave Sanders and his companions to Science Room 3 ..."[460]

The court determined that it could consider allegations of false promises of aid in conjunction with other facts alleged by the plaintiff in making its ruling.[461] The court concluded that:

> "... it was reasonable to infer that from approximately 12:30 p.m. to 4:00 p.m., the Command Defendants acted affirmatively to restrain the freedom of the occupants of Science Room 3, including Dave Sanders, to act on their own behalf. Thus, ... the Command Defendants entered into a special relationship with Dave Sanders

458 Sanders v. Board of County Commissioners of County of Jefferson, Colorado 192 F Supp 2d 1094, 1118 (D. Colo. 2001 (citing DeShaney).

459 Sanders v. Board of County Commissioners of County of Jefferson, Colorado 192 F Supp 2d 1094, 1118 (D. Colo. 2001 (citing DeShaney).

460 Sanders v. Board of County Commissioners of County of Jefferson, Colorado 192 F Supp 2d 1094, 1118 (D. Colo. 2001.

> during that time giving rise to a constitutional duty to protect and provide care."[462]

The trial court noted that it had to distinguish "between emergency action and actions taken after opportunity for reflection …" and it had to "… give great deference to the decisions that necessarily occur in emergency situations."[463]

As with its analysis concerning the special relationship doctrine, the trial court in Sanders again focused on 2 different time periods:

The first time period was the time between 11:00 a.m. and 12:30 p.m. (when Harris and Klebold committed suicide – and the police became aware of that). The court concluded that this first period of time was in essence an emergency, similar to a riot in a prison, necessitating "split-second judgments - in circumstances that are tense, uncertain, and rapidly evolving." Therefore "… the competing interests of public and officer safety outweighed the rescue needs

461 From Previous Page

Sanders v. Board of County Commissioners of County of Jefferson, Colorado 192 F Supp 2d 1094 (D. Colo. 2001. The plaintiff's allegations leading to the conclusion of involuntary confinement in Science Room 3 included the following:

"According to Plaintiff, from approximately 11:45 a.m. on, the Command Defendants, through dispatchers, were in telephone contact with the occupants of Science Room 3. … The Command Defendants directed dispatchers to: 1) assure the Science Room 3 callers that help was 'on the way' and would arrive 'in about ten minutes' (or words to that effect); 2) continue to provide such assurances until directed otherwise; and 3) order all Science Room 3 occupants not to leave Science Room 3 under any circumstances to seek aid or rescue for Mr. Sanders. … As a direct result of those assurances, for hours, the students and teachers in Science Room 3 forewent personal efforts to attempt to evacuate Dave Sanders to safety or obtain medical aid for him. … The Command Defendants knew until at least 3:00 p.m. such assurances were false because they had issued orders affirmatively prohibiting the assembled rescue personnel and SWAT/police officers from entering Columbine High School to rescue Dave Sanders. …"

"As hours passed and Mr. Sanders' condition deteriorated, the Science Room 3 students and teachers informed a police dispatcher by cell phone at about 2:00 p.m. that they were going to throw chairs through the exterior windows to get help for Mr. Sanders. … In response, the Command Defendants, through the dispatcher, threatened that breaking the Science Room 3 windows would draw the attackers attention to their location, despite their knowledge that Harris and Klebold had committed suicide at approximately 12:30 p.m. … Once again, the persons in Science Room 3 Changed their plans based on the Command Defendants' orders."

"In a third attempt to seek aid for Dave Sanders, a teacher left Science Room 3 between 2:30 and 3:00 p.m. but was physically forced back into the school building by a SWAT team member acting under orders of the Command Defendants. …" See Sanders 192 F Supp 2d at page 117. The court also noted that the wounds suffered by Mr. Sanders were survivable wounds had medical aid been provided on a timely basis.

462 Sanders v. Board of County Commissioners of County of Jefferson, Colorado 192 F Supp 2d 1094, 1119 (D. Colo. 2001

463 Sanders v. Board of County Commissioners of County of Jefferson, Colorado 192 F Supp 2d 1094, 1114 (D. Colo. 2001

of the students and staff inside Columbine High School, including Dave Sanders."[464]

The second period of time was between 12:30 p.m. and 4:00 p.m. As to this time period the court concluded otherwise, stating:

> "In this case, the pertinent time frame falls between approximately 12:30 p.m. when the Command Defendants learned that Harris and Klebold were dead and 4:00 p.m. when a SWAT team finally reached Dave Sanders in Science Room 3. Pursuant to Plaintiff's allegations, during that time, the Command Defendants knew Dave Sanders' exact location and the nature of his wounds. Yet they took repeated affirmative actions to block access to or rescue of Dave Sanders by private citizens or other state actors not withstanding his readily-accessible location. Under the factual allegations of Plaintiff's complaint I cannot say precisely at what moment between 12:30 p.m. and 4:00 p.m., the circumstances facing the Command Defendants Changed. I do conclude that at some point during the afternoon, the Command Defendants gained the time to reflect and deliberate on their decisions. At that point, the Command Defendants demonstrated a deliberate indifference towards Dave Sanders' plight shocking to the conscience of this federal court."[465]

Therefore, objective evaluation requires distinguishing between emergency situations and those situations in which there is adequate time for reflective deliberation. In the Sanders case, the trial court clearly distinguished between the first time period (when the officers were confronted with an emergency in locating and neutralizing the active shooter(s) and confirming that the same were neutralized) and the second time period (when the officers knew that the active

464 Sanders v. Board of County Commissioners of County of Jefferson, Colorado 192 F Supp 2d 1094, 1114 (D. Colo. 2001

465 Sanders v. Board of County Commissioners of County of Jefferson, Colorado 192 F Supp 2d 1094, 1115 (D. Colo. 2001

shooters were deceased yet still continued on their clearing actions as though it were a hostage situation).

L. Virginia Tech

With the above comments and concepts in mind, a review was made by this author.

Certain training records were provided to this author. Those records included: training requests, training information (such as instructors names, dates and location of training, and similar information), copies of power point presentations, attendance information, lesson plan cover sheets, outlines/lesson plans, and memoranda. In addition, the resume of one of the active shooter training instructors was also reviewed.

Moreover, this author had the opportunity to be present at Virginia Tech for certain aspects of the Archangel investigation and to meet with certain representatives of the Virginia Tech and Blacksburg Police Departments as well as with the team leaders of the response teams which actually responded to and entered Norris Hall. Those team leaders were Lieutenant Curtis L. Cook (Virginia Tech Police Department) and Sergeant Anthony Wilson (Blacksburg Police Department). In addition several telephonic interviews were also conducted by this author of Lieutenant Cook.

In addition, other material and documents were reviewed, such as the "Report of the Review Panel" presented to Governor Kaine, Commonwealth of Virginia. It should be noted that Lieutenant Cook was not interviewed by the Governor's Panel.

The training records and the discussions with the team leaders confirm that "active shooter"[466] training was undertaken by the Virginia Tech Police Department and the Blacksburg Police Department. In addition, these two departments also trained from time to time with the Christiansburg Police Department.

In addition, the training records provided confirm that the officers were trained in active shooter response and this type of

466 "Active shooter" training is also known from time to time as "Immediate Action – Rapid Deployment to Critical Incidents."

training is recorded as early as 2001 - 6 years before the events of April 16, 2007. Furthermore, the Virginia Tech and Blacksburg Police Departments trained on 2 separate occasions within the 12 months preceding Cho's rampage. The training included classroom as well as scenario based training concerning active shooter response and is consistent with acceptable active shooter training. Furthermore, the available training records reflect that actual, practical scenario training was given, not just qualification with a firearm.

The Governor's "Report" makes no claim and makes no key finding concerning a lack of training or inadequacy in training. In fact, the Governor's "Report" commented quite to the contrary stating:

> "The VTPD [Virginia Tech Police Department] and BPD [Blacksburg Police Department] were well trained and had conducted practical exercises together. They had undergone active shooter training to prepare for the possibility of a multiple victim shooter." Governor's "Report" at page 18. (Italics added.)

Additionally, the Governor's "Report of the Review Panel" made other complementary comments about the Virginia Tech and Blacksburg Police Departments' training:

> "They [the Virginia Tech and Blacksburg Police Departments] frequently train together, and had trained for an active shooter situation in a campus building before the incident. As will be seen, this preparation was *critical*." Governor's "Report" at page 11. (Italics added.)

> "Training together, working cases together, and knowing each other on a first-name basis can be critical when an emergency occurs and a highly coordinated effort is needed." Governor's "Report" at pages 12, 13.

> "The police were following standard procedure to surround the building in case the shooter or shooters emerged firing or trying to escape." Governor's "Report" at page 95.[467]

> "The two police forces trusted each other, had trained together, and did not have to take time sorting out who would go from which organization in which car." Governor's "Report" at page 94.

Review has uncovered no objective evidence from which a deficiency in training could, in this author's opinion, be inferred - nor is there any evidence of causation as required by case law. In this author's opinion, there appears to be no objective, reasonable basis to conclude that there is any viable "failure to train" issue present concerning the Virginia Tech and Blacksburg Police Departments. Those two departments were adequately trained.

Furthermore, review has uncovered no objective evidence whatsoever from which, in this author's opinion, either a special relationship or a state created danger claim could be inferred. In this author's opinion, there appears to be no objective, reasonable basis to conclude that there is any viable "special relationship" or "state created danger" issue present concerning the Virginia Tech and Blacksburg Police Departments.

Moreover, it should also be noted that a review reveals that the police were actively investigating leads to the West Ambler-Johnston murders. As noted above, law enforcement officers must rely upon specific and articulable facts when conducting investigations.

According to the time line in the Governor's "Report" Cho shot Emily Hilscher at about 7:15 a.m.; approximately 5 minutes later (at 7:20 a.m.) a caller on an administrative line of the Virginia Tech Police Department advises that a student possibly has fallen from her loft bed in room 4040 at WAJ; VTPD officer arrives at 7:24 a.m. and discovers two shooting victims.[468] From 7:42 a.m. (discovery of

467 This example of "following … standard police procedure" is also a reflection of the training which the Virginia Tech and Blacksburg Police officers received.

468 Governor's "Report" at page 25

two shootings victims) until about 9:41 a.m. (when a BPD dispatcher receives a call regarding the shooting in Norris Hall)[469] the investigation continued into the double murder at WAJ. This continuing investigation included the vehicle stop of the boyfriend and the gunpowder residue field testing of the boyfriend at the time period of 9:31 – 9:48 a.m.[470]

The police were also in the process of seeking a search warrant for the boyfriend's place of residence.

As the Governor's "Report" noted:

"The police had no evidence other than shell casings in the room, the footprints, and the victims. The VTPD police chief said that this murder might have taken a long time to solve, if ever, for lack of evidence and witnesses."[471]

Based upon the facts which the officers were developing at the time - [for example, and as more fully described in the Governor's "Report", the police were securing the crime scene, they were interviewing witnesses, they had information that Emily Hilscher had a boyfriend; that she had been visiting that boyfriend; he was the last known person to see her before the shooting; he owned a gun; he had been practicing with the gun at a target range; Emily Hilscher was found shot in her room; another male (not the boyfriend) was also found shot in her room] - it was a logical and professional inference to initially focus the investigation on the designated "person of interest" - namely the boyfriend of Emily Hilscher. This focus could also be used to eliminate the boyfriend as a suspect – which eventually happened – so that officers could focus elsewhere with their investigation.

469 Governor's "Report" at page 27. The Governor's "Report" indicated that the panel "estimates that the shooting [in Norris Hall] began at this time [namely, 9:40 a.m.] based on the time it took for the students and faculty in the room next door to recognize that the sounds being heard were gunshots, and then make the call to 9-1-1." Governor's "Report" at page 27, footnote 1.

470 Governor's "Report" at page 26

471 Governor's "Report" at page 79

However, Cho began shooting at "about 9:40 a.m."[472]

Within 3 minutes of VTPD receiving the active shooter 9-1-1 call, officers arrive at Norris Hall (9:45 a.m.)[473] and, as the Governor's "Report" noted: "By professional standards, this was an extra-ordinarily fast police response."[474]

At 9:51 a.m. Cho shoots himself in the head just as police reach the second floor.[475] That was the last shot heard by the police. At 10:08 a.m. Cho is found[476] and Lieutenant Cook is the officer who transmitted on radio "shooter down."

Reflecting upon the concept of "emergency response" verses "time for reflective deliberation" (as indicated in the United States Supreme Court's decision in County of Sacramento v. Lewis 523 US 833, 118 S Ct 1708, 140 L Ed 2d 1043 (1998), it would seem a reasonable conclusion that the officers and departments involved in the incident at Virginia Tech were being "forced to make split-second judgments – in circumstances which [were] tense, uncertain and rapidly evolving." In this author's opinion, the officers' actions were commendable.

In fact, the Governor's "Report" also noted:

"The close relationship of the Virginia Tech Police Department and Blacksburg Police Department and their frequent joint training saved critical minutes. They had trained together for an active shooter incident in university buildings. There is little question their actions saved lives." Governor's "Report" at page 99. (Italics added.)

Accordingly, it is this author's opinion that the Virginia Tech and the Blacksburg Police Departments and their officers acted reasonably in their actions and response on April 16, 2007 and that

472 The Governor's "Report" indicated that the panel "estimates that the shooting [in Norris Hall] began at this time [namely, 9:40 a.m.] based on the time it took for the students and faculty in the room next door to recognize that the sounds being heard were gunshots, and then make the call to 9-1-1." Governor's "Report" at page 27, footnote 1.

473 Governor's "Report" at page 27

474 Governor's "Report" at page 94

475 Governor's "Report" at page 28

476 Governor's "Report" at page 28

there appears to be no objective, reasonable basis to conclude that there is any viable substantive due process (special relationship or state created danger) issue present concerning the Virginia Tech and Blacksburg Police Departments and their officers.

Biography of Mark T. Baganz, ESQ.

Mark T. Baganz, Esq. is a former Madison, Wisconsin police officer and graduated from the University of Wisconsin-Madison Law School. He is admitted to practice law in the courts of Wisconsin and is also admitted to practice law before the United States Supreme Court, the Circuit Courts of Appeals for 6th, 7th, 9th and 11th federal circuits as well as before the Eastern and Western District federal courts in Wisconsin. He is a tenured faculty member in the Criminal Justice/Law Enforcement Program at Milwaukee Area Technical College (MATC) where he teaches, among other subjects, Arrest, Search & Seizure/Constitutional Law and Criminal Law. He also is an instructor in the MATC Police Recruit Academy and in MATC's Recertification (In-Service) Program. He formerly served in the capacity as a Police Training Specialist for MATC in its specialized and recertification programs in law enforcement as well as being the Police Recruit Academy Director for MATC. In addition, he is the former International Director of the American Society of Law Enforcement Trainers (ASLET). He has provided legal instruction and training to law enforcement officers throughout the United States. He has served on the Advisory Board for *Police Marksman* magazine and has written numerous articles for *Police Marksman* as well as other law enforcement publications. In his practice of the law, he has represented law enforcement officers involved in use of force incidents, including use of deadly force, and was himself, as a police officer, involved in an officer involved shooting. He has also been consulted on law enforcement issues by different attorneys, law enforcement agencies and individual officers. Attorney Baganz was present at Virginia Tech for certain aspects of the investigation and reviewed available information concerning the incident itself and training of the two primary responding agencies. He authored the opinion concerning the Federal Legal Standards for Law Enforcement in the United States in Similar Situations for this After Action Review.

Mark T. Baganz, Esq.
Attorney at Law
P.O. Box 1563
Brookfield, Wisconsin 53008-1563
(262) 797-7944

Contact Information

Archangel Group can be contacted at:

PO Box 16850
Golden, CO 80402
303-215-0779
info@archangelgroup.org
www.archangelgroup.org

The Virginia Tech Police Department can be contacted through:

Lt. Curtis L. Cook
Virginia Polytechnic Institute and State University
Sterrett Facilities Complex (0523)
Blacksburg, VA 24061
cookie@vt.edu

Index